Kaplan College

Fundamentals of Personal Financial Planning

by Jeffrey B. Mershon, MBA, CPA/PFS, CFP

D0943398

ISBN: 0-9726772-3-2

TABLE OF CONTENTS

Chapter 1: The Personal Financial Planning Process

Chapter 2: Data Gathering

Chapter 3: Client Attitudes and Behavioral Characteristics

Chapter 4: Personal Financial Statements and Budgeting

Chapter 5: Managing Debt

Chapter 6: Regulation of Financial Planning Activities

Chapter 7: CFP Board's *Code of Ethics and Professional Responsibility* and Related *Disciplinary Rules and Procedures*

Chapter 8: CFP Board's *Financial Planning Practice Standards*

Chapter 9: The Economic Environment

Chapter 10: Introduction to the Time Value of Money

Chapter 13: Business Law as it Relates to Financial Planning

Chapter 15: Introduction to Education Funding

Chapter 18: Planning for Divorce and Legal Separation

Chapter 19: Planning for Financial Windfalls

Chapter 20: Quantitative Analysis

Appendices

Index

PREFACE

This book has been designed to serve primarily as the textbook for the first (or introductory) course of a personal financial planning education program registered with Certified Financial Planner Board of Standards Inc. (CFP Board) and satisfying the education component of CFP Board's requirements for earning the Certified Financial Planner™ certification. Specifically, it covers topic numbers 1 through 20 of the 101 topics appearing in the CFP Board's 1999 Job Study Analysis.

This book has been written at the upper undergraduate level (junior and senior) and may be used in introductory courses in personal finance offered at colleges and universities. Also, it may be used by individuals interested simply in enhancing their knowledge of personal financial planning.

Each of the twenty chapters opens with an introduction of the chapter subject and a list of chapter learning objectives. At the end of each chapter, there is a list of important concepts, open-ended questions for review, and suggested additional readings.

The book is used as the textbook for the first course (Fundamentals of Personal Financial Planning) in Kaplan College's online Certificate in Financial Planning education program. In that course, it is supplemented by brief online readings, exercises, web field trips, questions for consideration, quizzes at the end of each of ten lessons, and a final examination containing 60 multiple-choice questions (some of which are related to a case situation) similar to those appearing on CFP Board's certification examination. Students in Kaplan's financial planning education program also have the use of a message board where they can pose questions online to qualified instructors.

ACKNOWLEDGMENTS

The author is indebted to all the academicians and personal financial planning practitioners who have created the body of knowledge contained in this text not only by practicing their respective professions in an exemplary manner but by participating in the several Certified Financial Planner™ job study analyses conducted by CFP Board of Standards. Moreover, I thank the countless volunteers who have donated literally lifetimes to the development and advancement of the personal financial planning profession by serving in various capacities with both CFP Board and the financial planning membership organizations.

I particularly thank Vickie Hampton, Ph.D., CFP®, Associate Professor at Texas Tech University, who performed a technical review of the manuscript of the first edition of this text and added significant value through her many useful suggestions for improvement in the content and wording. The first edition provided a solid foundation for the content of the second edition. Vickie has served on CFP Board's Board of Governors, and as Chair of CFP Board's Board of Examiners.

In addition, I wish to thank Kaplan College's Karen Baldeschwieler who conducted an exhaustive edit of the manuscript of the first edition of this text and substantially improved its readability and flow, while simultaneously performing her significant primary responsibilities. Also, I wish to thank Mike Wilson, instructor for Kaplan's online Fundamentals of Personal Financial Planning course, for passing on to me all the valuable feedback on the first edition of this text provided by Kaplan students. I have attempted to incorporate that feedback in this second edition. Finally, I wish to recognize the contribution of Kaplan's Mike Shevlin who endured countless rounds of revisions and produced the final document in a highly professional manner.

ABOUT THE AUTHOR

Jeffrey B. Mershon is Associate Executive Director of the Certificate in Financial Planning Online Education Program at Kaplan College, a Kaplan Higher Education school and a wholly owned subsidiary of The Washington Post Company. Mr. Mershon received his Bachelor of Arts degree in English Literature from Cornell University's College of Arts and Sciences and his Master of Business Administration degree in Accounting and Finance from Cornell University's Johnson Graduate School of Management. He developed Kaplan College's Insurance and Employee Benefits course, Income Tax Planning course, and a substantial portion of the Online Review course and Live Review materials.

Prior to joining Kaplan College, Mr. Mershon was Director of Curriculum Development at the College for Financial Planning, supervising the development and maintenance of the College's Certified Financial Planner™ and Master of Science in Financial Planning education courses and other education offerings. He served for five years as Assistant Executive Director and Director of Post-Certification at Certified Financial Planner Board of Standards in Denver, where he was instrumental in the development of CFP Board's *Code of Ethics and Professional Responsibility* and *Financial Planning Practice Standards*. He has practiced as a financial planner, consultant to various financial planning organizations, and as a partner in a local CPA firm, as well as in senior financial management in private industry. In addition to being a CPA, he has earned both the Certified Financial Planner™ certification and the Personal Financial Specialist designation. He is a member of the Financial Planning Association, the American Institute of CPAs, and the Colorado Society of CPAs.

CHAPTER ONE

The Personal Financial Planning Process

• • •

If you are reading this textbook as part of an education program leading to a professional designation in personal financial planning, or if you are just interested in learning more about this subject, you are about to embark on an exciting journey into this emerging profession. Financial planners play a critical role in the quality of life enjoyed by millions of people by functioning as their personal financial adviser and helping them to plan for and take control of their futures. Their role is every bit as critical as those played by physicians, attorneys, accountants, engineers, architects, and other service professionals. Financial planners are in a position to greatly enhance the well being of individuals and their families for generations to come. Because of the position they occupy as trusted advisers, they assume great responsibility for the management of their clients' financial health. Those individuals with the fortitude to make a career in this field will be rewarded financially and through the satisfaction of helping clients realize their dreams.

In this introductory chapter, we will establish the foundation for your study of personal financial planning by offering a definition of the term, and discussing its importance in achieving one's life goals and objectives. In addition, we will describe the six steps of the personal financial planning process and the personal financial planning subject areas, drawing a distinction between segmented (or modular) and comprehensive personal financial planning, and defining the terms **scope of the engagement**, **time horizon**, and **risk tolerance**.

CHAPTER ONE

The Personal Financial Planning Process

• • •

If you are reading this textbook as part of an education program leading to a professional designation in personal financial planning, or if you are just interested in learning more about this subject, you are about to embark on an exciting journey into this emerging profession. Financial planners play a critical role in the quality of life enjoyed by millions of people by functioning as their personal financial adviser and helping them to plan for and take control of their futures. Their role is every bit as critical as those played by physicians, attorneys, accountants, engineers, architects, and other service professionals. Financial planners are in a position to greatly enhance the well being of individuals and their families for generations to come. Because of the position they occupy as trusted advisers, they assume great responsibility for the management of their clients' financial health. Those individuals with the fortitude to make a career in this field will be rewarded financially and through the satisfaction of helping clients realize their dreams.

In this introductory chapter, we will establish the foundation for your study of personal financial planning by offering a definition of the term, and discussing its importance in achieving one's life goals and objectives. In addition, we will describe the six steps of the personal financial planning process and the personal financial planning subject areas, drawing a distinction between segmented (or modular) and comprehensive personal financial planning, and defining the terms **scope of the engagement**, **time horizon**, and **risk tolerance**.

The objectives of this chapter are:

- Discuss personal financial planning as a process.
- Identify the six steps of the **personal financial planning process**.
- Discuss each of the six steps of the personal financial planning process.
- Distinguish between **segmented (or modular)** and **comprehensive** personal financial planning.
- Define the terms **scope of the engagement**, **time horizon**, and **risk tolerance**.
- Identify the various personal financial planning subject areas.

PERSONAL FINANCIAL PLANNING DEFINED

Certified Financial Planner Board of Standards, Inc. (CFP Board)[1] has developed a definition of personal financial planning as "[T]he process of determining whether and how an individual can meet life goals through the proper management of financial resources."[2] This definition was carefully crafted, and it contains several key words. The first key word is "process." Students of personal financial planning need to understand that we are discussing an ongoing process, not a single transaction or one-time event, or even a series of transactions or events. Furthermore, the process is one of analysis, evaluation, recommendation, and perhaps implementation rather than simply one of selling products or services. The second key word is "whether." Personal financial planning must be able to determine *whether* a client can meet life goals. If a client has set unreasonable goals, it is the function of the financial planner to point that out to the client and, if possible, help the client adjust his or her goals to those that are reasonably achievable. The third key word is "how". One of the primary functions of personal financial planning, after it has ascertained *whether* a client can reasonably achieve his or her goals, is to determine *how*. This involves establishing a primary strategy or set of strategies, with perhaps alternative strategies, to accomplish the client's life goals.

The final key phrase in this definition is "through the proper management of financial resources." Personal financial planning must help the client identify what financial resources are or will be available to accomplish his or her goals. If we were to think of the personal financial planning process as a manufacturing process, financial resources would be the principal raw material consumed in the process.

---

[1] Founded in 1985 as a nonprofit professional regulatory organization, CFP Board fosters professional standards in personal financial planning so that the public values, has access to, and benefits from competent and ethical financial planning. It is an independent certifying organization that owns the certification marks Certified Financial Planner™, CFP®, and CFP flame logo (CFP marks). CFP Board regulates financial planners through trademark law by authorizing individuals who meet its certification requirements to use the CFP® marks.

[2] CFP Board's *Standards of Professional Conduct*, page 2.

The foregoing definition of personal financial planning should be expanded to include a couple of important ingredients. First, it is crucial to keep in mind that personal financial planning is an *ongoing* process. Second, for personal financial planning to reach its full potential it must be performed by qualified professionals. If planning were to be performed by those untrained in the discipline, it would most likely fall short of providing an optimum benefit to the client.

Accordingly, we offer the following definition of personal financial planning:

> **Personal financial planning is the ongoing process, conducted by professionals qualified in the discipline, of determining whether and how an individual can meet life goals through the proper management of financial resources.**

Note the consistent use of the term *personal* financial planning. This use is deliberate to make the point that this particular type of financial planning focuses on either an individual or family unit. It may include businesses or other entities (such as trusts or estates) that the individual or family owns or controls, or in which they participate. Another type of financial planning is delivered only to entities, rather than individuals or family units, for the benefit of the entity itself. This latter type of financial planning is not the type contemplated in the term personal financial planning and discussed in this book. Throughout this text, the terms personal financial planning and simply financial planning will be used interchangeably to connote the type of financial planning concerned with individuals or family units and related entities.

PERSONAL FINANCIAL PLANNING SUBJECT AREAS

The personal financial planning process can be applied to only one, a few, many, or all of the various subject areas of personal financial planning. Typically included in a list of financial planning subject areas are financial statement preparation and analysis (including cash flow analysis/planning and budgeting), investment planning (including portfolio design, asset allocation, and portfolio management), income tax planning, education planning, risk management and insurance, retirement planning, estate planning, and employee benefit planning. This list, while mentioning the principal subject areas, is not intended to be all-inclusive. Other subject areas certainly exist and will continue to evolve, subject only to the imagination of the financial planner and the client.

BENEFITS OF PERSONAL FINANCIAL PLANNING

The principal benefit of personal financial planning is that it makes possible the efficient acquisition, use, and control of one's financial resources, thereby improving one's standard of living. This efficient use of financial resources, while beneficial to individual clients, also has a more global, positive effect on the U.S. and world economies. Personal financial planning provides individuals with options, so they can deal with the future rather than being victims of it.

Essentially everyone can benefit from personal financial planning. This includes someone who has just graduated from college, singles, single parents, married working people in mid-career, senior-level corporate executives, business owners, and those approaching retirement or already retired. Individuals with established financial goals are at a decided advantage over those who merely react to events as they occur.

THE PERSONAL FINANCIAL PLANNING PROCESS

Many authors, when discussing the personal financial planning process, begin with the second step in the process—that of gathering client data including goals. This approach misses an extremely important step in the process—that of determining by mutual agreement between the client and the financial planner exactly what the proposed engagement will entail, prior to providing any financial planning service. It is unwise to gather data before determining what data will be sufficient and relevant to the services being provided.

In the early days of financial planning, most financial planners would produce for every client a voluminous document known as a comprehensive financial plan, regardless of the client's specific needs and objectives. Often these documents were prepared on canned computer software, which went through the same exhaustive analysis for every client and produced a document comparable in size to the current telephone yellow pages. These documents fill client shelves, files, and desk drawers, but few of them have been implemented successfully or completely. In many cases, these documents were used to make a one-time sale to the client of specific financial products or services. As such, they were not part of an ongoing process such as personal financial planning. Very often, the client had little input into the services to be provided by the financial planner and little understanding of his or her specific need for services or products.

> **NEED TO KNOW:**
> **STEPS IN THE PERSONAL**
> **FINANCIAL PLANNING PROCESS**
>
> Once we have established a definition of personal financial planning, what then is the personal financial planning process? For an authoritative standard for the steps involved in the process, we will adopt the six-step process specified by CFP Board. These steps include, but are not necessarily limited to, the following:
>
> - Establishing and defining the client-planner relationship
> - Gathering client data including goals
> - Analyzing and evaluating the client's financial status
> - Developing and presenting financial planning recommendations and/or alternatives
> - Implementing the financial planning recommendations
> - Monitoring the financial planning recommendations

Step 1: Establishing and Defining the Client-Planner Relationship

In this first step of the personal financial planning process, the client and the planner identify the specific services to be provided by the planner. This involves educating the client as to his or her needs and the appropriateness of specific services to address those needs. This involves the client's placing a high degree of trust in the planner. (In Chapter 6, we will discuss the fiduciary responsibility of a financial planner to his or her client.)

First, the planner and the client mutually define the "scope of the engagement." The **scope of the engagement** is the universe of services that the planner and the client agree is necessary and appropriate, and that the financial planner is qualified and willing to provide. The scope may include one or more subject areas and may be limited to specific activities. The process of mutual definition of the scope of the engagement is designed to provide realistic expectations for both parties. While there is no requirement that the scope of the engagement be in writing, this is a prudent practice for legal and ethics disclosure purposes. If an engagement letter is not executed by the parties, the financial planner should prepare file memoranda that document any oral understandings about the engagement objectives; the scope of services to be provided; the roles and responsibilities of the financial planner, the client, and other advisors; compensation arrangements; and scope limitations and other constraints. Also, it is important for both the client and the financial planner to realize that the scope of the engagement may, after initial mutual definition, be revised by mutual agreement.

In mutually defining the scope of the engagement, the client and the financial planner may agree to so-called **segmented (or modular) financial planning** rather than **comprehensive financial planning**. In segmented financial planning, the scope of the engagement is limited to a specific subject area or areas. For instance, a client who does not have a large estate, is in a relatively low income tax bracket, and has adequate insurance in place to protect him or her against the most significant personal risks, may have a specific need to have his or her investment portfolio and 401(k) plan evaluated to determine if both are achieving his or her goals consistent with his or her risk tolerance. On the other hand, a reasonably wealthy client who is middle-aged and has never used the services of a financial planner may require comprehensive financial planning in which all of the major subject areas of personal financial planning are evaluated.

It is conceivable that a financial planner who is licensed to sell securities and/or insurance may establish and mutually define a relationship with a client including no personal financial planning services. In other words, the scope of the engagement may not contemplate the provision of such services. The engagement may be confined to the purchase or sale of a financial product or service offered by the firm with which the financial planner is associated. Even though a planner may be qualified to provide personal financial planning services, it does not necessarily follow that such services will be provided in every client relationship.

Step 2: Gathering Client Data Including Goals

Once the planner and the client have established and defined the relationship and have determined that the scope of the engagement includes personal financial planning services, the second step of the personal financial planning process is to determine a client's personal and financial goals, needs, and priorities and to gather appropriate quantitative information and documents relevant to the client's personal financial situation.

In Chapter 2, we will discuss in greater depth the topic of gathering client data. This discussion will focus on just a few major points. First, an important distinction must be drawn between **qualitative** and **quantitative** information obtained from or about the client. Examples of qualitative data include the client's personal and financial goals, needs, priorities, time horizon, and risk tolerance. A client's **time horizon** is the period of time over which a specific goal needs to be accomplished. For example, if a client is accumulating funds for retirement, the time horizon is the period of time from the present until the client's desired retirement date. Similarly, if a client is planning for the education of a child, the time horizon is from the present until the child reaches college age, or it may include the period while the child attends college and conclude at graduation. In terms of an investment portfolio, time horizon refers to the number of years the client expects the portfolio to be invested before he or she must dip into principal. Alternatively, it can be the period of time during which the objectives stated for a specific portfolio will continue without substantial modification. Since the client subjectively selects a particular goal as being important, the selection of the appropriate time horizon is also considered to be qualitative in nature.

Another example of subjective or qualitative data is a client's **risk tolerance**. Some refer to this as risk tolerance *level*, as if it can be assigned a numerical value and mathematically compared among clients. A client's risk tolerance is the degree to which risk influences his or her choice of investments and is very subjective or qualitative, rather than quantitative. A client having a low risk tolerance will tend to avoid investments he or she perceives as risky. However, this avoidance of risk may negatively affect his or her potential return. This is the concept of the risk/reward trade-off, which is beyond the scope of this text. In Chapter 2, we will discuss in greater depth the concept of risk tolerance and attempts to quantify it.

Depending upon the type of client engagement and its scope, the financial planner will need to make a determination as to what quantitative information is both sufficient and relevant to the particular engagement. This information may be obtained either directly from the client or through other sources by interview, questionnaire, data-gathering form, client records, or other documents. Examples of quantitative information include copies of wills, trust documents, recent income tax returns, employer's current statement of employee benefits, investment account statements, copies of insurance policies currently in force, statements of projected social insurance benefits, ages and current health of client family members, fair market value of assets owned, current debts, cash flow, credit history, etc. All of these items constitute objective, factual data that can be expressed in quantitative terms.

Step 3: Analyzing and Evaluating the Client's Financial Status

Having gathered what is considered to be sufficient and relevant data (both qualitative and quantitative), the financial planner is now prepared to analyze this information and evaluate to what extent the client's goals, needs, and priorities can be met with the client's current and anticipated resources and current course of action. This will involve the use of client-specified, mutually agreed-upon, and/or other reasonable personal and economic assumptions. Personal assumptions could include retirement age(s), life expectancy(ies), income requirements, risk factors, time horizon, and any applicable special needs. Economic assumptions can include expected inflation rates, income, gift, and estate tax rates, and anticipated investment returns.

This step in the personal financial planning process is absolutely critical to the success of the financial planning provided. Successful completion of this step will identify strengths and weaknesses of the client's financial situation and current course of action. Moreover, the analysis and evaluation may point to the need to amend the scope of the engagement and/or obtain additional data.

Step 4: Developing and Presenting Financial Planning Recommendations and/or Alternatives

Once the financial planner has analyzed and evaluated the client's current situation, and prior to developing and presenting financial planning recommendations, the financial planner needs to identify alternative actions that reasonably could achieve the client's goals, needs, and priorities. The financial planner may need to consider multiple assumptions, and conduct research or consult with other professionals. The result of this analysis may be a single alternative, multiple alternatives, or no alternative to the client's current course of action. Clearly, the financial planner needs to evaluate such alternatives within the province of his or her competency and legal authority. The development and evaluation of alternatives is a highly subjective activity, and it is doubtful that any two financial planners would identify exactly the same alternatives.

Having identified and evaluated the possible alternatives and the client's current course of action, the financial planner is ready to develop recommendations expected to reasonably achieve the client's goals, needs, and priorities. The financial planner must be satisfied that there is sufficient relevant information to form the basis for any recommendations made. Relevant information may include an understanding of the client's goals, existing financial situation, available resources for achieving the goals, non-financial factors, and external factors. Any resulting recommendation must be consistent with and directly affected by the:

- mutually-defined scope of the engagement
- mutually-defined client goals, needs, and priorities
- quantitative data provided by the client
- personal and economic assumptions made
- financial planner's analysis and evaluation of the client's current situation
- alternatives selected by the financial planner

It is possible that a recommendation may be to continue the client's current course of action or to pursue alternative specific or general directions. Likewise, the financial planner may need to recommend that the client revise one or more of his or her goals.

After evaluating alternatives and developing recommendations, the financial planner must now communicate to the client in a manner and to an extent reasonably necessary to assist the client in making an informed decision. We recommend that such communications be in writing and include a summary of the client's goals and significant assumptions, a description of any limitations on the work performed, the recommendations made, and a statement that projected results may not be achieved. What follows is an example of a communication when recommendations are made only on selected goals and the financial planner communicates the parameters of the limited engagement:

> We have considered ways to achieve your goal of providing for the education of your children. However, you have instructed us not to consider other planning areas that might have an impact on that goal. If we had done so, it is possible that different conclusions or recommendations might have resulted.[3]

The financial planner is obliged to make a reasonable effort to assist the client in understanding his or her current situation, the recommendation(s) being made, the rationale for the recommendation(s), and the expected impact on the ability of the client to achieve his or her goals, needs, and priorities. Note that the financial planner is not responsible for making the client understand these issues but is required to make a reasonable effort to help the client understand them. Some of the factors the client needs to understand are:

- material personal and economic assumptions
- interdependence of recommendations
- advantages and disadvantages of each recommendation
- risks
- time sensitivity

The client needs to appreciate the sensitivity of changes in personal and economic conditions on the results that may be achieved by the recommendation(s). New tax laws, a change in family status, loss of or change in job or career, actual versus anticipated investment returns, and the client's health could all have a significant effect on the degree of achievement of the client's goals, needs, and priorities under a particular recommendation.

As you will learn in Chapter 7, Certified Financial Planner™ certificants are required to disclose conflicts of interest to their clients. At this step in the personal financial planning process, the financial planner needs to again disclose, if necessary, conflicts of interest that may have resulted from the recommendation(s) made. For instance, if the financial planner is recommending the purchase of a large quantity of securities or mutual funds from which the financial planner will receive a material amount of compensation, this must be disclosed to the client before the client acts on the recommendation.

The presentation of recommendations presents a good opportunity for the financial planner to determine whether those recommendations meet client expectations, whether the client is motivated to act on them, and whether they may need revision.

---

[3] *Statements on Responsibilities in Personal Financial Planning Practice,* American Institute of Certified Public Accountants.

Step 5: Implementing the Financial Planning Recommendations

After the financial planning recommendations have been developed and presented to the client, the financial planner and the client need to mutually agree on the responsibilities for implementing the recommendations consistent with the scope of the engagement. It is essential that the client take responsibility for accepting or rejecting the financial planning recommendations and for either implementing them personally or delegating implementation to others. Regardless of the level of assistance, implementation decisions are made by the client, not by the financial planner. If the financial planner is to provide implementation services, the specific services must be mutually agreed upon by the client and the financial planner. This may involve revision of the scope of the engagement. Some of the responsibilities that may be assumed by the financial planner include:

- identifying activities necessary for implementation
- determining the division of activities between the financial planner and the client
- establishing selection criteria for, selecting and referring to other professionals
- coordinating with other professionals
- sharing information as authorized
- selecting and securing products and/or services

This is another juncture at which the financial planner may be obliged to disclose conflicts of interest, sources of compensation, or material relationships with other professionals or advisers that have not been disclosed previously. For instance, if the financial planner refers the client to other professionals or advisers, the financial planner is obligated to indicate the basis for the referral, including any direct or indirect compensation that he or she may receive as a result.

It is entirely possible that the financial planner may have been selected to implement the recommendations of another financial planner. This will require the financial planner to revert back to Step 1 in the personal financial planning process to mutually define with the client the scope of the engagement, including such matters as the extent to which the financial planner will rely on information, analysis, or recommendations provided by others.

In addition, as you will learn in Chapters 7 and 8, the financial planner has an obligation to select appropriate products and services that are consistent with the client's goals, needs, and priorities. Not only does the financial planner need to select appropriate products and services that are in the client's interest, but he or she also needs to reasonably investigate and evaluate those products and services. Different financial planners might select different products or services for the same client, both of which may be suitable for the client and capable of achieving the client's goals, needs, and priorities. Clearly such a selection is subjective.

Finally, notice that Step 5 speaks of implementing financial planning *recommendations* rather than *financial plans*. It is a common misconception that personal financial planning always involves the preparation of a comprehensive financial plan. A series of recommendations may comprise what has historically been considered a comprehensive financial plan. But where there is only one or just a few recommendations to be implemented, it will, in most cases, be part of a segmented or modular plan which addresses perhaps only one or only a few of the personal financial planning subject areas (c.g. risk management or estate planning).

Step 6: Monitoring the Financial Planning Recommendations

The final step in the personal financial planning process is the monitoring of financial planning recommendations implemented in Step 5. The financial planner needs to mutually define with the client the responsibilities for periodic monitoring of the implemented financial planning recommendations. If the client wants the financial planner to monitor the progress and degree of success achieved by implementing the financial planning recommendations, this needs to be agreed upon between the parties. Such an agreement should specify exactly what is to be monitored, the frequency of monitoring, and how the results will be communicated to the client.

In determining a client's progress toward achieving established financial planning goals, the financial planner should (1) ascertain whether all recommended actions to achieve the goals were undertaken; (2) measure and evaluate the actual progress toward achievement of the goals; and (3) identify developments in the client's circumstances and in external factors that affect the financial planning recommendations. Then the financial planner should communicate to the client, ordinarily in writing, an evaluation of progress toward achieving the client's financial planning goals.

In certain cases, the results of monitoring may give rise to the re-initiation of earlier steps in the personal financial planning process and modification of the scope of the engagement. This further illustrates the point that personal financial planning is an *ongoing* process, not a single transaction or series of transactions. Monitoring can result in starting and restarting the process at various points in the process.

FINANCIAL PLANNING PRACTICE STANDARDS

In Chapter 8, we will discuss CFP Board's *Financial Planning Practice Standards*, which are based on the steps of the personal financial planning process discussed in this chapter.

LIFE CYCLE AND LIFE EVENT FINANCIAL PLANNING

Personal financial planning is a dynamic process. As clients move through various stages of their lives, their goals, needs, and priorities change and accordingly so does their need for financial planning. Some financial goals are important regardless of age or life situation, but certain life events, especially those that are unexpected, can trigger an acute need for financial planning. For example, obtaining one's first job, getting married, buying or selling a home, raising a family, losing one's job, starting a business, dealing with a divorce or death of a spouse, coping with a long illness, funding an education, needing to support adult children or aging parents, and retiring are all life events that may require financial planning. All of these events can be stressful or disruptive if not approached with care and forethought. We will discuss financial planning for some of these life events in subsequent chapters.

IMPORTANT CONCEPTS TO REMEMBER

Definition of Personal Financial Planning

Scope of the Engagement

Personal Financial Planning Process

Time Horizon

Personal Financial Planning Subject Areas

Risk Tolerance

Segmented (or Modular) vs. Comprehensive Financial Planning

QUESTIONS FOR REVIEW

1. What are the key elements in the definition of personal financial planning?

2. Why is it important that the client-planner relationship be mutually defined?

3. Why is it more difficult to gather client qualitative data than quantitative data?

4. Under what circumstances should a financial planner perform segmented (or modular) personal financial planning?

SUGGESTIONS FOR ADDITIONAL READING

Personal Financial Planning, 10th edition, by Lawrence J. Gitman & Michael D. Joehnk, South-Western/Thomson, 2004.

Personal Financial Planning, 7th edition, by G. Victor Hallman & Jerry S. Rosenbloom, McGraw-Hill, Inc., 2003.

The Tools & Techniques of Financial Planning, 6th edition, by Stephan R. Leimberg, Martin J. Satinsky, Robert T. LeClair, & Robert J. Doyle, Jr., The National Underwriter Company, 2002.

CHAPTER TWO

Data Gathering

• • •

Data gathering, the second step in the personal financial planning process, is one of the most critical steps in the process. Without sufficient, relevant information (both quantitative and qualitative) about the client and his or her financial and personal situation, the subsequent steps of the personal financial planning process cannot proceed with any realistic expectation of success in accomplishing the client's goals, needs, and priorities. Data gathering is one of the most important skills a financial planner needs to develop to be successful in helping clients achieve their goals. While obtaining quantitative information is reasonably straightforward (given well-designed data-gathering forms, a motivated and cooperative client, and helpful advisers), the gathering of qualitative data is usually much more problematic simply because it defies quantification and is highly subjective. And of even greater importance than gathering both types of data, is deciding what data is needed.

In this chapter, we will explore the aspects of data gathering, including the mutual definition of goals, needs, and priorities; determining risk tolerance; distinguishing between quantitative and qualitative data; using data gathering tools; and understanding the various personal financial planning subject areas.

The objectives of this chapter are:
- Describe the process of mutually defining client goals, needs, and priorities.
- Identify the essential characteristics of goals and objectives.
- Explain how clients' personal values and attitudes shape their goals and objectives and the priority placed on them.

- Distinguish between quantitative and qualitative client data.
- Describe the various types of quantitative client data.
- Describe the various types of qualitative client data.
- Explain the process of determining a client's risk tolerance.
- Use data gathering forms to obtain various types of client data.

QUALITATIVE DATA

Mutually Defining Client Goals, Needs, and Priorities

Why must the planner and the client mutually define client goals, needs, and priorities? Why not just ask the client for the information and accept his or her response at face value and proceed accordingly? Clearly, this is an option—and one that some financial planners follow. However, merely interviewing the client is not the same as mutually defining the client's goals, needs, and priorities. In order to reach a mutual definition, there must be a frank and open, two-way discussion between the financial planner and the client. This type of discussion should include an exploration of the client's values, attitudes, expectations, and time horizons as they are relevant to the client's goals, needs, and priorities. Personal values and attitudes shape a client's goals and objectives and the priority the client places on them. For instance, a client may place a high value on the education of his or her children; on providing for a spouse, children, or significant other in the event of the client's disability or premature death; on providing for parents who are near or below the poverty line or disabled; on retiring reasonably early at a meaningful income level; or on efficiently passing his or her estate to adult children. Once the financial planner has a reasonable understanding of the client's values, attitudes, and expectations, then he or she is in a better position to evaluate the consistency of the client's proposed goals, needs, and priorities. If the financial planner sets goals, needs, and priorities that do not align with a client's basic values, attitudes, and expectations, the result will usually be a lack of client commitment to their accomplishment.

In some cases, the client may not have given serious thought to such issues and may prefer to defer to the financial planner to suggest goals, needs, and priorities that are appropriate for the client. In this situation, the financial planner should avoid being placed in the position of having developed the goals, needs, and priorities unilaterally. If the client previously has not given a lot of thought to these issues, then the financial planner should attempt to focus the client on the issues so that the resulting goals, needs, and priorities truly represent the thinking of the client, rather than the financial planner. In Chapter 3, we will explore in more depth techniques for dealing with particular types of clients. A financial planner with a strong personality paired with a client who is somewhat timid, lacking in self-assurance, and inexperienced in financial matters can be a dangerous combination potentially resulting in the client's failure to take ownership of the goals, needs, and priorities. Conversely, a client with a dominant personality and a financial planner who is uncomfortable challenging such a client is a combination that may result in goals, needs, and priorities that the client firmly owns but that have not been subjected to informed inquiry and evaluation, and therefore may not be reasonable and realistic. Assisting clients in recognizing the implications of unrealistic goals and objectives is a critical financial planner responsibility. In most cases, there cannot be a final mutual definition of goals, needs, and priorities until all of the other data, both quantitative and qualitative, has been obtained and evaluated.

It is only after the client's goals, needs, and priorities have been mutually defined in this fashion that they rise to the level of working goals, needs, and priorities, subject to finalization as more client data is obtained and reviewed.

Important Characteristics of Goals and Objectives

Without mutually defined goals and objectives that are realistic and achievable, the personal financial planning process is doomed. Well-developed goals and objectives provide focus, purpose, vision, and direction for the personal financial planning process. Vague or imprecise goals that cannot be meaningfully measured are of limited value. To be optimally effective, goals must be clear, precise, consistent, and measurable.

A client may indicate that he or she wants to retire comfortably, start a business, purchase a vacation property, or put his or her children through college. These are typical client goals, but unless they are clarified with more specificity in quantifiable terms, they fail to serve as useful goals and objectives. For instance:

- At what age does the client want to retire and with what income and assets?
- Does the client have access to a qualified retirement plan or other savings vehicle?
- How much has the client accumulated already toward this goal?
- Does the client anticipate a significant inheritance in the time horizon involved?
- What other goals will require significant amounts of funding?
- What amount will the client need to save on a monthly basis, assuming a realistic return on investment and future inflation rate?

Regarding an education goal:

- How many children are there, and what are their current ages?
- When will they begin college?
- Will it be a state-supported or private educational institution?
- Will it be for just four years of undergraduate study, or will graduate school be involved?
- Will the student(s) live at home?
- Will the client's family qualify for financial aid?
- What type of savings vehicle will be employed?

Will the college costs be paid entirely from current income at the time, or will a portion or all of the costs be derived from savings?

Regarding starting a business:
- What kind of business?
- Will it be purchased or started by the client?
- What will it cost?
- When will it be launched?

What other income will be available to the client after he or she starts up or purchases the business?

And if the goal is a vacation property:
- Where will the vacation property be located?
- What will it cost?
- When will it be acquired?
- Will the client obtain a mortgage or pay cash?
- What resources are already available?

In order to increase the likelihood of the client's achieving his or her goals, these kinds of questions need to be asked and answered so that clearly defined, precise, consistent, and measurable goals are developed.

At Appendix A, there is a variety of sample data gathering forms. On pages A-4 and A-5, there are forms for gathering family goals and objectives. Pages A-13 through A-20 contain retirement planning, estate planning, education planning, tax planning, and a retirement planning questionnaire that are partially qualitative and partially quantitative in nature. Each of the above sample forms may be useful to the financial planner in gathering qualitative data.

Client Needs

Generally, client goals and objectives tend to be aspirational in nature. They are dreams that clients would very much like to accomplish, but rarely qualify as an absolute necessity. In that respect, they differ from client needs. For example, a client may need to provide for a disabled spouse, child or parent who has no other means of support; may have a legal obligation to pay alimony and/or child support in a specific amount over a given period of time; may have significant debt service requirements; or must honor a legal judgment entered against him or her. While it is true that a client may choose to ignore obligations of this type, either because of the fear of the repercussions of doing so or because of the client's value system, these obligations tend to fall into a somewhat different category than goals and objectives. Accordingly, they are considered to be needs, rather than goals and objectives.

Client Priorities

Once the financial planner and the client have mutually defined the client's goals and needs, they must then mutually define the client's priorities. Because the resources available to accomplish the goals and needs are probably limited, it is important that the client's priorities be established. This again involves an understanding of the client's values, attitudes, and expectations. The financial planner who knows, for instance, that the client places a very high value on education will find it easier to understand and assist the client in establishing that priority above other goals and objectives.

Risk, Risk/Return Tradeoff, and Risk Tolerance

Probably the most significant item of qualitative data other than a client's goals, needs, and priorities is his or her risk tolerance. Many of the recommendations that the financial planner will make will involve the purchase and/or sale of specific investments. Implementation of such recommendations should rely to a great extent on an assessment of the client's risk tolerance. The financial planner is under a legal and ethical obligation to help clients make investment choices that are "suitable" for their particular circumstances. Suitability must be based on the consideration of a number of different factors, including the client's goals, financial ability to sustain a loss, and psychological attitudes toward risk taking. Accurately matching the product to the client should lead to a lasting relationship that can be profitable to both parties.

The need for information about the client's ability to tolerate risk is especially critical when the financial planner is employing a computerized asset allocation program based on modern portfolio theory. To properly allocate the assets, a level of acceptable risk must be determined. Nearly all of the other calculations are a function of this initial determination. Other factors being equal, the client should be guided toward the investment with the higher return when faced with investments with equally tolerable levels of risk. Conversely, when the choice is between investments with equal levels of return, the client should be advised to select the one with the lower risk. Consequently, **risk, risk/return tradeoff,** and **risk tolerance** are concepts that need to be seriously considered by both the financial planner and the client during the development of financial planning recommendations.

Risk

Books on both risk management and investments explore the concept of risk, and in particular, speculative or financial risk. Here, we will provide only a general overview of investment risk.

In its broadest sense, the term **risk**, as used in an investment context, is the probability that an actual return on the investment will be lower than the expected return (or value). This risk is measured in terms of the volatility or variability in returns. By this definition, an investment that has low variability in returns from month to month, quarter to quarter, and year to year is less risky than an investment that fluctuates wildly in value during this same period. It is less risky because it is more predictable and less subject to surprises.

Risk/Return Tradeoff

In general, investment vehicles that produce higher average rates of return usually have greater variability in their returns. This is known as the risk/return tradeoff. In order to enjoy the possibility of relatively high returns, the client must also run the risk that the returns may be relatively low. In some cases, the value of an investment can fall below the amount of the initial investment, sometimes permanently and sometimes only temporarily. The term **risk**, when properly understood, includes not only the possible loss of principal but also returns that, although positive, are much lower than expected.

Risk Tolerance

The psychological makeup of each client is completely unique. Each differs in his or her willingness to be exposed to greater losses for the chance of getting greater returns.

As we discussed in Chapter 1, risk tolerance is a highly subjective and personal attribute that, while requiring evaluation and understanding by the financial planner, is not easily evaluated. Assessing a client's "level" of risk tolerance is a difficult process for a number of reasons. First, risk tolerance is an elusive, ambiguous concept to the average client. If they have no previous investment experience, it is especially hard for clients to specify how risk tolerant they are. Under such circumstances, the client is likely to resort to an analysis of his or her behaviors in other risky situations (e.g., physical activities such as skydiving, scuba diving, racing, motorcycling, etc.). However, research on risk taking demonstrates that a person's level of risk tolerance for physical activities is not a good gauge of risk taking in situations involving the potential loss of money, such as in investment decisions.

Second, while numerous approaches to assessing risk tolerance for financial matters have been proposed, the results of these procedures often vary greatly from one to the other. A client may seem risk-averse using one procedure and appear risk-tolerant when assessed using another technique. This is because each technique is subject to different sources of error.

Third, risk tolerance is not a fixed characteristic of an individual. The particulars of a given situation are as strong an influence on the person's willingness to accept risk as are his or her natural predispositions to either take or avoid risk. For example, most people are more willing to take risks with money acquired through a windfall than with money that they had to work hard to earn.

Finally, many clients fail to see their financial planner as a professional confidant and find it difficult to open up to the financial planner and provide the information needed to help them. In such a case, it can be difficult for the financial planner to acquire the information necessary to assess risk tolerance.

A variety of procedures have been used to analyze a client's risk tolerance, ranging from preferences for different gambles to choices the client has made in real life. Unfortunately, there are no standard instruments designed for application in a financial planning context. Most existing devices appear to have been created by various financial planning firms for their own use or are adaptations of techniques meant for use in scientific studies of risk-taking. Any measure of risk tolerance, like all measurement procedures and devices, needs to meet acceptable standards of reliability and validity, particularly when the information is being used to draw inferences for individuals rather than large groups of people. A properly constructed risk tolerance test must measure a characteristic consistently (reliability), and evidence must be obtained to document that the measuring device does, in fact, measure what it purports to measure (validity).

There is no one ideal method for completing this task. Each technique has its pitfalls. The research on assessing risk-taking propensity demonstrates clearly that a major cause for inaccurate results is that an insufficient number of questions are asked, particularly questions that elicit information about past behaviors, current attitudes, and intentions regarding the future. Even under ideal circumstances, though, it is impossible to truly peg the client's risk tolerance. At best, the results of the assessment are an approximation of the client's actual level of risk tolerance. The financial planner should not forget that risk tolerance is a dynamic characteristic of the client that can change with changing client circumstances such as age, income, number of dependents, and wealth. As a result, a client's tolerance for investment risk should be reevaluated periodically.

Information about the client's risk tolerance can be captured through the use of both formal and informal procedures. Formal procedures such as questionnaires have merit in that they permit standardization of the assessment process. Moreover, such questionnaires can serve as teaching tools almost to the same extent as they are assessment devices. Often it is possible to quantify the answers to a questionnaire and to develop some index of risk tolerance. In no case, however, should such an index be accepted blindly by either the client or the financial planner as the definitive measure of the client's risk tolerance.

Harold Evensky, in his writings on risk tolerance, provides the two basic principles of risk assessment. First, "[B]e aware of the potential conflicts between your objective view of risk and the client's emotional view. This is a major danger when the wealth manager is communicating on an intellectual frequency and the client is receiving on an emotional frequency," and second, "Do not assume client knowledge. Even the most successful and sophisticated business or professional client is likely to have a rudimentary knowledge of modern investment theory...".[4]

---

[4] *Wealth Management* by Harold R. Evensky, McGraw-Hill, 1997, p. 81.

In-Depth: Risk Tolerance Questionnaires

Many financial planning firms have developed their own risk tolerance questionnaires. While their primary role is to extract information regarding risk tolerance, they typically serve as an entree for client conversation, education, and management of the client's expectations. There tend to be four broad classifications of the methods used to assess how a person reacts to risk: (1) self-reported preferences for selected investment products; (2) preferences for probabilities/payoffs in various simulations; (3) choices made involving risk in naturally occurring life situations; and (4) self-reports of attitudes toward risk. These questionnaires may range from 5 to 10 pages and include anywhere from 5 to 25 questions. Questions will elicit information about the size of the client's investment portfolio and what percentage it represents of the client's total investments, whether there is an immediate or near term need for income from the portfolio, whether significant cash withdrawals of principal will be made over the next few years, whether the portfolio is taxable or partially taxable and the effective tax rate, the portfolio's investment time horizon, and the client's annual return goal based on an assumed inflation rate.

In addition, there are usually questions about the client's level of concern (expressed numerically) about such attributes as capital preservation, growth, low volatility, inflation protection, current cash flow, and aggressive growth. Some financial planners have devised a method to score this type of question in the form of a number between zero and 100 with zero representing an all-Treasury bill portfolio and 100 representing an all-equity portfolio. This score is often used in conjunction with the responses to the other questions to evaluate the client's tolerance for equity exposure.

Another useful question is one that asks the client if there are any specific asset class constraints. This can lead to further discussion with the client about certain asset classes with which the client is unfamiliar. This may enable the financial planner to educate the client about asset classes previously unknown to the client and to assure the client of a maximum exposure to those particular asset classes.

Often questionnaires have items directed at the client's feelings about failing to achieve his or her target rate of return, the portfolio's being worth less in "real" dollars because of inflation erosion, and short-term and long-term volatility. Also, the questionnaire should probe the client's concerns about an extended stock market downturn of up to four years, perhaps by asking how long a downturn the client is willing to tolerate if the portfolio produces a long-term return that permits the client to accomplish his or her goals. Other useful questions are those concerned with the client's feeling about being in or out of the stock market when it goes either down or up and questions that let clients choose from possible portfolios a risk/return intersection that best represents the balance between their goals for returns and their tolerance for risk. Finally, some form of gambling question (in which there is a certain result versus an uncertain one) is useful in eliciting additional information about the client's tolerance for risk. Frequently, the answers to this type of question indicate that the client does not wish to take risks to get rich but will take risks to keep from becoming poor. Starting at page A-16 of Appendix A, there appears a sample Investment/Risk Tolerance Questionnaire.

It should be apparent by now that a financial planner must take great care in framing questions to clients about risk tolerance. The answers provided could be significantly different depending on how the facts are couched in the question. The financial planner must make certain that his or her understanding of the terms used (for example, to express a probability statement) is the same as that of his or her clients.

An often-overlooked factor is the comparison between the client's *willingness* to assume risk and the client's *capacity* to assume risk. This involves analyzing other client data to determine the client's ability to absorb significant amounts of risk. A willingness to take risk should not exceed a capacity to take risk. Recent research on the use of risk tolerance questionnaires seems to support the superiority of a questionnaire addressing both risk attitude and risk capacity over a questionnaire containing questions that mostly address risk attitude.[5]

---

[5] "Assessing Risk Tolerance: Questioning the Questionnaire Method," Ken C. Yook, Ph.D. and Robert Everett, Ph.D., *Journal of Financial Planning*, August 2003.

Although assessing risk tolerance is a complex and inexact science, the financial planner nevertheless has an obligation to make such an assessment prior to proceeding with the subsequent steps of the personal financial planning process.

QUANTITATIVE DATA

Having discussed the principal types of qualitative client data, let us turn now to the gathering of quantitative client data. One of the most important types of quantitative data is the client's financial information, including cash inflows, cash outflows, assets, and debts. While we will discuss in this chapter how this financial information is obtained, we will defer until Chapter 4 our discussion of how this information is organized into meaningful personal financial statements and analyzed.

Quantitative data includes a large amount of information such as client and spouse names; dates and places of birth; social security numbers; home address and telephone number; previous marriages; names, age and dependency status of children; number and ages of grandchildren; name and relationship of others who are financially dependent on the client; significant health problems of family members (factual observations, such as the fact that a family member has cancer or diabetes); name and phone number of other professional advisers; current employer, position with employer, years employed with employer, and employer's phone number; other professional activities, paid or unpaid, outside of main employment; assets, liabilities, income sources and trends, expenditures (to be discussed in Chapter 4); insurance coverage; borrowing and credit considerations; Social Security eligibility; retirement plan participation and projected benefits; wills and trusts; and the degree of client involvement in planning, record-keeping and taxes. Quantitative data is confined to objective, factual information and does not require a judgment or opinion by either the client or the financial planner.

A large assortment of documents also should be gathered so that information can be collected directly from the original sources.

Many financial planners use a document request form to request necessary documents from the client.

Refer to Appendix A for some sample data gathering forms. Pages A-1 through A-3 in Appendix A, are designed to elicit basic personal client information. Pages A-6 through A-8 request detailed information about client assets. Page A-12 deals with the client's current insurance coverage, while page A-9 requests information about client liabilities. Page A-10 is concerned with client income sources. Page A-11 deals with client personal expenditures. Page A-21 addresses document storage and a statement from the client about the relative accuracy of the information submitted.

Important Documents to Collect

- estate planning documents, such as current wills, living wills, trust agreements, gift tax returns (if any), estate tax returns (if the client has been the beneficiary of any estates), guardian nominations, powers of attorney or appointment, and appraisals for significant assets
- income tax returns for perhaps the last three years
- closely-held business financial statements and income tax returns, deferred compensation plans, Keogh or SEP plans, pension or profit-sharing plans, stock option purchase agreements, buy-sell agreements, employment agreements, employee benefits booklets, articles of incorporation, merger/acquisition agreements, partnership agreements, sale or purchase contracts, and business insurance policies.
- matrimonial documents including divorce settlements, separation agreements, and prenuptial agreements
- investments
- notes and other debts
- notes receivable
- birth certificates and adoption decrees
- current statements of vested interests in pension or profit-sharing plans and IRAs as well as documents pertaining to other corporate benefit plans
- insurance-related documents, including copies of life insurance policies or a summary of policies owned; disability and medical expense insurance policies; auto and homeowners policies; and certain other insurance policies
- deeds, mortgages, leases, and land contracts
- previous financial planning documents
- copies of personal financial statements for the last three years

IMPORTANT CONCEPTS TO REMEMBER

Mutual definition of client goals, needs, and priorities

Essential characteristics of goals and objectives

Effect of client values and attitudes on client goals and objectives

Types of qualitative client data

Types of quantitative client data

Risk tolerance

Use of data gathering forms

Personal financial planning subject areas

QUESTIONS FOR REVIEW

1. What are some of the essential characteristics of well-developed client goals and objectives?

2. Distinguish between client goals and objectives and client needs.

3. What are some of the difficulties in assessing a client's risk tolerance?

4. What is meant by the risk/return tradeoff?

SUGGESTIONS FOR ADDITIONAL READING

The Tools & Techniques of Financial Planning, 6th edition, Stephan R. Leimberg, Martin J. Satinsky, Robert T. LeClair, & Robert J. Doyle, Jr., Chapter 17, The National Underwriter Company, 2002.

Wealth Management, Harold R. Evensky, pp. 23-36, McGraw-Hill, 1997.

"Assessing Risk Tolerance: Questioning the Questionnaire Method," Ken C. Yook, Ph.D. and Robert Everett, Ph.D., *Journal of Financial Planning*, August 2003.

"Assessing Risk Tolerance for Asset Allocation," William G. Droms, DBA, CFA and Steven N. Strauss, CPA/PFS

CHAPTER THREE

Client Attitudes and Behavioral Characteristics

• • •

In this chapter, we will explore how clients' thoughts, feelings, belief systems, and attitudes influence their behavior, financial decision-making, and reaction to money and property. Clients' attitudes toward money and investing are deeply rooted in their upbringings, cultural backgrounds, family situations, levels of knowledge, life experiences, stages in the life cycle, confidence levels, and risk tolerances. A financial planner's job, in developing financial planning recommendations, is to ferret out the emotions beneath the surface and try to help clients overcome fears and bad decisions. As a result, financial planners must not only act as financial guardians for their clients, but also as quasi-therapists.

While we will discuss each of the factors affecting client attitudes and behavioral characteristics (i.e., cultural, family, and emotional factors as well as life cycle and age, level of knowledge and experience, and risk tolerance), it is important to recognize that many of these factors are not independent but rather overlap, interrelate, and interact.

The objectives of this chapter are:

- Describe the effect of cultural influences on client attitudes and behavioral characteristics.
- Describe the effect of family influences on client attitudes and behavioral characteristics .
- Describe the effect of emotional influences on client attitudes and behavioral characteristics.

- Describe the effect of a client's age and stage in the life cycle on client attitudes and behavioral characteristics.

- Describe the effect of a client's level of knowledge, experience, and expertise on his or her attitudes and behavioral characteristics.

- Describe the effect of a client's risk tolerance on client attitudes and behavioral characteristics.

- Identify the basic fear-reducing activities employed by each of Doyle's four financial temperaments in his financial quaternary.

- Describe what is meant by sensing, intuitive, thinking, feeling, judging, and perceiving preferences according to the Myers-Briggs Type Indicator.

- Identify types of family/living arrangements other than the "nuclear family."

- Describe some of the principal methods of categorizing clients by their emotional or psychological types.

- Describe the specific psychological preferences that tell how people are energized, how they gather information, how they make decisions, and how they choose a particular lifestyle.

- Describe Keirsey's and Doyle's four basic temperaments.

- Discuss McKenna, Hyllegard, and Linder's suggested strategies for motivating and effectively communicating with the four general types of client temperaments.

- Explain the purpose of a financial planner psychological self-evaluation.

- Describe some of the most significant implications for financial planning of the concepts discussed in this chapter.

CULTURAL FACTORS AND INFLUENCES

In his book *The Social Meanings of Money and Property: In Search of a Talisman*, Professor Kenneth O. Doyle of the University of Minnesota theorizes that at some time in paleohistory, humans realized that someone else had *more or better*, and that difference constituted the first discernible wealth. This realization resulted in the fear that someone else might have more (envy) or that someone else might take what one has (jealousy).

Professor Doyle holds that, as a result of natural selection, systematically different varieties of man evolved around the world in Europe, Asia, Africa, and the Americas, each with a predominant temperament, along with distinguishable attitudes, values, and behavior patterns. Relying on the generally agreed source of human life as being the forests and savannas of east Africa (today's Ethiopia, Kenya, and the Sudan), Professor Doyle traces in the migration of man to different areas of the world the evolution of his attitudes, values, and temperament. On the basis of differences in art, myth, and ritual, Professor Doyle associates with European man a propensity for acquisition, achievement, and competition. With Asian man, he associates an inclination toward precision, hierarchy, demarcation, and a desire for order and harmony. With the ancient peoples of sub-Saharan Africa, he associates expressiveness, and with the early indigenous Americans, affiliativeness and amiability.

According to Professor Doyle's thesis, the social meanings that people attach to money and property reflect values, attitudes, and tendencies that are embedded in their **temperament** (personality). Psychologists define temperament as a pattern of consistently observable behaviors. McKenna, Hyllegard, and Linder[6] define temperament as "a unified configuration of inclinations, an innate pattern of attitudes and actions." It is generally agreed that one is born with his or her temperament, rather than temperament being learned. To a large degree, our behavior (including our financial decision-making) is the result of our innate temperament. Doyle believes that temperament is the result of genetic and environmental influences developed over long periods of history. Later in this chapter, in the section entitled "Emotional Factors and Influences," we will discuss temperament and behavior characteristics in greater depth.

As Professor Doyle goes to great pains to clarify, he does not even remotely suggest that all members of any geographical or cultural group possess the predominant characteristics of that group or that any culture is exclusively of one propensity or another. From his four groups, Doyle derives "four archetypal propensities" as the basic dimensions of personality that, to varying extents, explain the essential character of individuals, families, and communities.

Professor Doyle goes on to hypothesize that the central psychological purpose of money and property is to defend against threats to the ego, concluding that the central motive is fear and the central meaning is protection. He considers money and property to be one of several objects believed to impart magical powers to the possessor for the purpose of protecting him or herself against fear. Such objects are known as "talismans," or "preventatives."

Figure 3.1

The Basic Quaternary of Temperaments

II	I
Acquisitiveness/Driver	*Expansiveness/Expressive*
Galen's Choleric	Galen's Sanguine
Fear of incompetence	Fear of constraint
e.g., entrepreneurs, military officers	e.g., entertainers, sales representatives
III	**IV**
Concentration/Analytic	*Affiliativeness/Amiable*
Galen's Phlegmatic	Galen's Melancholic
Fear of disarray	Fear of abandonment
e.g., accountants, "hard" scientists	e.g., clergy, child care workers

Source: Copyright 1997 Kenneth O. Doyle. Used by permission

---

[6] "Linking Psychological Type to Financial Decision-Making" by Judy McKenna, Karen Hyllegard, and Ray Linder, *The Journal of the Association for Financial Counseling and Planning Education*, Volume 14(1), 2003.

The Quaternary

To better understand the four temperaments, Professor Doyle uses what is referred to as a quaternary, which is constructed on the intersection of two continuums (or dialectics). In his "Basic Quaternary of Temperaments," one end of the continuum is acquisition/affiliation while the other is expansiveness/concentration (see Figure 3.1). Four distinct types of people fall into the quadrants of the quaternary.

Beginning in the upper right quadrant, **Expressives** are said to enjoy engaging in lively and spontaneous behavior but do so mostly because they feel threatened by constraint. They tend to spend their wealth in ways that attempt to prove they are free spirits. **Drivers**, appearing in the upper-left quadrant, enjoy competition and accomplishment but act as they do primarily because of the fear of being found incompetent. They are inclined toward differentiation, categorizing people by levels of performance and ownership. The lower left quadrant contains the **Analytics**, who operate out of a fear of disarray or loss of control. They carefully guard their money and property because they fear they will lose control over it. Finally, the lower right quadrant is where the **Amiables** reside. They tend to avoid wealth because they fear abandonment by those close to them. Typically, they emphasize collectivity, socialism, and even communism. They seek to minimize differences among people to avoid anyone feeling disaffiliated. These four basic temperaments are discussed in more detail later in this chapter in the section entitled **Emotional Factors and Influences**.

Moreover, most individuals, families, and groups exhibit attitudes, values, and behaviors associated with more than one quadrant and one's position on the quadrants probably changes over time, in terms of life stage (discussed later), education and learning (also discussed later), and even shifts in the relative contribution of heredity versus environment. Most likely, people's values and behaviors change in response to situational factors such as role, context, and relationship, and how relatively uninhibited they feel at any particular time.

Another important phenomenon is that people belonging to any of the four groups tend to cling to the values and behaviors of their own group and not only disparage, but also fear, the values and behaviors of other temperaments, particularly those at the opposite pole.

The task of determining a client's position within the quaternary involves the use of assigning a value for each of the two axes. The vertical axis represents a client's degree of **introversion/extraversion**, which Carl Jung defined as the inclination to direct one's energy inward versus outwards. The horizontal axis plots what American psychologist William James referred to as tenderminded/toughminded. **Tenderminded** (or emotional) is defined as the inclination to evaluate the world according to gentle criteria like feeling and intuition, whereas **toughminded** (or rational) is the tendency to base evaluations and decisions on logic. If, by applying this methodology, a client ends up close to a quadrant border, it means he or she is a blend of two or more temperaments. Also, the closer one falls to the center point (the point at which the two axes intersect) of the quaternary, the more that person represents a blend of types. The further one strays from the center point, the more deeply entrenched their temperament and resulting behavior.

Figure 3.2

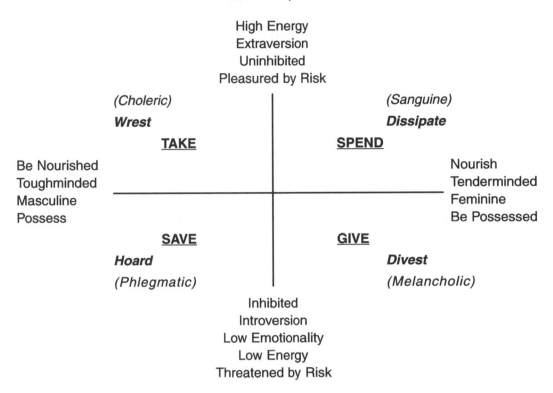

The Financial Quaternary—Individual Level

High Energy
Extraversion
Uninhibited
Pleasured by Risk

(Choleric)

Wrest

TAKE

(Sanguine)

Dissipate

SPEND

Be Nourished
Toughminded
Masculine
Possess

Nourish
Tenderminded
Feminine
Be Possessed

SAVE

Hoard

(Phlegmatic)

GIVE

Divest

(Melancholic)

Inhibited
Introversion
Low Emotionality
Low Energy
Threatened by Risk

Source: Copyright 1997 Kenneth O. Doyle. Used by permission.

The Financial Quaternary

In Figure 3.2, Professor Doyle illustrates the relationship between the four general temperaments he has identified in Figure 3.1 and four "financial temperaments" at the individual level. Reviewing his premise that the basic human motive is fear and that people use money and property as talismans to protect themselves from the particular fear that is associated with their temperament, he suggests that the basic fear-reducing financial activities are **give/take** and **save/spend**. Amiables tend to deal with their fear of abandonment by giving. Drivers assuage their fear of incompetence by taking. Analytics manage their fear of disorder by saving, and Expressives deal with their fear of constraint by spending.

FAMILY FACTORS AND INFLUENCES

Clearly, family plays a significant role in shaping a client's attitudes and behavioral characteristics. Of course, the whole concept of family has changed significantly over the past several decades. The traditional "family" composed of husband, wife, and two plus children with one main breadwinner has given way to a profusion of living arrangements, including dual income (where the breadwinners are married or unmarried and either with or without children), single, single parent, blended family, domestic partners, two- or even three-generation, and so-called boomerang children households.

With the rise of second marriages and second families, with many people delaying marriage and children, with some parents caught in the "sandwich" between toddlers and aging parents, and with some needing to fund their education just as they begin retirement, financial planning has had to adjust to these countless nontraditional family and living situations.

A financial planner whose psychological and historical orientation has been built around the so-called "nuclear family" may have a difficult time relating to clients in any of the other family/living situations described in the previous paragraph. In addition, clients who have recently entered into any of these alternative family/living situations may share the financial planner's view of the "nuclear family," both in psychological and historical orientation. This may be detrimental to such a client who does not fully appreciate the financial planning needs of his or her new family/living situation and who works with a financial planner who also lacks such an appreciation. Financial planners need to understand the attitudes and behavioral characteristics of clients in family/living situations other than that of the nuclear family. Moreover, financial planners need to help clients understand and appreciate the key financial planning factors applicable to the clients' new family/living situation. By educating clients in this fashion, the financial planner can influence the clients' attitudes and behaviors in a positive way and accordingly facilitate the client-planner relationship

As mentioned previously, the many factors that affect client attitudes and behavioral characteristics are not independent and tend to overlap and interrelate. This is certainly the case with cultural and family factors. In certain cultures, family is central to one's life and in such families there is either an implicit or explicit obligation to provide for all family members—both immediate and extended families. Often, this will be reflected in family living arrangements. For instance, three or more generations may reside in a single household. In other cultures, family is a less pervasive factor and adult and near-adult family members may be expected to be financially independent and self-maintaining. In these situations, families will tend to live in several households, rather than only one. If these differences in cultural/family factors are understood and appreciated by the financial planner, the client-planner relationship can be enhanced, thus permitting both parties to benefit from the relationship.

In Figure 3.3, we see the family level financial quaternary. Professor Doyle states that families can be characterized in the same way as individuals. Amiable families are emotionally needy and exhibit a propensity toward dependence. Driver families are acquisitive, with a tendency toward independence. Analytic families are retentive and inclined toward frugality and regulation, while Expressive families are inclined toward emotion, even dishevelment. And as with individuals, the more intense the fear, the more intense the behaviors used by families to cope with those fears: divesting, wresting, hoarding, and dissipating. Small individual discrepancies in financial values may produce some tension within a family (which may be healthy). However, larger individual discrepancies will produce conflict, and the weaker members will eventually either separate themselves or be separated by the stronger members.

Figure 3.3

The Financial Quaternary—Family Level

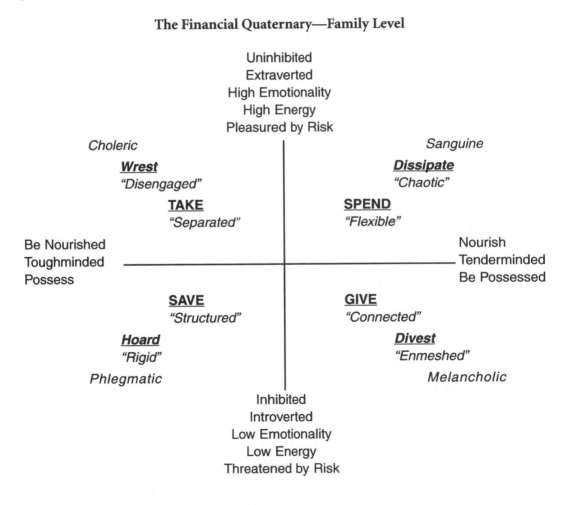

Source: Copyright 1997 Kenneth O. Doyle. Used by permission.
Note: Quoted terms are from Olson (1986).

EMOTIONAL FACTORS AND INFLUENCES

One of the two main schools of social scientists that studied peoples' perceptions of money and property was composed principally of economists. This group, originated by John Stuart Mill, was led over the years by economists Adam Smith, Stanley Jevons, John Maynard Keynes, Joseph Schumpeter, and Milton Friedman, and espoused **rational choice theory**, or **utility theory**, which holds that people make rational choices to maximize their overall "utility," or well-being. Specifically, Mill described the concept of **Economic Man**, the idea that humans are driven to achieve wealth in the most efficient manner, using complex objective information in the process. Mill and his followers committed income and consumption patterns to convenient formulas and did not address the psychological aspects of consumers.

But even the members of this school of thought recognized in varying degrees the importance of social and psychological considerations. They generally acknowledged that so-called rational motives are not necessarily what drive human behavior—that nonrational or irrational impulses may also be involved and may play a role in human motivation.

Later, a small group of psychologists challenged the premises of rational choice theory, demonstrating that this theory could not accommodate some common psychological phenomena. This laid the groundwork for considerable research into the psychological aspects of decision-making. Richard Herrnstein developed what has come to be known as **matching law**, which holds that people do not always try to maximize utility, but instead choose behaviors in direct proportion to the value they derive from each. In addition, people change their behavior in accordance with the amount of reinforcement they receive. If we accept the premise that people act and make decisions, particularly financial decisions, for reasons other than utility maximization, then we need to learn more about the source of these nonrational or irrational psychological factors.

A client's emotional or psychological makeup is certainly a very significant factor in the formation of the client's attitudes and behavioral characteristics. Again, as mentioned earlier, the various factors that affect a client's attitudes and behavioral characteristics, such as cultural, family, emotional, life cycle and age, client knowledge and experience, and risk tolerance, do not function independently and not only overlap but interrelate with each other. Consequently, when we speak of a client's emotional factors and influences, we necessarily are speaking simultaneously of the other factors just described to the extent that they have affected the client's emotional makeup.

Myers-Briggs Type Indicator (MBTI)

Various psychologists have developed methods of categorizing clients by "personality groups," some with a relatively large number of such groups. Peter B. Myers and Katharine D. Myers in their Myers-Briggs Type Indicator® (MBTI), have divided each of their four basic psychological types (Sensing-Introvert, Intuitive-Introvert, Sensing-Extravert, and Intuitive-

Extravert) into four sub-types (resulting in sixteen sub-types) by combining the additional factors of thinking, feeling, judging, and perceiving as the methods by which decisions are made and by which people orient toward the outer world.

The extraversion/introversion set of preferences defines how people are energized—either from the external world or internally. Extraverts prefer to talk things out and seek affirmation from friends and associates about their ideas. Introverts would rather think something through before discussing it with others and tend to be guarded about sharing personal information with people they do not know well.

Sensing and intuitive preferences refer to the process used by people to gather information. Sensing people tend to prefer dealing with the present and like dealing with concrete ideas and specifics. On the other hand, an intuitive will tend to use hunches and inspiration to brainstorm future options and take more of a "big picture" approach.

Thinking and feeling preferences tell how people make decisions. People who prefer thinking rely on logic and science, prefer numbers and figures, and value objectivity. Those who prefer feeling try to take into account the feelings of others and value harmony over clarity.

Under the MBTI scheme, judging and perceiving preferences describe lifestyle preferences. Judging persons are decisive, orderly, good planners, and have little trouble making decisions. They will tend to make lists of items to be accomplished and they are very aware of the time involved to accomplish these items. Those who have a perceiving preference are flexible, adaptable, and spontaneous. They prefer to keep their options open and have difficulty reaching closure on an item. Often, they work under last-minute pressure to complete a task. They enjoy gathering new information and new ideas before making a decision.

Allen and Brock[7] warn against the negative impact of labeling people under the MBTI. They indicate that the MBTI can be seen as a sixteen-room house in which each person has a favorite room, but necessarily uses all of the rooms in the house.

---

[7] *Health Care Communication Using Personality Type* by J. Allen and S.A. Brock, Routledge, 2000.

Keirsey's Four General Temperaments

Dr. David Keirsey[8], often considered the father of modern temperament theory, has identified four temperaments—**Guardians, Artisans, Idealists, and Rationals**. Keirsey refers to the **Guardian** as the preserving temperament who considers money management as a way to preserve a comfortable, secure and organized home and work environment. Being skilled in logistics, guardians are associated with measurement, sequential thinking, frugal spending, saving money, minimizing debt, preparing for the future, and protection of their families and loved ones. They tend to be dependable and responsible though conservative and conventional. Their primary needs are for stability, safety and security. However, guardians are frustrated by disorganization, uncertainty, and unanticipated change. They are said to be good with facts and figures and to exercise good self-control in financial decision-making. Financial security is important to a guardian; as a result, they tend to be risk-averse with a low tolerance for uncertainty and volatility. They look for investments that provide stable, consistent, and secure returns.

Keirsey refers to the **Artisan** as the "doing" temperament. They are quite spontaneous and spur-of-the-moment. With regard to money management, artisans want the freedom to do what feels good and to make an impression. Unlike guardians, who are skilled at logistics, artisans are adept at tactics. They can quickly read a situation and make an instant decision for the short term. They are associated with adaptation, contextual thinking (understanding the urgency of the moment as it relates to their finances), promotion (using money to advance and accomplish others' interests), and performance (expeditious completion of projects). They look for the most expedient way to do or fix something right away. They need action and spontaneous, fun-loving freedom and are impulsive, bold, and opportunistic. They shy away from limits, tend to take on too much financial risk, and are reluctant to establish and be guided by goals. Record-keeping and administration are not their cups of tea. They tend to be haphazard savers and have a high tolerance for risk.

Idealists are considered by Keirsey as the inspiring temperament. To an **Idealist**, money management is about cultivating relationships, growing personally and helping others achieve their potential. They are diplomats and promoters and are naturally disposed to interpretation (understanding the meaning of others' behaviors), integrative thinking (seeing how things can come together), counseling, and revelation (insight into underlying motives and desires). For an idealist, financial management is a low priority. They are more interested in sharing their financial resources to build relationships and to inspire others. They are naturally altruistic and willing to give to effect change in the lives of others. Their apathy about money and lack of interest in the typical quantitative measurements of money is often detrimental to their own financial well-being.

Keirsey's fourth temperament is that of the **Rational**, the achieving temperament. For rationals, money management is about acquiring the necessary competence to understand, explain, and predict, and therefore control, the financial forces that affect their lives. Skilled in strategy, rationals have a natural disposition for analysis, differential thinking (seeing differences, categories, classifications, and functions), designing, and marshalling (arranging plan components in the necessary order). They are ingenious and resourceful in developing financial strategies and in long-range planning. Rationals may develop overly complex plans that tend to stagnate and fall short in their accomplishment. Sometimes, they do not follow through on their plans. They are often highly skeptical, independent thinkers, who enjoy challenging conventional wisdom. As a result, they will only take advice from someone they perceive as having greater expertise than themselves. Their big picture approach often results in frustration with the mundane details of financial management. They will tend to accept any level of risk after determining by analysis that the rewards justify the associated risks.

---

[8] *Please Understand Me: Character and Temperament Types* by David Keirsey and Marilyn Bates, Prometheus Nemesis Book Company, Del Mar, CA, 1978 and *Please Understand Me II* by David Keirsey, Prometheus Nemesis Book Company, Del Mar, CA, 1998.

Given these four distinct temperaments, financial planners are challenged to develop financial planning recommendations that produce meaningful, psychological benefits.

Professor Doyle employs a similar typology in the use of the quaternary described earlier in this chapter. In the next section, he describes four general temperaments.

Doyle's Four General Temperaments

Expressives

Expressives (Quadrant I of the Quaternary) periodically experience a sort of psychological claustrophobia in which they feel confined and have a tremendous need to escape immediately. This is particularly true when confronted with a particularly heavy dose of rules and regulations. Expressives fear this boxed-in feeling. Ultimately their innate restlessness and current lack of stimulation result in their seeking different and interesting people, places, and different and interesting ways to attract similar people. Their relationships with spouses and other family members may be subject to wide swings of emotion and attachment. Their business relationships may be superficial as they indulge in flamboyant activities. This temperament is often drawn to sales and entertainment careers. Because a client's temperament has such a strong influence on his or her career choice, a client's profession can be, but is not necessarily, an important indicator of his or her temperament.

Expressives tend to enjoy competition, but they compete more for entertainment and recognition than to inflict serious injury to competitors. Moreover, they admire unusual behavior and appearance and tend to rebel against rules and regulations.

With regard to money and property, Expressives are constantly pursuing possessions that are different and interesting such as unusual clothing, autos, or investments. They almost invariably avoid budgets. They tend to spend, even recklessly at times, for the sake of self-image. As has been stated earlier, money and property are, for them, vehicles of expression, which serve to assuage their fear of constraint. As Expressives receive positive feedback on their activities, they will tend to become more deeply entrenched in their fundamental temperament. If they receive negative feedback, they tend to feel boxed in again, betrayed and depressed, and the reaction will be either to confront society or withdraw from it, more likely the former. Note the similarity of Doyle's Expressive with Keirsey's Artisan.

Analytics

While Expressives cannot bear to be boxed in, Analytics (Quadrant III of the Quaternary) cannot bear having things out of control. While Expressives are set off by a lack of stimulation, Analytics are uncomfortable if there is too much stimulation. They tend to be tense and shy and are, as a result, less spontaneous than Expressives but are certainly more steady and dependable.

Typically, they will seek an atmosphere of high structure and low risk and will avoid situations that they consider too exciting or upsetting. They are inclined to keep their financial affairs under control. Being tidy, stubborn, stingy, and retentive, they enjoy saving and hoarding. Their family relationships will, most likely, be structured, even rigid. Business relationships will be well defined. Typical professions for Analytics are computer programmer, accountant, actuary, and other "hard" sciences.

Analytics tend to be uneasy in large crowds and disdain flashy clothes and loud people. They try to maintain a composed life style. If their behavior is perceived as responsible or dependable, they are encouraged. They like to be thought of as thrifty, but not cheap or rigid. For the analytic, money and property cautiously employed have the power to reduce his or her fear of over-stimulation and disarray. Thus analytics use money and property to control and regulate their environments. Note the similarity of Doyle's Analytic with Keirsey's Guardian.

Drivers

While Expressives and Analytics represent different ends of a continuum of stimulation, Drivers and Amiables are at opposite ends of an independence/dependence continuum. Drivers tend to seek the objective elements of the environment, rather than the world of feelings or ideas. They abhor excessive nurturance and express few feelings of interpersonal sensitivity and attachment. They take, buy, compete, exploit, and make sure the world is aware of their achievement and independence. They often keep emotional distance from spouse and children, and they impart messages to their children of competition and toughness. In business relationships, they win by intimidating, and they enjoy it. Typical occupations include entrepreneur, corporate raider, and litigator.

Drivers reward aggressive behavior and punish timid behavior. They generally establish hierarchies based on accomplishment (a buttress to their need to feel masterful). If Drivers are made to feel weak, they will resist and will seek every opportunity to prove themselves. While they will generally appreciate having their style referred to as courageous and successful, they may not object to being referred to as overbearing or ruthless. Money and property are signs of success and independence, even "trophies" in a sense. Note the similarity of Doyle's Driver with Keirsey's Rational.

Amiables

Being at the opposite end of the nurturance continuum from Drivers, Amiables never have enough nurturance. This results in ever-increasing feelings of dependence and helplessness, and an increased inclination to perceive the emotional side of life. They feel full and complete when experiencing warmth and emotional closeness. With regard to money and property, Amiables believe that having more than one requires is evil and will result in their becoming less lovable. As a result, they disdain materialism and resent those who possess what they perceive as too much.

Amiables tend to minimize differences among people, and they detest the oppressiveness of the wealthy, as well as money in general. They often disregard the world of finance and tend to live modestly and not accumulate significant wealth. They reward redistribution of wealth and value personal relationships over personal possessions. An Amiable would like being referred to as sensitive and caring, but not syrupy, desperate, or manipulative. Amiables go to great pains to avoid hurting anyone's feelings, for this threatens nurturance and affiliation. By avoiding the accumulation of money and property, they attempt to control their fear of abandonment. Amiables use money and property to equalize the sense of value of all people. Note the similarity of Doyle's Amiable with Keirsey's Idealist.

Other Alternatives to Personality and Values Assessments

Of course, each of these assessment tools is only a tool. Unless they are accurate, reliable, and practical and used properly, they can give misleading results. Generally, these standardized assessments result in the placement of clients in categories or, if you will, boxes (typology). In addition, they tend to ask questions or request the client to respond to statements and use words often at opposite ends of a spectrum for the client to self-describe him- or herself. Some of the words used are open to interpretation by the person being evaluated. Moreover, since the person being evaluated is providing his or her self-perception often in an atmosphere that lacks context, rather than using the perception of third parties, the results are sometimes questionable.

It is important to distinguish between a personality assessment and a values assessment. In their article "Are You Putting Your Clients in a Box?"[9], authors Brian Wruk and Dean M. Hebert give the example of a client having a personality trait of being outgoing. They contrast this trait with having the value of enjoying being around people when they state that it is possible to enjoy being around people without being outgoing. Wruk and Hebert go on to introduce the concept of neuro-linguistic programming (NLP) as the study of communication and beliefs stemming from the blending of many disciplines. NLP is said by Wruk and Hebert to reveal a map of people's preferences instead of assigning labels and boxes. They contend that it is important to know how people take in and process information, make decisions, and how they are motivated to take action—that is, their beliefs and values.

Wruk and Hebert believe that an assessment should be context specific, allow (if not encourage) multiple answers or no answers as appropriate, consist of direct and not cleverly disguised questions, use unambiguous meanings for words, and permit mapping of individuals, couples, and groups. Dean Hebert has developed an NLP-based assessment called the Motivation Profile. It measures nine dimensions, including the client's preferred information-gathering system (seeing, hearing, sensing), major life preferences, tendency to avoid or move toward things, preference to make decisions by one's self versus seeking the advice of others, tendency to follow rules and procedures, tendency to take action or to assess or delay action, desire to maintain the status quo or to make changes, tendency to take a big-picture versus a detailed focus, and the extent to which one relies on past, present, or future events.

---

[9] "Are You Putting Your Clients in a Box?" by Brian Wruk and Dean M. Hebert, *Journal of Financial Planning*, March 2003.

NLP-based assessments as well as the typology employed by Myers-Briggs, Keirsey, Doyle, and others can be useful in screening, matching, and referring clients. Assigning planners who could most naturally work with a client, build rapport, and secure a long-term relationship can add significant value to a client-planner relationship.

Practical Application of the Four Basic Temperaments and Psychological Preferences in Financial Planning

In Table 3.1, you can see a side-by-side comparison of the four basic Myers-Briggs psychological preferences and the four basic temperaments as conceived by both Keirsey and Doyle.

Table 3.1

Comparsion of MBTI, Doyle, and Keirsey Categorization of Psychological Types		
Myers-Briggs Psychological Preferences	*Temperament Patterns*	
MBTI	Keirsey	Doyle
Sensing-Judging (SJ)	Guardian	Analytic
Sensing-Perceiving (SP)	Artisan	Expressive
Intuitive-Feeling (NF)	Idealist	Amiable
Intuitive-Thinking (NT)	Rational	Driver

Based on the profiles of these psychological preference types and temperaments which you read about earlier in this section of the chapter, strategies have been developed by McKenna, Hyllegard, and Linder[10] for motivating and more effectively communicating with these four general types of clients.

A financial planner dealing with a **Sensing-Judging (SJ)/Guardian/Analytic** type is well-advised to assume the role of a trusted, respected authority at the first meeting with such a client. It is important to share with this type of client the steps and the process to be used to help the client accomplish his or her goals. Equally important is for the planner to have had experience with comparable clients in terms of age, income, and life cycle stage. Once convinced of the planner's credentials, this type of client will tend to trust him or her and follow his or her direction. This type of client needs to be assured that by doing personal financial planning he or she is taking responsibility for his or her family. They will tend to be drawn to cautious, conservative financial planning recommendations with specific steps to implement.

---

[10] "Linking Psychological Type to Financial Decision-Making" by Judy McKenna, Karen Hyllegard, and Ray Linder, *The Journal of the Association for Financial Counseling and Planning Education*, Vol. 14(1), 2003.

To enhance communication with Sensing-Judging (SJ)/Guardian/Analytic types, it is important to appeal to their logistical skills and to communicate directly in a clear manner about the responsibilities of each party involved in the planning activity. It is helpful to use prior experiences with specific examples and to be thorough and accurate with facts and figures, allowing time for them to process the information. Finally, of utmost importance is meeting each of the planner's commitments to this type of client. Do what you said you would do and when you said you would do it, thus conveying your respect for the client.

In the case of **Sensing-Perceiving (SP)/Artisan/Expressive** types it is essential to be perceived as the facilitator of their enjoyment of life. Their concern is with the use of money, not its management. Accordingly, the planner must be sure to provide such clients with easy access to some reasonable amount of "mad" money to maintain their preferred lifestyle. This type of client is less concerned than are SJ/Guardian/Analytics with following accepted norms for accomplishing their goals. Being individuals who live for the moment, planning will be a challenge for them. Such clients are well-suited to automatic savings mechanisms so they can concentrate on any funds left over. It is important not to infringe upon their freedom of action and to show clearly identifiable results for their efforts. Planning recommendations will need to be designed to show short-term results rather than concentrating on the long-term.

Communication with SP/Artisan/Expressive types should appeal to their tactical skills to precipitate quick decisions on short-term needs and goals and should be simple (without being condescending) and free of financial jargon or buzzwords. Recommendations should be delivered briefly, getting quickly to the point, and with a sense of humor, as this builds trust with such clients. Finally, the planner should avoid any inference of rendering a judgment on this client's chosen free and easy lifestyle.

Dealing with **Intuitive-Feeling (NF)/Idealist/Amiables** requires the financial planner to assume at the first client meeting the role of a special companion or partner that will become an integral part of the client's life. Such clients are looking for a cooperative relationship with a financial planner based on shared values, philosophy, and outlook. Such clients need to feel that the financial planning activities being undertaken pursuant to the financial plan are consistent with their personal value system. It is essential to keep such clients focused on their ideals and the persons for whom the planning is intended to benefit. Unless the financial planning recommendations result in a meaningful and significant life for such clients, it will be difficult to obtain client buy-in. As clients of this type shun being defined by their money, planners need to avoid references to such clients as "upper class" or "affluent" or similar terms. A planner is well-advised to communicate to such clients that he or she has heard their dreams and visions for the future and understands their personal concerns, especially their relationships. Such clients can easily discern a lack of sincerity and the presence of hidden motives; so it is essential to be truthful and genuine with such clients.

Intuitive-Thinking (NT)/Rational/Driver types require the financial planner to assume the role of an independent-minded expert. They will feel more comfortable knowing that the planner is a continuing student of financial markets and investment vehicles and is well-versed in the various disciplines that constitute personal financial planning. Such clients will tend to listen to such experts, but not necessarily implement their recommendations. Like SP/Artisan/Expressives, they are not particularly concerned with following accepted norms for accomplishing their goals. This type of client must be acknowledged as knowledgeable and competent and will be impressed with plans that provide the maximum "bang for the buck." Intellectual curiosity is a key trait of such clients and they will appreciate being provided with research studies or papers reflecting the current thinking on financial planning and markets. Planners who attend meetings for financial planning professionals or subscribe to professional journals should make a point of sending copies of interesting articles or presentations to this type of client.

Planners should appeal to the strategic intelligence of NT/Rational/Driver types by first describing the ends of the planning process and then providing the detailed steps to achieve them. Such clients may be skeptical and challenge the planner by playing devil's advocate. Planners need to avoid any inference that they are attempting to direct the lives of such clients.

As McKenna, Hyllegard, and Linder indicate in the article cited earlier, "[I]f financial planners, counselors and educators lack knowledge about what motivates clients to follow recommendations, they will be handicapped in helping individuals understand and apply financial information."

Financial Planner Self-Evaluation

According to Richard W. Siroka, Ph.D., the director of the Center for the Psychosocial Study of Financial Behavior in New York, a prerequisite for becoming a competent financial planner is to ".....deal first with your own feelings and attitudes."[6] Dr. Siroka compares this to the common practice of psychoanalysts undergoing psychoanalysis themselves before treating patients. He suggests that financial planners need to be aware of certain attitudes in their clients as well as in themselves, including the degree of financial literacy and attitudes toward money, earning, giving, and receiving. It is through a financial planner's self-knowledge of his or her attitudes and behavior characteristics toward money and property that he or she is better able to ascertain the client's sub-surface emotions and help clients avoid bad decisions and deal with their fears.

---

6 "The Many Moods of Money" by Caitlin Mollison, *Ticker*, April 1998.

LIFE CYCLE AND AGE FACTORS AND INFLUENCES

Relying on the work of major developmental theorists, Professor Doyle suggests four important adult life stages. The first he calls the **discovery stage** (typically ages 20-30), in which money and property serve as media through which people send and receive information in order to evaluate other people and be themselves evaluated. The information is not confined to economic status: It can include the values, attitudes, conflicts, and fears that are illustrated in the Quaternary discussed earlier.

Clients in the discovery stage, particularly those with young children, probably will not be thinking about writing wills, setting up investment plans, or buying life insurance, but each of these actions is actually very important to them at this stage of life. Also, when children arrive, either one parent needs to stay home to take care of the children or there is a need for paid child care. This may be only the tip of the iceberg as the realization of the total costs of raising a child begins to sink in. Then there is the need to begin to build an emergency fund of three to six months' living expenses, to start a college fund for the children, and some sort of regular savings plan.

In the second stage, referred to as the **effectance stage** (typically ages 30-45), the adult has achieved expertise in the ways of the world and is concentrating on his or her career, relationships, and other adult activities. At this point, personality is fairly well established and adult actions are more and more consistent with the individual's general temperament. Also, people in this stage tend to have more responsibilities and are becoming more aware of the concept of risk.

The pressures on clients in the effectance stage can be substantial as they attempt to fund education expenses for their children (or even for themselves), save adequately for their retirement, pay for life, disability, and long-term care insurance, and possibly assist aging parents.

In the third stage, the **modeling stage** (typically ages 45-60), middle-aged adults become interested in passing their wisdom and their property on to the next generation. Estate and business-succession planning usually take place during this stage.

The fourth and final stage, the **evaluation stage** (age 60 and older), brings contemplation of the sum total of one's life. Money and property come into play as measures of a person's disappointment or satisfaction. People in this stage are generally more open to philanthropy, particularly if they are content with their lives.

At this stage, clients are generally freer to concentrate their efforts more on their own well-being. Usually, children are now self-sustaining, the home mortgage may be paid off (or close to it), and funds have been accumulated for retirement. However, just as a client at this life stage begins to feel comfortable, children may decide to marry or get divorced or may need help with a home down payment or expenses of the grandchildren. At the same time, clients at this stage often want to arrange their financial affairs so that they are not now nor do they become a burden to their children. Estate planning and gifting programs become even more important during this life stage as well as the need for a durable power of attorney (either for health care or for property) and a living will. Some financial planners contend that financial planning decisions are influenced less by the client's age as by the age of the client's children and the client's parents. These financial planners believe that retirement planning may be the only financial planning area dependent upon the client's age.

These stages can be plotted on Professor Doyle's quaternary by adding a third axis (driver/amiable by expressive/analytic by stages of development.) In this fashion, the meanings of money and property can be examined not only in quadrant terms, but also in terms of the evolving meanings over the individual's life span.

LEVEL OF CLIENT KNOWLEDGE, EXPERIENCE, AND EXPERTISE

Other significant factors that affect a client's attitudes and behavior are the levels of a client's knowledge, experience, and expertise in financial matters. Clearly a client who has acquired little knowledge and has had limited experience and expertise in financial matters represents a serious challenge to a financial planner. The planner will need to simultaneously provide the client with a significant amount of education about the personal financial planning process and the financial planning subject areas and also seek to instill in the client a strong sense of trust of the planner. One of the disadvantages of working with such clients is that they may fail to act because of their lack of knowledge and experience and because they have not yet begun to trust the financial planner to act in their best interest. This necessitates additional effort by the financial planner to build a working level of trust with such a client. After the client has received some financial education and has been involved in the financial planning process, it should become easier to work with him or her.

Other clients will have extensive education in financial matters, experience with financial planning and its various aspects, and perhaps even some expertise in one of the many areas of financial services. Generally, these types of clients will make it easier for the financial planner to provide financial planning services. They require much less education and the planner should not have to expend as much effort building the level of trust. Some clients may have previous experience as financial planning clients or they may have some familiarity with investments, insurance, retirement plans, employee benefits, or estate planning. Certain clients may have work experience in one or more of the various financial services. Generally, such clients will be quicker to build a good working relationship with their financial planner. Of course, this result is not guaranteed since the client and planner may still be at the opposite ends of one of the continuums described in Professor Doyle's quaternary (extraverted-introverted or toughminded-tenderminded) and, accordingly, may have difficulty communicating and working well together.

RISK TOLERANCE FACTORS AND INFLUENCES

The subject of a client's risk tolerance was discussed at length in Chapter 2. In that discussion, you learned that a client's risk tolerance is a highly subjective and personal attribute that, while requiring evaluation and understanding by the financial planner, is not easily evaluated. Risk tolerance is (1) an elusive, ambiguous concept to the average client, (2) not easily assessed, (3) not a fixed characteristic of an individual, and (4) often not easily imparted to a financial planner by a client. Therefore, its assessment is a complex and inexact science. Just as in the assessment of a client's psychological or emotional makeup, the result achieved is only as good as the reliability and validity of the assessment tool employed.

Also, as discussed earlier in this chapter, the many factors that affect a client's attitudes and behavior characteristics interact to varying degrees simultaneously. Consequently, a client's risk tolerance has been shaped to some extent by cultural, family, and emotional factors as well as by his or her stage in the life cycle and level of knowledge and experience in financial matters.

IMPLICATIONS FOR FINANCIAL PLANNING

How can the concepts discussed in the section on emotional factors and influences be applied to the financial planning process? To the extent that financial planning involves the sale of products or services, it would appear that the psychological preferences and temperaments described there should be quite useful. Sales personnel are trained to estimate a prospect's temperament, or social style, on the basis of a variety of verbal and physical cues and then design the sales presentation around this assessment. A skilled salesperson should find these concepts useful in quickly evaluating and influencing a client.

However, when dealing with two or more sales prospects simultaneously (e.g., business partners or married couples) who represent different temperaments, the salesperson can either alternate the approach between the prospects or direct most of the presentation to the presumed decision maker with the attendant risk of offending the other party and possibly losing the sale.

Use of these concepts can also help the financial planner determine a client's propensity to save for retirement or for other financial goals. SJ/Guardian/Analytics will have a tendency to save more systematically than other types, but may be inclined to invest in more conservative investments, leaving themselves exposed to the ravages of inflation. NT/Rational/Drivers will generally save more than NF/Idealist/Amiables and SP/Artisan/Expressives, but NT/Rational/Drivers can be expected to tap their retirement accounts for what they consider to be important or profitable short-term opportunities. NF/Idealist/Amiables will tend to avoid saving effectively unless they come to understand that no one else will take care of them if they don't take care of themselves. An NF/Idealist/Amiable can be expected to defer to his or her partner's savings plan. SP/Artisan/Expressives may invest from time to time, but they are as likely as NT/Rational/Drivers to raid their accounts impulsively and to invest in risky ventures.

Another important application of these psychological preference and temperament concepts is in qualitative client data gathering. Knowing generally into which quadrant a client falls and where he or she may be along the life stage continuum can be very useful information to the financial planner in addressing that client's goals and objectives. As we have seen, every temperament has a characteristic fear. According to Professor Doyle, fear, which often hides behind other emotions, is the strongest motive because the human brain is most sensitive to threat. A client's particular fear can be inferred by knowing the client's temperament (quadrant). In financial planning terms, clients' fears may include not having evaluated their financial situation, not having developed goals and objectives, not having put in place financial recommendations to accomplish their goals and objectives, and not knowing their progress in implementing financial recommendations. To a large degree, personal financial planning involves the reduction of clients' fears by helping them to accomplish their goals, needs, and priorities.

Another benefit of these concepts is that the better clients understand their financial temperaments and those of people who are important to them, the more effective they can be as financial planning clients and financial decision-makers. When couples make an effort to adjust their individual positions to one that is closer to the intersection of the two axes of the financial quaternary, they will automatically move toward each other. This can be very helpful in developing financial planning recommendations that are attractive to both parties. Since money is very often a powerful source of friction between couples, effective use of these concepts can improve their ability to deal with each other over money issues. An additional benefit of these concepts is that clients can make sure that the financial planning recommendations they receive are generally consistent with their financial temperaments.

Financial planners can use these concepts in assessing their clients' risk tolerance, a concept that was discussed in Chapter 2 and, to a lesser extent, in this chapter. Generally, as mentioned earlier, NT/Rational/Drivers and SP/Artisan/Expressives tolerate risk quite well while SJ/Guardian/Analytics and NF/Idealist/Amiables are generally more risk-averse. In fact, NT/Rational/Drivers and SP/Artisan/Expressives can be blind to risks that more temperate people would avoid. And the reluctance of SJ/Guardian/Analytics and NF/Idealist/Amiables to enter the market can prove to be an expensive weakness. Again, if clients are in tune with their characteristic temperament and the associated risk tolerance, they can make wiser financial decisions. Financial planners need to be able to determine a client's characteristic temperament in order to improve communication with the client and to better understand how a client's thoughts, feelings, belief systems, and attitudes influence his or her behavior, financial decision-making, and reaction to money and property.

Going beyond the psychological preference and temperament concepts discussed earlier, in more general terms, financial planners need to determine who their clients are, including how they feel about money, risk, and investments, and attempt to get them to open up about how they were raised and what their parents' and grandparents' attitudes toward money and investing were. Clients should be encouraged to discuss their fears, no matter how irrational they may appear. To the extent that financial planners demonstrate to clients that they recognize their emotions about investing and respect those feelings, they are more likely to gain their clients' trust. Clients often impart to their financial planners what they perceive the planners want to hear. For example, they may exaggerate their levels of risk tolerance and financial sophistication. A financial planner needs to dig beneath the client's emotional facade to determine his or her real attitudes about money and property and how these attitudes may be expected to affect his or her financial behavior characteristics.

IMPORTANT CONCEPTS TO REMEMBER

Cultural, family, emotional, life cycle and age, knowledge and experience, and risk tolerance factors and influences on client attitudes and behavioral characteristics

Temperament

Rational choice theory or utility theory

Myers-Briggs Type Indicator

Keirsey's four basic temperaments

Doyle's four basic temperaments

Neuro-linguistic programming

Financial planner self-evaluation

Adult life stages

QUESTIONS FOR REVIEW

1. What is meant by the statements, "The central motive of money and property is fear," and, "The central meaning of money and property is protection"?

2. According to Professor Doyle, with what specific fear are each of his four basic temperaments associated?

3. In the financial quaternary, what are the basic fear-reducing financial activities?

4. How can a financial planner evaluate clients at various life stages?

5. Describe in your own words the four general human temperaments or psychological preferences. How would you classify yourself within these temperaments/preferences?

6. How can you use temperament/psychological preference information about a client to motivate the client to accomplish his or her goals, to enhance client communication, and to build client trust?

7. What are some of the shortcomings of standard assessment tools for categorizing clients by "personality groups"?

8. What is neuro-linguistic programming (NLP) and how does it differ from the typology used by Myers-Briggs, Keirsey, Doyle, and others?

9. Why is it important for a financial planner to assess his or her own attitudes and behavior characteristics toward money and financial decision-making?

SUGGESTIONS FOR ADDITIONAL READING

The Social Meanings of Money and Property: In Search of a Talisman by Kenneth O. Doyle, Sage Publications, 1999.

"Linking Psychological Type to Financial Decision-Making" by Judy McKenna, Karen Hyllegard, and Ray Linder, *The Journal of the Association for Financial Counseling and Planning Education*, Volume 14(1), 2003.

"Health Care Communication Using Personality Types" by J. Allen and S.A. Brock, Routledge, 2000.

Please Understand Me: Character and Temperament Types by David Keirsey and Marilyn Bates, Prometheus Nemesis Book Company, Del Mar, CA, 1978.

Please Understand Me II by David Keirsey, Prometheus Nemesis Book Company, Del Mar, CA, 1998.

"Are You Putting Your Clients in a Box?" by Brian Wruk, CFP® and Dean M. Hebert, M.Ed., *Journal of Financial Planning*, March 2003.

"The Many Moods of Money" by Caitlin Mollison, *Ticker*, April 1998.

Your Money Personality: What It Is and How You can Profit from It by Kathleen S. Gurney, Doubleday, 1988.

The Secret Meaning of Money by Cloe Madanes, Jossey-Bass, 1994.

Frozen Desire: The Meaning of Money by James Buchan, Farrar Straus Giroux, 1997.

"Hearts, Minds & Money" by Donald Jay Korn, *Financial Planning*, February 1999.

"The Psychology of Money" by Mary Rowland, *Modern Maturity*, March/April 1996.

"How Assessing Personality Type Can Benefit You and Your Practice" by Neale C. Bringhurst, Ph.D., *Journal of Financial Planning*, January 2001.

"Know Your Client, Part Two" by Carol M. Kauffman, *Financial Planning*, March 2003.

CHAPTER FOUR

Personal Financial Statements and Budgeting

• • •

Having gathered financial quantitative client data, as discussed in Chapter 2, the financial planner is now ready to take the data gathered and place it in a format that will be useful in determining the client's financial status, reviewing the client's recent financial activities, and developing and using a budget to assist the client toward the accomplishment of his or her goals and objectives. This involves understanding the basic personal financial statements, knowing how to analyze them, advising clients about their record-keeping systems, and helping clients develop and use a personal budget.

This discussion generally will avoid technical accounting terms, as it is not our intent to provide instruction in accounting but to provide introductory information to financial planners about personal financial statements. Readers who have received formal education and have significant experience in accounting may elect to skim this chapter.

The objectives of this chapter are:

- Identify the basic personal financial statements.
- Describe the function of the personal balance sheet.
- Describe the function of the personal cash flow statement.
- Describe what is meant by a personal emergency fund.
- Determine the appropriate amount of a personal emergency fund in a given client situation.
- Evaluate a client's financial performance and status through the use of ratio analysis in a given client situation.

- Discuss useful record-keeping systems to manage and control a client's personal financial affairs.
- Explain the process of developing and using a personal budget.

THE PERSONAL BALANCE SHEET

A **personal balance sheet**, or statement of personal financial position, is designed to show a client's financial status at a particular moment in time, usually at the end of a month, quarter, or year. A balance sheet essentially takes a "photograph" of the client's financial position at that particular instant. A client's financial status is his or her **net worth**, which is the sum of the current fair market value of his or her **assets** minus the client's debts (or **liabilities**). This financial statement is referred to as a balance sheet because the statement is divided into two general columns with the assets on the left side and both the liabilities and net worth on the right side. By convention and for control purposes, the mathematical values in each of these two columns must balance, or be equal to each other; just as in algebra, each side of an equation must be of equal value.

A balance sheet is organized into three distinct categories—total assets (what is owned), total liabilities (what is owed), and net worth (what one is worth). The financial planner needs to understand the relationships among these three categories. The relationship can be described mathematically with the following equation: Total Assets = Total Liabilities + Net Worth. This equation can be manipulated and remain true. For example, Net Worth = Total Assets – Total Liabilities. Likewise, Total Liabilities = Total Assets – Net Worth. There is no need to memorize these formulas if the reader keeps in mind the fact that everything on the left side of the balance sheet (the assets) has to equal the sum of the items on the right side of the balance sheet (the liabilities and net worth). See Figure 4.1 for an example of a statement of personal financial position, or personal balance sheet.

Figure 4.1

STATEMENT OF PERSONAL FINANCIAL POSITION, OR PERSONAL BALANCE SHEET			
Name _____		Date _____	

ASSETS		LIABILITIES AND NET WORTH	
Liquid Assets		**Current Liabilities**	
Cash on hand	$	Utilities	$
In checking		Rent	
Savings accounts		Insurance premiums	
Money market funds and deposits		Taxes	
Certificates of deposit (<1 yr. to maturity)		Medical/dental bills	
Other		Repair bills	
Total Liquid Assets		Bank credit card balances	
Investments		Dept. store credit card balances	
Stocks		Travel and entertainment card balances	
Bonds		Gas and other credit card balances	
Certificates of deposit (>1 yr. to maturity)		Bank line of credit balances	
Mutual funds		Other current liabilities	
Real estate		**Total Current Liabilities**	
Other			
Total Investments		**Long-Term Liabilities**	
Retirement Funds		Primary residence mortgage	
Vested employer pension benefits		Second home mortgage	
IRAs		Real estate investment mortgage	
Rollover IRAs		Auto loans	
Other		Appliance/furniture loans	
Total Retirement Funds		Home improvement loans	
Personal Use Assets		Single-payment loans	
Primary residence		Education loans	
Second home		Other long-term loans	
Auto(s):		**Total Long-Term Liabilities**	
Auto(s):			
Recreational vehicles			
Household furnishings		(II)Total Liabilities	$
Jewelry and artwork			
Other		Net Worth [(I) − (II)]	$
Total Personal Use Assets			
(I) Total Assets $ _____		Total Liabilities and Net Worth $ _____	

Assets

Now let us consider some of the items that properly fall into the Total Assets category (the left side of the balance sheet). First, an asset is something one owns, whether he or she paid cash for it, borrowed to purchase it, or received it as a gift or inheritance. An example is one's personal residence, which is usually subject to a mortgage loan. But suppose a client leases an automobile. Does that constitute an asset to the client? No, it would not, because the client does not have ownership of the automobile.

The normal convention for a personal balance sheet is to categorize assets into four general categories. Typically, the first category is **cash or cash equivalents**. This includes checking accounts, savings accounts, money market accounts, money market fund accounts, certificates of deposit with less than one year to maturity, U.S. Treasury bills, the cash value of life insurance, and similar items. Another term for these types of assets is "liquid" assets. This means that they can be converted readily to cash without a resulting loss of the original amount invested (the principal) and with minimal transaction costs.

The second category is **investments**. It is usually composed of stocks, bonds, mutual funds, annuities, commodities, futures, options, partnership interests, certificates of deposit with a maturity of more than one year, real estate held for investment purposes, a client's ownership interest in a business, and other similar items. As a general rule, investment assets are acquired to accomplish long-term goals. Such assets, while not considered liquid, may or may not be considered "marketable." Marketability refers to the ability to sell an item quickly and thereby convert it to cash (such as stocks, bonds, mutual funds, etc.), regardless of whether or not there is a resulting loss of principal. Certain investment assets are not considered to be readily marketable (e.g., real estate, ownership interest in a business, etc.).

Typically, the third category consists of the client's **retirement funds**. This can include the present lump-sum value of the client's pension benefits in which the client is vested, or to which he or she is currently entitled. In other words, if the client is permitted to receive these benefits in a single lump sum, the value of that lump sum on a given date is listed on the balance sheet. Other retirement funds include IRAs and Keogh accounts owned by the client and the current vested balance held in employee savings plans, such as 401(k), 403(b), SEP, and ESOP accounts.

The fourth and final category is **personal use assets**. The main items in this category are the client's personal residence, any second or vacation homes, timeshares, and items of personal property such as automobiles, recreational equipment, home furnishings and appliances, clothing, furs and jewelry, home electronics, collectibles/art/antiques, and similar items.

Each of the items in the four categories discussed above must be assigned a current **fair market value**. Fair market value can and often does differ from the original purchase price of an asset. It represents the actual value of the asset (such as the balance in a bank account) or the price that a willing seller with full knowledge of its value and who is not compelled to sell would sell it for to a buyer who had full knowledge of its value and who is not compelled to buy it. Generally, the financial planner may find this information from client documents or from other published sources. In some cases, the financial planner or client may need to contact a valuation expert or to refer to other sources to determine current fair market value. After values have been assigned to each item they are subtotaled by category and the category totals are summed to arrive at Total Assets. We have now completed the left side of the balance sheet.

Liabilities

A liability represents a debt that is owed and for which there is an obligation to repay in the future. Typically, in a personal balance sheet, such items are categorized as current (or short-term) and long-term. **Current or short-term liabilities** are due within one year of the balance sheet date, and **long-term liabilities** are due after one year. Examples of current liabilities can include, but are not limited to, unpaid utility bills, rent, insurance premiums, taxes, medical/dental bills, repair bills, alimony, child support, credit card purchases, gas and other credit card balances, and bank line of credit balances. These types of items should be included only if the client owes the funds now (that is, has an unpaid invoice or bill). The amount of liability on any of these items at the balance sheet date is the total of the various balances outstanding, not the minimum required monthly payments.

The primary long-term liability of most clients is the unpaid mortgage balance(s) on their personal residence or second residence(s). Note that the amount placed on the balance sheet is not the original amount of the mortgage loan but the current unpaid balance as of the balance sheet date. In addition, it includes the unpaid balance on any home equity loans or home equity lines of credit, depending upon how they are used. (Remember: home equity loans may be categorized as current or short-term liabilities if they are due within one year of the balance sheet date). Other typical long-term liabilities include life insurance policy loans, employee savings plan (401(k)) loans, credit union loans, student loans, and automobile loans due more than one year after the balance sheet date.

Net Worth

As discussed earlier, net worth is the mathematical difference between the Total Assets and the Total Liabilities determined above. It can also be referred to as the actual wealth or equity a client possesses in owned assets. It is least confusing to think of net worth as the amount of money that would remain if all the assets were sold at their current fair market value and all the current balances of the liabilities were paid (ignoring transaction costs and taxes).

By analyzing sequential personal balance sheets, the financial planner can track a client's financial progress over time. For an individual client, net worth is the statistic most closely watched by the financial planner. With proper financial management, net worth should tend to grow over a period of several years, except in certain cases such as when a client retires and depletes assets or when a family pays for a child's education. Net worth could also decline from period to period simply as a result of fluctuating market conditions.

The Total Liabilities plus the Net Worth complete the right side of the balance sheet. If the calculations were performed correctly, the total of the left side (Total Assets) is equal to the total of the right side (Total Liabilities and Net Worth).

THE PERSONAL CASH FLOW STATEMENT

A personal cash flow statement summarizes the items of income that were actually received (cash inflows) and the expenditures actually made (cash outflows) during a specific period of time (usually a month, quarter, or year). While the balance sheet is like a photograph of a client's financial status at a particular moment, the cash flow statement is more like a videotape of the financial activity during a particular period of time. It shows a summary of all the cash activity (both in and out) over a period of time. Refer to Figure 4.2 for an example of a personal cash flow statement.

Just as the personal balance sheet (or statement of personal financial position) has three general sections (Total Assets, Total Liabilities, and Net Worth), so does the cash flow statement. These three parts are **Cash Inflows**, **Cash Outflows**, and **Cash Surplus (or Deficit)**. Cash surplus or deficit is merely the difference between cash inflows and cash outflows. Another name for a cash surplus is **discretionary income**. It represents the amount of cash remaining after all expenditures have been made and is therefore, presumably, available to the client for whatever purpose the client chooses (e.g., savings, investment, debt reduction, or major purchase). However, the financial planner must be confident that the cash outflow data is accurate, since what appears to be a cash surplus may actually be unidentified cash outflows (expenditures the client has not included in the cash flow statement).

Cash Inflows

Cash inflows ordinarily include earnings in the form of wages, salaries, self-employment income, bonuses, and commissions; investment earnings such as interest, dividends, and capital gains; and proceeds from the sale of assets (e.g., securities or autos). Other examples are retirement income from pensions or annuities, gross rents from assets leased to others, alimony, child support, scholarships, grants, social security benefits, tax refunds, gifts, and other similar items. Earned income should be included on a gross basis (i.e., before payroll deductions for taxes and benefit contributions). The items withheld from one's gross income should be shown as expenditures in the Cash Outflows section of the Cash Flow Statement.

Figure 4.2

PERSONAL CASH FLOW STATEMENT		
Name(s) _____		
For the _____ Ending _____		
CASH INFLOWS		
Wages and salaries	Name:	
	Name:	
	Name:	
Self-employment income		
Bonuses and commissions		
Pensions and annuities		
Investment income	Interest received	
	Dividends received	
	Rents received	
	Sale of securities	
	Other	
Other income		
	(I) Total Income	$ _____
CASH OUTFLOWS		
Housing	Rent/mortgage payment (include insurance and taxes, if applicable)	$
	Repairs, maintenance, improvements	
Utilities	Gas, electric, water	
	Phone	
	Cable TV and other	
Food	Groceries	
	Dining out	
Autos	Loan payments	
	License plates, fees, etc,	
	Gas, oil, repairs, tires, maintenance	
Medical	Health, major medical, disability insurance	
	(payroll deductions or not provided by employer)	
	Doctor, dentist, hospital, medicines	
Clothing	Clothes, shoes, and accessories	
Insurance	Homeowner's (if not covered by mortgage payment)	
	Life (not provided by employer)	
	Auto	
Taxes	Income and social security	
	Property (if not included in mortgage)	
Appliances, furniture, and other major purchases	Loan payments	
	Purchases and repairs	
Personal care	Laundry, cosmetics, hair care	
Recreation and entertainment	Vacations	
	Other recreation and entertainment	
Other items		
	(II) Total Expenditures	$ _____
	CASH SURPLUS (OR DEFICIT) [(I) − (II)]	$ _____

Cash Outflows

Just as cash inflow items are included in the personal cash flow statement on the basis of cash actually received, so we include cash outflow items strictly on the basis of cash actually expended. This means that if a client purchases an item such as an automobile, major appliance, or home improvement through the use of credit, only the amount actually paid out in cash (purchase price less amount borrowed) in the current period is considered to be an expenditure, or cash outflow. The item purchased is shown as an asset, and the amount borrowed is shown as a liability on the client's personal balance sheet.

Examples of typical client expenditures include housing (mortgage payments, rent, repairs and improvements, and household services), utilities, food (consumed both at home and out), transportation (auto expenses, commutation, parking), medical and dental bills including health insurance premiums, clothing, various types of insurance, taxes, major purchases, personal care (laundry and dry cleaning, cosmetics, hairdresser/barber), recreation, entertainment, and vacation, charitable contributions, and countless miscellaneous personal expenses.

Various conventions are used for categorizing expenditures. To make the cash flow statement more useful for clients, cash outflows are often categorized into **living expenses**, **asset purchases**, **tax payments**, and **debt repayments**. In addition, some financial planners categorize cash outflows as to whether they are fixed or variable in nature. This latter distinction can prove very useful when it is necessary to make reductions in expenditures either to create a cash surplus (by eliminating a cash deficit) or to increase the size of a cash surplus (or discretionary income). **Variable expenditures** are those over which the client is said to have some degree of discretion or control in the short-run. For example, one can decide how much to spend on this year's vacation. So-called **fixed expenditures** would include such items as the monthly mortgage payment or rent, over which the client has very little, if any, control in the short-run.

Analysis of the cash flow statement can help a financial planner track a client's annual savings rate and determine whether the client is living within his or her means. Clients who are unable to do so may be good candidates for budgeting, which will be discussed later in this chapter.

THE RELATIONSHIP BETWEEN THE BALANCE SHEET AND THE CASH FLOW STATEMENT

It is important that financial planners and clients understand the interplay between the balance sheet and the cash flow statement. A client's cash flow statement will show how the client's financial position changed between two balance sheet dates. For instance, if a client accumulates a cash surplus (that appears on the cash flow statement) in the most recent period, his or her net worth (that appears on the balance sheet) increases by the amount of the cash surplus (and conversely, if there is a cash deficit). Why is this true? Think of the accounting that underlies the cash flow statement and the balance sheet as a scale that must at all times balance. Or for those who are mathematically inclined, think of it as following the same rule used in algebra (i.e., both sides of the equation must balance). So if the client uses cash (assume $1,000) to repay debt, the cash balance will be reduced, but so will the liabilities balance, also by $1,000. As a result, the assets (the left side of the balance sheet) are reduced by $1,000 and the liabilities (on the right side of the balance sheet) also by $1,000. Everything is still in balance.

Likewise, if an asset is purchased for $1,000 with cash, the asset will appear as an asset on the balance sheet. Cash, which is also an asset, will be reduced by $1,000 and other assets will be increased by $1,000. As a result, total assets will not change, nor will liabilities and net worth (the right side of the balance sheet). Suppose the client used $1,000 of cash to pay a personal living expense. Cash (a balance sheet asset) is reduced by $1,000 and cash outflows (in this case, an expense) are increased by $1,000. If there were no other transactions, what is the effect on net worth? The cash flow statement would show zero cash inflows and $1,000 of cash outflows (representing the $1,000 of expenses), resulting in a net cash outflow (or deficit) of $1,000. At the end of each accounting period (month, quarter, year, etc.), the cash flow statement is always closed (any net balance is reduced to zero) and that net balance is transferred to the balance sheet as either an increase or decrease in net worth. In this case, we would have to reduce the net cash outflow (or deficit) of $1,000 by $1,000 to bring it to a zero balance. But remember that we must keep both sides of the scale (or equation) in balance. As a result, we will have to reduce net worth (on the balance sheet) by $1,000.

Whenever we reduce cash, either we must increase cash outflows, increase assets, or decrease liabilities in order to maintain balanced accounts. These are the only three uses to which cash can be applied.

If you think carefully about how the Cash Flow Statement and the Balance Sheet interact, you should be able to figure out why a cash surplus

APPROPRIATE EMERGENCY FUND ASSETS

What types of assets are appropriate for inclusion in an emergency fund? By its very nature, an emergency fund should be invested conservatively. It should provide almost complete security of principal and liquidity (ability to be converted to cash quickly with very little or no resulting loss of principal). Therefore, the kinds of accounts or investments that are suitable for this purpose typically include cash and/or cash equivalents such as checking accounts, savings accounts, credit union accounts, money market accounts or funds—all of which can be converted to cash quickly. If a certificate of deposit has a short maturity (say less than 90 days), it may be appropriate. CDs with longer maturities are probably inappropriate because of the early withdrawal penalties usually imposed. The cash surrender value of life insurance policies may also qualify but may be subject to insurance company delay in payment and could affect what might be valuable life insurance coverage. The use of life insurance cash values may depend upon the nature of the personal emergency. Periods of unemployment or disability are not good times to tap life insurance cash values as they result in increased debt and possible loss of valuable coverage. However, this source may be appropriate for very temporary emergencies, such as a major unexpected repair. The use of credit cards or lines of credit is generally not an appropriate substitute for liquid assets.

increases net worth. If we increase cash (an asset), we increase the left side (Total Assets) of the balance sheet. However, the balance sheet must balance, so we need to increase something on the right side. A cash surplus is an increase in cash without a corresponding increase in liabilities. The only category left (besides assets and liabilities) is net worth. Since every entry must balance (hence the name balance sheet), we must increase net worth to keep things in balance.

But realize the time differential in the two statements. As discussed previously, a cash flow statement covers a period of time, such as a month, a quarter, or even a year. A balance sheet is as of a specific date, in other words, as of just one point in time. If you attempt to reconcile the changes on a quarterly cash flow statement with a point-in-time balance sheet, you may not directly "see" all of the changes on the balance sheet caused by the three months of cash flow—especially if the statements have different ending dates.

To summarize, a cash surplus will increase net worth. Conversely, a cash deficit decreases net worth. Increasing net worth is a sign of growing financial strength, while decreasing net worth signals declining financial strength.

THE EMERGENCY FUND

As a matter of financial prudence, every client should have an emergency or contingency fund to meet unexpected expenses. An emergency fund is a certain amount of liquid assets accumulated with the purpose of providing coverage for some or all of a client's expenses during a period of reduced cash flow due to disability, unemployment, or other personal emergency. The presence of such a fund will prevent a client from having to either borrow money or liquidate investments at a time when their value may be temporarily depressed. Depending upon the client's health and employment history, number of income earners, the nature of his or her employment or self-employment, and the degree of financial dependency of others on the client, the size of the fund should be equivalent to anywhere from three to six months' continuing expenditures (cash outflows). If the client has several sources of income, or if the sources are particularly stable, three months' expenses may be adequate. Some client situations may dictate emergency funds greater than six months' expenses due to an unstable income source or potential for more frequent or greater financial emergencies. Failure to accumulate such a fund can have devastating effects on a client's financial health.

Some financial planners recommend supplementing an emergency fund with an unsecured line of credit or home equity line of credit. As long as the emergency fund is of the recommended size (3-6 months' ongoing expenditures), it is prudent to also have lines of credit available. However, lines of credit should not substitute for the necessary emergency fund. For instance, if the reason a client needs to tap a liquid emergency fund is the loss of a job and he or she is unable to locate employment within a reasonable period of time, the last thing the client needs is more debt.

RATIO ANALYSIS

Having developed the basic personal financial statements, the balance sheet (or statement of financial position) and the cash flow statement, now the financial planner needs to know how to analyze those statements to determine the client's current financial health and its trend. Typically, this is accomplished through the calculation of certain key financial ratios. While ratio analysis is not directly applicable to personal financial statements, it is used more often in evaluating small business interests owned by the client. One very important ratio is the **current ratio**, which is the ratio of current assets to current liabilities. The higher the ratio, the greater is the client's ability to satisfy current debts with current assets. An even more telling ratio is the **acid test ratio**, or **quick ratio**, which is the ratio of cash/cash equivalents and current amounts receivable by the client to the client's current liabilities. Note that these two ratios are calculated using the personal balance sheet (or statement of financial position).

When evaluating the cash flow statement, a financial planner often calculates the **savings ratio**, the ratio of the current period's cash surplus (excess of cash inflows over cash outflows) to the current period's income after taxes. Most families save about 5 to 8 percent per year but families saving to achieve an important goal would need to save a much higher percentage. Financial planners help their clients determine how much in savings is required to meet their financial goals. The ability to handle debt can be assessed using the **consumer debt ratio**. This is the ratio of monthly consumer debt payments to monthly net (after-tax) income. Generally, consumer debt refers to debt other than mortgage indebtedness. A generally accepted rule in the personal financial planning profession is that this ratio should not exceed 20 percent.

Other important financial ratios are those used by lenders to qualify borrowers for home mortgage loans. These include the **housing cost ratio** (the total of the monthly mortgage payments [including principal and interest], plus $1/12^{th}$ of the annual real estate taxes, plus $1/12^{th}$ of the annual homeowners insurance premium plus $1/12^{th}$ of any annual condominium association fees divided by the gross [before-tax] monthly income). As a general rule of thumb and depending on the mortgage program involved, this ratio should not exceed 33 percent. A second key debt service ratio is the **total debt ratio** calculated by dividing the total monthly loan payments by the gross [before-tax] monthly income. The numerator of this ratio should include the monthly housing amount (used in the housing cost ratio) plus other installment and personal loan obligations. This includes such items as automobile loans, student loans, installment/revolving credit payments, monthly mortgage payments on non-income producing property, installments on personal loans from individuals, and monthly alimony and child support payments. Generally, this ratio should not exceed 36 percent. For short-term adjustable rate mortgage loans, the applicable ratios are generally 28 percent and 38 percent.

PERSONAL RECORD-KEEPING

A good record-keeping system is important for many reasons. The integrity and reliability of financial statements are based on the accuracy of the data included, and the process of data collection and financial statement preparation is much easier when clients have good records. With the variety of personal record-keeping software currently available to clients, the previously unpleasant and tedious task of maintaining personal records and preparing personal financial statements has been simplified.

In addition to maintaining good records of income and expenditures, assets, and liabilities, clients need to maintain other records and documents. Among the more important of these items are:

- a list of bank accounts and the latest twelve monthly statements;
- a list of credit card numbers;
- major home improvement expenditures;
- current insurance policies and a list of policies and insurance agents;
- individual income tax returns and the tax returns of any business in which a client is either an owner or principal;
- investment and retirement account statements including purchase and sale confirmations and records of stock splits;
- current trust agreements and wills (originals to the client's attorney and a copy maintained at home);
- photos and fingerprints of children and medical records;
- current powers of attorney and living wills; and
- current statements of employee benefits.

PREPARING AND USING A BUDGET

After working with certain clients for a while, it becomes obvious that they do not possess the self-discipline to live within their financial resources. This type of client may benefit from the use of a cash budget. A cash budget is used to plan and evaluate income and spending patterns. It is a realistic estimate of income and expenditures, prepared from actual historical information and client goals, which serves as a control document for future cash flow. A client with no record of historical income and expenditures will have a difficult time developing a realistic initial budget. However, he or she can get started by keeping detailed expenditure records for a few weeks before starting the budgeting process.

While a budget is focused on short-term financial performance (usually the coming year), it can be of significant assistance in achieving a client's long-term financial goals. A budget helps clients achieve disciplined spending and eliminate unnecessary expenditures. A budget should be thought of as a guideline rather than a document requiring rigid adherence to exact budget category totals. Funds are often transferred from one category to another as the year progresses and new information becomes available.

Budgeting offers certain advantages including providing motivation to a client to accomplish financial goals, serving as a financial measurement device, pointing out excessive or inefficient spending, and planning for future transactions rather than being surprised by them. Of course, a budget is only as useful as the information used to develop it and if it is used too rigidly, it can stifle the client's creativity in achieving his or her goals. In addition, some clients have a difficult time maintaining accurate records, which are a requirement for meaningful budgeting. Clients tend to be more motivated if they can visualize the accomplishment of specific goals by adherence to the cash budget. For instance, a client saving for his or her child's education who sees the funds accumulating monthly in an account for this purpose, and who can identify the source of these funds as the savings realized by budgeting, should tend to be more motivated to adhere to the budget.

In Depth: How a Budget is Developed

Normally, a budget is developed in several steps. It is very useful to already have determined the client's goals and the savings necessary to accomplish them. Next is a realistic estimate of the amounts of income from various sources and the anticipated expenditures for the budget period. Achievement of all short-term goals as well as current or short-term contributions to the accomplishment of long-term goals should be incorporated into the expenditures estimate. This should include scheduled additions to savings and investments, provided the budget still balances. It may be necessary to cut certain expenditures to keep the budget in balance.

For control purposes, it is useful to divide the expenditures between fixed and variable categories. After income and expenditures are compared, it can be determined if the expected expenditures are equal to or less than the anticipated income. It is at this point that additional income sources may need to be identified or expenditures may need to be reduced. Finally, it is useful as an additional control device to present each category of income and expense as a percentage of the total.

Finally, a budget only has value if used and if used properly. In order for a cash budget to work effectively, the client must make a comparison of actual monthly income and expenditures to the monthly amounts budgeted to identify variances from the budget—in particular, unfavorable variances. Once unfavorable variances have been calculated, they need to be analyzed to determine why they occurred. Perhaps the unfavorable variance is a one-time event due to a specific reason. If the unfavorable variance persists over several months, then either the amount budgeted was inadequate or spending on that item is out of control. Refer to Appendix B, pages B-3 through B-6 for an example of a cash budget and page B-7 for an example of a budget control schedule (in which actual cash inflows and cash outflows are compared to the amounts budgeted for those items, by category).

IMPORTANT CONCEPTS TO REMEMBER

Personal Balance Sheet or Statement of Personal Financial Position

Interrelationship of Assets, Liabilities, and Net Worth

Personal Cash Flow Statement

Emergency Fund

Ratio Analysis

Personal Cash Budget

QUESTIONS FOR REVIEW

1. What is the primary purpose of a personal balance sheet or statement of personal financial position?

2. What critical function does a personal cash flow statement perform?

3. Why is it important that individuals have an emergency fund, and how should the amount be determined?

4. What role is played by ratio analysis in determining a client's financial status?

5. How can a personal cash budget contribute to the accomplishment of a client's goals and objectives?

SUGGESTIONS FOR ADDITIONAL READING

Personal Financial Planning, 10th edition, by Lawrence J. Gitman and Michael D. Joehnk, South-Western/Thomson, 2004.

CHAPTER FIVE

Managing Debt

• • •

In this chapter, we will discuss the *responsible* use of debt to assist clients in the achievement of their goals and objectives. If not used in a responsible manner, debt may not only fail to contribute to the accomplishment of a client's goals, but may cause the deterioration of the client's current and future financial position. There are certain situations in which taking on debt makes sense and many others in which it does not. We will explore the various types of debt (both short-term and long-term) and when each type may be appropriate, the importance of developing and maintaining good credit, regulation of credit, buying versus leasing, getting debt under control, and bankruptcy.

The objectives of this chapter are:
- Identify the situations in which debt makes sense and those in which it does not.
- Describe the various types of consumer debt.
- Distinguish among the many types of home mortgage loans.
- Analyze a given client situation to determine whether the client should refinance his or her existing mortgage loan.
- Describe the principal advantages and disadvantages of home equity loans and home equity lines of credit.
- Analyze a given client situation to determine whether the client should purchase or lease a particular asset.
- Discuss the importance of good credit in achieving a client's goals and objectives.
- Describe the main provisions of some of the most significant federal legislation regulating personal credit.
- Distinguish between the two most commonly used types of personal bankruptcy.

WHEN DOES DEBT MAKE SENSE?

Probably the most obvious examples of responsible borrowing (assuming one is able to service the debt) are for large purchases, such as personal residences and automobiles.

Home Mortgages and Auto Loans

In many respects, purchasing a home using mortgage debt is self-policing (at least initially) in that the lending institution will not allow a home buyer/borrower to borrow beyond his or her capacity to repay the loan (based on verifiable information available at the time the loan is initiated). However, if the borrower's financial situation should deteriorate thereafter, the lending institution will most likely not become aware of that information, and the borrower will still be obligated to service the debt. Similarly, a borrower must qualify initially for an automobile loan but his or her financial situation could change negatively afterward. As a result, it is important that clients taking on debt for large purchases not only meet the initial qualifications for that debt but have a reasonable basis for believing that they will continue to be able to service it over the life of the loan.

Emergencies

Another appropriate reason for taking on debt is to pay the costs related to an unanticipated financial emergency. Examples of such emergencies include the need for living expenses during a period of unemployment, travel expenses to visit a close relative who is seriously ill or to attend a funeral, or major home repairs/replacements such as a failed furnace, water heater, or air conditioning unit. As discussed in Chapter 4, everyone should have a reasonable emergency fund available to cover such expenses. However, if a client is relatively young or has not yet been able to accumulate the requisite emergency fund, debt may be the only option available in these situations.

Margin Leverage

Many clients use loans known as "margin accounts" to partially finance the purchase and holding of securities typically purchased through a securities broker/dealer firm. Like home mortgages and automobile loans, these are secured loans that use a valuable asset as collateral for repayment. While such loans involve some risk if the value of the securities purchased in this fashion declines significantly, it can also provide substantial "leverage" (if the securities increase in value) in that the investor has used much less of his or her own funds to achieve what may be a large gain.

Education

In addition, many people incur debt in the process of obtaining a college or trade/professional education. As long as the education leads to a significant increase in one's earning power and can be serviced comfortably, such debt can make sense.

Credit Card Float

Others use credit cards purely as a convenience so that they do not need to carry large amounts of cash or write personal checks where they may not be accepted, to receive a more or less interest-free loan or "float" on their purchases, and to provide good documentation for their expenditures. Such credit card debt is only justified *if the credit card statement is paid in full each month*. We will discuss credit card use in greater detail later.

WHEN DOES DEBT NOT MAKE SENSE?

Some people use consumer credit, particularly credit cards, to finance living beyond their means. They may pay even everyday expenditures using their credit cards. How often have you seen people on their lunch hour from work in a delicatessen or fast food restaurant paying for their $5.00-$6.00 lunch every day by credit card? Then when they receive their monthly credit card statement, they realize that they are overextended and cannot pay the balance in full. This is usually the start of a dangerous trend. Many fail to acknowledge that they are spending too much because they can still make the minimum required monthly payment on their debts. However, making the minimum required monthly payment on an original balance due of $2,000 can take 13.5 years to repay in full and result in the payment of over $1,700 in interest (about 85% of the original balance).

Some of the types of expenditures that are inappropriate for the use of credit include basic living expenses, unnecessary spur-of-the-moment purchases, and goods and services that have a very short life.

TYPES OF DEBT

Consumer Debt

Generally, consumer debt is short-term debt used to purchase products and services; for example, auto loans, credit card debt, and personal lines of credit are consumer debt. Usually, secured consumer debt, such as an auto loan, bears a lower interest rate than unsecured debt.

Open Account Credit

One important type of consumer debt is **open account credit**. It is extended to a consumer prior to any purchases, up to a preauthorized credit limit. Such credit can be granted by a retail establishment or a financial institution, such as a bank, savings and loan association, major stock brokerage firm, commercial finance company, or a credit union. Generally, as long as the consumer pays the monthly statement balance in full each month, there is no interest charged.

Bank Credit Cards

The largest source of open account credit is bank credit cards. VISA and MasterCard are the most commonly used. They offer the advantage of being usable for the purchase of almost any type of product or service or for borrowing money within a pre-established credit limit. Many credit cards today offer **buyer protection plans**, which protect items purchased with the cards against loss, theft, or damage for up to 90 days. Some even extend the manufacturer's warranty up to one year. Certain cards offer price-protection plans, discounts on long distance phone calls, lost-card registration, full-value auto rental insurance coverage, high value travel accident insurance, cash rebates, merchandise rebates, airline tickets, or even investments. However, these so-called cardholder benefits are expensive for the card issuer to provide, and these costs are passed on to the cardholder in the form of a higher interest rate, ranging from 14 to 18 percent.

In addition to the interest rate charged, consumers need to consider other costs such as annual fees, transaction fees, and the "grace period" offered. The grace period is the period of time after a purchase is made and before interest begins to be charged. Many credit cards offer a grace period of 25 days. This means that if a purchase is paid for within the 25-day grace period, no interest will be charged. Some cards have either very short or no grace periods. Note that grace periods apply only to purchases. When a consumer takes a cash advance on a credit card, interest is charged from the date the cash is withdrawn.

Credit cards, if used responsibly, can provide interest-free loans, simplified record keeping, returns and resolution of unsatisfactory purchase disputes, convenience and security, and availability for emergencies; but this is offset by high interest rates on unpaid balances and a built-in temptation to overspend. The interest rates charged on credit cards are generally higher than any other form of consumer credit.

Credit Lines

Banks, brokerage houses, and other financial institutions offer revolving lines of credit usually accessed by writing checks on regular checking accounts or specially designed credit line accounts. These accounts are variously referred to as overdraft protection lines, unsecured personal lines of credit, and home equity credit lines. As mentioned in Chapter 4, total monthly payments on consumer debt should not exceed 20% of one's net income, or take-home pay (gross income minus taxes). In addition, with the exception of home equity credit lines, interest paid on consumer debt is considered personal interest and, as a result, is not deductible for federal income tax purposes.

Investment Debt

Loans that are offered by securities firms to their customers for the purpose of purchasing or carrying securities are referred to as **margin accounts**. These accounts permit investors to "leverage" the securities they own by using them as collateral for loans to purchase more securities. In order for this type of debt to make economic sense, the interest rate paid on the debt must be less than the potential rate of return from the investment. When an investor purchases securities through a securities firm, the investor is required to provide a certain percentage of the purchase price in cash, and the balance is borrowed from the securities firm using the purchased securities as collateral. Also, investors who already own securities may deposit them with a securities firm and borrow up to certain limits against the deposited securities. These so-called "initial margin" and "maintenance margin" percentages change from time to time.

While margin accounts can provide the investor with a substantial amount of leverage to improve his or her rate of return, they also expose the investor to potentially large "margin calls" (requests for additional cash deposits when the value of securities decline substantially), and if the investor is unable to make a margin call, the securities could be sold by the broker to satisfy the margin requirement.

Investors may borrow from other sources, such as banks, credit unions, finance companies, or from friends or relatives, to purchase or carry investments. This type of debt is also referred to as investment debt. Interest paid on investment debt is deductible for federal income tax purposes to the extent of **net investment income**, or investment income minus investment expenses.

Mortgage Debt

In general, debt is best used for large purchases. This is especially true when the item purchased has the potential to appreciate in value, such as a personal residence. The interest rate charged on home mortgage loans is affected by prevailing long-term interest rates in the market. The rates offered by different lenders may vary, so comparison shopping is often very beneficial. In addition to the basic interest rate charged, mortgage loans come with other attendant up-front costs, such as loan-origination fees (commonly known as **points**), appraisal fees, credit reporting fees, title searches, various amounts required to be placed in escrow, etc.

A point is 1% of the amount of the mortgage loan. If, for example, the lender charges 2 1/2 points on a $150,000 loan, the cost of the points would be $ 3,750. Generally, the higher the number of points, the lower the interest rate on the mortgage loan. Borrowers should request the lender to provide the **Annual Percentage Rate (APR)** under different loan assumptions so that a valid comparison can be made. However, if the buyer plans to be in the home for only a short period of time, it may make sense to pay a lower amount in points with a corresponding higher interest rate in order to minimize the overall short-term costs.

Points paid on a mortgage loan in connection with the purchase of a primary residence are generally deductible as interest paid for federal income tax purposes in the year the home is purchased, provided the payment of points in the local area is customary and the number of points paid is the going amount for the area. On the purchase of a second home or when refinancing a primary or second home, points are deductible, but the deduction must be prorated over the term of the mortgage. If a portion of the loan proceeds are used to improve the home, the portion of the points allocable to the improvements may be deducted in the year paid.

TYPES OF MORTGAGES

Fixed-Rate Mortgage

Probably the best known and most widely used type of mortgage is the **fixed-rate mortgage**. Under this type of loan, the interest rate does not change over the entire repayment period, which is typically either 15 or 30 years. The monthly payment amount is fixed based upon the interest rate charged, the life of the loan, and the original amount borrowed. The monthly payment includes interest and an amount allocated to repayment of the principal amount borrowed. The interest portion declines over time as the unpaid principal balance gradually declines. Since the monthly payment is fixed, this means that the portion allocable to repayment of principal gradually increases over time. We will learn more about the monthly amortization of mortgage loans using a financial function calculator in Chapters 10 and 11.

Biweekly Mortgage

Sometimes the lender structures the payments on a fixed rate mortgage loan so that they are due every two weeks (26 payments per year) rather than once per month. The biweekly payment amount is one half of the monthly payment amount. Because of the higher frequency of payments, these loans will have a shorter life and result in lower total interest costs.

Adjustable Rate Mortgage (ARM)

In this type of loan, both the interest rate and the monthly payment are adjusted upward or downward in accordance with the movement of interest rates in the market. Usually the change in the interest rate is tied to a stated interest rate index and adjusted at specific intervals (usually once or twice per year). Because the borrower is assuming nearly all of the interest-rate risk, the initial rate on an ARM is usually between two to three percentage points below the current rate on a fixed-rate mortgage loan.

A potentially undesirable feature of ARMs is the possibility of **negative amortization**. This is most likely to occur if the ARM has a payment cap rather than an interest rate cap. This occurs when the adjusted interest rate on the loan increases the required monthly payment to a point beyond the payment cap. Since the homeowner is paying a lesser amount than what is really required to pay the interest due (based on the higher interest rate), the underpaid amount is added to the loan balance (principal). In a negative amortization situation, the borrower may end up with a larger unpaid mortgage balance at the end of an adjustment period than he or she had at the beginning of the period. This is because the unpaid interest has been added to the principal balance. Financial planners need to advise their clients to find out if the ARM for which they are applying can result in negative amortization.

Convertible ARM Mortgage

These loans permit the borrower, for a fee, to convert from an adjustable-rate mortgage loan (ARM) to a fixed-rate loan at any time between the 13th and 60th month, if interest rates decline. Usually, it will take a significant decline in interest rates to compensate for the fee paid at the time of conversion. Typically, the fixed rate is one quarter to one half percent above the current fixed-rate loan interest rates.

Balloon Mortgage

This type of mortgage is one in which the borrower makes fixed payments based on a fixed rate for a long-term mortgage, typically 30 years. However, these payments are made only for a limited number of years, often five or seven years, and then the unpaid balance on the loan must be paid in full in a lump sum. In some cases, the payments are limited to interest only. This type of mortgage makes sense for a borrower who plans to sell the home before the balloon payment is due. Generally, the interest rate charged on such loans is lower than that charged on the typical 30-year loan, resulting in lower payments (particularly where only interest is paid).

Graduated Payment Mortgage (GPM)

Typically a **graduated payment mortgage** loan is a 30-year loan with a fixed interest rate. However, the difference between this type of loan and a 30-year fixed-rate mortgage loan is that in the case of the GPM payments are lower for the first few years (or increase annually for the first few years), then adjust to a higher fixed payment for the balance of the repayment period. These loans are appropriate for clients who, with some certainty, anticipate significant increases in income over the next few years. One disadvantage is the possibility of negative amortization in the early years as lower payments fail to pay the total interest charged during that period.

Growing Equity Mortgage (GEM)

Under a GEM, the monthly payments increase each year for a specific period of years (e.g., 5 or 7 years), after which the payments level off. The loan term is shorter than usual because the payments include more principal than under normal amortization.

Two-Step Mortgage

This type of mortgage is also referred to as either a 5/25 or 7/23 mortgage. The term is 30 years with the rate fixed during the first either five or seven years and then going to an adjusted rate when the first phase ends. Generally, they offer a lower rate than regular fixed-rate mortgages and make the most sense for an owner who plans to sell the home before the initial five- or seven-year period expires.

Reverse Annuity (or Amortization) Mortgage (RAM)

This type of mortgage loan is designed primarily for a retiree who wants to use what may be a substantial equity in his or her personal residence (i.e., in some cases, the original mortgage may already be paid off) to provide a monthly income either for a certain period of years or for the remainder of his or her life. With certain clients who are elderly, have significant equity in their personal residences, and have limited other income to live on, this type of mortgage loan can make a lot of sense. Clearly they could sell the home and use the proceeds or take out a second or new mortgage loan. However, in these cases, either the owner does not want to move from the current residence or cannot qualify for a new loan because of insufficient income, or both.

Under this type of loan, the homeowner obtains a loan for a percentage of his or her equity in the home. The homeowner continues to live in the home while the lender, usually a bank, makes periodic (usually monthly) payments to the owner for a certain term or for the duration of his or her life. Under some RAMs, the owner receives a lump sum rather than periodic payments. The lending institution is repaid, including interest, by the sale of the home after the owner's death. If the owner opts for the life annuity option, the RAM may end up paying more than the fair market value of the home. In these cases, the lender will usually have its own insurance that will make up for any losses it may incur.

SOURCES OF MORTGAGE LOANS

Conventional Mortgage Loans

These are loans made by commercial lenders, who assume all the risk of loss. Typically, such lenders require a **down payment** of 20 percent of the purchase price of the home. However, down payments can be as low as 5 percent, if the borrower is willing to pay a **private mortgage insurance** (**PMI**) premium to insure the lender for the additional risk involved. The premium is paid at closing and then annually, usually as part of the monthly payment, until sufficient equity has built up in the house.

Federal Housing Administration (FHA) Loans

The federal government, to promote home ownership, offers lenders mortgage insurance on high loan-to-value loans. The insurance premium, similarly to PMI, is paid by the borrower at the closing plus on an annual basis thereafter. Down payments on such loans are as low as three percent of the first $25,000 and five percent of the amount in excess of $25,000. The maximum mortgage amount insurable by the FHA is based on the national median price of homes and varies depending on the area of the country. As a result, these loans are not available for expensive homes.

U.S. Department of Veterans Affairs (VA) Loan Guarantees

Lenders who make loans to eligible veterans of the U.S. Armed Forces and their unmarried surviving spouses may obtain **VA loan guarantees** for such loans. Under these plans, an eligible veteran may be able to purchase a home with no money down and is required only to pay the closing costs. The requirements to qualify for such a loan are more liberal than conventional loans as a fringe benefit for those who have served in the armed services.

REFINANCING

Homeowners refinance their mortgage loans for various reasons. Usually, it is because mortgage interest rates have declined significantly below the rate they are currently paying on their home mortgage and they want to reduce their monthly payments and free up the difference in payments for other uses. Also, they may be able to reduce the time period for repayment, thereby reducing total interest costs. Another reason is to consolidate other debts that require monthly payments into a single monthly mortgage payment. The desire to consolidate may be unrelated to current mortgage interest rates. In fact, current interest rates may even be higher than the rate being paid on the existing mortgage loan. The result, in this case, may be higher payments and/or a longer repayment period.

Figure 5.1

MORTGAGE REFINANCING ANALYSIS		
Name _____	Date _____	
Item	**Description**	**Amount**
1	Current monthly payment (Terms: _____)	$_____
2	New monthly payment (Terms: _____)	_____
3	Monthly savings, pretax (Item 1 – Item 2	$_____
4	Tax on monthly savings [Item 3 × tax rate (____%)]	_____
5	Monthly savings, after-tax (Item 3 – Item 4	$_____
6	Costs to refinance:	$_____
	a. Prepayment penalty $_____	
	b. Total closing costs (after-tax) _____	
	c. Total refinancing costs (item 6a + Item 6b)	$_____
7	Months to break even (Item 6c ÷ Item 5)	_____

If the objective is to reduce monthly payments over the term of the loan, the economic feasibility analysis is fairly straightforward. See Figure 5.1 for a mortgage refinancing analysis. The key information for this analysis is the additional period of time the homeowner intends to own the home, the difference between the original interest rate being paid currently and the new proposed rate under the refinance, the resulting difference in mortgage payments on an after-tax basis, and the amount of closing and other refinancing costs payable. In effect, what is being calculated is a breakeven point for the refinancing costs. In other words, how long will it take to recover via monthly cost savings the closing and other refinancing costs payable in cash (or deducted from the loan proceeds) at the time of refinancing?

In Depth: How to Determine Whether to Refinance

The first step is to determine the new monthly mortgage payment and to subtract it from the current monthly mortgage payment. The difference is the monthly pretax savings. Theoretically, in order to convert this amount to an after-tax savings, it is necessary to break down the total monthly mortgage payments (both current and proposed) between interest and principal repayment. But because these amounts change each month as the mortgage is gradually paid off, the amounts involved are difficult to determine with great accuracy. For the sake of expediency, we assume for the purpose of the calculation that the difference in monthly mortgage payments is entirely interest. Since mortgage interest is tax-deductible and assuming the client can itemize deductions (ignoring state income taxes), multiply the payment difference by one minus their federal marginal tax rate to calculate the after-tax difference in payments. For example, if refinancing will save a person with a 30 percent marginal tax rate $100 a month before taxes, the savings will be $70 a month on an after-tax basis.

Next, we need to calculate the total closing and other refinancing costs incurred. This can include a mortgage application fee, an appraisal fee, points, credit report fees, inspection fees, title search and title insurance premiums, mortgage recording fees, legal fees, mortgage prepayment penalty (though these have become fairly rare), etc. These costs will vary based on the state and particular locality. They will often be as much as, or more than, the closing costs incurred in connection with the original mortgage. As a general rule of thumb, it is usually not beneficial to refinance unless the new mortgage interest rate is at least two percentage points lower than the existing rate.

Then, divide the total closing and other refinancing costs by the monthly after-tax cost savings to determine the number of months it will take to break even (to recover the refinancing costs via monthly cost savings). If the homeowner plans to remain in the home for at least this period of time, then refinancing probably makes sense. Again, theoretically, one should take into account the time value of money and reduce the future after-tax cost savings back to a present value and then compare it to the total refinancing costs. This more sophisticated calculation will be considered in Chapters 10 and 11 when we address the time value of money.

Some of the options that homeowners have available to them upon refinancing include:

- Replacing a fixed-rate loan with a lower-interest fixed-rate loan of the same term. The effect will be to reduce the amount of the monthly fixed payment.
- Replacing a 30-year fixed-rate loan with a 15-year fixed-rate loan. The effect may be that the monthly payment does not change that much, although the loan will be repaid much more quickly.
- Replacing a fixed-rate loan with an ARM. In most cases, the monthly payment will be reduced but the homeowner will now be exposed to the possibility of higher payments in the future.
- Replace an ARM with a fixed-rate loan. In most cases, this will result in higher monthly payments, but the amount will now be stable (rather than subject to periodic adjustment).

The economic feasibility analysis is more complex where the homeowner's sole objective is to reduce the total costs of the mortgage over the life of the loan, rather than just reduce the monthly payment. An important factor is the term of the new loan versus the term of the existing loan. If a 30-year loan has been in existence for 10 years and it is replaced with another 30-year loan, the loan maturity has been extended 10 additional years to a total of 40 years. And in this case, even with a lower interest rate, the homeowner may end up paying more total interest. So, in order to use the mortgage refinancing analysis discussed above, the maturity of the replacement loan needs to match the maturity of the original loan.

HOME EQUITY LOANS AND HOME EQUITY LINES OF CREDIT

The difference between the fair market value of one's personal residence and the unpaid balance on any existing mortgages represents a **homeowner's equity** in the property. This is a valuable asset that can be employed to help achieve the client's goals. A **home equity loan** usually takes the form of a second mortgage on the home. The maximum loan amount is calculated as a percentage of the homeowner's equity in the property. (Of course, the homeowner has to qualify to make both the required first and second mortgage payments.) Typically, a lender will permit total debt on the property (including the first and second mortgages) of 70 to 80 percent of the fair market value. In some cases and in certain areas of the country, lenders will loan up to 100% of the fair market value or even beyond that amount. Also, in certain areas of the country, where real estate values have declined, homeowners often owe more than their home is worth. This type of loan is useful where the homeowner has an immediate and readily determinable cash need.

A home equity line of credit is similar to an unsecured personal line of credit in its operation except that the line is secured by a second mortgage on the home. These lines of credit are offered by banks, savings and loan associations, major brokerage firms, and many credit unions. The credit limit is established through the calculation in the previous paragraph, and then the homeowner is free to write checks (or, in some cases, use a credit card) to draw on the credit line up to its limit. Usually, once the homeowner has drawn on the line, he or she receives a monthly statement showing the amount owed and the minimum required monthly payment. Interest rates are usually flexible and adjusted periodically with reference to an interest rate index. Obviously, as more funds are drawn from the credit line, the monthly payment increases.

One of the primary advantages of home equity loans and home equity lines of credit is the income tax treatment of the interest paid. Currently, a homeowner is permitted to deduct the interest charges paid on home equity loans and lines of credit of up to $100,000. This is the only type of consumer loan that still qualifies for such tax treatment. It is irrelevant what the original cost of the house was or how the loan proceeds are used. One overall restriction is that the amount of total indebtedness cannot exceed the fair market value of the home. Typically, home equity loans and lines of credit carry lower interest costs than other types of consumer credit.

However, the loan application process for this type of debt can be extensive, including an appraisal of the property and the payment of some amount of closing costs (usually substantially less than the amount incurred upon refinancing). Therefore, the set-up costs for home equity loans and lines of credit are typically more expensive than other forms of consumer credit.

Financial planners should advise their clients to use these highly advantageous forms of credit with caution. Just because a lending institution may grant a line of credit to a homeowner for, say, $100,000 does not mean that the homeowner has adequate cash flow to service this amount of debt. Also, the collateral for the line of credit is one's home. Failure to repay the loan as agreed can result in the loss of one's home. Finally, clients may be tempted to use the normally long repayment schedules (10 or 15 years) to keep their payments artificially low while purchasing items with an economic life well short of the repayment term. For instance, if an automobile having a useful life of perhaps five years is purchased through a home equity line of credit repayable over fifteen years, perhaps the client could not afford the car in the first place.

BUY VERSUS LEASE DECISIONS

One of the more common financial decisions faced by clients is whether to purchase or lease an asset such as a personal residence or automobile. In most cases, the decision to buy or lease is guided by one's values and goals in addition to economic factors.

Buy versus Lease for a Personal Residence

The economics of renting or buying a personal residence depend primarily on the following factors: (1) the price of homes and mortgage interest rates in a particular area; (2) income tax benefits of home ownership; (3) the extent to which home prices increase or decrease over time; and (4) the period of time one expects to live in the home and the degree of uncertainty of this issue. Refer to the Home Rent-Or-Buy Analysis at Figure 5.2. Under the leasing option, there are really only two costs involved—the annual rent and the tenant's insurance policy premium. The tenant's insurance policy covers the tenant's personal property (furniture, clothing, and other personal effects), provides liability coverage for invitees injured in the leased premises, and for acts of the tenant no matter where they may occur. With the exception of coverage for the real estate, it is the tenant's equivalent of a homeowner's policy. Therefore, the total cost of leasing is the annual rent plus the tenant's annual insurance policy premium. It could be argued that the interest foregone by having to provide the landlord with a security deposit constitutes an additional cost. Normally these interest earnings foregone are not a significant amount of money. Of course, this assumes that the property is returned to the landlord in good condition and that the full security deposit is refunded to the tenant. If part or all of the security deposit is forfeited to the landlord, then this cost could be significant.

With regard to the cost of buying equivalent housing, there are many costs involved. First are the annual mortgage payments, to which we add the annual real estate taxes, the annual homeowner's insurance policy premium, maintenance of the property, and the interest income that was foregone on the funds used for both the down payment and the closing costs. (Note: Some refer to this last item as an opportunity cost because if the home were leased, funds would not have been used for the down payment and closing costs and therefore these funds would have continued to earn interest. The decision to purchase resulted in having to use these funds and therefore forego the interest income that would have been earned.) Maintenance costs tend to be lower on newer homes than on older homes. If one does not have a clear idea of what those costs may be, an assumed factor, such as 0.8 percent of the price of the home, can be used as an estimate. Additional costs to consider when helping a client make housing decisions are costs such as appliances, furniture, window coverings, and landscaping.

Figure 5.2

HOME RENT-OR-BUY ANALYSIS
A. Cost of Renting   1. Annual rental costs   (12 × monthly rental rate of $ _____)
2. Renter's insurance
Total cost of renting (line A.1 + line A.2)
B. Cost of Buying   1. Annual mortgage payments (Terms: $ _____, _____ months, _____%)   (12 × monthly mortgage payment of $ _____)
2. Property taxes   (_____% of price of home)
3. Homeowner's insurance   (_____% of price of home)
4. Maintenance   (_____% of price of home)
5. After-tax cost of interest on down payment and closing costs   ($ _____ × _____% after-tax rate of return)
6. Total costs (sum of lines B.1 through B.5)
Less: 7. Principal reduction in loan balance (see note below)
8. Tax savings due to interest deductions   (Interest portion of mortgage payments $ _____ × tax rate of _____%)
9. Tax savings due to property tax deductions   (line B.2 × tax rate of _____%)
10. Total deductions (sum of lines B.7 through B.9)
11. Annual after-tax cost of home ownership   (line B.6 − line B.10)
12. Estimated annual appreciation in value of home   (_____% of price of home)
Total cost of buying (line B.11 − line B.12)

When the total costs of buying have been determined, we need to subtract certain items to reduce the gross costs to economic reality. For instance, part of the annual mortgage payments represents repayment of principal on the mortgage loan. This amount needs to be subtracted because, in effect, it represents a savings account in the form of an increase in the homeowner's equity in the home. Next, we need to take the total annual mortgage interest and multiply it by the homeowner's marginal income tax rate (the highest income tax rate at which his income is taxed) in order to determine the income tax savings due to mortgage interest deductions. Technically, if mortgage interest is also tax-deductible in the state in which the homeowner resides, we need to use the combined effective tax rate for both federal and state purposes, but that type of calculation is beyond this text. Then, we calculate the tax savings resulting from the deduction of the annual real estate taxes on the property by multiplying those taxes by the same tax rate used for the mortgage interest deduction calculation. After deducting the three items we just calculated in this paragraph, we arrive at the after-tax cost of home ownership. Of course, we are making an assumption that the homeowner will be able to itemize his or her deductions in determining his or her federal income taxes. If this is not the case, and the homeowner must instead claim only the standard deduction, the result will be different.

Many analysts would end the calculations at this point and compare the after-tax costs of home ownership to the total costs of leasing and make a decision accordingly. In most cases, the cost of leasing will be lower. However, we have left out a critical ingredient–the estimated annual appreciation in the value of the home. This will need to be determined by analyzing the average annual appreciation in the value of comparable homes over several years and factoring in the current status of the residential real estate market. If it is in an up-trend, the financial planner may want to use a factor higher than the historical average (vice versa in a down trend). After calculating the estimated annual appreciation, one subtracts it from the annual after-tax costs of home ownership to arrive at the total cost of buying. This total cost of buying is then compared to the total costs of leasing to determine which option makes better economic sense.

Obviously, just running the numbers is not the entire answer. The financial planner must factor in the client's personal situation and needs and the general condition of the housing market.

Buy versus Lease for an Automobile

In Figure 5.3, we have a worksheet for performing a lease versus purchase analysis for an automobile used for personal purposes (rather than business purposes). The basic reasoning that we used in the home lease versus purchase analysis will still apply, except that we will not be concerned with tax deductions since neither lease payments nor interest paid on an automobile loan are tax-deductible unless the vehicle is used in a business context.

Figure 5.3

AUTOMOBILE LEASE VERSUS PURCHASE ANALYSIS		
Name _____ Date _____		
Item	**Description**	**Amount**
Lease		
1	Initial payment:	
	a. Down payment (capital cost reduction): $_____	
	b. Security deposit: _____	$_____
2	Term of lease and loan (years)*	_____
3	Term of lease and loan (months) (Item 2 × 12)	_____
4	Monthly lease payment	$_____
5	Total payments over term of lease (Item 3 × Item 4)	$_____
6	Interest rate earned on savings (in decimal form)	_____
7	Opportunity cost of initial payment (Item 1 × Item 2 × Item 6)	$_____
8	Payment/refund for market value adjustment at end of lease ($0 for closed-end leases) and/or estimated end-of-term charges	$_____
9	**Total cost of leasing (Item 1a + Item 5 + Item 7 + Item 8)**	$_____
Purchase		
10	Purchase price	$_____
11	Down payment	$_____
12	Sales tax rate (in decimal form)	_____
13	Sales tax (Item 10 × Item 12)	$_____
14	Monthly loan payment (Terms: _____, _____, months, _____%)	$_____
15	Total payments over term of loan (Item 3 × Item 14)	$_____
16	Opportunity cost of down payment (Item 2 × Item 6 × Item11)	$_____
17	Estimated value of car at end of loan	$_____
18	**Total cost of purchasing (Item 11 + Item 13 + Item 15 + Item 16 − Item 17)**	$_____
Decision		
If the value of Item 9 is less than the value of Item 18, leasing is preferred; otherwise the purchase alternative is preferred.		

*This form is based upon assumed equal terms for the lease and the installment loan, which is assumed to be used to finance the purchase.

To calculate the total cost of leasing, we start with the down payment (commonly called the **capital cost reduction**) and the security deposit most leasing organizations require. Next we need to determine the total dollar amount of lease payments to be made over the life of the lease. It is important for the purposes of this analysis that the term of the lease and the term of the auto loan are identical. If the lease term is 36 months, we simply multiply the required monthly lease payments by 36 to arrive at the total lease payments over the life of the lease. Then we need to determine the interest rate that the client was earning on the funds used for the capital cost reduction and security deposit. This rate is applied, for the term of the lease, to the total of the capital cost reduction and security deposit paid upon signing the lease. Next, in the case of an open-end lease, we need to either add or subtract the assumed **market value adjustment** made at the end of the lease. If the automobile is returned in good condition with the agreed-upon number of miles or less, there may be an amount refunded to the lessee. Conversely, if the condition of the automobile is considered poor and the mileage is higher than permitted in the lease, there may be an amount charged to the lessee. In the case of a **closed-end lease**, there is no adjustment for market value but there may be additional charges for excess miles. After making this either positive or negative adjustment, we arrive at the total cost of leasing.

In order to calculate the total cost of purchasing, we add the required down payment, the total sales tax paid, the total monthly loan payments over the term of the loan (assumed to be the same term as the lease) and the opportunity cost of the interest foregone on the down payment. Then we subtract the estimated value of the automobile at the end of the loan payments to arrive at the total cost of purchasing.

Then, we compare the total cost of leasing to the total cost of purchasing to determine which makes better economic sense. Again, as was the case in leasing versus purchasing a personal residence, there are factors other than numbers to be considered. One of the downsides of leasing is that it costs more than buying a car for cash and generally costs more than buying a car subject to a loan. Also, there are usually mileage restrictions, and it is very expensive to break an automobile lease before the end of the term.

Clearly, the analysis would look quite different where a high percentage of the car's use is for business purposes. In that case, the business portion of the lease payments, the business portion of the interest paid on the loan, and the business portion of the depreciation for the automobile would be tax-deductible. This type of analysis is beyond the scope of this text. Again, from a theoretical point of view, the cash flows involved in the preceding analysis should be adjusted for the time value of money. We will discuss the time value of money in Chapters 10 and 11.

THE IMPORTANCE OF GOOD CREDIT

If used responsibly, open account credit is an effective method of purchasing goods and services. Today, most households take advantage of 30-day charge accounts to pay such items as their utility and phone bills. In addition, most households have one or more retail charge cards, at least two bank credit cards, and often a travel and entertainment card, such as American Express. They may also have one or more revolving credit lines (e.g., overdraft protection, unsecured personal line of credit, or a home equity line). As a result, many families may have substantial amounts of credit available to them.

NEED TO KNOW: KINDS OF INFORMATION THAT APPEAR IN A CREDIT REPORT

- Name, social security number, age, number of dependents, and current and previous addresses.

- Employment record, including current and past employers, and income data if available.

- Credit history, including loans and credit lines, credit cards, payment record, and account balances.

- Public record information such as bankruptcies, tax liens, foreclosures, civil suits, and criminal convictions.

- Names of firms and financial institutions that have recently requested copies of one's file.

Many people do not appreciate the value of having good credit. The ability to borrow large amounts of money and to repay it in an agreed-upon fashion is essential to a client in meeting his or her personal and financial goals. Good credit means that there is no delinquency in one's loan payments and that debts are repaid according to the terms of any contract, agreement, or invoice. Clients can obtain (and it is advisable that they do so periodically) their credit report from national credit reporting agencies such as Equifax Credit Information Services, Trans-Union, or Experian (formerly TRW Credit Data). If clients authorize it, their financial planner can obtain the report for them. The information included in the credit report should be checked for accuracy by the consumer and incorrect or incomplete information corrected or added. This is particularly true for young adults and married women to verify that all accounts for which they are either individually or jointly liable are listed in their credit files, because lenders will usually shy away from credit applicants with little or no credit history.

Consumers and creditors can purchase a credit score based on the information included in a consumer's credit report. The score is calculated by the firm of Fair, Isaac and Company, Inc. (FICO) using a mathematical equation that evaluates many types of information included in a consumer's credit report. Credit bureau scores are often called **FICO scores** because most credit bureau scores used in the U.S. are produced from software developed by Fair, Isaac. FICO scores are provided to lenders by the three major credit reporting agencies: Equifax, Experian, and TransUnion. There is no single "cutoff score" used by all lenders and there are many additional factors that lenders use to determine one's actual interest rate. Credit bureau scores are not the only scores used. Many lenders use their own scores, which often will include the FICO score as well as other information about the consumer. It is also possible that a consumer's credit score can be different at each of the three main credit-reporting agencies. This is because each agency may have somewhat different information on a consumer. Included with each score report is a list of up to four **score reason codes** that explain why the score was not higher. This is very useful information in putting together a remedial plan to increase one's score. It is strongly recommended that clients periodically obtain their credit score and take remedial action to improve it to maintain a consistently high score.

If there is a pattern of payment delinquencies or a personal bankruptcy, this information will remain in the credit report for a long time. Delinquencies are retained for seven years and bankruptcies for ten years.

IMPORTANT CONSUMER CREDIT LEGISLATION

Over the past 35 years or so, many important pieces of legislation have been enacted to protect creditors and regulate lenders. Following is some of the most important federal legislation.

Consumer Credit Protection (Truth in Lending) Act

This act, also known as Regulation Z, requires lenders, prior to extending credit, to disclose both the dollar amount of finance charges and the annual percentage rate (APR) charged (within 1/4 of 1 percent), as well as other loan terms and conditions. The APR is calculated by dividing the average annual finance charge by the average loan balance outstanding. Every credit card must contain some form of user identification—generally a picture or signature. The credit card owner's liability for a lost or stolen card is limited to a maximum of $50 per card. Companies may not send out unrequested credit cards, but they are permitted to send unsolicited credit card applications.

Equal Credit Opportunity Act (ECOA)

This act prohibits credit discrimination on the basis of sex or marital status. It makes it illegal for lenders to ask questions about an applicant's sex, marital status, and childbearing plans. Lenders are required to view women's income the same as men's and include alimony and child support as part of that income. It further prohibits credit discrimination based on race, national origin, religion, age, or the receipt of public assistance. Finally, joint debt of a husband and wife must be reported to credit bureaus in the name of both parties.

Fair Credit Billing Act

Under this act, consumers must notify the creditor in writing of any billing errors within 60 days of the date they receive the statement. Creditors have 30 days to respond to the consumer about billing errors and 90 days to resolve the complaint, during which time creditors may not collect the bill or issue an unfavorable credit report. Credit cardholders may withhold payment from the bank (known as a holder in due course) for unsatisfactory goods or services charged to their accounts if, after good-faith attempts, they cannot satisfactorily resolve their disagreement with the seller. Merchants are permitted to give cash discounts of any size to customers who pay cash instead of using credit.

Fair Debt Collection Practices Act

This act requires creditors to notify customers in writing within five days of the first contact by a collector of the amount owed, to whom, and how to dispute the claim. The collector must cease collection efforts until sending the customer written verification of the debt. The customer can prevent a collector from communicating with him or her by notifying the collector in writing. Collectors are not permitted to (1) use abusive language, threaten the customer, or call at inconvenient times or at the place of work; (2) misrepresent themselves; (3) use unfair tactics in an effort to collect the debt; (4) contact anyone else about the customer's debt unless they are trying to locate him or her; and (5) collect an amount greater than the debt or apply payments to another disputed debt.

Fair Credit and Charge Card Disclosure Act

Card issuers are required by this Act to provide full disclosure of all fees, grace periods, and other financial terms in unsolicited application invitations. Also, they must notify consumers when their accounts are about to be renewed.

Consumer Credit Reporting Reform Act

Enacted in 1996 as an update to the Fair Credit Reporting Act of 1971, this legislation requires credit bureau reports to contain accurate, relevant, and recent information about the personal and financial situation of credit applicants. It restricts access to credit files to only bona fide users of financial information. Applicants who are denied credit or whose borrowing costs increase as the result of a credit investigation must be told why and given the name and address of the reporting credit agency. Consumers were given the right to review their credit files personally and correct any inaccurate information. Credit bureaus are required to have toll-free phone numbers and provide consumers with one low-cost credit report every two years. Credit information disputes must be resolved within 30 days and must consider the consumer's documentation. Credit bureaus must establish and maintain formal procedures for correcting credit reports. Creditors can be sued by consumers for not correcting reporting errors. Finally, employers must get written permission from employees or prospective employees to review their credit files.

DEALING WITH PROBLEMATIC DEBT

Many factors may contribute to a client taking on problematic debt. Probably the most common reason is misuse of credit cards by overextending and making only the minimum monthly payment. This can be exacerbated by the loss of one's job or by serious illness or injury. Another contributing factor is purchasing automobiles that the client cannot really afford. Auto dealers make the purchase sound appealing by offering zero percent loans while correspondingly refusing to reduce the sticker price of the auto. The result is that there may be little, if any, savings. Many consumers suffer from compulsive spending, an emotional disorder similar to compulsive gambling, which may require professional help. Others are simply attempting to keep up with their neighbors, peers, and relatives. The real issue is losing focus on one's long-term goals. If well-established goals are in place, there is less temptation to stray from accomplishment of those goals.

In Depth: Getting Help with Debt

If a client comes to the conclusion that he or she has taken on too much debt, there are some options that can help.

Obviously, the first is to reduce one's spending by reclassifying some purchases from "needs" to "wants." Those spending categories that most would agree are discretionary include entertainment, travel, clothing, gifts, new autos, and home improvements. These are fruitful grounds for cost cutting. Paying off credit card balances can actually be a very good investment by eliminating the payment of 15% or more in annual interest.

Another useful tactic is to consolidate or transfer debt to a different creditor. This would include finding cheaper credit cards, taking out a home equity loan or home equity line of credit, or working with a consumer credit counselor to develop a repayment schedule.

Others have found switching from credit cards to debit cards very useful so that they think twice about purchasing an impulse item when they know that the charge will hit their bank account immediately.

Another useful strategy may be to pay off debts with accumulated savings. Generally, this should not include the use of one's emergency fund unless that is the only available resource. If the emergency fund is used for this purpose, the client should immediately begin a plan to rebuild the fund to its required level of three to six months' living expenses.

Finally, one should consider borrowing money from one's relatives at a rate that is higher than the relative is currently earning on liquid accounts but much less than the rate being paid on the existing debt, particularly credit card debt.

Bankruptcy

During the 1980's and 1990's, consumers used credit at unprecedented levels. The heavy debt loads combined with occasional periods of economic recession have resulted in a real financial crisis for many consumers. According to the Administrative Office of the U.S. Courts, personal bankruptcy filings rose 15.2 percent to a total of 1,464,961 in the twelve months ended March 31, 2002. Individuals account for about 97 percent of all bankruptcy filings. Households that cannot resolve serious credit problems on their own may need to turn to the courts. The filing of bankruptcy should be considered a measure of last resort for an overextended borrower. It is not a satisfactory means of credit or debt management.

Chapter 13

There are two major forms of bankruptcy available to a consumer—the **Wage Earner Plan** and **Straight Bankruptcy**. The Wage Earner Plan, established under Chapter 13 of the U.S. Bankruptcy Code, provides for a workout procedure under which the borrower's debts are restructured by developing a debt repayment schedule that is more compatible with the debtor's ability to repay. There is a good possibility that such a plan will be approved by a majority of the creditors if a plan can be structured:

- to pay off the debt within three to five years
- if the debtor has a steady source of income
- secured debt is $750,000 or less and unsecured debt of $250,000 or less

Interest and late-payment penalties are waived during the revised repayment period. Upon approval of the plan by a majority of the creditors, the debtor makes payment to the court, which in turn pays off the creditors. The debtor is able to retain the use of and title to all of his or her assets.

Chapter 7

Straight bankruptcy, provided for under **Chapter 7** of the U.S. Bankruptcy Code, places the emphasis on giving the debtor a fresh start. The majority of consumer bankruptcy filings are filed under Chapter 7. Chapter 7 filings during the twelve months ended March 31, 2002, increased 17.2 percent over the previous twelve-month period to 1,059,777. This form of bankruptcy does not, however, eliminate all of the debtor's obligations and does not necessarily result in the loss of all of the debtor's assets. Under federal law, certain types of debt are generally not dischargeable in bankruptcy. These include, most notably, child support and alimony payments incurred as a result of a divorce decree, student and government loans, unpaid income tax liabilities for the last three years, and income tax withholding and FICA obligations for employees.

Certain assets are exempt from distribution under the Bankruptcy Code. Debtors can claim either the federal exemption amounts or the usually more favorable state exemption amounts. This includes such items as a debtor's personal residence (subject to a maximum excludible amount), a nominal amount of personal property, pension or retirement benefits (usually without limitation), and wages of a family member who is providing more than one half of the support of a child or other dependent. Federal exemptions include civil service or railroad workers' pension benefits, veterans' benefits, and certain Social Security and disability payments.

Chapter 11

Another bankruptcy option may be available under **Chapter 11** of the U.S. Bankruptcy Code to those who qualify. Generally it is for individuals who do not qualify under Chapter 13 either because they exceed the debt limitations or do not have a regular source of income but nevertheless wish to restructure their debt. Chapter 11 had previously been reserved primarily for businesses but the U.S. Supreme Court ruled that it is also available to individuals who qualify. In a Chapter 11 bankruptcy, the creditors vote on the reorganization plan and they may vote to block it. The result may be very lengthy delays and significant legal fees.

"Chapter 20"

A fairly recent development is the so-called **Chapter 20 bankruptcy**, which contains a blend of Chapter 7 and Chapter 13 provisions. It permits debtors to eliminate their unsecured debt under Chapter 7 and to restructure their secured debt under Chapter 13.

Bankruptcy and the Financial Planner's Liability

The subject of bankruptcy is a complex specialty in law and, should a financial planner recommend bankruptcy for a client, it is strongly suggested that competent legal counsel be consulted. Indeed, simply recommending that a client file bankruptcy may be considered the "unauthorized practice of law" and will most likely subject the financial planner to professional liability.

IMPORTANT CONCEPTS TO REMEMBER

Appropriate and inappropriate uses of debt

Various types of consumer debt

Types of home mortgages

Refinancing a home mortgage

Home equity loans and home equity lines of credit

Lease vs. Buy analysis

Maintaining good credit

Truth in Lending Act

Fair Credit Billing Act

Consumer Credit Reporting Reform Act

Types of bankruptcy

QUESTIONS FOR REVIEW

1. What are some of the situations in which debt makes sense and some in which it does not?

2. What are some of the various types of consumer debt?

3. Under what circumstances does investment debt make sense?

4. What are some of the most commonly used types of mortgage loans?

5. When does it make economic sense to refinance an existing home mortgage loan?

6. What is the principal advantage of home equity loans and home equity lines of credit?

7. What is the process for determining whether a client should purchase or lease an automobile for personal purposes?

8. How does the Truth in Lending Act protect borrowers?

9. Under what circumstances should a client consider filing bankruptcy under Chapter 7 versus under Chapter 13?

SUGGESTIONS FOR ADDITIONAL READING

Personal Financial Planning, 10th edition, by Lawrence J. Gitman and Michael D. Joehnk, South-Western/Thomson, 2004

CHAPTER SIX

Regulation of Financial Planning Activities

• • •

In this chapter, we will discuss the regulation of the principal activities conducted by financial planners. Of primary importance is the regulation of the provision of investment advice, in which nearly every financial planner engages. It is important that financial planners know which individuals and entities are excluded from the regulatory definition of investment adviser and which individuals are exempted by law from having to register as an investment adviser. Once registered as an investment adviser, the financial planner takes on several legal obligations including reporting on his or her activities to the Securities and Exchange Commission and/or state(s) in which he or she operates, providing disclosure to clients and potential clients, and functioning in the capacity of a fiduciary (a very high legal duty).

In addition to investment adviser regulation, financial planners who sell or offer to sell securities are subject to further regulation at both the federal and state levels. Financial planners who sell or offer to sell insurance products or provide advice about insurance are subject to regulation at the state level. Moreover, financial planners who provide legal advice, income tax preparation, or income tax advice need to understand their regulatory obligations in these areas. Finally, recent federal legislation has imposed on financial planners an obligation to protect clients' personal financial information and to act appropriately when taking custody of clients' assets. We will discuss the various regulatory requirements in each of these areas.

The objectives of this chapter are:

- Identify the principal regulated activities in which a financial planner may participate.

- State the definition of an investment adviser under the Investment Advisers Act of 1940.
- Describe the types of individuals or entities excluded from the definition of investment adviser under the Investment Advisers Act of 1940.
- Describe the types of individuals exempted from having to register as an investment adviser under the Investment Advisers Act of 1940.
- Describe the initial and continuing SEC reporting requirements of a registered investment adviser.
- Identify the **brochure rule** applicable to registered investment advisers.
- Explain what is meant by a registered investment adviser's **fiduciary duty**.
- Describe how the sale of securities is regulated.
- Describe how the sale of insurance products and offering of advice about insurance is regulated.
- Discuss legislation that is intended to protect the privacy of clients' personal financial information.
- Discuss legislation designed to protect clients in situations where a registered investment adviser has custody of client assets.

REGULATION OF FINANCIAL PLANNING ACTIVITIES

At this time, personal financial planning, per se, is not subject to either federal or state regulation. To many, this may come as a bit of a surprise. If you ask most people who are directly or indirectly involved with personal financial planning whether the profession is regulated, they will most likely respond that it is. What *is* subject to regulation are certain activities that, in some cases, are integral to the provision of personal financial planning services. Chief among these activities is the provision of investment advisory services. While it is theoretically possible to practice personal financial planning without providing investment advice, as a practical matter, it is quite difficult. In fact, most financial planners would agree that providing investment advice is an integral part of personal financial planning. But technically, it is the act of providing investment advice that is regulated—not personal financial planning. One reason that the personal financial planner is becoming the investment adviser of choice for many people is that the financial planner, unlike some other financial advisers, recognizes that a client's investment portfolio should be constructed only in the context of explicit client goals and as the result of an initial and ongoing financial planning process.

Other financial planning activities that are subject to regulation are the sale of securities, the sale of insurance products, and in certain states, the provision of advice about insurance. Also, to the extent that a financial planner is involved in the sale of real estate, he or she may be subject to regulation in that area, as well. If a financial planner provides legal advice as part of his or her financial planning practice, he or she will be subject to licensure as an attorney. Moreover, financial planners who prepare income tax returns or provide income tax advice, while not necessarily subject to regulation, may elect voluntarily to be regulated in order to increase their credibility with clients or potential clients.

Moreover, the use of the title "financial planner" is largely unregulated. Currently, essentially anyone may use the title "financial planner" and hold him or herself out as such to an unsuspecting public. The person using this title may have no education or experience in personal financial planning or may not have passed a rigorous professional examination in the subject. In essence, such a person may lack any qualifications in personal financial planning and yet is able to hold out to the public as an expert in the field. At this time, neither the federal government nor the various states have shown any serious interest in regulating the practice of personal financial planning, per se.

Of course, financial planners who elect to earn and use various designations in personal financial planning, such as Certified Financial Planner™ or CFP®, Chartered Financial Consultant, or Personal Financial Specialist, subject themselves voluntarily to the regulation of the organizations awarding those designations.

Regulation of Investment Advisers

The Securities and Exchange Commission (SEC) regulates investment advisers and investment adviser representatives, having assets under management above a certain dollar amount, at the federal level primarily under the Investment Advisers Act of 1940 and the adopting rules. The primary element of this regulatory program is that an individual meeting the definition of an investment adviser under the Act (last amended in 1996) must register with the SEC, unless exempted or excluded from registration. In addition, the various states, in cooperation with the SEC, regulate investment advisers and investment adviser representatives, having investment assets under management below a certain dollar amount, under their securities laws (**blue sky laws,** so named because the issuance of fraudulent securities, common before the passage of federal securities laws, were referred to as patches of "blue sky.")

What is the definition of an **investment adviser** under the Investment Advisers Act of 1940? Generally, it "means any person who, for compensation, engages in the business of advising others, either directly or through publications or

NEED TO KNOW: "ENGAGING IN THE BUSINESS"

The definition of "engaging in the business" depends primarily upon how frequently and regularly a person provides advice or analysis or reports concerning securities and whether such advisory services are provided under conditions that suggest that their provision constitutes a business activity. SEC Release 1092 indicates that the giving of advice need not constitute the principal business activity or any particular portion of the business activities in order for a person to be an investment adviser. The SEC staff considers a person to be "in the business" of providing advice if the person:

- holds him or herself out as an investment adviser or as one who provides investment advice;

- receives any separate or additional compensation that represents a clearly definable charge for providing advice about securities, regardless of whether the compensation is separate from or included within any overall compensation, or receives transaction-based compensation if the client implements the investment advice; or

- on anything other than rare, isolated and non-periodic instances, provides specific investment advice. To make a definitive determination if a person is an investment adviser, one needs to consider all of the relevant facts and circumstances.

writings, as to the value of securities or as to the advisability of investing in, purchasing, or selling securities, or who, for compensation and as part of a regular business, issues or promulgates analyses or reports concerning securities...". Obviously, this is a very broad definition. It consists of three elements, each of which must be satisfied for an entity to be covered by the Act.

- The entity must be engaged "in the business" of providing advice or of issuing analyses or reports concerning securities.
- The advice, analysis, or report must be with respect to "the value of securities" or the "advisability of investing in, purchasing or selling securities."
- The advice, analysis, or report must be provided in return for "compensation."

These three elements are interrelated in that the principles underlying one element are often relevant to the other elements.

"Holding out" as an investment adviser may be evidenced by public advertising seeking advisory clients (yellow pages, professional listings, newspapers, etc.), designating one's self as an investment adviser on business stationery or on a business card, or encouraging word-of-mouth referrals from existing clients.

If the facts show that a fee, though charged for a collection of services for establishing a nonadvisory service, varies according to whether investment advice is provided, then "special or additional compensation" is deemed to be present. The compensation received need not be paid by the client, it could be paid by a third party.

"Specific investment advice" is considered to include advice respecting specific securities or categories of securities, allocation of capital in specific percentages between various investment media including life insurance, particular types of mutual funds, and high yield bonds, but not "advice limited to a general recommendation to allocate assets in securities, life insurance and tangible assets."

What is meant by providing advisory services "concerning securities?" The advisory services provided must be with respect to an instrument or instruments which satisfy the Act's definition of a "security." As a result, advice that is limited to whether to invest directly in commodity futures, real estate, art work, a non-security business opportunity, or some other non-security medium does not subject its provider to regulation as an investment adviser. An additional factor is whether the provider exercises professional judgment in rendering the service. Merely providing information or performing record-keeping or other ministerial duties does not constitute advisory activity. But a person who advises others on the selection of an investment adviser is providing advisory services, since judgment is involved.

Finally, what does it mean to provide advisory services "for compensation?" SEC Release 1092 states that the "compensation element is satisfied by the receipt of any economic benefit, whether in the form of an advisory fee or some other fee relating to the total services rendered, commissions or some combination of the foregoing."

In Depth: Investment Adviser Exclusions

Certain individuals or entities are excluded from the definition of investment adviser under the Investment Advisers Act:

- A **bank** or any bank holding company that is not an investment company (subsidiaries providing investment advisory services, foreign banks, and savings and loan associations are not entitled to rely on this exclusion—they must register). Effective 5/12/01, departments or divisions of banks or bank holding companies serving as the investment adviser to a registered investment company must register.

- Any **lawyer, accountant, engineer**, or **teacher** whose performance of advisory services is **solely incidental** to the practice of his or her profession (does not apply to those who provide investment advice as an independent business). Advisory services will not be considered "solely incidental" if the professional holds himself or herself out as providing investment advice to the public, if the investment advisory services are not connected with and reasonably related to provision of primary professional services, and if any fee charged for the advisory service is not based on the same factors as are used in developing fees for primary professional services.

- Any **broker or dealer** whose performance of advisory services is **solely incidental** to the conduct of his or her business as a broker or dealer and who receives no special compensation therefor (e.g., development of a financial plan for a substantial number of clients is arguably not solely incidental). Where a differential in fees offered a client could be said to be "primarily attributable" to the rendering of investment advice, a finding of special compensation will be made. Also, a registered rep of a broker/dealer who has an independent financial planning or other advisory business, not subject to the broker/dealer's control, cannot rely on the broker/dealer exclusion.

- The **publisher** of a bona fide newspaper, news magazine or business or financial publication of general and regular circulation.

- Any person whose advice, analyses or reports relate to no securities other than **securities which are direct obligations of or obligations guaranteed as to principal or interest by the United States, or securities issued or guaranteed by corporations in which the United States has a direct or indirect interest** which shall have been designated by the Secretary of the Treasury as exempted securities for the purposes of this Act

- Such **other persons not within the intent of the Act**, as the SEC may designate by rules and regulations or order

These individuals and entities need not register with the SEC and are not regulated under the Act's provisions, including the Act's anti-fraud provisions.

Investment Adviser Exemptions

Certain individuals are **exempt from having to register** as an investment adviser, even if they do not come under an exclusion (see box). The primary exemption is any adviser that during the previous twelve months has had **fewer than 15 clients** and does not hold himself or herself out generally to the public as an investment adviser. A second exemption is an adviser **all of whose clients are residents of the state** within which such adviser maintains his or its principal office and place of business, and who does not furnish advice or issue analyses or reports with respect to securities on any national securities exchange.

In addition, any adviser who currently has **less than $25 million of assets under his or her own management** should, instead of registering with the SEC, register with the state securities commissioner in his or her state of residence. If the total assets under management increase to $25 million or more, but not $30 million, an investment adviser may register with the SEC, but he or she is not required to do so. If an adviser reports on his or its annual updating amendment (to be discussed later) that total assets under management have increased to $30 million or more, the adviser **must** register with the SEC within 90 days after filing that annual updating amendment. Also, if an adviser reports on his or its annual updating amendment that total assets under management have decreased to less than $25 million, he or it must withdraw from SEC registration within 180 days after the end of his or its fiscal year by filing Form ADV-W. If the adviser has his or its principal office and place of business in a state that has no investment adviser statute (as of early 2004, only the State of Wyoming), he or it is permitted to register with the SEC. Doing so can afford some degree of prestige as well as help to dispel some of the public's fear in selecting a financial planner.

A final category of exemption is an investment adviser whose **only clients are insurance companies**.

Investment advisers exempt from registration are still subject, however, to certain anti-fraud provisions in Section 206 of the Investment Advisers Act of 1940, as will be discussed later.

SEC Registration Procedures

Prior to 1997, investment advisers were regulated directly by both the SEC and the securities commissions in each state in which the adviser transacted business. The regulatory scheme changed with the passage of the National Securities Markets Improvement Act of 1996. Title III of that act, known as The Investment Advisers Supervision Coordination Act amended the Investment Advisers Act of 1940 to put an end to federal and state overlapping adviser regulation. Effective July 8, 1997, the SEC became generally responsible for larger advisers while the states assumed responsibility for smaller advisers.

After determining that an individual or entity is required to register as an investment adviser with the SEC, how does one go about doing so? First, the applicant must file a so-called Form ADV electronically with the Investment Adviser Registration Depository (IARD). The adviser must file simultaneously a "notice filing" with the state or states in which he or she plans to provide investment advisory services. The fee for filing Form ADV is currently $150. Form ADV may be obtained electronically at the SEC's IARD Home Page (http://www.sec.gov/divisions/investment/iard.shtml) or by calling the Publications Unit of the Commission in Washington, D.C. There are commercial organizations that will complete the entire registration process for a fee.

Part 1 (formerly Part I) of **Form ADV** is principally for use by regulators. Part II serves as the basis for the disclosure document the adviser must provide to each of its advisory clients. We will discuss Part II of Form ADV later under **The Brochure Rule**. At the time of publication of this book, the SEC has proposed amendments that would revise many of Form ADV's reporting and disclosure requirements. In September 2000, the SEC adopted some of the proposals dealing with Part 1 but it has deferred consideration of the amendments to Part II. Part 1 is now divided into Parts 1A and 1B. Part 1A sets forth those items to which all advisers must respond and Part 1B sets forth additional items to which only state-registered advisers must respond. Part 1A is primarily concerned with adviser background information, information about the adviser's business, conflicts of interest, custody, persons controlling the adviser, disciplinary history, and small business information. Part 1A is required to be completed by both SEC-registered and state-registered advisers. Part 1B is required only of state-registered advisers and is concerned primarily with state-specific adviser matters such as bond and net capital requirements.

After the initial filing, investment advisers are required to amend their Form ADV each year by filing an **annual updating amendment** (Schedule I) within 90 days after the end of their fiscal year. In addition to the annual updating amendment, an adviser must amend Form ADV by filing additional amendments promptly if the information provided for certain items in Part 1 or the information provided in Part II becomes materially inaccurate. Failure to update one's Form ADV is a violation of SEC rules and similar state rules and can lead to revocation of one's registration.

If an adviser reports that he or she no longer needs to register, registration must be withdrawn by filing a Form ADV-W, Notice of Withdrawal from Registration, within 180 days after the end of the fiscal year. The penalty for not complying with the registration requirements is the bringing of a possible civil or administrative action against the adviser by the SEC.

Note that an individual who has registered with the SEC as an investment adviser is not entitled to use the initials **RIA (for Registered Investment Adviser)** after his or her name. He or she must spell out "Registered Investment Adviser" rather than using the aforementioned abbreviation. The purpose of this rule is to minimize the possibility that these initials (RIA) may, in effect, confer some sort of professional designation or educational degree on the holder.

The Brochure Rule

The primary practical consequence of having to register with the SEC as an investment adviser is the requirement of complying with Rule 204-3 (commonly known as the brochure rule) under the Investment Adviser Act of 1940. This rule requires each registered investment adviser to deliver to each advisory client and prospective advisory client a written disclosure statement, or brochure, describing the adviser's services, qualifications, and potential conflicts of interest. This brochure (usually satisfied by providing Part II of Form ADV) must be delivered to each and every client not less than 48 hours prior to entering into an advisory contract or, if the client has the right to cancel the advisory contract without penalty for a period of five days, at the time the client enters the contract. The only situation in which an investment adviser is not required to deliver the brochure is if he or she provides services to a client for which compensation of less than $200 will be received. In addition, the adviser must each year deliver, or offer in writing to deliver, to each advisory client a copy of his or her updated disclosure statement.

Moreover, an anti-fraud rule requires that advisers disclose to their clients promptly material financial and disciplinary information. Under this rule, advisers with custody or discretionary authority over client funds or securities, or advisers that require prepayment of advisory fees of more than $500 per client six months or more in advance, must disclose a precarious financial condition *to those clients involved*. This would generally include insolvency or bankruptcy. Also under the rule, material legal or disciplinary actions taken against the adviser or a member of the adviser's management must be disclosed *to all clients*.

Fiduciary Duty

The anti-fraud provisions of the Investment Advisers Act of 1940 and most state laws impose a duty on investment advisers to act as fiduciaries in dealing with their clients. This means that the adviser must hold the client's interest above his or her own in all matters. Conflicts of interest should be avoided at all costs. However, there are some conflicts that will inevitably occur, such as a person being licensed as a securities agent (registered representative) as well as an investment adviser. In these instances, the adviser must take great pains to clearly and accurately describe those conflicts and how the adviser will maintain impartiality in its recommendations to clients.

The primary duties of investment advisers and practices they should avoid are shown in the In Depth on the next page. There are other situations that require disclosure of conflicts, including:

- The adviser or its employees are also acting as a broker/dealer and/or securities agent
- The adviser is receiving transaction-based compensation, including 12(b)-1 or other marketing fees, related to securities recommended to its clients
- The adviser receives any type of compensation from any source for soliciting or referring clients to another adviser or a broker/dealer
- Hidden fees in the form of undisclosed service charges, wrap fees or expenses reimbursed by other parties

Compliance

On December 3, 2003, the SEC adopted Rule 206(4)-7 under the Investment Advisers Act of 1940. This new rule requires investment advisers to (1) establish and implement compliance policies and procedures, (2) annually review and update their compliance policies and procedures, and (3) designate a chief compliance officer responsible for supervising the adviser's compliance with federal and state laws which govern the adviser's business activities. This new rule became effective on February 5, 2004. The mandatory compliance date for this new rule and rule amendments is October 5, 2004. On or before the compliance date, the adviser must:

NEED TO KNOW: DISCLOSURE

The most important duty of an investment adviser is the disclosure of all information relating to the relationship between the adviser and a client. Advisers have great leeway in tailoring their client services as long as clients know up front about such things as:

- What kinds of services are available?
- Who is providing those services?
- What fees and other expenses will the client be subject to and are these fees negotiable?
- Is the adviser being compensated from other sources?
- Is the adviser affiliated with another investment adviser, a broker/dealer or an issuer of securities?
- Can the client implement a financial plan with someone else or does the client only get to keep the plan if he or she implements it through the adviser?
- What other potential conflicts of interest exist that might affect the adviser's recommendations?

- designate a chief compliance officer; and
- adopt compliance policies and procedures that satisfy the requirements in the new rule

Regulation of Securities Salespersons

In addition to SEC requirements, a registered investment adviser who sells or offers to sell securities may also be subject to rules of the **National Association of Securities Dealers (NASD)**. The NASD, established in 1938, is a self-regulatory membership organization made up of approximately 5,200 securities firms with some 92,000 branch offices and over 653,000 securities industry professionals throughout the United States. It is an organization that creates and enforces rules for its members designed for the ultimate benefit and protection of investors and based on the federal securities laws. It is overseen by the SEC to ensure that NASD is carrying out these rules. NASD Regulation was established in 1996 as a subsidiary of the NASD. It was created to separate the regulation of the broker/dealer profession from the operation of The Nasdaq Stock Market. NASD Regulation helps ensure that member firms and their employees comply with NASD and Municipal Securities Rulemaking Board (MSRB) rules, as well as federal and state securities laws and regulations.

In Depth:

Duties the SEC Expects of an Adviser

- Make reasonable investment recommendations independent of outside influences
- Select broker/dealers based on their ability to provide the best execution of trades for accounts where the adviser has authority to select the broker/dealer
- Make recommendations based on a reasonable inquiry into a client's investment objectives, financial situation and other factors
- Always place client interests ahead of its own

Practices Investment Advisers Should Avoid

- Acting as an issuer or affiliate of an issuer of securities
- Recommending unregistered, non-exempt securities or the use of unlicensed broker/dealers
- Any activity that acts as a fraud or deceit on clients
- Charging unreasonable fees
- Failing to disclose to all customers the availability of fee discounts
- Using contracts that seek to limit or avoid an adviser's liability under the law (hedge clauses)
- Limiting a client's options with regard to the pursuit of a civil case or arbitration
- Borrowing money from or lending money to clients

Among NASD Regulation's many functions is the maintenance of the qualification, employment, and disciplinary histories of registered securities employees of member firms through the Web Central Registration Depository (CRD) system. The CRD system is a registration data bank and application processing facility. It processes applications for agent registration in all states, the District of Columbia, Puerto Rico, and for the securities exchanges. It permits individuals seeking registration with multiple organizations and states

NEED TO KNOW: TYPES OF REGISTRANTS

Registered representatives can be registered to sell a large variety of products. These various registrations are each referred to as a **series**. The registration providing the broadest authority is **Series 7**, general securities representative, which qualifies a registered representative for the solicitation, purchase, and/or sale of all securities products, including corporate securities, municipal securities, options, direct participation programs, investment company products, and variable contracts. Another very popular registration is **Series 6**, which qualifies the holder primarily for the solicitation, purchase, and/or sale of mutual funds, variable contracts, and annuities. In addition there are separate registrations for direct participation programs, corporate securities, government securities, private securities offerings, equity trader, registered options, municipal securities, and assistant representative. Series 7 or Series 6 registered reps may also need to register under **Series 63** (Uniform Securities Agent State Law Examination), **Series 65** (Uniform Investment Adviser Law Examination), or under **Series 66** (Uniform Combined State Law Examination).

Prospective principals of securities firms must pass additional examinations that test their knowledge of supervisory rules in the areas of investment banking, trading, and market making, retail sales activities, and financial responsibility rules. Financial and operational principals must further demonstrate a thorough knowledge of the requirements regarding record keeping, net capital, customer reserves, financial reporting, and credit.

to do so by submitting a single form and a combined payment of fees to the NASD. In addition to individual registration, the Web CRD system also processes the membership registration and withdrawal forms for broker/dealers.

Records of securities professionals are available to the public through the NASD Regulation Public Disclosure Program, which extracts data from the Web CRD system.

The requirements of NASD rules and regulations come into play when a financial planner associates with a broker or dealer in the selling of security products, as is often the case. Any securities professional associated with an NASD member firm (including partners, officers, directors, branch managers, department supervisors, and salespersons) must register with the NASD. The registration application requires information about the individual's prior employment and disciplinary history. The NASD prescribes two levels of qualification and registration:

- Registered representatives, generally sales personnel

- Principals, generally officers of the firm and other management personnel involved in the day-to-day operation of the firm's investment banking or securities business.

As part of the registration process, securities professionals must pass an examination administered by NASD Regulation to demonstrate competence in the areas in which they will work. These mandatory qualification examinations cover a broad range of subjects on the markets, as well as the securities industry and its regulatory structure, ensuring a minimum level of understanding and expertise. The areas in which candidates are tested include federal securities laws, SEC and NASD rules and regulations, securities products, the operation and interrelation of financial markets, economic theory and kinds of risk, corporate financing, accounting, and balance sheet analysis, portfolio theory and analysis, fair sales practices, including solicitation and presentation, types of customer accounts, and tax treatment of various investments. NASD Regulation may grant qualification examination waivers for its requirements based on registration filing errors, continuing registrations with other regulatory authorities, experience in the securities industry (including other examinations taken by the applicant, such as those for Certified Financial Planner™ certificant or Chartered Financial Analyst); educational achievement; or regulatory experience.

An individual's broker/dealer firm registers the individual with NASD Registration by filing a Uniform Application for Securities Industry Registration or Transfer, **Form U-4**. This form lists other self-regulatory organizations (SROs) such as the securities and options exchanges and the states with which the individual wishes to register. If an individual submits misleading information or omits material information, particularly with regard to personal history and past disciplinary or law enforcement encounters, he or she is subject to disciplinary action including possibly being barred from the securities industry. Even after the initial filing of the U-4 form, a registered representative has a continuing obligation to update his or her U-4 if any of the information changes or becomes inaccurate. This includes the registered rep's home address or any of the questions involving customer complaints, criminal disclosure, regulatory disciplinary actions, civil judicial actions, terminations, or financial judgments.

If a registered rep leaves his or her broker/dealer firm for any reason, the firm has up to 30 days to supply the registered rep with a copy of the Uniform Termination Notice for Securities Industry Registration, **Form U-5**, which it is required to file with NASD Regulation. The Form U-5 indicates the date the rep left the firm and a brief reason why he or she left. Registered reps are advised to review this Form for accuracy. If the information is inaccurate or incomplete, the registered rep should notify his or her prior employer promptly. The new broker/dealer employer must obtain and review a copy of a registered rep's most recent Form U-5. The broker/dealer employer is required to report on the Form U-5 any customer complaint, criminal action, regulatory action, investigation, internal review alleging rule violations, any investigation it may currently be conducting, and the reason for any involuntary termination.

For regulatory purposes, NASD Regulation does not distinguish between an employee or an **independent contractor**. Regardless of one's technical employment status, he or she is obligated to follow all applicable securities laws and regulations. An example of this is the requirement to get clearance from one's broker/dealer employer for certain personal financial activities, including any financial accounts held by the registered rep or members of his or her immediate family with other securities firms, relationships with other businesses, and any forms of compensation received from any source other than the broker/dealer employer. Also, every registered rep must be supervised by a registered principal, and they must have at least one meeting annually to formally discuss regulatory and compliance matters.

After registration, a registered rep may conduct a securities business as an agent only while under the direct supervision of his or her broker/dealer firm. He or she cannot conduct any securities transactions other than with his or her member firm unless receiving prior written approval to do so.

Continuing Education

A registered rep is required to adhere to certain continuing education requirements during the course of his or her career. On July 1, 1995, the NASD and other SROs adopted a mandatory Continuing Education Program for the securities industry. The Program is intended to ensure that the registered rep stays up to date on products, markets, and rules. Under the Program, registered reps are required to attend periodic computer-based training in regulatory matters (referred to as the **Regulatory Element**) and to participate in the annual training programs provided by the broker/dealer employer to keep the registered rep informed on job- and product-related subjects (referred to as the **Firm Element**).

Depending upon the registration(s) held by the registered rep, he or she must complete one of the Regulatory Element computer-based training programs on the second anniversary of his or her initial securities registration and then every third year thereafter. If a registered rep becomes the subject of a significant disciplinary action (a suspension, fine of $5,000 or more, or a statutory disqualification) or is otherwise ordered to do so by a securities regulator, he or she is required to complete a Regulatory Element computer-based training session immediately and the subsequent requirement anniversaries will be adjusted accordingly. The **General Program**, which applies to most registered reps, focuses on compliance, regulatory, ethical, and sales-practice standards.

If a registered rep fails to satisfy a Regulatory Element requirement within 120 days beginning with his or her anniversary date, his or her securities registration becomes inactive until the requirement is satisfied. If the registration remains inactive for two years, it will be administratively terminated and the individual will be required to re-qualify for registration by examination.

The Firm Element has a different but complementary focus to the Regulatory Element training. At least annually, a registered rep's broker/dealer firm is required to evaluate and prioritize its training needs and prepare a written training plan designed to enhance the registered rep's securities knowledge, skill, and professionalism. The training programs in the broker/dealer firm's Firm Element plan are required to cover the general investment features and associated risk factors, suitability and sales practice considerations, and applicable regulatory requirements of the securities products, services, and strategies offered to the public. If a registered rep fails to participate in the training programs stipulated by his or her firm as part of its compliance with the Firm Element, the registered rep will be sanctioned by his or her firm, including possible termination.

Obligations to Securities Customers

The foundation of the securities industry is fair dealing with customers. A registered rep has an obligation to serve his or her customers with honesty and integrity by putting their interests first. A large part of this is based on **knowing your customer**. A registered rep must obtain a clear understanding of each customer's financial condition. Some of this information is obtained when opening a new customer's account with the registered rep's broker/dealer firm. Other information may be obtained through conversations with the customer or through credit checks made by the broker/dealer firm with credit agencies or other financial institutions. Account records concerning a customer's financial status must be kept up to date.

An additional obligation of a registered rep is for each customer as well as the registered rep to have a clear understanding of the customer's investment objectives. Once these customer objectives have been obtained and recorded in the customer's file, the registered rep must make certain that specific recommendations for that customer fall within these objectives (and accordingly, are suitable). Just as a customer's financial status may change, so too may the customer's investment objectives. As a result, they should be reviewed periodically and a written record made of the changes as they occur.

In addition, a registered rep must discuss each order with his or her customer prior to entering it, unless the customer has given written discretionary authority to the registered rep, which has been approved by his or her broker/dealer firm. An oral grant of discretionary authority is not sufficient and acting on such authority violates NASD rules.

In Depth: The Public Disclosure Program

In 1987, the NASD created the **Public Disclosure Program (PDP)** for investors to gain convenient access to information about securities firms and their associated personnel. Using this Program, investors can learn about the professional background, business practices, and conduct of NASD member firms or their brokers by obtaining a public report of disclosable background information. The PDP reports contain information required to be reported under securities industry rules including, generally:

- final disciplinary actions taken by NASD Regulation and other SROs or by federal, state, and foreign securities agencies;
- civil judgments and arbitration decisions;
- certain criminal convictions, information, and indictments;
- settlements of $10,000 or more of customer complaints, arbitration claims, or civil suits and allegations of sales practice violations;
- employment terminations after allegations were made involving violations of investment-related statutes or rules, fraud, theft, or failure to supervise investment-related activities;
- bankruptcies filed within the last 10 years and outstanding judgments and liens;
- bonding company denials of coverage, payout, or revocation;
- any suspension or revocation to act as an attorney, accountant, or federal contractor;
- pending disciplinary actions taken by industry regulators;
- pending arbitrations and civil proceedings;
- pending complaints alleging sales practice violations and compensatory damages of $5,000 or more; and
- open examinations that are deemed formal investigations involving regulatory or criminal matters.

It is important to remember that a number of items in the PDP report involve pending actions or allegations that may be contested and have not been resolved or proven. It is possible that they may be withdrawn or dismissed, resolved in favor of the registered rep, or concluded through a negotiated settlement with no admission or conclusion of wrongdoing. In spite of this, if used effectively by customers, they leave a wayward registered rep no real place to hide.

Another obligation owed to a registered rep's customer is that charges to customers must be reasonable and not unfairly discriminatory among customers. Depending upon the type of security being traded, rarely is a markup on equity securities above 5 percent considered fair or reasonable. Indeed, depending on the circumstances and the type of security involved, markups at or even below 5 percent may be considered unfair or unreasonable. Commissions approaching or exceeding 5 percent are subject to close regulatory scrutiny and must be justified, taking into account all relevant circumstances.

Other Securities Industry Regulated Areas

Advertising, sales literature, business cards, e-mail, communications with the public (such as seminar announcements), and most print and electronic correspondence in the securities industry are subject to regulatory review and approval. Some items may require scrutiny by the broker/dealer's compliance officer or even advance filing with NASD Regulation. Other items require formal record keeping. Registered reps need to obtain their supervisor's approval of any written material prepared by the registered rep or that the registered rep wishes to use before delivering it to a customer or prospect.

So-called **microcap** security and penny stock fraud have resulted in increased regulatory, enforcement, and rulemaking efforts. In spite of the fact that information about most of these thinly capitalized companies is difficult to obtain, a registered rep, as in all recommended transactions, must ensure that he or she has adequate information about the issuer to form a reasonable basis for a recommendation and to ensure the suitability of the investment. Proposed rules, if adopted, will require the review of specific information prior to such recommendations.

Following is a list of specific practices that constitute serious violations of securities industry regulations. They may harm the customer, another member firm, the integrity of the marketplace, the issuer of the securities, or the public in general.

- Rumors, knowingly false and misleading statements, and incomplete information. Advising a client to buy or sell a security based on a "hot tip" constitutes securities fraud. If the "hot tip" is not real, or is not "hot," the customer can be misled. If it is a "hot tip," the registered rep may be violating insider-trading rules. Registered reps involved in these types of activities may be subject to civil liability, disciplinary action, and even criminal charges.

- Trade practice rules including insider trading (illegal use or passing on to others material, non-public information or entering into transactions while in possession of such information); backing away (failing to honor the quoted bid and ask prices for a minimum quantity); trading ahead of customer limit orders; front-running (prohibited buying or selling of a security or an option on a security while in possession of material, non-public information concerning an imminent block transaction in the security or option); trading ahead of research reports; and anti-intimidation/coordination (coordinating a member firm's prices, trades, or trade reports with any other member firm or threaten, harass, coerce, intimidate, or otherwise improperly influence another member firm).

- Commingling—placing customer funds intended for securities transactions in the registered rep's account or insurance business account.

- Churning—frequent trading, or trading that is not consistent with the financial goals and risk tolerance of a customer, in a discretionary account.

- Suitability—the registered rep must have reasonable grounds for believing each recommendation to a customer is suitable on the basis of the customer's other securities holdings and financial situation, among other factors.

- Free-riding and withholding—new issues of securities that immediately begin trading at a higher price than originally offered must be distributed to the public. They cannot be placed in the accounts of the registered rep under any circumstances.

- Selling away—selling securities without processing the order through the broker/dealer firm with which the registered rep is associated and without the firm's permission or knowledge

- Sharing in accounts—sharing profits or losses in an account with a customer is generally prohibited.

- Conflicts of interest—registered reps should avoid even the appearance of conflict, let alone any actual conflict of interest, in transactions with customers.

- Switching and break-point sale for mutual funds—switching the customer among funds with similar investment objectives is usually a violation if it has no legitimate investment purpose and may needlessly impose another commission charge and increased tax liability on the customer. Also, recommending to a customer a mutual fund purchase for a quantity just beneath the point where the customer could save commission charges significantly by purchasing a few more shares is usually a violation.

- Unauthorized trades—entering an order without the expressed and detailed permission of the customer unless the registered rep and his or her firm have been granted written discretionary authority by the customer.

- Parking securities and maintaining fictitious accounts—holding or hiding securities in someone else's or a fictitious account is misleading and strictly prohibited.

- Failure to cooperate with NASD staff can result in a fine, suspension, or bar from the industry. In this connection, a registered rep must keep NASD Regulation informed of his or her current home address.

- Cheating on exams—prohibits an applicant from receiving assistance while taking a qualification exam. Penalty is normally being barred from the securities industry.

Dispute Resolution

NASD Dispute Resolution, Inc. operates the largest arbitration and mediation forum in the securities industry. NASD Dispute Resolution resolves disputes in a fair, expeditious, and cost-effective manner between customers and securities firms and their associated persons and between associated persons and securities firms. Although filing, processing, and hearing fees are required, arbitration is typically less expensive and less time-consuming than court proceedings.

For more information about NASD regulations and registration procedures, please consult its website: http://www.nasdr.com.

The Role of NASAA

Organized in 1919, the North American Securities Administrators Association (**NASAA**) is a voluntary association of 66 state, provincial, and territorial securities administrators. In the United States, this organization is the voice of the state securities administrators and agencies charged with state law enforcement. As noted above, these administrators are the major regulators for the smaller investment advisers, i.e., those with less than $25 million of assets under management at any one time. In addition, NASAA has been instrumental in implementing the provisions of the Uniform Securities Act, model legislation that coordinates state securities throughout the U.S. State administrators are also charged with administration of state **blue sky** security statutes.

For more information about NASAA regulation and registration procedures, please consult its website: http://www.nasaa.org.

Regulation of Insurance Producers and Insurance Advisers/Counselors/Consultants

While the sale and offering of securities is primarily a federally regulated process, insurance industry regulation is administered by the states. Each state enacts laws governing the conduct of the insurance industry within its borders. These laws also cover the licensing and registration of insurance producers (same as salespersons) who offer insurance products, such as life, health, and property insurance and annuities, or provide advice about insurance. Certain states regulate persons known as insurance advisers, counselors, or consultants who do not sell insurance products but rather render advice about such products to the general public.

The central figure in this regulation is the State Insurance Commissioner, who has the ultimate responsibility for the administration of state insurance laws. These Commissioners have membership in a voluntary association known as the National Association of Insurance Commissioners (**NAIC**), which, while having no legislative power, is nevertheless extremely influential in the shape and future of insurance laws and regulation in the states. For example, the NAIC has established standards to evaluate the financial health of insurance companies that may be used by financial planners and others to determine whether an insurance product is one that he or she wishes to offer to clients.

For more information about NAIC model regulations and licensing procedures, please consult: http://www.naic.org. For a list of individual state insurance regulators, please visit: http://www.naic.org/state_contacts/sid_websites.htm.

Other Regulated Activities

Financial planners are sometimes placed in the position of being asked questions by clients pertaining to the law. While the financial planner may be quite confident of his or her understanding of the particular law or laws involved, responding to such questions or, alternatively, offering opinions about the law not necessarily in response to a client question, may be considered in some states to be the **unauthorized practice of law**. In most areas of the law, only a licensed attorney can render legal advice. If a financial planner decides to render legal advice on a reasonably consistent basis, he or she should be licensed as an attorney.

It is recommended that financial planners who are not attorneys respond to client legal questions by first indicating that they are not licensed as an attorney. Second, if they choose to respond to the legal question, they should indicate that their answer is their understanding of the relevant law but that the client should consult a licensed attorney to confirm the financial planner's understanding.

Another area of potential regulation for financial planners is the sale of real estate. At times, clients will ask the financial planner to assist with the purchase or sale of real property. The financial planner needs to be cautious in this area as the activity engaged in on behalf of the client may require licensing as a real estate salesperson or broker. It is important that financial planners consult the applicable state's real estate laws as to the requirements for licensing in that area.

Some financial planners prepare income tax returns and/or render income tax advice for clients. Generally, anyone can prepare an income tax return for another person without needing to be licensed to do so. However, the rendering of income tax advice is generally restricted to licensed attorneys and certified public accountants (or other licensed accountants). The same approach as recommended for the rendering of general legal advice should apply here. First, the financial planner should indicate to the client that he or she is neither a licensed attorney nor a CPA. Then, he or she should indicate that his or her advice is based on their understanding of the law but that the client should consult either a licensed attorney or CPA to confirm the financial planner's understanding.

Financial planners who prepare income tax returns should consider becoming either a CPA or an IRS Enrolled Agent, not for regulatory purposes but simply because of the credibility they can achieve with clients and potential clients. Financial planners who provide income tax advice on a regular and consistent basis and who are not either licensed attorneys or CPAs, should either become appropriately licensed or use the approach described in the previous paragraph.

Client Privacy Protection

Initial compliance with the privacy protection provisions of the **Gramm-Leach-Bliley Act** (GLBA) and related Federal Trade Commission regulations was required on or before July 1, 2001. The GLBA requires "financial institutions" to protect the privacy of most information they obtain from individuals who use their products and services. "Financial institutions" include investment advisers, broker-dealers, investment companies, and insurance agents and brokers. Professionals who provide individual clients with "financial products or services" must have notified, by the July 2001 compliance date, their individual, non-business clients of their policies that protect the privacy of their clients' personal financial information. After this initial compliance, this information must be provided to new clients before acceptance of engagements and to continuing clients annually, generally with the same language included in client engagement letters.

"Financial products or services" includes, among many other things, personal financial planning. The notification to clients must include the types of nonpublic personal information collected by the financial planner, the types of nonpublic personal information the financial planner discloses about the client, the parties to whom the information is disclosed, the client's right to opt out of the disclosure, the financial planner's policies with respect to sharing information on a person who is no longer a client, and the financial planner's practices for protecting the confidentiality and security of client non-public personal information.

SEC CUSTODY RULE

On September 25, 2003, the Securities and Exchange Commission approved a revised rule to clarify circumstances under which a SEC-registered investment adviser or one required to be so-registered has custody of client assets. The revised rule became effective November 5, 2003, but compliance was not required until April 1, 2004. Revised Rule 206(4)-2 makes it a fraudulent, deceptive, or manipulative act for such advisers to have custody of client funds or securities unless they are maintained by a broker/dealer, bank, or other "qualified custodian." A qualified custodian is a bank, savings association, a broker/dealer, a registered futures commission merchant, or a foreign financial institution that customarily holds assets for its customers in accounts separate from its proprietary assets. The qualified custodian must hold the funds or securities in an account either under the client's name or under the adviser's name as agent or trustee for its clients. If the qualified custodian sends account statements directly to an adviser's clients, the adviser is relieved from sending its own account statements and from undergoing an annual surprise examination. The amendments also add a definition of "custody" and clarify when an adviser is considered to have custody of client funds or securities. Finally, the amendments remove the Form ADV requirement that advisers with custody include an audited balance sheet in their disclosure brochure to clients.

An adviser is considered to have custody of client assets when it holds "directly or indirectly, client funds or securities or has any authority to obtain possession of them." The rule provides three examples of what constitutes having custody of client assets. The first example is where the adviser has possession of client funds or securities, even briefly. Under this example, holding clients' stock certificates or cash, even temporarily, puts those assets at risk of misuse or loss. Inadvertent receipt of such client assets can be corrected by returning the assets within three business days of receipt. If the adviser has possession of a client's check made payable to a third party, it does not constitute possession for purposes of the custody rule.

The second example is where an adviser has authority to withdraw funds or securities from a client's account. This includes the situation where an adviser has power of attorney to sign checks for a client, can dispose of client funds or securities for any purpose other than authorized trading, or can deduct advisory fees or other expenses directly from a client's account.

The third example of an adviser being considered to have custody of a client's assets is where the adviser acts in any capacity that gives the adviser legal ownership of, or access to, the client's funds or securities. The example cited is that of a firm acting as general partner and investment adviser to a limited partnership. Because of its position in the limited partnership, the adviser has authority to dispose of funds and securities in the limited partnership's account and, as a result, has custody of client assets.

An adviser may use a mutual fund transfer agent in lieu of a qualified custodian to hold mutual fund shares for a client. In addition, the revised rule excepts advisers with respect to privately offered uncertificated securities in their clients' accounts if ownership of the securities is recorded only on the books of the issuer or its transfer agent, is in the name of the client, and transfer of ownership is subject to prior consent of the issuer or holders of the issuer's outstanding securities.

In the common situation where an SEC-registered investment adviser is also a registered representative with a NASD member firm, such persons were formerly permitted (under an SEC no-action letter) to forward stock certificates on behalf of their clients without triggering the custody rule. This will continue to be true under the revised custody rule. However, investment advisers are still prohibited from forwarding stock certificates unless acting in the capacity of a securities registered representative.

While this revised rule applies only to SEC-registered investment advisers and those who are required to be registered with the SEC, it is anticipated that most states will eventually adopt similar custody rules. Accordingly, state-registered investment advisers will most likely be required at some point to comply with such rules.

IMPORTANT CONCEPTS TO REMEMBER

Definition of an Investment Adviser

Investment Adviser Exclusions and Exemptions

Form ADV, Parts 1 and II

Investment Adviser reporting requirements

Brochure Rule

Fiduciary Duty

NASD

Central Registration Depository (CRD)

Forms U-4 & U-5

NASAA

NAIC

Gramm-Leach-Bliley Act

QUESTIONS FOR REVIEW

1. To what extent is personal financial planning, per se, regulated?

2. What are the three elements of the definition of an investment adviser?

3. Which individuals or entities are excluded from the definition of an investment adviser?

4. Which individuals or entities are exempt from having to register as an investment adviser?

5. How does Form ADV Part 1 differ from Part II?

6. What is the principal purpose of the brochure rule?

7. What does it mean to have a fiduciary duty to a client?

8. Which securities registered representative registration provides the broadest authority to sell securities?

9. How does the Regulatory Element differ from the Firm Element of the securities industry continuing education requirement?

10. What requirements placed on registered representatives by the securities industry are intended to achieve fair dealing with customers?

11. What are some of the specific practices that constitute serious violations of securities industry regulations?

12. What role does the National Association of Insurance Commissioners (NAIC) play in the regulation of the insurance industry?

13. What activity is the Gramm-Leach-Bliley Act designed to prevent?

SUGGESTIONS FOR ADDITIONAL READING

Investment Adviser Regulation: A Step-by-Step Guide to Compliance and the Law by Clifford E. Kirsch, Practising Law Institute, New York, 2003.

Registered Representative & Other Security Industry Professionals published by NASD Regulation, Inc., 2001.

The Continuing Education Program for Securities Professionals published by The Securities Industry/Regulatory Council on Continuing Education, 2001.

"Ten Deadly Sins" by Steven K. McGinnis, *Financial Planning*, February 2004

"The Compliance Heat is On" by Steven K. McGinnis, *Financial Planning*, August 2003

"SEC Tripwires" by Richard J. Koreto, *Financial Planning*, May 2003

CHAPTER SEVEN

CFP Board's *Code of Ethics* and *Professional Responsibility* and Related *Disciplinary Rules and Procedures*

• • •

One of the cornerstones of any respected profession is a codification of the standards of ethical and professionally responsible conduct expected of its professionals. In the medical, legal, accounting, and other learned professions, these codes of ethics have been in place for over 100 years. In spite of being a relatively young profession, personal financial planning, under the leadership of Certified Financial Planner Board of Standards, has promulgated an ethics code (most recently revised in July 2003) covering the ethical and professional conduct of those authorized to use CFP Board's certification marks. While a code of ethics was already in place at the time, during 1992 CFP Board substantially revised that code resulting in the *Code of Ethics and Professional Responsibility*, which became effective January 1, 1993. In this chapter, we will discuss the principal provisions of this ethics document as revised from time to time.

Having promulgated its code of ethics, CFP Board then turned to the task of creating a mechanism to enforce it, in those cases where such enforcement was necessary. As indicated in the Compliance section of the code of ethics, compliance depends on each CFP Board designee's knowledge of and voluntary compliance with the Principles and Rules, on the influence of fellow professionals and public opinion, and on disciplinary proceedings, when necessary, involving CFP Board designees who fail to comply with the applicable provisions of CFP Board's code of ethics document. Correspondingly, CFP Board created a subsidiary board known originally as the Board of Ethics and Professional Review, currently known as the Board of Professional Review (Board). The Board is responsible for investigating, reviewing, and taking appropriate action with respect to alleged violations of the

Code of Ethics and Professional Responsibility and alleged noncompliance with the *Financial Planning Practice Standards*, which are discussed in Chapter 8 of this text. It has original jurisdiction over all such disciplinary matters and procedures, and it follows the *Disciplinary Rules and Procedures* in its enforcement activities. We will discuss the key provisions of these disciplinary rules and procedures later in this chapter after we have discussed the principal components of the *Code of Ethics and Professional Responsibility*.

The objectives of this chapter are:

- Define the terms included in the "Terminology" section of CFP Board's *Code of Ethics and Professional Responsibility*.
- Identify the categories of persons to whom CFP Board's *Code of Ethics and Professional Responsibility* is applicable.
- Discuss the interrelationship between the Principles and the Rules of the *Code of Ethics and Professional Responsibility*.
- Describe the seven Principles of the *Code of Ethics and Professional Responsibility*.
- Describe the primary Rules that support each of the seven Principles of the *Code of Ethics and Professional Responsibility*.
- Identify the key aspects of CFP Board's *Disciplinary Rules and Procedures*.

CODE OF ETHICS AND PROFESSIONAL RESPONSIBILITY

Prior to reading the following sections on the *Code of Ethics and Professional Responsibility* (the Code) and the *Disciplinary Rules and Procedures*, the reader is encouraged to first download copies of the current versions of CFP Board's *Code of Ethics and Professional Responsibility* and the *Disciplinary Rules and Procedures* at CFP Board's website, http://www.CFP.net.

Terminology

In this section of CFP Board's *Code of Ethics and Professional Responsibility*, CFP Board defines twelve terms commonly used in the personal financial planning profession. One of the more contentious terms defined is that of **client**. As the definition reads, even a person who asks a practitioner a financial planning question informally without compensating the practitioner (the so-called "over the back fence" or "cocktail party" question) and who reasonably relies upon the practitioner's answer, could be considered to be a client. This definition has the potential to become a legal time bomb for a practitioner. In light of this definition, practitioners should be extremely careful that they do not inadvertently become "engaged" by a person they do not consider a client. For instance, if a neighbor, friend, or relative were to ask a financial planning question of a practitioner with the implication being that the neighbor, friend, or relative does not intend to pay for the professional advice, it would seem prudent that the practitioner either decline to answer the question or provide an answer accompanied by a disclaimer (preferably written) that makes clear that the practitioner does not consider that person to be the practitioner's client.

The second term defined is **CFP Board designee**. It includes current CFP® certificants, candidates for certification, and anyone else having any direct or indirect entitlement to the CFP certification marks.

In its January 1, 2003 revision of the Code, CFP Board added a new definition—that of **compensation**. Since this term had previously been used elsewhere in the Code without being defined, CFP Board considered it prudent to add this definition. It is defined as "any economic benefit a CFP Board designee or related party receives from performing his or her professional activities."

Another important term defined is **conflict(s) of interest**. This definition was slightly reworded effective January 1, 2003. Basically, it is any set of circumstances, relationship, or other facts about the CFP Board designee that reasonably may keep the designee from rendering disinterested advice, recommendations, or services. The most common example is when a financial planner is a securities registered representative associated with a broker/dealer firm and will receive compensation as a direct result of his or her client implementing the planner's recommendations through the planner. As we will discuss later, this situation requires, at a minimum, that the planner disclose this relationship to the client. If the client is aware of the relationship and still wishes to proceed with the implementation of the planner's recommendations through the planner's broker/dealer, then the planner has discharged his or her ethical responsibility.

Another contentious definition is that of **fee-only**. As the definition now reads, it is a method of compensation in which the personal financial planning practitioner is *compensated only by his or her client*. This means that the practitioner is paid a fee by the client and does not receive any other type of compensation from any other source. This seems straightforward, but in **Advisory Opinions 97-1 and 97-2**, (rescinded by CFP Board in January 2002), CFP Board provided further guidance on this definition. In Advisory Opinion 97-1, CFP Board addressed the issue of how a CFP certificant dealt with a specific client versus how the CFP certificant dealt with the general public with regard to claiming to provide fee-only services. If a CFP certificant did, or was willing to, provide to a client services which conformed to CFP Board's fee-only definition, it was proper for a CFP certificant to indicate that he or she offered fee-only services even though he or she may have been compensated by other methods with other clients. As a result, CFP certificants were able to provide fee-only services and advertise them even if they also provided other financial planning services wherein they are compensated by a different method. Accordingly, in Advisory Opinion 97-1 (now withdrawn), the method of compensation was from the perspective of a specific client, not from that of the general public. In this Advisory Opinion, CFP Board concluded that competency and ethical practice, not a method of compensation, are the most important issues for the public in choosing a financial planning practitioner.

In Advisory Opinion 97-2 (now withdrawn), CFP Board expanded on Advisory Opinion 97-1 by distinguishing between the use of the term "fee-only" when offering specific financial *services* as opposed to its use with respect to an *individual* CFP certificant or a financial planning *practice*. The Board clarified that in Advisory Opinion 97-1, a CFP certificant was able to offer fee-only services to a client and advertise them as such, even if the certificant also received commissions from that same client or other clients for other services. Accordingly, CFP certificants were free to offer multiple services to clients with different compensation methods. If a certificant offered fee-only services to a client, such services must in fact have been available to that client. If the certificant never intended to provide such a service or he or she only intended to provide the service as an introduction to other services not on a fee-only basis, without disclosing that fact to the client, advertising containing such information was considered false and misleading and in violation of the Code. CFP Board stated unequivocally in Advisory Opinion 97-2 that this type of device, known as the "bait and switch" tactic, was neither addressed nor condoned nor was a loophole created to permit it in Advisory Opinion 97-1. Advisory Opinion 97-2 emphasized the requirement that CFP certificants disclose fully to clients the methods of compensation available to the client and that subsequent changes in the method(s) of compensation be disclosed to and approved by the client.

Advisory Opinion 97-1 did not address the circumstances in which a CFP certificant uses the term "fee-only" to describe himself or herself as an individual *practitioner* or the *practice* with which he or she is associated. In Advisory Opinion 97-2, CFP Board addressed this issue concluding that a CFP certificant could use the term "fee-only" to refer to himself or herself as an individual practitioner or to his or her practice in advertisements and other general statements to the public *only* if the CFP certificant and/or practice was compensated solely by clients in *all* client relationships. To use "fee-only" to describe an individual or practice compensated from sources other than the client was considered by CFP Board to be false and misleading and a violation of the Code.

As mentioned earlier, both of these Advisory Opinions have now been withdrawn by CFP Board in light of their apparent conflict with the position taken by regional offices of the Securities and Exchange Commission during audits of investment advisers registered with the SEC. CFP Board elected to withdraw these two Advisory Opinions in order to minimize confusion for CFP certificants who are also registered investment advisers with the SEC.

In early 2003, CFP Board's Board of Professional Review (BOPR) issued **Advisory Opinion 2003-1** in which it requires CFP Board designees to avoid misrepresentation when using the term "fee-only." The BOPR departs from the Code definition of "fee-only"—"a method of compensation in which compensation is received solely from a client with neither the personal financial planning practitioner nor any related party receiving compensation which is contingent upon the purchase or sale of any financial product." The BOPR takes the position in this Advisory Opinion that in order for a CFP Board designee to describe his or her compensation as "fee-only," *all* compensation from *all* clients must be derived solely from fees. The Opinion allows for minimal exceptions provided the compensation is inconsequential and independent of the purchase of any product or service. It requires CFP Board designees, when using such terms as "fee-only" and "fee-only firm," to meet the foregoing requirements of deriving *all* compensation from *all* clients solely from fees.

In Advisory Opinion 2003-1, the BOPR defines fees as (1) hourly, fixed or flat fees; (2) percentage fees based on some aspect of the client's financial profile, such as assets under management or earned income; and (3) performance-based fees, which are tied to the profitability of the client's invested assets. Other types of compensation not qualifying as fees include: (1) commissions generated from a product or service, including traditional sales commissions, 12(b)1 fees, trailing commissions, surrender charges, and contingent deferred sales charges, even if used to reduce or offset other fees; and (2) referral compensation providing compensation or other economic benefit to the CFP Board designee for recommending, introducing, or referring a product or service provided by another person or entity, even if used to reduce or offset other fees. In this Advisory Opinion, the BOPR states its belief that the public regards compensation structure as important information when choosing a financial planning professional. Accordingly, it believes that the appropriate use of the term "fee-only" by CFP Board designees in all public discourse demonstrates professionalism by avoiding casual use of the term. Similarly, the BOPR advises CFP Board designees to avoid the use of other terms (such as "fee-based") designed to induce the public into a distorted belief that the designee receives "fee-only" compensation when in fact the designee receives commissions, referral compensation, or any other form of compensation not defined as fees by the BOPR. The BOPR enumerates several Rules in the Code which may be involved in cases involving misrepresentation of compensation arrangements or failure to disclose compensation arrangements, but concentrates on Rules 401, 402, and 101(a) and (b). We will discuss these Rules later in this chapter.

Another definition added to the Code in early 2003 on the recommendation of CFP Board's Disclosure Task Force is **financial planning engagement**. Such an engagement is said to exist when a client, based on the relevant facts and circumstances, reasonably relies on information or services provided by a CFP Board designee using the financial planning process. This definition is interrelated with the definition of "client" discussed earlier. Again, CFP Board designees must be careful to not create a situation where a person relies upon information or services provided by the CFP Board designee, unless the designee intends to create such a relationship.

One of the most important definitions in the Terminology section is the definition of **personal financial planning** or **financial planning**. It is defined as a *process* of determining whether and how an individual can meet life goals through the proper management of financial resources.

The next definition offered is that of **personal financial planning process** or **financial planning process**. This definition recites the six steps of the process as follows:

- Establishing and defining the client-planner relationship
- Gathering client data including goals
- Analyzing and evaluating the client's financial status
- Developing and presenting financial planning recommendations and/or alternatives
- Implementing the financial planning recommendations
- Monitoring the financial planning recommendations

Personal financial planning subject areas or **financial planning subject areas** are described as follows:

- Financial statement preparation and analysis (including cash flow analysis/planning and budgeting)
- Investment planning (including portfolio design, asset allocation, and portfolio management)
- Income tax planning
- Education planning
- Risk management and insurance
- Retirement planning
- Estate planning
- Employee benefit planning

This list, while mentioning the principal subject areas, is not intended to be all-inclusive. Other subject areas certainly exist and will continue to evolve, subject only to the imagination of the financial planner and the client.

One of the more confusing issues for students of personal financial planning is the difference between a "personal financial planning professional" and a "personal financial planning practitioner." A **personal financial planning professional** is anyone who is capable and qualified to offer objective, integrated, and comprehensive financial advice to or for the benefit of individuals to help them achieve their financial objectives. In other words, the individual has to have the ability to provide financial planning services to clients, using the personal financial planning process covering the basic financial planning subject areas. Presumably someone who holds a professional designation in personal financial planning, such as the CFP® certification, would qualify as a personal financial planning professional. However, someone qualifying as a personal financial planning professional is not, automatically, a personal financial planning practitioner. Many holders of professional designations in personal financial planning choose not to practice personal financial planning. Accordingly, those persons are *not* personal financial planning practitioners. Only those personal financial planning professionals who choose to engage in personal financial planning using the personal financial planning process in working with clients are considered **personal financial planning practitioners**.

Preamble and Applicability

The Preamble of the *Code of Ethics and Professional Responsibility* explains that the Code has been developed to provide principles and rules to all CFP certificants, who are obligated not only to comply with the mandates and requirements of all applicable laws and regulations but also to act in an ethical and professionally responsible manner in all professional services and activities. It clarifies that the Code applies to all CFP Board designees in the performance of any professional responsibility in which CFP Board's marks are used. This makes it clear that the provisions of the Code are not confined to CFP certificants who practice personal financial planning.

In addition, the Code applies to candidates for the CFP certification who are registered as such with CFP Board as well as individuals who have been certified in the past and retain the right to reinstate their CFP certification without passing the current CFP certification examination.

Composition and Scope

This section explains the design of the Code. Part I covers the seven **Principles** which are general statements of the ethical and professional goals that CFP Board designees are expected to aspire to in their professional activities. Each Principle is followed by comments, which are not part of the Principle, but which further explain the meaning of the Principle.

Part II includes the **Rules**, which flow from and modify the Principles. What this means is that the Rules numbered in the 100 series, for instance, relate to Principle 1—Integrity, while those Rules relating to Principle 2—Objectivity are numbered in the 200 series. The Rules provide practical (and more easily enforceable) guidelines derived from the tenets embodied in the Principles. For instance, it is only an aspirational or idealistic statement to say that a CFP Board designee should display integrity (Principle 1). But to prohibit a CFP Board designee from making a false or misleading communication about the size, scope, or areas of competence of the designee's practice or of any organization with which he or she is associated is a much more specific, practical, and enforceable standard (Rule 101(a)). Rule 101(a), therefore, provides one of several practical guidelines derived from the tenet of integrity embodied in Principle 1.

An important point made in this section of the Code is that the Rules apply to specific activities performed by CFP Board designees. So if a particular CFP Board designee does not engage in the specific activities covered by the Rules, then those Rules do not apply to that designee. It cites the example of Rule 402, which is a disclosure rule directed at personal financial planning practitioners. If a CFP certificant only sells securities as a registered representative, he or she is not subject to this Rule. However, the certificant still may have disclosure responsibilities under Rule 401.

Compliance

CFP Board designees are required to adhere to the Code. To the extent that a CFP Board designee knows the Principles and Rules, chooses to voluntarily comply with them, and is influenced by fellow professionals and public opinion, adherence to the Code is not an issue. Those designees who fail to comply with the Code are subject to disciplinary proceedings.

The Principles

The Code is composed of seven Principles, which, as discussed earlier, are aspirational statements that apply to all CFP Board designees and provide guidance to them in the performance of their professional services. The seven Principles can be said to form the skeleton of the Code and each Principle is "fleshed out" with a series of Rules that pertain to it.

Integrity

Frequently, clients bestow both trust and confidence in financial planners. It is integrity, the first Principle, that is the true source of such public trust. It is derived from a sense of honesty and candor not influenced by personal gain and advantage, and free of deceit or subordination of one's principles.

Objectivity

The second Principle, objectivity, requires intellectual honesty, impartiality, and maintenance of the integrity of one's work and professional judgment. For instance, if a designee determines objectively that a particular recommendation is in the best interest of a client, then the designee should stand by that decision and not allow his or her judgment to be subordinated by others or by influences of personal gain and advantage.

Competence

The competence Principle requires that CFP Board designees deliver professional services competently. This requires that designees initially attain and subsequently maintain the knowledge and skill necessary to provide the particular services they offer and that they apply this knowledge and skill effectively in providing those services. In addition, designees must know when they do not possess the requisite knowledge and skill to deliver a specific service. In those cases, they must either refer their client to someone who has the required knowledge and skill or they must consult with such experts before attempting to provide service to their client. A CFP Board designee is presumed to be qualified to practice financial planning at the time that he or she is first certified to use CFP Board's marks but is required to make a continuing commitment to learning and professional improvement.

Fairness

The fourth Principle, fairness, calls for the CFP Board designee to deliver professional services in a fair and reasonable manner to clients, principals, partners, and employers and to disclose conflicts of interest in so doing. It is with this Principle that the disclosure rules are associated. It is difficult for a financial planner to completely avoid conflicts of interest. In those cases where they cannot reasonably be avoided, in order to treat the client fairly, they must be disclosed to the client. Such disclosure empowers the client to decide whether or not to proceed with the particular CFP Board designee in light of the disclosed conflict(s) of interest. Failure to inform the client of a conflict of interest constitutes treating the client unfairly.

Confidentiality

Under the Principle of confidentiality, the CFP Board designee is precluded from disclosing confidential client information without the client's specific consent, unless under certain specific legal restraints. As discussed under Principle 1, integrity, clients are often interested in creating a relationship of personal trust and confidence. One of the foundations of such a relationship is that of confidentiality. A client has a right to expect that his or her personal financial information will be safeguarded by the financial planner.

Professionalism

The sixth Principle, professionalism, is concerned with actions that bring credit upon the personal financial planning profession. This is directed not only at actions taken with respect to clients but also with respect to fellow professionals and those in related professions. It involves the maintenance of a professional image with all parties involved and the avoidance of acts that may bring discredit upon the profession.

Diligence

The final Principle, diligence, requires a CFP Board designee to provide professional services expeditiously and thoroughly. In other words, if a client reasonably expects to receive specific services within a particular timeframe, the services should be delivered within that timeframe. Moreover, the designee should not compromise the completeness and quality of the services in order to deliver them within the agreed-upon timeframe. An additional requirement is that designees plan properly for the provision of the agreed-upon services and properly supervise those selected to provide the services. This includes making a reasonable investigation of the products and services recommended to clients.

The Rules

Rather than discussing each of the 36 Rules in detail, we will concentrate on the Rules with the greatest impact.

Rules 101-102

Rule 101 prohibits CFP Board designees from attempting to obtain clients through false or misleading communications or advertisements. Rule 102 is even broader in that it precludes a CFP Board designee from engaging in conduct involving dishonesty, fraud, deceit or misrepresentation or making a false or misleading statement to anyone—not just a potential client.

Rule 103

Rule 103 deals with custody of client funds or other property. The key points here are that the CFP Board designee (1) must act only in accordance with the authority granted to him or her in the governing legal instrument; (2) shall identify and keep complete records of all property in his or her custody; (3) will promptly deliver to the client or third party any property which they are entitled to receive and render an accounting therefor (4) shall not commingle client funds with his or her own funds, though commingling of several clients' funds is permitted if accurate records are maintained; and (5) shall maintain custody of client funds with the care required of a fiduciary. Acting as a fiduciary means that the financial planner must hold the client's interest above his or her own in all matters. In terms of legal liability, a fiduciary takes on a high level of responsibility.

Rule 201

Consistent with the principle of objectivity, this Rule requires a CFP Board designee to exercise reasonable and prudent professional judgment in providing professional services. This Rule is cited often in Board of Professional Review disciplinary cases. A CFP Board designee must be able to demonstrate that he or she exercised the requisite professional judgment in dealing with clients. Not surprisingly, this Rule is coupled with Rule 202, explained next.

Rule 202

Rule 202 requires a financial planning practitioner to act in the interest of the client. This is akin to a fiduciary duty. Of course, if a financial planning practitioner is a registered investment adviser, he or she is, by law, a fiduciary as determined by the U.S. Supreme Court and the SEC.

Rule 301–302

Rule 301 requires CFP Board designees to keep up-to-date in professional knowledge and, as a minimum, to meet the CFP Board's continuing education requirement. Rule 302 requires a CFP Board designee to offer advice only in those areas where he or she has competence. In those areas where he or she is not professionally competent, he or she must seek the counsel of qualified individuals and/or refer clients to such parties. Simply put, if you don't know what you're doing in a particular area, get advice from someone who does or refer the client to that person or firm.

The Disclosure Rules

Rules 401 through 404 (the disclosure rules) can be somewhat confusing. Before we discuss the Rules as they now exist, the reader should be aware that the CFP Board created a Disclosure Task Force (Task Force), which began work in March 2001, to:

- Encourage disclosure that provides consumers with the desired information to make decisions during a financial planning engagement
- Encourage disclosure that meets the needs of the client but is not unduly burdensome on the practitioner
- Encourage discussion of disclosure between clients and practitioners so that trust in the financial planning profession is enhanced

Key concepts that were considered critical by the Task Force in successfully rewriting the Principle 4 Rules included:

(a) Proposed Rules 402, 403, and 404 should apply to a CFP Board designee "in a financial planning engagement."

(b) The proposed Rules should focus on compensation, not costs to the client.

(c) The proposed Rules should be compensation neutral.

(d) The proposed Rules should not necessarily disturb longstanding client relationships.

(e) Where possible, the proposed Rules should incorporate existing forms of disclosure within the financial planning community and avoid being unnecessarily onerous to the practitioner, while still addressing the client's needs.

(f) The proposed Rules should accommodate three points of disclosure:

  (i) Initial—which should be general in nature.

  (ii) At time of recommendation—where the practitioner can generally only estimate compensation.

  (iii) Retrospective—once the amount(s) and type(s) of compensation is (are) actually known.

The Task Force developed several proposed revisions to the 400 series of Rules using feedback received from two exposure drafts exposed to interested parties for comment during 2001 and 2002. These proposed revisions have been incorporated in the February 2003 revision of the 400 series of Rules.

Rule 401

Rule 401, which was revised only slightly in early 2003, applies to the rendering of *all* professional services by a CFP Board designee. It requires that the designee disclose "material information relevant to the professional relationship." This includes conflicts of interest, the designee's business affiliation, address, telephone number, credentials, qualifications, licenses, compensation structure, and any agency relationships, and the scope of the designee's authority in his or her capacity as an agent plus the information required by all laws applicable to the relationship. To understand Rule 401, assume that the relationship with a client is not one involving personal financial planning services. This would be the case if the designee was a registered representative with a securities broker/dealer firm and the client had limited the engagement to filling an order for the purchase or sale of specific securities. Clearly, this is not a relationship involving the rendering of personal financial planning services. Accordingly, the CFP Board designee needs to be certain that the client has been informed that the designee is a securities registered representative who works for a specific broker/dealer firm and receives commissions for the client's purchase or sale of securities. In addition, as discussed earlier, this Rule requires the designee to advise the client of the designee's current business affiliation, address, telephone number, credentials, qualifications, licenses, and compensation structure. In this type of client relationship, the designee need not comply with Rule 402, which is discussed next.

Rule 402

Rule 402 *applies only to CFP Board designees in a financial planning engagement*. This Rule requires the timely written disclosure of all material information relative to the professional relationship (one of personal financial planning, which is a fiduciary relationship) *prior to the engagement*. These disclosures must always include conflicts of interest and sources of compensation. For example, if a financial planner is providing personal financial planning services and he or she will receive commissions from the sale of products recommended to the client, he or she has a conflict of interest and it must be disclosed to the client. Added in the early 2003 revision of this Rule is a new requirement to inform the client or prospective client of his/her right to ask at any time for information about the compensation of the CFP Board designee.

In its revision of Rule 402, the Task Force substituted the term "CFP Board designee in a financial planning engagement" for the term "personal financial planning practitioner" as used previously. The Task Force clarified that the required disclosure must take place prior to the engagement and, as discussed earlier, introduced a new requirement to inform the client or prospective client of his/her right to ask at any time for information about the compensation of the designee.

Rule 402 provides a "safe harbor" guideline for written disclosures, including five items which may be provided via SEC Form ADV, Part II, a CFP Board Sample Disclosure Form, or an equivalent document. The five items to be included in the disclosure include:

- The basic philosophy of the CFP Board designee (or firm) in working with clients. This includes the philosophy, theory and/or principles of financial planning which will be utilized by the designee.
- Information about the educational background, professional/employment history, professional designations and licenses held by those principals and employees of a firm who are expected to provide financial planning services to the client and a description of those services.
- A statement that in reasonable detail discloses (as applicable) conflict(s) of interest and source(s) of, and any contingencies or other aspects material to, the designee's compensation.
- A statement describing material agency or employment relationships a designee (or firm) has with third parties and the nature of compensation resulting from such relationships.
- A statement informing the client or prospective client of his/her right to ask at any time for information about the compensation of the designee.

This additional information required by Rule 402 follows very closely the information included in Form ADV, Part II, which a registered investment adviser must provide to a client under the SEC's "brochure rule." Based on a review of the foregoing requirements, it should be clear that a CFP Board designee *must* disclose conflicts of interest, the background and client philosophy of those who will provide services to the client, how the designee is being compensated and, if requested by the client, the details of such compensation. These requirements are in keeping with the status of a fiduciary, which is assumed by a CFP Board designee in a financial planning engagement.

Rule 403

New Rule 403, just as revised Rule 402, *applies only to CFP Board designees in a financial planning engagement.* This Rule covers the situation where a client elects to avail him- or herself of the opportunity, provided in the disclosure statement required by Rule 402, to obtain information about the compensation of the CFP Board designee. The Rule clarifies that the designee, upon request, will provide reasonable detail about his or her compensation relating to the client's engagement, including compensation derived from implementation. The designee may provide approximate dollar amounts or percentages or a range of dollar amounts or percentages. To the extent that the designee cannot reasonably ascertain the requested compensation information, he or she still must make the required disclosure when such information first becomes available. The designee may use estimates of compensation provided they are based on reasonable assumptions.

Also, after a designee has provided the required disclosure in response to a client request, if that information is subsequently determined to be significantly inaccurate, he or she will provide the client with corrected information in a timely manner. This makes it clear that a designee who has responded to a client's request for compensation information has a continuing obligation to keep the client informed, should the information initially provided turn out to be materially inaccurate.

Rule 404

This Rule, like Rules 402 and 403, *applies only to CFP Board designees in a financial planning engagement.* Patterned after the SEC's Form ADV, Part II annual requirement, this Rule requires the CFP Board designee to *offer* to provide at least once per year the disclosure initially made under Rule 402. It is strongly recommended that the designee make such offer in writing annually and request a definitive response from the client as to whether he or she wishes to receive the disclosure document. As a minimum, the designee should be able to demonstrate that the annual offer to provide the disclosure document was in fact made to each current client. It would seem preferable to have in one's file a written response from the client electing to either receive or not receive the disclosure document. Also, where the client has requested to receive the disclosure document annually, the designee should be able to demonstrate that it was in fact provided as requested.

Rule 405

This is one of the shortest Rules, simply requiring that a designee's compensation be fair and reasonable. This requirement precludes charging the client or receiving from other sources compensation considered by a reasonable person to be unconscionable in amount. If a client has never before been a financial planning client and is unaware of the typical compensation received by financial planners, the designee may not take advantage of the client's ignorance or lack of experience by charging and/or receiving unreasonable amounts of compensation.

Rule 407

In effect, this Rule requires a designee to inform his or her employer of conflicts of interest which may be created by the designee's outside affiliations. For instance, a designee may be affiliated with an outside organization in a capacity which is in direct competition with his or her employer. This requirement precludes a designee from entering into such relationships without first informing his or her employer.

In addition, if a designee's right to use the CFP marks is suspended or revoked or has lapsed due to failure to properly renew, he or she must inform his or her employer.

Finally, if a designee changes employers, he or she must give his or her clients timely notice of the change. In some cases, employers do not permit an employee by contract to contact his or her former clients upon leaving the employer and becoming employed by a competing employer. If this is the case, then the designee is not required to inform those clients of his or her employment change.

Rule 408

Under this Rule, a designee is not permitted to receive additional compensation for providing services to his firm's clients without advising the firm of such additional compensation. If one recalls that the 400 series of Rules pertain to the Principle of Fairness, it seems appropriate that one's employer, like one's clients, be treated fairly.

Rule 409

This Rule deals with the situation where a CFP Board designee enters into a business (as distinguished from a professional) relationship with a client. It requires the designee to establish the terms to be fair and reasonable to the client, to disclose the risks involved, to disclose any conflicts of interest which the designee may have, and to provide any other relevant information that makes the transaction fair to the client. One such CFP Board designee/client business relationship is where there are loans between the two parties. This situation is addressed in CFP Board Advisory Opinion 2001-1, which was published in the Third Quarter 2001 *CFP Board Report*. CFP Board's Board of Professional Review (BOPR) has taken a skeptical view of such loans and held them to be a violation of Rule 202 (acting in the interest of the client). Even borrowing from clients who are relatives or financial institutions may still be found to violate Rule 202 if (1) the terms and conditions of the loans were not clearly and objectively disclosed to the client, taking into account the client's level of sophistication; (2) the terms and conditions of the transaction were not fair and reasonable under the circumstances; and (3) the client did not fully understand the terms and conditions of the transaction and the impact of the transaction on his/her financial situation.

Loans running from a CFP Board designee who is a personal financial planning practitioner to a client (not as common as the reverse situation) are also considered not to be in the best interest of the client because they may lock the client into the relationship with the practitioner, even when the client's financial planning needs are not being met. The BOPR will also consider loans to clients used as an enticement for the client to enter into a financial transaction or loans bearing a below market interest rate (a form of rebate) as violations of Rule 202. The BOPR has held that such loans between clients and practitioners violate Rule 607 (discussed later) inasmuch as they reflect negatively on the integrity of the designee, the CFP marks, and the financial planning profession. As a result, the BOPR, in Advisory Opinion 2001-1, urges all CFP Board designees to avoid the practice of borrowing from or lending to clients. It would appear to the author that such loans may be a violation of Rule 409, if the conditions specified in that Rule are not satisfied by the CFP Board designee.

Rule 501

Rule 501 is another very important Rule that addresses confidentiality of client information. The Rule not only prohibits revealing client information without the client's consent but also prohibits using client information for the CFP Board designee's own benefit. The only exceptions to this Rule are (1) to set up an account for a client in order to effect a transaction for a client (where the client has specifically requested the designee to do so); (2) to comply with legal requirements or legal process; (3) to defend the designee against charges of wrongdoing; (4) in connection with a civil dispute between the designee and the client. An important point on Rule 501 is that it does not matter whether the designee's unauthorized use of client information actually caused harm to the client; it is still a violation of the Code. Rule 503 extends confidentiality requirements to a designee's business partners as well, both while working together and after terminating the relationship.

Rule 601

Rule 601 is a Rule that most CFP Board designees seem to forget about. It requires a designee to use the CFP® and CERTIFIED FINANCIAL PLANNER™ marks in compliance with CFP Board rules and regulations. The most common violation of this Rule is the use of the CFP® or CERTIFIED FINANCIAL PLANNER™ marks as nouns. They should *never* be used as nouns—only as adjectives. A CFP Board designee can use the marks directly after his or her name if he or she has been certified by CFP Board to do so. But in every other case, the marks must be used as adjectives. An example is "John is a CFP certificant or CFP practitioner" rather than "John is a CFP" (which violates the Rule). The reason for this Rule is that CFP Board must not allow the usage of these marks to fall into the public domain and therefore threaten their uniqueness (which is a requirement to keep them registered with the U.S. Patent and Trademark Office). An example of how this happened to other organizations is the use of "Kleenex" instead of "tissue" and "Xerox" rather than "photocopy." Unless registered marks are used correctly, they can become valueless, and clearly this is not in the best interest of CFP Board or of those who have been authorized to use its marks.

Rules 602–611

Rules 602 through 605 impose an obligation on a CFP Board designee to report alleged violations of this Code by other CFP Board designees, alleged violations of law by other designees or by other financial professionals, and alleged illegal conduct within the designee's employer organization. Rule 606 requires a designee to comply with all applicable laws, rules, and regulations of governmental agencies, other authorities, and CFP Board. Rule 607 is a general Rule that prohibits conduct that reflects adversely on the CFP Board designee's integrity or fitness as a CFP Board designee, upon the marks, or upon the profession. A designee who is registered with the SEC as an investment adviser is prohibited from using "RIA" or "R.I.A." after his or her name. Only the term "registered investment adviser" is permitted after the name of a person who is registered as such with the SEC.

Rule 610 prohibits a CFP Board designee from holding the client's records "hostage" for the collection of unpaid fees. A client's original records are to be returned promptly upon client request whether or not the client has paid the entire amount owed to the designee. While Rule 603 requires a designee to report alleged violations of the Code by another designee, Rule 611 prohibits using this tactic solely to harass, maliciously injure, embarrass and/or unfairly burden another CFP Board designee.

Rule 701

This Rule requires a CFP Board designee to provide services diligently. What does it mean to provide services diligently? Primarily, it involves providing services in a reasonably prompt and thorough manner, and it includes proper planning for, and supervision of, the rendering of those services. This is another Rule often cited in Board of Professional Review disciplinary cases.

Rule 702

Rule 702 requires a designee to determine whether a client relationship is warranted by the potential client's individual needs and objectives. It may be that the client has already had a particular service performed satisfactorily and recently by another practitioner and there is no justifiable reason for the designee to perform it again for compensation. This Rule prohibits the designee from providing unnecessary services to the client. The other part of this Rule is that the designee must have the ability to provide the requested service or to involve other professionals who are qualified to do so.

Rules 703–705

Rule 703 could be considered redundant for those CFP Board designees who are also registered representatives with a securities broker/dealer firm because they are already required to only make and/or implement recommendations that are suitable for the client. CFP Board makes the same requirement of its designees, even those who are not registered representatives. Rule 704 is related to Rule 703 in that it requires making a reasonable investigation of financial products recommended to clients. Finally, Rule 705 makes the designee responsible for work performed by his or her subordinates.

DISCIPLINARY RULES AND PROCEDURES

CFP Board enforces the *Code of Ethics and Professional Responsibility* as well as the *Financial Planning Practice Standards* (Practice Standards) (discussed in Chapter 8) through the *Disciplinary Rules and Procedures*. The Board of Professional Review (BOPR) is charged with the duty of investigating, reviewing, and taking appropriate action with respect to alleged violations of the Code and alleged non-compliance with the Practice Standards. CFP Board Staff Counsel reviews documents and materials provided in response to a notice of investigation to determine if there is probable cause to believe grounds for discipline exist. Matters not dismissed by Staff Counsel advance to a Hearing Panel composed of at least one member of the BOPR and at least two CFP certificants. One member serves as chair and rules on all motions, objections, and other matters presented in the hearing.

Grounds for Discipline

The following, which need not have occurred in the course of a client relationship, are considered grounds for discipline:

- Any act or omission that violates the Code
- Any act or omission that fails to comply with the Practice Standards
- Any act or omission that violates the criminal laws of any state or of the U.S. or of any province, territory, or jurisdiction of any other country.

- Any act that is a proper basis for professional suspension
- Any act or omission that violates these disciplinary procedures or which violates an order of discipline
- Failure to respond to a request by the BOPR without good cause shown, or obstruction of the BOPR
- Any false or misleading statement made to CFP Board
- Any other acts amounting to unprofessional conduct may be grounds for discipline

Forms of Discipline

If no grounds for discipline (discussed earlier) have been established, the BOPR may dismiss the complaint as being without merit or may issue a cautionary letter to the designee. Where grounds for discipline have been established, the BOPR may impose any of the following forms of discipline:

- The BOPR may require additional continuing education or other remedial work instead of or in addition to any other discipline.
- Private Censure—an unpublished written reproach mailed to the designee involved.
- Public Letter of Admonition—a written reproach that may be published in a press release or other form of media unless there are mitigating circumstances.
- Suspension of the Right to Use the Marks—for a specified period of time, not to exceed 5 years, for those designees who the BOPR deems can be rehabilitated. Notice of the suspension is published unless there are extreme mitigating circumstances. The designee *may* qualify for reinstatement after the suspension.
- Revocation of the Right to Use the Marks—permanent revocation of the right to use the marks. Notice is published unless there are extreme mitigating circumstances.
- If the person charged by the BOPR with violating the Code or failing to comply with the Practice Standards is a candidate for the CFP certification, the candidate may be:
  1. Certified, if the requirements are met, with a private censure placed in the candidate's record
  2. Certified, if the requirements are met, with a letter of admonition published as applicable and placed in the candidate's record
  3. Suspended (delayed) certification for up to 5 years—may be published at the discretion of the BOPR
  4. Denied certification—may be published at the discretion of the BOPR

Also, the BOPR may issue a temporary suspension for a definite or indefinite period of time while disciplinary proceedings are conducted. This is known as an **interim suspension** and may be issued when a CFP Board designee has been convicted of a serious crime, been professionally suspended, converted funds or other property, participated in conduct that poses an immediate threat to the public, or has engaged in conduct the gravity of which impinges upon the stature and reputation of the marks. The CFP Board designee involved must respond in writing. If there is no response, the allegations are deemed admitted, and the interim suspension goes into effect. If the designee does respond, a show cause hearing is held before at least a quorum of the BOPR.

Investigation Procedure

An investigation is either commenced upon a written request from a complainant or by a recommendation from the CFP Board Staff Counsel. An investigation adheres to the following procedure:

- If the complaint involves the Practice Standards, the request must be from a person who has a contractual relationship with the CFP Board designee, or from CFP Board Staff Counsel.
- The designee is given written notice that he or she is under investigation and advised of the general nature of the allegation(s).
- The designee has 30 days to file a written response.
- If there is no response within 30 days, the matter is referred to a hearing panel.
- If the designee responds within 30 days, CFP Board Staff Counsel determines if there is probable cause to believe that grounds for discipline exist and then must either:
  - Dismiss the allegations as being without merit
  - Dismiss with a letter of caution recommending remedial action and entering other appropriate orders
  - Refer the matter to the BOPR for preparation and processing of a complaint against the designee
- Staff counsel conducts an investigation as expeditiously as reasonably possible.
- The complaint is forwarded to the designee.
- The designee must answer within 20 days from the date of service. The designee may request appearance at the panel's hearing.
- If there is no answer, the designee is deemed in default and the allegation(s) is (are) deemed admitted.
- Discovery takes place only after the complaint is issued. The designee may obtain copies of unprivileged documents in the disciplinary file that are relevant to the pending action.
- The designee may generally submit up to 100 pages of documents. No evidence will be accepted less than 30 days prior to the scheduled hearing date. If more than 100 pages are needed, the designee must justify the reason for such evidence with the BOPR then determining which documents will be permitted.
- All witnesses are to be identified and the nature and extent of their testimony must be made available no later than 30 days prior to the scheduled hearing.
- At least 30 days prior to the hearing date, notice of the hearing must be given to both the designee and his or her legal counsel, if any.

- The designee may be represented by legal counsel, can cross-examine witnesses, and present evidence.
- Proof of misconduct must be established by a preponderance of the evidence.
- The hearing panel must record its findings of fact and recommendations in writing and submit them to the BOPR.
- The panel can recommend dismissal of charges or refer the matter to the BOPR with a recommendation that discipline is appropriate.
- The BOPR then reserves the authority to review the determination of the hearing panel and modify it without reviewing the record. If it does modify it, it must state its reasons for modification.
- Finally, appeals can be made to CFP Board's Board of Appeals within 30 days after the notice of order is sent to the designee. However, if not appealed within 30 days, the order becomes final.

If a CFP Board designee has been the subject of an order of professional suspension or is convicted of a serious crime (felony; crime involving misrepresentation, fraud, extortion, misappropriation, or theft; or an attempt or conspiracy to commit such a crime; or solicitation of another to commit such a crime), he or she must notify CFP Board in writing within 10 days after the date the designee is notified of either. A professional suspension shall include a recorded suspension or bar as a disciplinary measure by any governmental or industry self-regulatory authority or a license as a securities registered representative, broker/dealer, insurance or real estate salesperson or broker, attorney, accountant, investment adviser, or financial planner.

After a complaint has been issued and prior to final action by the BOPR, a designee can make a settlement offer in writing on one occasion only. If an offer is rejected, the matter is returned to the hearing panel.

Legal Reinstatement

Following are the key provisions of the legal reinstatement rules and procedures:
- As discussed earlier, there is no reinstatement of a designee's right to use the CFP® marks after revocation of the right to use the marks.
- If the designee is suspended for one year or less, reinstatement is automatic if the designee files, within 30 days of the expiration of the suspension period, an affidavit that he or she has complied with the suspension order.

- If the designee is suspended for longer than one year, he or she must petition for a reinstatement hearing within six months of the end of the suspension period. If he or she fails to file the petition in a timely manner, the right to use the marks is administratively relinquished.
- Before a reinstatement hearing will be scheduled, the designee must meet all administrative requirements for recertification including paying the hearing costs and providing evidence that all prior hearing costs have been paid.
- The designee must prove by clear and convincing evidence that he or she has been rehabilitated and is now fit to use the marks.
- If the petition for reinstatement is denied, the designee must wait two years to file a new petition. If the second petition also is denied, the right to use the marks is administratively relinquished.

With a few exceptions, all proceeding records are confidential and are not made public.

Finally, the cost of proceedings is assessed against the CFP Board designee and must be paid at least 30 days prior to the hearing date. Such costs may be refunded if the BOPR dismisses the matter as being without merit.

IMPORTANT CONCEPTS TO REMEMBER

Terms defined in the Terminology Section of the Code

Principles of the Code

Rules of the Code

Key aspects of the *Disciplinary Rules and Procedures*

Fee-only and Advisory Opinions 97-1, 97-2, and 2003-1

CFP Board's Disclosure Task Force

QUESTIONS FOR REVIEW

1. What are some of the legal liability implications of the current definition of "client"?
2. What is a common example of a conflict of interest?
3. What are some of the primary issues that make the definition of "fee-only" such a controversial topic?

4. What is the difference between a personal financial planning professional and a personal financial planning practitioner?

5. To what categories of individuals does the Code apply?

6. What is the interrelationship of the Code's Principles and the Rules?

7. Which of the existing Rules are referred to as the "disclosure" Rules?

8. What are some of the grounds for discipline under the *Disciplinary Rules and Procedures*?

9. What are the permitted forms of discipline under the *Disciplinary Rules and Procedures*?

SUGGESTIONS FOR ADDITIONAL READING

CFP Board's *Standards of Professional Conduct*

CFP Board's Disclosure Task Force *Exposure Draft of Proposed Revisions to the Rules and Terminology that Relate to the Principle of Fairness in CFP Board's Code of Ethics and Professional Responsibility* (CFP Board Report, First Quarter 2002) available at http://www.CFP.net

CFP Board's *Financial Planning Practice Standards*

• • •

In any true profession, particularly in the so-called learned professions of law, medicine, and accounting, standards of good practice have been established to provide professional guidance to practitioners of those professions. With the promulgation of CFP Board's *Financial Planning Practice Standards*, as well as the *Code of Ethics and Professional Responsibility,* personal financial planning has taken another significant step toward increased professionalism. The practice standards, like the Code, rely for their effectiveness upon the peer review process, which is the hallmark of any true profession.

Practice standards establish the level of professional practice and the process that a client should reasonably expect a CFP Board designee to use in a financial planning engagement. As we will discuss in this chapter, practice standards differ from ethics standards (as embodied in the *Code of Ethics and Professional Responsibility*) and from so-called practice aids. Compliance with these Practice Standards is mandatory for a CFP Board designee in a personal financial planning engagement, but other financial planning practitioners are encouraged to consider them when providing financial planning services.

The objectives of this chapter are:
- Distinguish among ethics rules, practice standards, and practice aids.
- Identify the purposes for the development and promulgation of financial planning practice standards.
- Discuss the role of the Board of Practice Standards in developing CFP Board's *Financial Planning Practice Standards*.

- Describe the interrelationship between the personal financial planning process and CFP Board's *Financial Planning Practice Standards*.
- Identify the ten CFP Board *Financial Planning Practice Standards*.
- Describe an additional source of professional guidance in the provision of personal financial planning services.

ETHICS RULES VERSUS PRACTICE STANDARDS VERSUS PRACTICE AIDS

Many people tend to treat the above terms as being interchangeable and, therefore, equivalent. It is important, especially for those individuals who are obliged to comply with these dictums, that they understand how they differ.

Ethics Rules, specifically those included in the CFP Board's *Code of Ethics and Professional Responsibility*, are concerned with one's ethical and professionally responsible *conduct* toward clients, professional colleagues, employers, the personal financial planning profession, and the public. They are concerned with how a CFP Board designee *behaves* and the manner in which he or she *treats or deals with* the parties mentioned in the previous sentence. In other words, does his or her conduct or behavior in dealing with the aforementioned parties display, as a minimum, integrity, objectivity, competence, fairness, confidentiality, professionalism, and diligence?

Practice Standards, on the other hand, are focused on the content and professional rigor of the *process* used by the CFP Board designee in providing specific personal financial services covered by the standards. While the ethics Rules require a CFP Board designee to attain and maintain competence, they do not specify the minimum requirements for providing personal financial planning services. That is the role of the Practice Standards. As mentioned in the introduction to this chapter, the Practice Standards establish the level of professional practice and the process that a client should reasonably expect a CFP Board designee to use in a financial planning engagement. Stated differently, practice standards establish the black line between good practice and malpractice.

It should be apparent by now that a CFP Board designee may be fully in compliance with the ethics rules in the Code in that he or she behaves in an ethical and professionally responsible manner toward clients and others, but the services he or she delivers do not meet minimum practice requirements as specified in the Practice Standards. Similarly, a designee's services may be provided in full compliance with the Practice Standards but he or she may not behave in an ethical and professionally responsible manner and, therefore, violate the Code. It is important that CFP Board designees understand the distinction between these two types of requirements.

In addition to ethics rules and practice standards, there are **practice aids**, which are intended to prescribe step-by-step procedures for providing a specific service. The Practice Standards establish the minimum professional requirements for providing a specific service but they do not provide detailed instructions for how to do so. That is the function of practice aids, which have been developed by various financial planning membership organizations and commercial providers. Practice aids do not represent standards or rules but rather a suggested formula or set of instructions for how to provide a specific service (i.e., a "how-to" book).

Purpose of Financial Planning Practice Standards

CFP Board has provided three justifications for the development and promulgation of financial planning practice standards. First, it assures that the practice of financial planning by CFP Board designees is based on agreed-upon norms. As discussed earlier, by establishing the minimum requirements for providing specific financial planning services, practice standards delineate both the area of good practice and the area of sub-standard practice or malpractice.

Second, they advance professionalism in financial planning. This is accomplished by identifying the requirements of good practice and requiring CFP Board designees to adhere to those requirements. This, in turn, helps the profession achieve a greater level of consumer confidence.

Finally, it enhances the value of the personal financial planning process. By using the personal financial planning process it promulgated as the foundation for the Practice Standards, CFP Board has lifted the stature of that process from an aspirational statement to the very basis for good practice.

Legal Status of Practice Standards

An important point made in one of the introductory sections of the Practice Standards is that they apply to CFP Board designees performing the tasks of personal financial planning *regardless of the person's title, job position, type of employment or method of compensation*. This statement should remove any doubts by designees employed in various employment settings that if they provide personal financial planning services, they will be expected to comply with the Practice Standards.

The Practice Standards contain legal disclaimer language similar to that appearing in the Code. The point is made that conduct inconsistent with a Practice Standard, in and of itself, is not intended to give rise to a cause of action nor to create a presumption that a legal duty has been breached. In other words, failing to comply with a Practice Standard does not by itself give an aggrieved party grounds for a lawsuit for malpractice. Other factors may have to be present before such a suit may have a reasonable expectation of success. It is also stated that the Practice Standards are not designed to be a basis for legal liability, but it is clear that they may be used to establish the standard of care a client may expect from a CFP Board designee in a personal financial planning engagement.

However, unlike the Code, a person filing a complaint against a CFP Board designee for an alleged violation of the Practice Standards, must stand in a position of **privity**. In law, privity is a legally recognized relationship between two parties (e.g., between members of a family, between an employer and employees, or between others who have entered into a contract together). In the context of a personal financial planning engagement, this would include primarily a client but it could also include a business partner of the practitioner. In the case of an alleged violation of the Code, a written request for investigation may be made by *any person*, not just a client or business partner.

ORIGIN AND HISTORY OF PRACTICE STANDARDS AND THE BOARD OF PRACTICE STANDARDS

CFP Board, as an independent professional regulatory organization founded in 1985 to benefit the public by establishing and enforcing education, examination, experience, and ethics requirements for CFP professionals, first established its certification process. The initial step was to determine fundamental criteria for competency in the financial planning profession. This was accomplished through the development of a financial planner job study analysis first conducted in 1987, updated in 1994, and again updated in 1999. The job study analysis asked experienced practitioners to enumerate the tasks they perform in the delivery of personal financial planning services. This formed the basis of the CFP and Certified Financial Planner body of knowledge and helped to establish the education, examination, and experience requirements for certification as a CFP Board designee. Administration of the certification process was vested in a subsidiary board known as the Board of Examiners composed of volunteers who have expertise in these areas.

With regard to the ethics requirement, the CFP Board initially adopted the code of ethics of the membership organization then known as the Institute of Certified Financial Planners. To some extent, it was revised to meet the needs of a professional regulatory organization as opposed to a membership organization. In order to enforce this early code of ethics, the CFP Board established a second subsidiary board known initially as the Board of Ethics and Professional Review, later changed to the Board of Professional Review. However, it was not until 1991 that the CFP Board, then known as the International Board of Standards and Practices for Certified Financial Planners, decided to completely revise the code of ethics. During 1992, the CFP Board's Post-Certification Committee developed a revised document, which it titled *Code of Ethics and Professional Responsibility*. This document was exposed to CFP Board designees, consumer organizations, regulators, related membership organizations, and others for public comment. It was revised to reflect many of the comments received from various parties and the document was approved by the CFP Board's Board of Governors and became effective January 1, 1993. The Board of Governors believed that CFP Board designees may be more inclined to comply with the new Code if they were at least familiar with its contents and requirements. As a result, coincident with the promulgation of its ethics document, the CFP Board revised its continuing education (CE) requirement for CFP Board designees to include two continuing education units in knowledge of the Code, to be obtained from providers pre-approved by the CFP Board. This CE requirement was subsequently extended to practice standards. CFP Board designees now must successfully complete biennially a two-CE unit program covering either the Code or the Practice Standards, or both.

Near the completion of the development of the code of ethics document, CFP Board determined in September 1993 that it also should develop and promulgate standards for the practice of personal financial planning consistent with its role as a professional regulatory organization charged with benefiting the public. As a result, it created in September 1994 a third subsidiary board known as the Board of Practice Standards. This subsidiary board purposefully was composed of nine volunteer CFP Board designees who were engaged in the practice of personal financial planning.

Beginning in 1995, the Board of Practice Standards (BPS) began the work of drafting proposed practice standards. In the process of working on its first standard, the BPS determined that the personal financial planning process, as it was then defined, needed to be revised to add a new first step. It discovered that a practitioner cannot effectively begin to gather client data and determine the client's goals and objectives without first establishing and defining the relationship with the client. If the relationship contemplated is a personal financial planning relationship, then the subsequent steps of the financial planning process follow logically. Of course, it is essential that there be a clear understanding between the designee and the client about the scope of the engagement. Specifically, what financial planning services will be provided? How will the practitioner be compensated? Which responsibilities will be assumed by the practitioner and which by the client? How long will the engagement last? If the relationship is one, for instance, of simply filling a customer's order to buy or sell securities, then the financial planning process may not be relevant.

Moreover, the BPS discovered that in order for the engagement to be fully effective, the scope of the engagement had to be *mutually defined* by both the financial planning practitioner and the client, rather than by only one party. The BPS believed that a client who does not understand why a particular service is being provided or does not agree with the necessity of a particular service being provided is less likely to make a commitment to the accomplishment of his or her goals.

After revising the personal financial planning process to include this vital first step and revising the wording of certain other steps, the BPS was ready to develop practice standards using the revised financial planning process as the framework. The practice standards were developed over a seven-year period using a development process similar to that adopted for the development of the Code. Exposure drafts of each practice standard were distributed to CFP Board designees, consumer organizations, financial planning organizations, regulators, and others for written comment during an exposure period. The comments received from these parties were considered by the BPS in developing the final language of each practice standard. In late 2001, the BPS was disbanded at the successful completion of its prodigious task.

DESIGN OF PRACTICE STANDARDS

As discussed earlier, the Practice Standards hang on the framework of the personal financial planning process. Each series of Practice Standards corresponds to a step of the personal financial planning process. For instance, Practice Standard 100-1, Establishing and Defining the Relationship with the Client: Defining the Scope of the Engagement, is based on Step 1 of the personal financial planning process, establishing and defining the client-planner relationship.

Each Practice Standard is only one sentence long. The Practice Standard is followed immediately by an explanation to give the Practice Standard context and a statement as to how the Practice Standard is related to the *Code of Ethics and Professional Responsibility*. Finally, the anticipated impact of the Practice Standard on a) the public, b) the financial planning profession, and c) the financial planning practitioner is given.

THE PRACTICE STANDARDS

Practice Standard 100-1: Establishing and Defining the Relationship with the Client: Defining the Scope of the Engagement

The financial planning practitioner and the client shall mutually define the scope of the engagement before any financial planning service is provided.

The essential element of this first standard is that the scope of the engagement shall be *mutually* defined by the financial planning practitioner and the client *prior to providing any financial planning service*. Rather than the practitioner telling the client what services he or she needs, the client needs to be informed as to the reasons for providing particular services and needs to agree that those services will be beneficial to him or her. Also, the client needs to know what the practitioner's compensation arrangements will be, what responsibilities both the client and the practitioner will assume, the estimated duration of the engagement, and the exact scope of the engagement. The explanation indicates that the scope of the engagement need not be in writing (though it is recommended that this be done), but the disclosures required by the Code may need to be in writing. The other important point here is that the scope of the engagement needs to be mutually defined *before* any services are rendered. This permits the client to control the extent of his or her commitment to the engagement. Of course, the scope of the engagement may change by mutual consent. Clients who understand the reason why particular financial planning services are being provided, the practitioner's compensation arrangements, the responsibilities of both the practitioner and the client, how long the engagement is expected to last, and exactly what services are being provided are more likely to make a commitment to the accomplishment of his or her goals and objectives. In short, the client will tend to be better informed, more highly motivated, more empowered, and more comfortable with the specific engagement and with the practitioner relationship if the practitioner and the client conform with the terms of Practice Standard 100-1.

Practice Standard 200-1: Gathering Client Data: Determining a Client's Personal and Financial Goals, Needs and Priorities

The financial planning practitioner and the client shall mutually define the client's personal and financial goals, needs and priorities that are relevant to the scope of the engagement before any recommendation is made and/or implemented.

In the 200 series, there are two Practice Standards both dealing with gathering client data. Practice Standard 200-1 focuses on gathering *qualitative* information from the client including his or her personal and financial goals, needs and priorities relevant to the engagement and the services being provided. As in Practice Standard 100-1, this standard requires that this information be *mutually defined* and that this be accomplished *prior to making and/or implementing any recommendations*. Again, the point here is that the practitioner cannot unilaterally decide what the client's goals, needs, and priorities are. Conversely, the client cannot simply dictate these items to the practitioner without there being a two-way conversation and exchange of relevant information. It is often to the client's advantage to use the practitioner as a sounding board in developing his or her goals, needs, and priorities. The practitioner needs to educate the client about possible goals, needs, and priorities, to explore the client's values and attitudes as they relate to them, and then arrive at an agreement as to what they are. Failing to agree upon clear, precise, consistent, and measurable goals and objectives will, most likely, doom the engagement to failure. One of the practitioner's most important responsibilities here is to assist clients to recognize the implications of unrealistic goals and objectives.

Practice Standard 200-2: Gathering Client Data: Obtaining Quantitative Information and Documents

The financial planning practitioner shall obtain sufficient quantitative information and documents about a client relevant to the scope of the engagement before any recommendation is made and/or implemented.

Practice Standard 200-2 addresses the gathering of *quantitative* information. It requires the practitioner to obtain sufficient and relevant quantitative client information and documents applicable to the scope of the engagement and the services being provided *prior to making and/or implementing any recommendations*. The practitioner first needs to determine what quantitative information and documents are sufficient and relevant and then proceed to obtain it directly from the client or other sources through an interview, questionnaire, client records, or other relevant documents. It is important that the practitioner communicate to the client that the practitioner intends to rely on the completeness and accuracy of the information provided and what the effect of incomplete or inaccurate information will have on his or her conclusions and recommendations.

Another key point is that if the practitioner is unable to obtain sufficient and relevant quantitative information and documents to form a basis for recommendations, the practitioner will either (1) restrict the scope of the engagement to those matters for which sufficient and relevant information is available, or (2) terminate the engagement. Finally, the practitioner needs to communicate to the client any limitations on the scope of the engagement, as well as the fact that these limitations potentially can impact the conclusions and recommendations.

Practice Standard 300-1: Analyzing and Evaluating the Client's Financial Status: Analyzing and Evaluating the Client's Information

A financial planning practitioner shall analyze the information to gain an understanding of the client's financial situation and then evaluate to what extent the client's goals, needs and priorities can be met by the client's resources and current course of action.

Practice Standard 300-1, which covers the subject of analyzing and evaluating the client's financial status, is the only practice standard in the 300 series. The practitioner is required to analyze the information obtained in the 200 series of practice standards to gain an understanding of the client's financial situation and to evaluate to what extent the client's goals, needs and priorities can be met by the client's resources and current course of action. The practitioner needs to factor in not only any mutually agreed-upon and/or other reasonable assumptions, but also consider any economic assumptions such as inflation rates, tax rates, and investment returns. Analysis of the client's information may result in revision of the scope of the engagement.

Practice Standard 400-1: Developing and Presenting the Financial Planning Recommendations: Identifying and Evaluating Financial Planning Alternative(s)

The financial planning practitioner shall consider sufficient and relevant alternatives to the client's current course of action in an effort to reasonably meet the client's goals, needs and priorities.

There are three practice standards in the 400 series. Practice Standard 400-1 requires the practitioner to consider sufficient and relevant alternatives to the client's current course of action and to evaluate the effectiveness of such alternatives in reasonably achieving the client's goals, needs and priorities. In most cases, there will be alternatives that a client may reasonably pursue and the practitioner is obligated to consider multiple assumptions, conduct research or consult with other professionals to determine if these alternatives are viable for the specific client situation.

Practice Standard 400-2: Developing and Presenting the Financial Planning Recommendations: Developing the Financial Planning Recommendations

The financial planning practitioner shall develop the recommendation(s) based on the selected alternative(s) and the current course of action in an effort to reasonably meet the client's goals, needs and priorities.

Practice Standard 400-2 requires the practitioner to develop his or her recommendations based on the selected alternatives (developed pursuant to Practice Standard 400-1) and the client's current course of action, so as to reasonably meet the client's goals, needs and priorities. These recommendations need to be consistent with and directly affected by (1) the mutually defined scope of the engagement; (2) the mutually defined client goals, needs and priorities; (3) the quantitative data obtained about the client; (4) any personal and economic assumptions considered; (5) the practitioner's analysis and evaluation of the client's current situation; and (6) the alternatives selected by the practitioner.

It is possible that the practitioner's recommendation may be to continue the current course of action or, alternatively, that the client should modify a specific goal or goals. A key point here is that the recommendations developed by a particular practitioner may or may not agree with those that might be developed by another practitioner given the same client situation and information. And yet the recommendations of different practitioners may reasonably achieve the client's goals, needs and priorities.

Practice Standard 400-3: Developing and Presenting the Financial Planning Recommendations: Presenting the Financial Planning Recommendations

The financial planning practitioner shall communicate the recommendation(s) in a manner and to an extent reasonably necessary to assist the client in making an informed decision.

Practice Standard 400-3 calls for the practitioner to communicate his or her recommendations in a manner and to an extent reasonably necessary to assist the client in making an informed decision. In this connection, the practitioner needs to communicate the factors critical to the client's understanding of the recommendations including, but not limited to, personal and economic assumptions, interdependence of recommendations, the advantages and disadvantages of the recommendations, the associated risks and/or time sensitivity. An important point here is that the practitioner avoid presenting his or her opinion as fact. The practitioner needs to make sure the client understands that the recommendations *may* achieve the client's goals, needs and priorities but that changes in personal and economic conditions could alter the intended outcome. These changes can include legislative, family status, career, investment performance and/or health considerations. Also, this step is an additional opportunity for the practitioner to advise the client of any conflicts of interest and how they may impact the practitioner's recommendations. It is also the final opportunity to assess whether the recommendations will meet the client's expectations, whether the client is willing to act on the recommendations, and whether these expectations need to be modified.

Practice Standard 500-1: Implementing the Financial Planning Recommendations: Agreeing on Implementation Responsibilities

The financial planning practitioner and the client shall mutually agree on the implementation responsibilities consistent with the scope of the engagement.

The 500 series contains two Practice Standards which became effective January 1, 2002, and which address the subject of implementing the financial planning recommendations. Not surprisingly, Practice Standard 500-1 requires that there be mutual agreement on the implementation responsibilities consistent with the scope of the engagement. It emphasizes that the client is responsible for accepting or rejecting the practitioner's recommendations and for retaining and/or delegating the implementation responsibilities. The practitioner's responsibilities may include, but are not limited to, identifying activities necessary for implementation, determining the division of activities between the practitioner and the client, referring the client to other professionals, coordinating with other professionals, sharing of information as authorized, and selecting and securing products and/or services. In some cases, the scope of the engagement may need to be revised. This is an additional opportunity to disclose any conflicts of interest. If the implementation is referred to other professionals, the practitioner is obligated to disclose the basis for the referral.

Practice Standard 500-2: Implementing the Financial Planning Recommendations: Selecting Products and Services for Implementation

The financial planning practitioner shall select appropriate products and services that are consistent with the client's goals, needs and priorities.

In Practice Standard 500-2, the practitioner is obligated to select appropriate products and services that are consistent with the client's goals, needs and priorities. It would appear to the author, that the selection should also be consistent with the client's current financial situation, the analysis performed in earlier steps of the financial planning process, and with the practitioner's recommendations made previously. The selection is to be made in the client's best interest and a reasonable investigation of the recommended products and services must be made. As a result, the practitioner will have a reasonable basis for believing that the products or services selected are suitable for the client's situation. Finally, the practitioner must make all required disclosures about the products or services recommended necessary to comply with applicable laws, rules, and regulations. These latter requirements of suitability and disclosure are already incorporated in the Code.

Practice Standard 600-1: Monitoring: Defining Monitoring Responsibilities

The financial planning practitioner and client shall mutually define monitoring responsibilities.

This last Practice Standard also became effective January 1, 2002. It requires the practitioner to mutually define with the client the monitoring responsibilities associated with implementation of the plan. The purpose of this standard is to clarify the role, if any, of the practitioner in the monitoring process. The practitioner must make a reasonable effort to define and communicate to the client those monitoring activities that the practitioner is able and willing to provide. The monitoring process may reveal the need to reinitiate the steps of the personal financial planning process, which in turn, can result in revision of the scope of the engagement.

OTHER PROFESSIONAL GUIDANCE IN PROVIDING PERSONAL FINANCIAL PLANNING SERVICES

While they are not directly applicable to nor enforceable against CFP Board designees (unless they are also Certified Public Accountants and members of the American Institute of Certified Public Accountants), the AICPA's *Statements on Responsibilities in Personal Financial Planning Practice* offer additional guidance in this area. These Statements have been published for the guidance of members of the AICPA and do not constitute enforceable standards under the AICPA *Code of Professional Conduct* (the equivalent of the CFP Board's *Code of Ethics and Professional Responsibility*). Nevertheless, they offer useful guidance for practitioners of personal financial planning. It should be kept in mind that these Statements were prepared specifically for CPA members of the AICPA who practice personal financial planning and are not designed for general use.

Statement No. 1–Basic Personal Financial Planning Engagement Functions and Responsibilities

The AICPA's Personal Financial Planning Executive Committee has developed five Statements. In Statement No. 1, *Basic Personal Financial Planning Engagement Functions and Responsibilities,* the AICPA provides its definition and scope of personal financial planning. It states that "personal financial planning engagements are only those that involve developing strategies and making recommendations to assist a client in defining and achieving personal financial goals." It specifies the activities which are involved in *all* personal financial planning engagements, namely (1) defining the engagement objectives; (2) planning the specific procedures appropriate to the engagement; (3) developing a basis for recommendations; (4) communicating recommendations to the client; and (5) identifying the tasks for taking action on planning decisions. In addition, it lists other services that *may* be included in such engagements, including (1) assisting the client to take actions on planning decisions; (2) monitoring the client's progress in achieving goals; and (3) updating recommendations and helping the client revise planning decisions. The Statement also makes clear that personal financial planning does not include services limited to such tasks as (1) compiling personal financial statements; (2) projecting future taxes; (3) tax compliance, including, but not limited to, preparation of tax returns; or (4) tax advice or consultations.

The Statement then recites existing AICPA professional standards and published guidance applicable to personal financial planning engagements, including applicable Rules of the AICPA *Code of Professional Conduct, Statements on Responsibilities in Tax Practice, Statements on Standards for Consulting Services,* and statements applicable to the preparation of personal financial statements and financial projections.

The Statement continues with guidance on how to define the engagement objectives. Its content is, in effect, parallel to the 100 and 200 series of CFP Board Practice Standards. It calls for a mutual definition of the scope of the engagement, as does Practice Standard 100-1, except that it espouses written documentation (preferably an engagement letter) of the understanding reached between the client and the practitioner. It also discusses the gathering of client data, including goals. In addition, it suggests that the engagement be carefully planned so that it can be demonstrated that a systematic approach was taken and that there is an adequate basis for the recommendations made. The communication of recommendations to clients generally parallels Practice Standard 400-3 except that it suggests making recommendations only in writing and including delineation of any restrictions on the scope of the engagement imposed by the client as well as a statement that projected results may not be achieved.

Moreover, guidance is provided in this first Statement on identifying the tasks for taking action on planning decisions in a manner similar to that specified in Practice Standard 500-1. The Statement concludes by making clear that the practitioner is not responsible for the additional services of assisting the client to take action on planning decisions, monitoring progress in achieving goals, nor updating recommendations and revising planning decisions, unless undertaken by specific agreement with the client. This position is consistent with Practice Standard 100-1, which provides guidance on reaching a clear understanding with the client of the specific services to be provided and those that will not be provided.

Statement No. 2—Working With Other Advisers

This Statement provides guidance on the use of the work of other advisers by a practitioner. It will be of most value to practitioners whose compensation is derived solely from client fees. It covers the situations where (1) the practitioner may use advice provided by others in developing client recommendations, including advice suggesting that action be taken as well as advice providing information; (2) the practitioner refers a client to other advisers who assist the client in securing products or services identified in the practitioner's financial planning recommendations; or (3) the practitioner refers a client to advisers who provide services in areas in which the practitioner is not a licensed provider, does not practice, or chooses not to practice, in a specific engagement.

Where other advisers are engaged, the practitioner should restrict the scope of his or her engagement accordingly. If the client declines to engage another recommended adviser, the engagement may still proceed but the practitioner should communicate to the client any limitation on the scope of the engagement as well as the potential effect on the conclusions and recommendations developed. The Statement cites the example of the need for a business valuation, which the client declines to complete due to cost considerations.

This second Statement suggests that the practitioner become satisfied concerning the professional qualifications and reputation of another adviser before referring clients to that adviser. When referring such an adviser to a client, the client should be advised of the nature of the work to be performed by the adviser and the extent to which the practitioner will evaluate that work.

If the practitioner uses the opinions of another adviser in completing the personal financial planning engagement, the practitioner should understand and evaluate the adviser's opinions and the procedures used to develop them. If the other adviser's opinions were used without evaluation by the practitioner, that fact should be communicated to the client. The Statement provides examples of written communications to clients in this situation.

Statement No. 3—Implementation Engagement Functions and Responsibilities

This statement provides guidance applicable to implementation engagements. It goes beyond the guidance in Practice Standards 500-1 and 500-2. It defines implementation engagements as those that involve assisting the client to take action on planning decisions developed during the personal financial planning engagement. It includes activities such as selecting investment advisers, restructuring debt, creating estate documents, establishing cash reserves, preparing budgets, and selecting and acquiring investments and insurance products. The Statement is limited to those situations in which the practitioner is engaged by a client to assist with the implementation activities. It does not extend to those situations in which the practitioner is functioning in a fiduciary or agency relationship. In the situations described in the Statement, the practitioner may (1) refer the client to other advisers; (2) coordinate and/or review the delivery of services and/or products by other advisers; (3) participate in implementation by establishing selection criteria; or (4) participate in implementation by participating in the selection of service providers and/or the selection and acquisition of products.

The Statement suggests that the practitioner and the client identify and agree on the level of the practitioner's assistance in implementation. It also clarifies that regardless of the level of assistance by the practitioner, implementation decisions are made by the client, not the practitioner. In addition, it suggests documenting the practitioner's understanding of the nature and scope of the implementation services to be provided and the roles and responsibilities of the practitioner, the client, and other advisers.

If the practitioner is engaged to establish selection criteria, he or she should identify those attributes or other specifications that are required to accomplish the client's objectives. Selection criteria may be expressed in ranges if the practitioner and the client agree that such practice is useful. Moreover, if the practitioner is engaged to participate in selecting and acquiring products, the practitioner should gather data that provides a reasonable basis for determining whether the alternatives meet the selection criteria. Finally, if the practitioner is engaged to assist the client in taking action on planning decisions developed in a personal financial planning engagement in which the practitioner did not participate, the practitioner should obtain a sufficient understanding of the planning decisions to effectively assist in implementation. He or she should consider factors such as the client's goals, existing financial situation, the available resources for achieving the goals, non-financial factors, and external factors. Relevant information may also include estimates, projections, and assumptions.

The Statement provides two appendices containing illustrations of possible procedures to be followed by the practitioner who is engaged by a client to assist in implementing a personal financial planning decision. In each example, the initial personal financial planning engagement is presumed to have been completed before implementation, either by the practitioner in the illustrations or another adviser.

Statement No. 4–Monitoring and Updating Engagements– Functions and Responsibilities

This Statement provides guidance on the topics of monitoring implemented recommendations and updating services. It defines monitoring engagements as those that involve determining the client's progress in achieving established personal financial planning goals. Updating engagements are defined as those that involve revising the client's existing financial plan and financial planning recommendations, as appropriate, in light of the client's goals, current circumstances, and current external factors. The Statement indicates that these services are typically undertaken after implementation of actions and recommendations developed during a personal financial planning engagement and they may be either separate or combined engagements.

With regard to monitoring engagements, the Statement's guidance parallels the guidance provided in Practice Standard 600-1. It calls for documentation of the practitioner's understanding of the nature and extent of the monitoring and/or updating services to be provided and the roles and responsibilities of the practitioner, the client, and other advisers. Practice Standard 600-1 requires mutual definition of the monitoring responsibilities by the client and the practitioner. However, the Statement provides much more detailed guidance than that offered in Practice Standard 600-1. It discusses the varying complexity and scope of monitoring engagements as including (1) undertaking some, or all, of the monitoring services; (2) coordinating and/or reviewing monitoring services performed by other advisers; and (3) monitoring the progress toward goals in a financial plan developed by other advisers.

The Statement suggests that the practitioner, in determining the client's progress toward achieving established financial planning goals, should (1) ascertain whether all recommended actions to achieve the goals were undertaken; (2) measure and evaluate the actual progress toward achievement of the goals; and (3) identify developments in the client's circumstances and in external factors that affect the financial plan. The client and the practitioner should agree on the frequency of monitoring activities and the practitioner should use monitoring criteria that are appropriate and consistent with the criteria used to establish the financial planning goals being monitored. The Statement suggests that the items monitored may change in importance over time and more emphasis may need to be placed on specific aspects at a particular time. Monitoring may result in a recommendation to the client to review or update the existing financial plan.

Practice Standard 600-1 indicates that the monitoring process may reveal the need to reinitiate steps of the financial planning process and/or revise the scope of the engagement. Statement No. 4 refers to such activities as "updating engagements." The Statement suggests that the practitioner communicate to the client that updating a personal financial plan affects all aspects of the plan and that all existing financial planning recommendations should be reviewed as part of the updating process. It indicates that in updating a personal financial plan and financial planning recommendations the practitioner should consider the integrated nature of financial planning and the effect of revising recommendations to achieve one financial planning goal on the client' ability to achieve all other financial planning goals.

Statement No. 5—Developing a Basis for Recommendations

This Statement offers guidance in establishing a solid foundation for making specific financial planning recommendations. It indicates that developing a basis for recommendations involves:

(1) collecting relevant quantitative and qualitative information which may include but is not limited to:

(a) the client's goals, existing financial situation, and available resources;

(b) non-financial factors such as client attitudes, risk tolerance, family considerations, age, health, and life expectancy;

(c) external factors such as estimates of inflation, taxes, economic conditions, legislative activity, investment markets, and interest rates; and

(d) reasonable estimates, projections, and assumptions furnished by the client, provided by the client's advisers, or developed by the practitioner.

(2) analyzing the client's current situation as it relates to the client's goals and objectives and identifying strengths and weaknesses of the existing financial situation

(3) formulating, evaluating, and recommending appropriate strategies and courses of action for achieving the client's goals

Much of this guidance is included in the 200, 300, and 400 series of the Practice Standards. In the section of the Statement entitled "Analyzing Information", valuable guidance is offered on testing the sensitivity of estimates, assumptions, and projections used and communicating to the client those that are significant to the plan and those that have a high probability of variation that could materially affect the plan.

IMPORTANT CONCEPTS TO REMEMBER

The differences between ethics rules, practice standards, and practice aids

Privity

Mutually defining the scope of the engagement

Qualitative versus quantitative client data

Analysis and evaluation of the client's financial situation and information

Identifying and evaluating alternatives

Developing and presenting recommendations

Implementing recommendations

Monitoring recommendations

AICPA *Statements on Responsibilities in Personal Financial Planning Practice*

QUESTIONS FOR REVIEW

1. How do ethics rules differ from practice standards?

2. What are the three justifications offered by CFP Board for the development and promulgation of financial planning practice standards?

3. From which parties will CFP Board accept complaints alleging violation(s) of the Code versus alleged noncompliance with the Practice Standards?

4. What is the purpose of a job study analysis and how is the resulting information used by CFP Board?

5. What does it mean to "mutually define" the scope of the engagement?

6. A financial planning practitioner's recommendations should be consistent with and directly affected by what other aspects of the personal financial planning engagement?

7. According to the AICPA's *Statements on Responsibilities in Personal Financial Planning Practice,* for what financial planning services is the practitioner *not* responsible unless undertaken by specific agreement with the client?

SUGGESTIONS FOR ADDITIONAL READING

CFP Board's *Standards of Professional Conduct* available at http://www.CFP.net.

American Institute of Certified Public Accountants' *Statements on Responsibilities in Personal Financial Planning Practice, AICPA Professional Standards,* American Institute of Certified Public Accountants, Inc., 2003 available by contacting the AICPA at http://www.aicpa.org.

CHAPTER NINE

The Economic Environment

• • •

In addition to those techniques that are in the financial planner's direct control to implement for the client, there is a greater economic context in which the personal financial planning process is conducted. The economic environment is really under the control of others, such as the Federal Reserve Board, Congress, and marketplace forces. In addition, financial intermediaries, such as banks, securities brokerage, and insurance companies play an important role in the economy. This chapter outlines how the economic environment impacts personal financial planning and the ability of the financial planner to help his or her clients achieve their financial goals.

The economic environment transitions from good economic conditions to less favorable conditions. These transitions — from expansion to peak, through contraction or recession to trough, and back again to expansion — are better know as **the business cycle**. We will discuss how fiscal policy and monetary policy are used to influence the business cycle and to control the inflation that occurs in certain stages of the business cycle.

The objectives of this chapter are:
- Identify the various phases of the business cycle.
- Describe the dynamics taking place during each phase of the business cycle.
- Identify the forces internal to the economic system that drive the business cycle.
- Describe what constitutes a recession.
- Describe how a recession differs from a depression.

- Describe inflation and how it is created.
- Identify the items that make up the **market basket of goods and services** included in the Consumer Price Index.
- Describe the ten items that constitute The Conference Board's composite index of leading economic indicators.
- Describe the Gross Domestic Product and what it indicates about the economy.
- Distinguish between monetary policy and fiscal policy as tools to affect the economy and inflation.
- Identify the two methods of monetary policy employed by the Fed to affect inflation or influence output and employment.
- Discuss the role played by financial institutions and financial intermediaries.

THE BUSINESS CYCLE

Boom and bust, prosperity and recession, the good times, the bad times, and all the times in between, form what is known as the business cycle. Every capitalistic economy in the modern era has endured periods of growth and confidence trailing off into periods of despair. See Figure 9.1 for an analysis of business cycle expansions and contractions since 1854.

The Order of the Cycle

While the U.S. economy has endured the Roaring '20s and the Great Depression, it has experienced a long series of less severe expansions and contractions until the present time. One basic truth is that we are always in a business cycle. Business expands and then contracts ad infinitum. Business cycles tend to follow a repetitive pattern. Periods of **expansion** are characterized by significant increases in demand, production, income, wealth, employment, and profits. The construction of both homes and factories, and the addition of machinery and equipment flourish, with the value of these assets growing as home prices and common stock prices increase. Predictably, a period of **contraction** follows when demand, production, employment, and income decline. Construction levels and the addition of machinery and equipment are reduced substantially. Asset values decline, including the prices of homes and common stock. Some contractions worsen into a recession bottoming out at a **trough**. This is normally followed by a **recovery** as the economy again expands, sometimes even reaching the previous level of prosperity, known as the **peak**. At the peak, unemployment is low, personal income and business profits increase, and consumer demand rises.

To review, the general order of the business cycle is as follows: expansion, peak, contraction, and trough. The expansion phase brings about the contraction phase. During expansion, companies tend to increase their productive capacity beyond their needs and produce more product than can soon be absorbed by customers. Both the resulting build-up in inventory and the funds invested in unsold products and services cause price reductions to stimulate demand. Competitors usually match the price reductions but some are unable to survive financially at these lower price levels and, as a result, become bankrupt. The result is higher unemployment and less borrowing as businesses cease to invest. Banks and other lenders then reduce interest rates to attract more borrowers. As the downward spiral continues, those companies still in business borrow at the lower rates to reduce their debt. Soon unemployment reaches a plateau, and it becomes apparent that the contraction has put in place the basic ingredients for the coming recovery phase. As individuals and businesses adapt to the current situation and begin to see a brighter future, they stimulate the economy by spending. Businesses, in particular, invest in more efficient processes at the low interest rates, and the expansion phase starts all over again.

The dynamics taking place during each phase of the business cycle can be summarized as follows:

- **Recovery to expansion**—Inflation declines, employment and personal income increase, consumer sentiment and consumer demand rise, resulting in higher auto sales, retail sales, consumer credit, and housing starts; inflationary pressure builds.

- **Expansion to peak**—Gross domestic product (discussed later in this chapter) and industrial production increase, as do the purchasing managers' index and capacity utilization; labor productivity declines; unit labor costs and producer prices increase, with even more inflationary pressure.

- **Peak to contraction**—Consumer price index increases; employment and personal income decline; consumer sentiment and consumer demand decline as auto sales, consumer credit, housing starts, and retail sales drop, eventually reaching a trough.

- **Trough to recovery**—Gross domestic product (discussed later in this chapter) and industrial production decline as do the purchasing managers' index and capacity utilization; labor productivity increases while both unit labor costs and producer prices decline, resulting in lower inflation and launching the next round of the business cycle.

Companies attempting to react to the business cycle are usually frustrated by the difficulty of determining exactly where the economy is in the cycle, how long it will be there, and when it will achieve either peak or trough. Business cycles may last less than a year, a year or two, or as much as a decade, accompanied by false troughs and peaks. Within each major cycle, there may be many minor cycles. Cycles do not occur with any particular regularity or last for any easily predictable period of time.

Figure 9.1

U.S. BUSINESS CYCLE EXPANSIONS AND CONTRACTIONS Contractions (recessions) start at the peak of a business cycle and end at the trough.					
Business Cycle Reference Dates		Duration in Months			
Peak	Trough	Contraction	Expansion	Cycle	
Quarterly Dates are in parentheses		*Peak to Trough*	*Previous Trough to this Peak*	*Trough from Previous Trough*	*Peak from Previous Peak*
	December 1854 (IV)	--	--	--	--
June 1857 (II)	December 1858 (IV)	18	30	48	--
October 1860 (III)	June 1861 (III)	8	22	30	40
April 1865 (I)	December 1867 (I)	*32*	*46*	*78*	*54*
June 1869 (II)	December 1870 (IV)	18	18	36	50
October 1873 (III)	March 1879 (I)	65	34	99	52
March 1882 (I)	May 1885 (II)	38	36	74	101
March 1887 (II)	April 1888 (I)	13	22	35	60
July 1890 (III)	May 1891 (II)	10	27	37	40
January 1893 (I)	June 1894 (II)	17	20	37	30
December 1895 (IV)	June 1897 (II)	18	18	36	35
June 1899 (III)	December 1900 (IV)	18	24	42	42
September 1902 (IV)	August 1904 (III)	23	21	44	39
May 1907 (II)	June 1908 (II)	13	33	46	56
January 1910 (I)	January 1912 (IV)	24	19	43	32
January 1913 (I)	December 1914 (IV)	23	12	35	36
August 1918 (III)	March 1919 (I)	*7*	*44*	*51*	*67*
January 1920 (I)	July 1921 (III)	18	10	28	17
May 1923 (II)	July 1924 (III)	14	22	36	40
October 1926 (III)	November 1927 (IV)	13	27	40	41
August 1929 (III)	March 1933 (I)	43	21	64	34
May 1937 (II)	June 1938 (II)	13	50	63	93
February 1945 (I)	October 1945 (IV)	*8*	*80*	*88*	*93*
November 1948 (IV)	October 1949 (IV)	11	37	48	45
July 1953 (II)	May 1954 (II)	*10*	*45*	*55*	*56*
August 1957 (III)	April 1958 (II)	8	39	47	49
April 1960(II)	February 1961 (I)	10	24	34	32
December 1969 (IV)	November 1970 (IV)	*11*	*106*	*117*	*116*
November 1973 (IV)	March 1975 (I)	16	36	52	47
January 1980 (I)	July 1980 (III)	6	58	64	74
July 1981 (III)	November 1982 (IV)	16	12	28	18
July 1990 (III)	March 1991(I)	8	92	100	108
March 2001 (I)	November 2001 (IV)	8	120	128	128
Average, all cycles: 1854-2001 (32 cycles)		17	38	55	*56
1854-1919 (16 cycles)		22	27	48	**49
1919-1945 (6 cycles)		18	35	53	53
1945-2001 (10 cycles)		10	57	67	67
Average, peacetime cycles: 1854-2001 (27 cycles)		18	33	51	***52
1854-1919 (14 cycles)		22	24	46	****47
1919-1945 (5 cycles)		20	26	46	45
1945-2001 (8 cycles)		10	52	63	63

*31 cycles, **15 cycles, ***26 cycles, ****13 cycles

Figures printed in **bold italic** are the wartime expansions (Civil War, World Wars I and II, Korean War, and Vietnam War); the wartime contractions, and the full cycles that include the wartime expansions.

Sources: NBER; the U.S. Department of Commerce, Survey of Current Business, October 1994, Table C-51.

Economic Forces

As we have discussed, it is impossible to predict with accuracy the length and severity of a business cycle. However, we know the forces that drive the business cycle and that they come from within the economic system rather than being external to it.

Supply and Demand

Of primary importance are the forces of **supply and demand**. A business cannot enjoy increasing income without producing greater quantities of its product or service; however, those larger quantities must be sold in order to produce a profit. When demand is adequate, the level of production will be sustained and will grow as income increases. If demand is not adequate, the opposite will occur. During the expansion phase of the cycle, demand and supply are aligned in a way that results in the growth of production and income. During the contraction phase, their relative alignment dictates a decrease in production and income.

Credit

A second potent force is the use of **credit**—the ability to borrow money and spend more than one earns. Borrowing has the effect of inflating demand and bidding up the level of production, thereby feeding the expansion phase of the cycle. As soon as the availability of credit declines (perhaps due to market saturation or fewer profitable investment opportunities and higher interest rates), so does demand and, ultimately, the level of production and income, leading to contraction.

Capacity

A third factor is the creation of **excess capacity** (overexpansion of productive capability), either by companies making excess investment in new plant and equipment or by consumers who borrow to excess to purchase homes, autos, or other goods. When this excess investment and borrowing reach an extreme, companies and consumers suddenly curtail their spending, which causes a decline in production and income.

Efficiency

Fourth, a contraction brings about a decline in production and income to a level that can be realistically sustained (without a constant flurry of borrowing). In other words, contraction restores **efficient levels of operation**, thus creating the conditions needed to head the economy back into expansion.

Cyclicality

Based on the experience of the 1990s, when the U.S. economy recovered from a trough in March 1991 to grow at an unprecedented rate for a decade, some economists began to believe that the business cycle had been repealed. It appeared that the expansion would never peak. However, in November 2001, the Business Cycle Dating Committee of the National Bureau of

Economic Research determined that this unprecedented period of expansion reached its peak in March 2001: This unusually long period of prosperity ended, just like any sustained period of contraction eventually ends.

Recession

While there is some debate about what constitutes a recession, most economists would agree that a **recession** is characterized by two consecutive quarters of decline in real Gross Domestic Product (GDP). The National Bureau of Economic Research (NBER) defines a recession as a "period of significant decline in total output, income, employment, and trade, usually lasting from six months to a year, and marked by widespread contractions in many sectors of the economy."

A **growth recession** is a recurring period of slow growth in total output, income, employment, and trade, usually lasting a year or more. A growth recession may encompass a recession, in which case the slowdown usually begins before the recession starts, but ends at about the same time. **Slowdowns** also may occur without recession, in which case the economy continues to grow, but at a pace significantly below its long-run growth.

Depression

A recession that is major in both scale and duration is defined as a **depression**. The affliction is not confined to isolated areas of the country but rather affects the entire country to varying degrees and lasts for several years, accompanied by substantial declines in total output, income, employment, and trade.

THE POST-WORLD WAR II ECONOMY

The economic after-effect of virtually all wars is slump and contraction. However, after World War II, the U.S. economy behaved differently than after other wars. Prior to World War II, inflation had seldom been of much concern in the U.S. After that war, thousands of young soldiers returned home, got married, started having children and wanted things like homes, cars, kitchen appliances, and all the modern conveniences. While credit had been used as early as the 1920s for the purchase of larger durable goods, it had not been used extensively. For example, pre-war home buying typically required very large down payments and short mortgage terms. However, after World War II, credit became a normal part of buying consumer goods.

During the war, nearly half of all items produced had been for the war effort. As a result, consumers had gone without many things. No automobiles had been made, few new homes had been built, and few appliances had been available for consumers. Individuals invested what they could in the war effort by buying War Bonds. After the war, considerable pent-up demand was unleashed, with this demand far exceeding the supply of virtually everything. This unprecedented demand, in turn, created inflation.

Inflation

Inflation is generally defined as an increase in prices due to excessive spending on credit, or "too many dollars chasing too few goods." Economists believe that inflation occurs when demand exceeds supply at current prices, leading to the bidding up of prices.

The driving force behind inflation is supply and demand. A business has limited capacity to produce whatever it provides. The extent to which this capacity is used is known as "capacity utilization." Few, if any, businesses (particularly manufacturing businesses) produce at 100 percent of capacity. Operating at 100 percent of capacity would require all equipment to be operating 100 percent of the time. In the real world, this does not happen for a number of reasons. Equipment must be shut down for routine maintenance periodically. It may also require replacement or major repairs. Any time the equipment is down, capacity is reduced. Employees also take time off for sick leave, vacation time, company meetings, or any number of reasons, during which times they do not produce. Consequently, a business operating at 85% capacity utilization is generally considered at full capacity.

As demand increases for products or services, companies attempt to work as close to capacity as possible. However, operating at effective capacity typically requires more employees, so companies increase capacity by hiring new workers. Newly hired employees are seldom as efficient as more experienced employees, resulting in increased errors and production slowdowns. If, for example, experienced employees can produce 25 items per hour and new employees can produce only 20 items per hour, the labor cost per unit, the energy cost per unit, and the equipment cost per unit increase. Additionally, as the level of production increases, routine maintenance is reduced because equipment is nearly always in use, resulting in a higher level of breakdowns. The time that equipment is down forces a shutdown in production until it is repaired, but meanwhile the labor costs go on. These combined factors push the cost of production up for every item produced. The business is then required to increase its selling prices to cover its higher costs and still make a reasonable profit — this is the start of inflation. As long as demand remains strong, few consumers will decline to buy the products at the higher prices. But as demand declines, this situation changes.

An additional factor to be considered is the increased direct costs of doing business. When demand is high and the resources to meet the demand are limited, the cost of materials and labor go up. In a rapidly growing economy, there is very low unemployment, with employers competing with one another to attract the best workers by offering higher pay, shorter working hours, or additional benefits. As this happens at each level of the production chain, raw materials and components cost more, labor costs go up and the output at increasing levels is priced higher. As long as the supply is less than the demand, and the higher prices alone do not deter buyers, production continues.

But the cycle cannot continue forever. As Company A starts making higher-than-normal profits making widgets, Company B decides to jump on the bandwagon and starts making widgets as well, to take advantage of existing demand. All may go well until Company C gets into the widget business. All of a sudden, there are more widgets being produced now than consumers are willing to purchase. In an effort to maintain market share, keep employees working, or unload excess inventory, the widget competitors start to reduce their prices. One or more of them might decide to cut its production, laying off workers to save money. As this happens to more and more companies, the economy contracts and inflation slows as buying slows. A recent example may help to illustrate the point. In 2000 and 2001, home and business computer sales started to decline sharply. As expected, computer manufacturers continued to put out faster, smaller computers, but consumers appeared to be unimpressed by the added features. Accordingly, there has been a significant contraction in the manufacture of PCs and a reduction in their prices.

Credit accelerates the volatility of the inflationary cycle. The widespread use of credit makes demand rise faster than it could in the pre-war era, when consumers could only purchase items for which they had the cash in hand. When demand rises significantly, so does inflation. This may not always occur in the short-run, but, ultimately, increased demand will result in inflationary pressures. Since incomes historically have not increased at the same rate as inflation, real income, the buying power in the hands of consumers, goes down.

Consumer Price Index

The terms **consumer price index (CPI)** and inflation are typically used interchangeably. Sometimes the CPI is called a cost-of-living index. In reality, it is not. It is a measure of the economy as a whole (although there are regional versions available) and is not specifically applicable to any particular individual or group of individuals. Each person's cost of living changes as his or her personal situation changes. Any parent who has a grown child leave home realizes that his or her household cost-of-living drops noticeably. The CPI is based on a **market basket** of goods and services that is static. The CPI market basket includes items such as food, medical care, housing, utilities, clothing, transportation, and the like. Each item is weighted according to its perceived relative importance. However, except for the regional indexes published, it fails to reflect differences in specific parts of the country. In some areas of the country, new housing demand may be relatively strong, while in other areas there may be virtually no demand for new housing. Additionally, products tend to cost less when purchased close to their source of production. Small towns tend to have higher prices for some consumer goods because the economies of scale for transporting goods to those towns do not exist.

The basket changes only infrequently and only after a survey to determine how consumer buying patterns may have changed. The last big change was in the early 1980s when the Bureau of Labor Statistics removed the cost of home ownership and replaced it with an imputed cost of renting owner-occupied homes. This change was made to reflect the fact that homeowners who have lived in their homes for five or more years usually do not experience a significant change in living costs.

Government Influence on the Business Cycle

Most early students of economics arrive at the impression that the business cycle is independent and autonomous — it seems to just happen, like the weather. In fact, in more recent times, the American business cycle has been influenced by a variety of attempts to guide and direct it. Before we discuss the tools available to the U.S. Government to affect the business cycle, we will discuss the mechanism that has been created to monitor the business cycle so that it can be determined when use of these tools is necessary or desirable and what the effect is of their use.

LEADING ECONOMIC INDICATORS

An **economic indicator** is a measure of how a specific sector of the overall economy is performing. For example, new housing starts constitute an economic indicator because consumers will build houses only when their incomes and levels of confidence are high. Similarly, the inflation rate is an economic indicator that can provide valuable information about consumers' buying power. Economists analyze information reflecting recent economic activity to make forecasts of future economic activity.

There is no one indicator that by itself can consistently provide an accurate estimate of future economic activity. That is why economists use a group of indicators, watched as a whole, to make such estimates. The Conference Board has developed a composite index of leading economic indicators that is used by many economists to forecast economic activity. See **In Depth: The Conference Board's Composite**.

To be effective, a composite index of this type must include only indicators that truly *lead* the business cycle with reasonable accuracy, cover the breadth of the economy comprehensively, and are available monthly relatively soon after the measurement period. The use of ten indicators tends to provide both stability and ease of prediction. Of course, no composite index is completely reliable since leading economists disagree on the outlook for future activity based on identical information. Nevertheless, the composite index of leading economic indicators has proven to be an effective predictor of economic activity throughout its history.

One of the shortcomings of a national index of leading economic indicators is that it is only useful in forecasting the general direction of the economy as a whole. If one's interest is in a particular sector, he or she must use only the indicators for that sector. Moreover, national leading economic indicators generally are not useful in forecasting economic activity for a specific geographic region. The 2000 census showed that certain parts of the country are losing population and industry while others are gaining. As a result, some geographic areas will suffer deflating housing prices and higher-than-average unemployment and others just the opposite. Therefore, use the indices with care.

In Depth: The Conference Board's Composite

1. Average weekly hours of production workers in manufacturing industries
2. Average weekly initial claims for unemployment insurance
3. Manufacturers' new orders in 1996 dollars, consumer goods and materials industries
4. Vendor performance—slower deliveries diffusion index; measures the relative speed at which industrial companies receive deliveries from their suppliers
5. Manufacturers' new orders in 1996 dollars, non-defense capital goods industries
6. New private housing units authorized by local building permits (housing starts)
7. Stock prices, 500 common stocks (S&P 500)
8. Money supply—M2—in 1996 dollars
9. Interest rate spread, 10-year U.S. Treasury bonds less federal funds rate; often called the yield curve
10. University of Michigan index of consumer expectations

Other Economic Indices

There are many other indices that can provide hints as to what is going on in the economy. One of these is **Personal Income**, which is an unadjusted number that reflects income (e.g., wages, salary, fringe benefits, profit, rent, royalties, etc.) plus "transfer payments" such as veterans' benefits, social security payments (minus social security taxes paid), unemployment compensation, and welfare payments. It is a cumulative number for the nation rather than an individual amount.

Employment Data includes the unemployment rate, changes in the number of people employed, the average workweek, and factory overtime. These numbers give an idea of how well companies can meet demand without extra hours being worked by employees, and indicate how close to capacity an industry may be operating.

The **Index of Consumer Sentiment** is maintained by the University of Michigan. It attempts to measure how the public feels about the economy. Consumer sentiment is of paramount importance because if enough people believe a recession is coming, they will curtail spending and otherwise act in a manner that will tend to bring about a recession. Typically, when there is high inflation, consumer sentiment is negative about the economy, and conversely when inflation is low.

There are a number of measures of **Consumer Demand** but three tend to get the most attention: (1) new vehicle sales; (2) consumer credit; and (3) housing starts. These measures can provide valuable evidence how people feel about the future of the economy. People who are afraid they will soon lose their jobs will not buy a home, new car, or take on additional debt. Conversely, if current consumer sentiment is one of feeling secure in their jobs, they will be more inclined to do these things. Two other measures of consumer demand also are mentioned frequently in the press. These are the level of home sales and retail sales.

Industrial Production is a measure of changes in the output of a number of industries including manufacturing, mining, and utilities. **Capacity Utilization** measures the extent to which the total production capacity of businesses is being employed. The **Purchasing Managers' Index** measures the amount of purchasing currently being undertaken by purchasing managers of large corporations. A baseline of 50 is used. If the index is higher, there is expanding activity; if lower, business activity is contracting.

Labor Productivity and Unit Labor Costs is a measure of the efficiency of the work force. This is a very important measure to follow, as it is critical that productivity increase if personal income is to increase. The **Producer Price Index**, previously known as the Wholesale Price Index, is a measure of changes in prices charged to wholesale customers by the producers of products.

Gross Domestic Product (GDP)

For those who took economics many years ago, GDP has replaced Gross National Product (GNP) as the measure of national production. Where GNP measured all levels of production and earnings of all Americans and American-owned enterprises wherever they were, **GDP** measures the final output of goods and services produced in the U.S. regardless of who produced it. Likewise, measuring only the final output rather than output at all levels eliminated multiple counting. For example, the farmer produces wheat that is sold to a miller to produce flour, which in turn is sold to a baker to produce bread, which in turn is sold to a retailer to sell to consumers. The cost of the wheat, milling, and baking are all included in the final price of the loaf of bread as a measurable unit.

GDP is the most commonly used single measure of the economy. It indicates if the economy grew, contracted, or was stagnant during the reporting period. It is not a predictor of events but rather a reporter of events. There are a number of adjusted versions of the GDP. The most commonly used is the Constant-Dollar GDP, a.k.a. real GDP. This takes out fluctuating prices so that relative changes can be more easily evaluated, with a base year of 1992 currently being used. Some reports use a Seasonally-Adjusted Annual Rate. This attempts to remove the bumps in the road, such as the 4th quarter holiday season retail sales bump, to give a more realistic view of the year as a whole.

MONETARY POLICY

The U.S. Government uses two general methods to influence the performance of the economy. One of these methods, which we will discuss later in this chapter, is known as fiscal policy involving the use of governmental taxation and spending and conducted primarily by Congress. The other general method, conducted by the Federal Open Market Committee (the FOMC) of the Federal Reserve System (the Fed), is known as monetary policy and is conducted mainly by raising and lowering short-term interest rates to affect consumer spending.

Established in 1913 as the country's central bank, the Fed consists of seven members of its Board of Governors located in Washington, D.C. and twelve Federal Reserve District Banks. The Fed, while accountable to Congress and subject to government audit and review, is independent of congressional appropriations and administrative control. It is, by design, intended to be independent of congressional and executive branch political pressure. It provides Congress with regular reports on its activities and finances and the executive branch with information about its economic programs. The Fed's FOMC meets eight times per year in Washington to make decisions on monetary policy.

The two basic goals of monetary policy, as prescribed by law, are (1) to promote "maximum" output and employment, and (2) to promote "stable" prices. With regard to the first goal, the Fed's actions can impact the level of output and employment only in the short-term. For instance, when a contraction of demand has moved the economy toward recession, the Fed may lower interest rates to stimulate consumer spending. Long-term levels of output and employment are influenced to a greater degree by technology, consumers' willingness to save and incur risk, and by other factors. So while the Fed cannot affect these long-run levels, it can help to smooth out the peaks and valleys that can be disruptive to the economy.

NEED TO KNOW: HOW THE FED REMAINS INDEPENDENT

Certain checks and balances have been created to help to maintain the Fed's independence, including the following:

1. Appointment of the seven Fed governors for 14-year staggered terms by the President with confirmation by the Senate. The length of a governor's term and the fact that the terms are staggered prevents any one president from appointing a significant number of Governors.

2. Appointment of the twelve Reserve Bank presidents for 5-year terms by their respective Board of Directors, subject to the final approval of the Board of Governors.

3. Reserve Board directors are not political appointees, but rather are chosen to represent a broad cross section of regional interests (e.g., depository institutions, nonfinancial businesses, labor, and the public).

4. Financially self-sustaining by meeting its operating expenses primarily from its portfolio of securities and not from congressional appropriations.

If the Fed were to attempt to stimulate the economy continuously, rather than just during periods of recession, such an attempt would strain capacity limitations and increase the level of inflation without providing the desirable effects of lower unemployment or higher long-run output. When inflation is at a high level, its variability increases correspondingly, which has the negative effect of increasing uncertainty and thereby hindering economic growth. As a result, long-term interest rates take on a risk premium, and the ability of businesses and households to plan and contract—so essential for capital formation—becomes more complicated. Moreover, as a result of inflation being indexed in the income taxation system, high inflation has the insidious effect of distorting economic decision making. Rather than engaging in productive activities, consumers spend their time and resources trying to hedge against inflation.

By keeping inflation at a very low level, the Fed accomplishes its second goal of stabilizing long-term prices. When inflation is maintained at relatively low levels over a sustained period, economic decision making tends to minimize the impact of inflation. However, there are times when the Fed's two goals of maximizing output and employment and stabilizing long-term prices are at odds from a priority standpoint. As a result, the Fed walks a tightrope between short-term price stabilization and long-term maintenance of low inflation levels. In addition, even though the Fed is independent within the government, it is still subject to political pressure from those seeking short-run results rather than being concerned with the longer-run health of the economy.

The Fed's Tool Chest

The actions of the Fed work in an indirect, rather than direct, manner through the market for bank reserves (the federal funds market, explained later) by raising or lowering short-term interest rates. Banks and other depository institutions (herein referred to as "banks") are required by law to keep a minimum amount of funds, known as **reserves**, either as cash in their vaults or as deposits with the Fed. Currently, banks are required to hold between 3 percent and 10 percent of the funds they have in interest-bearing and non-interest-bearing checking accounts as reserves. It is rare that the Fed changes reserve requirements as a monetary policy tool.

Because the amount of reserves a bank needs to maintain fluctuates with its deposits and daily transactions, a bank may need to borrow additional funds on a short-term basis from other banks that happen to hold more than the minimum required reserves. Such short-term borrowing (often overnight) is transacted in a private financial market known as the **federal funds market**. The interest rate on these loans is referred to as the **federal funds rate**, or simply the **funds rate**; this rate fluctuates in response to the levels of supply and demand for reserves. For instance, if the amount of reserves made available to the federal funds market increases, the funds rate will decline. Conversely, a decrease in the supply of reserves will cause the funds rate to increase.

Having discussed the bank reserve requirement, the federal funds market, and the federal funds rate, let us turn now to an explanation of the major tool used by the Fed to impact the supply of reserves in the banking system, **open market operations**. The Fed conducts open market operations by buying and selling government securities on the open market through the Federal Reserve Bank of New York. To lower the funds rate the Fed would, for instance, purchase government securities from a bank. Rather than transferring cash to pay for the securities, the Fed simply increases the bank's reserves, thereby providing the bank with reserves in excess of its minimum requirement. This permits the bank to make those excess reserves available to other banks that may need additional reserves. The net effect of the Fed's purchase of securities is to increase the aggregate supply of reserves and to lower the federal funds rate. It should be apparent that the Fed can *increase* the funds rate by *selling* government securities to decrease the supply of reserves in the banking system.

NEED TO KNOW: REGIONAL CONDITIONS

Many times the national economy is quite healthy while certain states or regions of the country are in recession. Why can't the Fed target such areas for economic stimulation? The problem is that the Fed works through nationally linked credit markets so its actions are broadcast throughout the economy. Clearly, some states or regions may need economic stimulus more than others but the Fed has no effective way to direct its efforts to any particular area of the country. Also, if the Fed were to apply its tools every time a state was in recession, it would be providing stimulus on a continuous basis resulting in overstimulation of other areas of the country. Of course, when the Fed assesses the current economic health of the country, it takes into account regional economic conditions.

Banks, instead of borrowing from other banks, may also borrow from one of the twelve Federal Reserve Banks at what is referred to as their "discount windows." The rate charged on such borrowings is called the **discount rate**. While this rate is set by the boards of directors of the Federal Reserve Banks, it is subject to the approval of the Fed's Board of Governors. This type of borrowing, discouraged by the Fed, is minimal. The main effect of changes in the discount rate is to telegraph either a more restrictive or more expansionary future policy. As a result, discount rate changes tend to be made at the same time as funds rate changes.

Interest Rates

By raising and lowering interest rates, the Fed is attempting to influence consumers' demand for goods and services. However, what really stimulates demand is **real interest rates**, not published market interest rates (so-called **nominal rates**), such as the **prime rate** (commercial loan rate quoted by some major banks, which is not always the lowest rate). Real interest rates are defined as nominal interest rates minus the expected rate of inflation. Clearly, wide swings in the expected inflation rate can have a significant effect on the choice of monetary policy. For example, in 1978 the nominal funds rate averaged 8 percent, but the inflation rate was 9 percent. So, even though nominal interest rates were high, monetary policy still stimulated demand with a negative real funds rate of minus 1 percent. By contrast, in early 1999, the nominal funds rate was 4.75 percent, and the inflation rate was approximately 2 percent. The result was a positive 2.75 percent real funds rate. Accordingly, the nominal funds rate of 8 percent in 1978 was more stimulative than the 4.75 percent nominal funds rate in early 1999.

Changes in real interest rates bring about corresponding changes in borrowing costs, the availability of bank loans, and household wealth, which in turn affects the level of demand for goods and services. Lower borrowing costs result in increased business investment and personal spending on big-ticket items, such as autos and homes. Also, lower real rates may encourage banks to increase their lending to businesses and households (resulting in greater spending) and stimulate the stock market by making common stocks and similar investments more attractive than bonds and other debt instruments (thus increasing household wealth and willingness to spend).

Another favorable effect of lower real interest rates is the resulting reduction in the value of the U.S. dollar in the international market. A lower value for the U.S. dollar enables the U.S. to sell overseas more competitively but increases the cost of foreign imports, bringing about higher aggregate spending on U.S.-produced goods and services.

The Impact of Monetary Policy

By increasing aggregate demand for goods and services, firms are encouraged to increase production and employment and to spend more on capital goods. The resulting increased level of economic output leads to higher income and, in turn, to higher consumption.

However, there is a lag of between three months and two years from the Fed's monetary policy actions and the resulting effect on the economy. Inflation is a bit more stubborn, and Fed actions may take one to three years to have their desired effect in this area. So much of the effectiveness of a Fed action is dependent on how it is perceived by consumers. For instance, if people believe that a tightening of policy reflects the Fed's determination to control inflation, they will act accordingly in ways that help support the Fed's intention. On the other hand, if consumers are doubtful of the Fed's resolve to control inflation, they will act in a manner that feeds the current inflation. This long and variable lead time for policies to take effect is one of two main factors that make the Fed's job more difficult in stabilizing output in the short run and promoting price stability in the long run. If these lags were very short and predictable, the Fed could take an action, observe the result soon thereafter, and then adjust as necessary to accomplish its goals for the economy. Unfortunately, the Fed is not in the position to wait for inflation to actually occur and then take action. By then it is too late. Therefore, it must project the effect of its actions sometimes well into the future and make adjustments long before inflation rears its ugly head.

The second issue is the effect of factors other than monetary policy on the economy, such as fiscal policy (discussed later in this chapter); the availability and price of key natural resources, such as oil; economic developments in the world economy (outside the U.S.); financial conditions at home and overseas; and the introduction of new technologies. The Fed must consider all of these factors and design its actions to either reinforce or offset them. This is not an easy task as the timing and size of these factors is difficult to estimate. For instance, new technologies can substantially improve worker and capital productivity. In fact, this may have occurred in the 1990s, but the Fed needs to confirm that such productivity advances are permanent, rather than temporary.

It should be clear that the Fed cannot predict the timing and effectiveness of its actions on the economy. It attempts to fine-tune its crystal ball by examining the indicators of future output, employment, and inflation. These indicators include the money supply, real interest rates, the unemployment rate, nominal and real GDP growth, commodity prices, exchange rates, various interest rate spreads, and inflation expectation surveys. While the Fed has sophisticated economic forecasting models available to it, policymakers must apply human judgment after discussion and debate.

Example: The Asian Currency Crisis

The 1997-98 currency crisis in East Asia is a good example. Over this period, economic activity in several countries in that region either slowed or declined, and this reduced their demand for U.S. products. In addition, the foreign exchange value of most of their currencies depreciated, and this made Asian-produced goods less expensive for us to buy and U.S.-produced goods more expensive in Asian countries. By themselves, these factors would reduce the demand for U.S. products and therefore lower our output and employment. As a result, this is a factor that the Fed has had to consider in setting monetary policy.

FISCAL POLICY

As mentioned earlier, fiscal policy is the use of government spending and taxation by Congress to influence the health of the economy. In the 1800s and early 1900s, economics paid homage to **Say's Law**, which held that supply creates its own demand. Under this theory, recession and depression and their resulting unemployment were viewed as temporary, self-correcting events. It was assumed that prices and wage rates were totally flexible and that they would adjust until unsold goods were sold and the available work force was hired. Say's Law was the law of supply and demand taken to the extreme, as it shunned governmental interference in the corrective process. The approach was known as *laissez faire*—letting market forces prevail. Say's Law was doing fine until 1929 when the Great Depression began, reaching its trough in 1933. This devastating depression did not behave as Say's Law would have predicted and, as a result, economists went back to the drawing board.

President Franklin D. Roosevelt was convinced that the panacea for the Depression was to inject the economy with massive amounts of money by **priming the pump**, involving heavy government spending and hiring. This action was expected to increase demand and stimulate a recovery. President Roosevelt established enormous public works programs (such as the Works Progress Administration, the Tennessee Valley Authority, and the Civilian Conservation Corps) and paid for them by incurring huge federal budget deficits. The president was following the thinking of English economist **John Maynard Keynes** who, in 1936, abandoned the basic tenets of Say's Law by theorizing that it was possible that there could be chronically insufficient demand, unused productive capacity, and unemployment. Keynes knew his economics too well to accept the premise of Say's Law that wage and price cuts would triumph over the economy. He concluded that demand must be stimulated through government spending even if it was necessary to run deficits. Keynes introduced the concept of a **multiplier effect**, which is caused by the millions of civic works employees spending their earnings on privately produced goods and services to increase aggregate demand and return the country to full employment. Keynesian theory was later referred to as **demand-side economics**.

Later economists added to Keynesian economic theory by suggesting that a tax cut could have the same effect on aggregate demand as increasing government spending. This combination of government taxation and spending adjustments is known as **fiscal policy**, and it is used not only to stimulate demand but also to control inflation. It is important to understand the difference between monetary policy (the actions of the Federal Reserve System, discussed earlier) and fiscal policy (the actions of the federal government). Monetary policy works through its effect on the banking system, the money supply, bank lending, and interest rates, while fiscal policy works through its direct impact on aggregate demand and inflation.

As discussed earlier, during World War II, the United States government spent huge amounts of money on defense, including the hiring of thousands of people to produce war materials. But unlike the Great Depression when civic works employees spent their earnings to stimulate the economy, there were huge shortages of goods available for purchase resulting in unsatisfied demand and corresponding inflation during World War II. In response, the government resorted to rationing of goods to try to stabilize prices and the existence of a black market served to reduce inflationary pressures.

In the 1970s, a new school of economics developed known as **supply-side economics**. This school of thought supported the concept of increasing the economy's ability to supply or produce more goods, rather than stimulating demand. This was to be accomplished by simultaneously reducing federal income taxes and federal spending to eliminate deficits. President Reagan was one of the strongest supporters of this approach as he advocated tax reductions to encourage greater output of goods. By more nearly balancing the supply and demand of goods, it was believed that inflation could be kept in check. Similarly, tax reductions would increase disposable income, resulting in greater savings, which would provide funding for investment. Some have characterized supply-side economics as "smaller government."

In summary, fiscal policy can be used to stimulate the economy and create jobs by increasing government spending and reducing taxes. Conversely, taxes are raised and/or government spending is reduced in order to cool off the economy. Unlike monetary policy, fiscal policy can be directed at specific sectors of the economy, such as home ownership (by permitting tax deductions for home mortgage interest and real estate taxes). Similarly, charities are supported through tax deductions for charitable contributions. In the 2001 Tax Act, tax benefits were expanded in the areas of retirement savings and education funding.

ROLE OF FINANCIAL INSTITUTIONS AND FINANCIAL INTERMEDIARIES

Financial intermediaries are financial institutions functioning as middlemen in the daily operation of our economy. Specifically, financial intermediaries transfer funds from ultimate lenders (i.e., financial institutions) to ultimate borrowers (e.g., consumers). They do this by borrowing, in effect, "from Peter to pay Paul." Financial intermediaries acquire funds by issuing their own debt obligations to the public (e.g., savings accounts and certificates of deposit) and then turn around and use this money to buy securities (e.g., stocks, bonds, and mortgages) for themselves.

These institutions give people options beyond hiding their money in coffee cans or stuffing it under mattresses. Savers can invest in savings accounts and CDs, or another financial asset with comparable (or greater) security than a mattress, and still earn some interest income. Such savings are magnified throughout the economy by what is referred to as the money multiplier effect. Similarly, the institutions with whom they invest may sell their securities to other financial intermediaries rather than to the original saver. In addition, the saver/investor always has the option of purchasing corporate stocks or bonds if his or her risk tolerance level will accommodate this type of purchase.

The role of financial intermediaries is critical in our economy, in part because competition among them for the investor's dollar forces lending interest rates lower. Financial institutions in their roles as intermediaries are also in a better position than individuals to diversify their portfolios and spread the risk of security ownership. They are expert in evaluating borrower characteristics and can take advantage of economies of scale in the large-scale buying and selling of securities.

Since financial intermediation tends to drive down interest rates, or at least to temper any increase, it has been highly beneficial to our rate of growth. A high rate of economic growth requires a large volume of consumer investment. The lower the rate of interest the ultimate borrower must pay, the greater the potential investment.

Commercial Banks

The most common financial institutions are **commercial banks**. There are probably in excess of 10,000 of these institutions, ranging in size from the gargantuan Bank of America, JP Morgan Chase, and Citibank to the thousands of small community banks scattered throughout the country. Their major source of funds continues to be demand deposits (checking accounts) as well as money market accounts and time deposits. Commercial banks have either a federal or state charter to conduct their business. If they have a federal or national charter, the bank is subject to the authority of the Comptroller of the Currency, the Federal Reserve, and the Federal Deposit Insurance Corporation (FDIC). A state-chartered bank is subject to the regulatory authority of the particular state in which it is located, the Federal Reserve, and the FDIC.

Savings and Loan Associations

In recent years, the importance of **savings and loan associations** in our economy has been diminished. Probably, this is because of the savings and loan financial scandals of the 1980s. Traditionally, they have acquired almost all their funds through time deposits that are then used to make mortgage loans thereby encouraging home ownership. Like banks, savings and loan associations may be federally or state chartered, and are now regulated by a branch of the FDIC (the successor to the Federal Savings and Loan Insurance Corporation [FSLIC]) and the Federal Home Loan Bank Board.

Insurance Companies

Life Insurance Companies have historically ranked third in size to banks and savings and loan associations. They insure people against the financial consequences of death and, because of their need for immediate liquidity, invest their funds very conservatively. This is changing, however, as the newer types of variable life (VL) and variable universal life (VUL) policies are implemented with assets that are invested more aggressively. Life insurance companies are regulated directly by the state insurance department of the state in which they offer policies.

Property and Casualty Insurance Companies insure homeowners against theft and fire, automobile owners against liability, collision, and theft, and businesses against negligence, property loss, and other types of financial risks. Essentially, they are regulated in the same manner as life insurance companies.

Mutual Funds

There are many different types of mutual funds. These funds pool the funds of many people of moderate assets, and then invest the money in a wide variety of securities, as outlined in their prospectuses, thereby attaining important diversification of risk. Mutual funds are the investment of choice for many middle class individuals, since they permit participation in the stock market without the risk of direct ownership. The funds are regulated by the U.S. Securities and Exchange Commission (SEC).

Broker/Dealer Firms and Investment Bankers

Brokerage firms, or brokerage houses, act as agents in executing orders to buy and sell securities on the various stock exchanges, most notably the New York Stock Exchange (NYSE). Merrill Lynch is an example of a brokerage firm that participates in the sale of securities in what is known as the secondary market (i.e., markets that trade existing, already outstanding securities.) Brokerage firms often serve both in a broker capacity (executing securities transactions for the accounts of their customers) and as dealers (where they trade for their own account, hoping to realize a profit). The SEC, as well as the individual exchanges, regulate brokerage firms and their registered representatives through the National Association of Securities Dealers (NASD).

Other securities professionals include **investment bankers** who operate similarly to the brokerage houses, except that they deal in the primary securities market. The primary market refers to the sale and distribution of securities when they are originally issued by the money-raising corporation or governmental unit. These are the individuals who offer or "float" so-called **IPOs (initial public offerings)** of securities.

Credit Unions

Credit unions are a rapidly growing form of financial institution and perform much the same function as banks and savings and loan associations. They are organized as cooperatives for individuals with some form of common interest. For example, employees of a large business, such as AT&T, may charter a credit union. Credit union members buy shares, which are the same as deposits, and this makes them eligible to borrow from the credit union. They may be federally or state-chartered, with the former regulated by the National Credit Union Administration (NCUA) and the latter by the state in which they operate.

Federal Deposit Insurance Corporation (FDIC) Coverage

The FDIC provides insurance for depositors who have accounts in commercial banks and other FDIC-covered institutions. The basic insurance amount for each depositor is $100,000 per institution. This amount has not been adjusted since 1980. All types of deposits received by a financial institution in its usual course of business are insured (e.g., savings deposits, checking deposits, deposits in NOW accounts, Christmas Club accounts, and time deposits [including certificates of deposit, or CDs]). Cashiers' checks, officers' checks, loan disbursement checks, outstanding drafts, negotiable instruments, and money orders drawn on the institution also are insured.

FDIC coverage is not, however, determined on a per-account basis, but rather on a per-institution basis. This means that all accounts of the same depositor in the same institution are aggregated to determine the amount of insurance coverage for that depositor. Therefore, one cannot increase the amount of FDIC insurance coverage by dividing funds among different accounts of the same type in the same institution. However, if the same depositor opens accounts in different institutions, the depositor receives up to $100,000 of FDIC coverage at each institution.

Deposits maintained in different categories of legal ownership within the same institution are separately insured. As a result, a depositor can have more than $100,000 insurance coverage in a single institution. For example, one can increase the amount of FDIC insurance to the allowable limit by titling assets in joint ownership, as well as single (or individual) ownership. A depositor cannot increase FDIC insurance by dividing funds owned in the same ownership category among different accounts. The type of account (e.g., checking, savings, or CD) has no bearing on the amount of insurance coverage.

In addition, separate ownership and insurance coverage is available for retirement plans held with a bank as trustee, such as an IRA, Keogh, or pension or profit-sharing plan. Testamentary or "payable on death" (P.O.D.) accounts are also covered. Each person's interest in a joint ownership account is assumed to be equal, unless bank records indicate otherwise. So if Tom and Mary have a joint checking account with a balance of $20,000, each is insured for only $10,000 of coverage for that account. The following example may help to clarify the amount of FDIC coverage in a specific situation:

> Assume a client has $50,000 in a joint checking account, $50,000 in an IRA, and $50,000 in a CD in her name alone. Because the FDIC views these accounts as three different categories of accounts, the client has $125,000 of total insurance coverage (remember that only half of the $50,000 joint checking account is insured for her). If instead she had two CD accounts in her name alone with a total balance of $150,000, her coverage would be limited to just $100,000 (because she has only one category of account).

In recent years, and with the continuing trend of financial services deregulation, a number of nontraditional deposit products or investments have been offered by FDIC-covered institutions. Unlike traditional investment products such as savings and time deposits, these non-deposit investment products are not insured. Examples of uninsured investment products include:

- Annuities
- Mutual funds
- Stocks
- Bonds
- Municipal securities
- U.S. Treasury securities (Treasury bills, notes, and bonds)

Starting July 1, 1998, FDIC insurance covers the account of a deceased deposit owner for six months after the owner's death just as if the owner were still alive. This is particularly beneficial to the surviving owner of an account held as joint tenancy with right of survivorship where the survivor has other solely owned accounts at the same institution.

The financial planner needs to verify that his or her clients have been informed about the distinction between FDIC-insured and uninsured investments.

The Glass-Steagall Act

The Banking Act of 1933, popularly known as the Glass-Steagall Act, separated commercial banking and investment banking. This prohibited commercial banks from becoming involved in new offerings of corporate stocks or bonds. As a result, commercial banks lost a considerable source of funding for their operations, leading to numerous calls for and attempts to repeal such prohibitions. In the late 1990s, these calls for reform succeeded, and the Act was repealed. However, many of the vestiges of the Act remain and there are still questions as commercial banks move into this new arena. Nevertheless, repeal of the Act has contributed to the wave of financial services deregulation that has been taking place in recent years. Financial planners looking to offer and implement investment products to their clients can only stand to benefit from this atmosphere.

IMPORTANT CONCEPTS TO REMEMBER

Phases of the business cycle

Forces internal to the economic system that drive the business cycle

Recession

Depression

Inflation

Consumer Price Index

Composite index of leading economic indicators

Other economic indices

Gross Domestic Product

Monetary policy

Fiscal policy

Role of financial institutions and financial intermediaries

Federal Deposit Insurance Corporation (FDIC) Coverage

Glass-Steagall Act

QUESTIONS FOR REVIEW

1. What are the various phases of the business cycle and what are the dynamics during each phase?

2. What are the forces internal to the economic system that drive the business cycle?

3. What is the most commonly understood definition of a recession and how does that definition differ from the one offered by The National Bureau of Economic Research?

4. How does a depression differ from a recession?

5. How does demand for goods and services create inflation?

6. What are the items that make up the "market basket" of goods and services included in the Consumer Price Index?

7. What are the items that comprise The Conference Board's composite index of leading economic indicators and how is this index used to affect the economy?

8. What is the Gross Domestic Product and how is it used to determine the status of the economy?

9. How does monetary policy differ from fiscal policy as tools to affect the economy and inflation?

10. What are open market operations and how do they differ from adjusting the Fed's discount rate in terms of their effect on the economy?

11. What role is played by financial institutions and financial intermediaries in the daily operation of the U.S. economy?

12. How does a depositor determine the amount of FDIC coverage available to him or her on various types of accounts maintained with commercial banks and other FDIC-covered institutions?

13. What effect, if any, has the repeal of the Glass-Steagall Act of 1933 had on financial services organizations?

SUGGESTIONS FOR ADDITIONAL READING

The Irwin Guide to Using The Wall Street Journal, 6th edition, by Michael B. Lehmann, McGraw-Hill, a division of the McGraw-Hill Companies, 2000.

The Federal Reserve System: Purposes and Functions, Board of Governors of the Federal Reserve System, 1994.

CHAPTER TEN

Introduction to The Time Value of Money

• • •

Money has time value—that is to say, its value changes with the passage of time. A dollar today is worth more than a dollar to be received in the future because today's dollar can be invested to earn interest thereby increasing the owner's wealth. In an inflationary environment (which has been the state of the economy certainly since the end of World War II), the "real" value of the dollar declines over time. Conversely, since a future dollar is worth less today, why would an investor ever trade the present dollar for one to be received in the future? Primarily, this occurs because individuals hope to have more future dollars by deferring use of their current dollars. Of course, individuals will do this only if future growth in their dollars is possible; in other words, if they can compound their money. This chapter examines the concept of compounding as well as its counterpart in converting from future value back to present value, a process known as discounting.

For a financial planner, the **time value of money (TVM)** is one of the most critical concepts to master. Success on the certification examinations for various personal financial planning designations is dependent upon a good working knowledge of time value of money concepts and the ability to apply those concepts in performing calculations using a financial function calculator. In this chapter, the reader will learn the basic TVM calculations, such as present value and future value of a sum of money, as well as ordinary annuity calculations in which payments are received or made at the end of each period over an assumed number of time periods and annuity due calculations where payments are received or made at the beginning of each period. At the end of this chapter, the reader should know what the foregoing concepts involve and understand when and how to apply them. In Chapter 11, we will explore some more advanced concepts of the time value of money.

In order for the reader to understand and apply the concepts discussed in this chapter, he or she must have access to a financial function calculator. The discussions of calculator keystrokes will be based on the Hewlett Packard Model 10BII calculator. Other calculators may be used but the reader will need to determine the correct keystrokes for calculators other than the HP 10BII. The reader should strive to understand the reasoning behind the calculations and the process of using the calculator, rather than simply memorizing sets of keystrokes.

The objectives of this chapter are:

- Explain common elements involved in solving time value of money problems.
- Use a financial function calculator to solve time value of money problems.
- Calculate sample future value applications.
- Calculate sample present value applications.
- Calculate sample ordinary annuity and annuity due applications.

TIME VALUE OF MONEY BASICS

The principal advantage of using time value of money (TVM) concepts is that it permits a comparison of sums of money at different points in time so that an investor can make reasonable decisions about receiving, disbursing, or investing money. In most time value of money calculations, three given variables will be used to calculate a fourth unknown variable. It is possible to solve TVM problems by using a calculator with exponential functions, TVM tables, a computer programmed to do so, or a financial function calculator. Without any question, the latter method is the easiest and the one that will be employed in this text.

Future Value of a Single Sum

Probably the easiest TVM concept to understand is that of the future value (FV) of a single sum. What is meant by a "single sum"? It refers to a lump-sum either paid or received at a specific point in time. The FV of a single sum is that amount of money to which a present sum will accumulate when compounded for a given number of periods and at a given interest rate. In the first period, the single sum earns interest, which is added to the original sum; in subsequent periods, interest is earned not only on the original sum but also on the interest earned in each of the previous compounding periods. This process of interest being earned on increasing sums over time is known as **compounding**.

For example, if $100 is deposited in a savings account at the beginning of a particular year, and this account pays an interest rate of 10 percent annually, how much will the investor have in the account at the end of that same year? The answer is $110 — the original $100 plus $10 of interest earned. This simple calculation may be expressed arithmetically (see Appendix C), but suffice it to say that the 10 percent interest rate is multiplied by the principal of $100 and the product is added to the original principal with the total as the correct answer. This is pretty straightforward.

Now, however, what happens at the end of the second year, presuming this same 10 percent interest payment? The answer is now $121 or, again, the interest rate of 10 percent multiplied by the new principal amount of $110 and the product added to the previous principal amount. The $1 in excess of the $10 interest on the original principal of $100 further illustrates the principle of compounding. By continuing with these calculations, it is possible to determine the amount that will be in the account at the end of a considerable number of years, but it will obviously take some time and work. Fortunately, there is a much easier way to determine how much money will be in the account after a specified number of years. This can be determined by using a financial function or business calculator to compute the amount. Through the inputting of variables for N (the number of years), I/YR (the annual interest rate), and PV (the original principal or present value), we can determine the amount that will have accrued at a set future date, or FV (future value). (Note: When using a financial function calculator, such as the HP 10BII, it is important to enter cash outflows (payments or investments) as a *negative number*. Cash inflows are treated as positive amounts.)

In our example, $100 (the PV or beginning value) will grow at 10 percent interest per year (I/YR) after 20 years (N) to $672.75 (the FV or ending value). This amount is derived easily with the use of the recommended HP 10BII calculator by inputting the given numbers for PV, N, and I/YR on the appropriate keys and solving for FV. But before you perform the calculation, be sure to set the calculator for one payment per period (1 P/YR) by entering 1, Shift (colored key directly above the C/C All key), P/YR (second key from the right in the top row of keys). (Note: The reader is responsible for reading the owner's manual for the financial function calculator used to identify variations in keystrokes from those shown for the HP 10BII). Be sure to enter the PV of $100 as a negative number or cash outflow (or investment) in order to obtain a positive answer of $672.75. Also, the annual interest rate (10 percent in this example) is referred to as the compound rate in these types of problems.

Another view that shows the importance of understanding present value versus future value is contained in the following example:

> Assume that you received a 5-year certificate of deposit (CD) that was purchased for $1,000. The certificate paid an interest rate of 6.8 percent per year and you want to know what it will be worth tomorrow, when it matures at the end of its five-year term.

Since the beginning deposit was $1,000, that is entered as the PV, or present value, as a negative number. (In this case, it is very important to remember that the PV on the calculator has nothing to do with the present day. It is simply the beginning value). N is equal to five, the term of the CD, and I/YR is 6.8. After you have entered these three values, press FV to calculate the future value (also called the ending value). If you entered all the values correctly, you will discover that the CD will be worth $1,389.49 tomorrow, at its maturity.

Present Value of a Single Sum

The preceding section considered the question of how much a single sum is worth, when compounded over time. Now consider the reverse. What is the value today of a single sum that will be received in the future when discounted for a given number of periods and at a given interest rate? It should be intuitive that the $672.75 to be received 20 years from now, in our first example, using a 10 percent annual reduction factor is equal to $100 today. This annual reduction factor is referred to by the term **annual discount rate** in the time value of money process. Discounting determines the worth of money to be received in the future in terms of its current or present value.

As with the compounding (or future value) process, the present value of a dollar depends on:

1. the length of time before it will be received, and
2. the annual (or some other time period) interest rate

The further into the future the dollar will be received, and/or the higher the interest (or discount) rate, the lower the present value of the dollar. For example, a dollar to be received after 20 years is worth considerably less than one to be received after five years when both are discounted at the same rate. To prove this, compute the present value of the $672.75 future value from the previous problem using an N of 5 rather than 20 at the discount rate (I/YR) of 10 percent. You should get an answer of $417.72. Since we know from the previous problem that $672.75 when discounted for 20 years at 10 percent is equal to $100, we have just proven the accuracy of the second statement in this paragraph.

Remember, while a financial function calculator eases the arithmetic computation, one still must first determine whether the problem concerns a future or present value. It is here that a thorough understanding of the compounding and discounting concepts is critical.

The Future Value of an Annuity

In our earlier discussion, we presented the present value and future value of a single sum. Of course, as an individual identifies a financial goal, many times the implementation of a systematic savings program is necessary to meet this goal. Examples of financial goals that typically require the investment of monthly or annual payments are the funding of a college education for a child or saving for one's own retirement. If these payments are equal and regular, the series of payments is called an **annuity**. (Note: The use of the term annuity for time value of money purposes should be distinguished from the commercially available insurance product of the same name). The accumulation of funds to meet a financial goal is then referred to as the **future sum of an annuity**. If each payment is made at the *beginning* of each period, as is the case with insurance policy premiums or lease payments, the series is called an **annuity due**. If the payments are made at the *end* of each period, as is the case with mortgage loan payments or auto loan payments, the series is known as an **ordinary annuity**.

Example: Remember the individual from our earlier example who deposited $100 in a savings account that pays 10 percent annual interest. Let us now assume that he deposits not only the initial $100 but an additional $100 per year for the next two years. If he deposits these amounts at the beginning of each year, how much will he have at the end of the three-year period? How much will he have at the end of the same period if he deposits these amounts at the end of each year? In the first case, the answer is $364.10, which is calculated on the HP 10BII by setting the calculator to the BEGIN mode and then inputting +/– 100 in the PMT key, 10 I/YR, 3 N, and then solving for FV. In the next case (that of the ordinary annuity), the FV is $331.00. To derive this amount, use the same keystrokes as in the annuity due case, but set the calculator to the END mode.

The difference between the ending values of the two types of annuity payments will be quite substantial as the number of periods increases and/or the interest rate rises. Consider a savings account where the individual deposits $1,800 annually for 25 years at 8 percent annual interest. If the deposits are made at the end of each year (an ordinary annuity), the ending amount is $131,590.69. If these deposits are made at the beginning of each year (an annuity due), the ending amount is $142,117.95, a difference of $10,527.26. Now, use the same savings amounts over the same period of time, but increase the annual interest rate to 12 percent. The future sum of the ordinary annuity is now $240,000.97, while the annuity due sum is $268,801.08, a difference of $28,800.11.

Accordingly, there are two points to be made here:

1. We have just demonstrated that the larger the number of time periods and the higher the interest rate per period (or rate of return), the greater the sum that is accumulated in the future.
2. The sooner dollars are invested, the greater their accumulated value at the end of a specified period of time.

The Present Value of an Annuity

Just as with the future value and present value of a dollar analysis, it is often necessary to reverse the future value of an annuity calculation to that of the present value of an annuity. Oftentimes, a potential investor is not so much interested in a future value of his or her periodic payments but rather its present value. This is particularly true where the investor wants to compare several investment alternatives, such as whether to buy one bond over another.

If the annuity is an ordinary annuity, the present value of the future payments could be determined by obtaining the present value of each periodic payment and adding them together. However, this is a long and tedious process. Using the financial function calculator can simplify it.

Consider an example of an individual who wants to withdraw $10,000 annually from her savings account at the *end* of each year for the next ten years. She can earn 8 percent annually on these funds over this time period. Accordingly, use this rate as the applicable discount rate.

What is the present value of that future cash flow? Another way to ask it is: How much does she need in her savings account before she starts the withdrawals? The answer is $67,100.81. Using the HP 10BII, input +/− 10,000 as PMT, 8 I/YR, and 10 N. Then solve for PV.

Compare this amount to payments to be withdrawn at the *beginning* of each year, i.e., the present value of an annuity due. The keystrokes on the HP 10BII calculator are exactly the same, but you first place the calculator in the BEGIN mode. The answer is $72,468.88. Again, notice the difference in amount that time makes. By withdrawing these payments at the beginning of each year rather than at the end, our individual will need an additional $5,368.07 in his or her savings account.

As with the present value of a dollar, the present value of an annuity is related to the interest rate and the total period of time over which the annuity payments are made. The lower the interest rate and/or the longer the period of the annuity, the greater the present value of the annuity.

Application of Compounding and Discounting Concepts

All time value of money problems use the concepts of compounding and/or discounting, although there are variations on the theme (discussed later in this chapter). In answering time value problems, one must first determine whether the problem involves a lump sum or one-time payment, or a series of payments (i.e., an annuity). After that, one needs to ascertain if the problem concerns going from the present to the future (i.e., a future value computation) or from the future back to the present (a present value computation).

Consider the example of funding a college education. If the problem is asking you to compute the cost of this education using some presently known figure but over some time period in the future at a given rate of increase, you are being asked to compute the future value of a lump sum (or a dollar, in the earlier explanation). Conversely, if you want to calculate the amount of life insurance you would need to pay for the future cost of a child's college education if your client were to die tomorrow, you are being asked to compute a present value amount. Alternatively, if one is being asked to save for the estimated cost of an education at some time in the future (for example, beginning saving for a one-year-old child to attend college when he or she is age 18), one is being asked to compute an annuity amount.

In working time value of money problems, trust your intuition as to what the question is asking. You will usually be correct. Thinking about the kind of answer you are looking for will usually tell you what kind of calculation is needed. The important thing is to think the problem through. Once you understand the time value of money concepts, you will be able to look at your answer and know if it makes sense. You will not likely be able to know if it is exactly correct, but when you look at your answer, you should be able to tell if it is reasonable considering the facts.

Compounding and Payments Made Other Than Annually

All of the previous examples used annual interest rates and series of payments that were made only once per year. Of course, compounding can and does often occur more than once per year. For example, interest on a savings account may be paid monthly, or at a frequency of twelve times per year.

Fortunately, adjusting for these payments that are made other than annually is quite simple, particularly with the use of a financial function calculator. First, you must indicate to the calculator the number of payments there are each year. For example, if you have twelve payments per year, press: 12, SHIFT, P/YR. To determine the number of payments per year for which the calculator is set, press: SHIFT, C ALL, holding down the C ALL key for a moment while viewing the display. It will show the number of payments per year for which the calculator is set. With this done, when entering the annual interest rate, the calculator will automatically adjust the interest rate for compounding periods that are less than a year in length.

When it is necessary to enter the number of compounding periods, enter the number of years, press SHIFT and then the xP/YR key (same key as N). These keystrokes cause the calculator to multiply the number of years by the number of compounding periods per year to determine the total number of compounding periods. For example, if one is investing $100 at the beginning of each month for 15 years at 8 percent per year, the following keystrokes can be used:

- Set to BEGIN mode
- 12 SHIFT P/YR
- 100 +/– PMT
- 8 I/YR
- 15 SHIFT xP/YR
- Solve for FV

The correct answer is $34,834.51. When 15 SHIFT xP/YR was entered, the display showed 180, or 15×12, which is the total number of compounding periods. Use of this calculator function should emphasize the importance of clearing the calculator between calculations. Clearing the calculator is the way to find out for how many payments per year the calculator is set.

Inflation-Adjusted Rate of Return

In some cases, it is necessary to calculate a "real" rate of return, which is defined as the nominal rate of return adjusted for inflation. For example, if an investor can earn an 8 percent nominal return on his or her investments over the next year, and inflation is expected to be 2 percent over this same time period, what is the investor's real rate of return adjusted for inflation? While it would be intuitive to simply subtract the anticipated inflation rate of 2 percent from the nominal rate of return of 8 percent to arrive at an inflation-adjusted rate of return of 6 percent, mathematical theory requires a somewhat more complicated calculation.

The intuitive result of 6 percent is a good approximation of the correct answer, but to be precise, we need to use the following formula:

$$[(1 + r)/(1 + i) - 1] \times 100$$

Where r = the expected nominal rate of return on investments for a given period of time and i = the expected inflation rate over the same period of time.

Solving the above problem by substituting the 8 percent and 2 percent rates, we get the following:

$$= [(1 + .08)/(1 + .02) - 1] \times 100$$
$$= [1.08/1.02 - 1] \times 100$$
$$= [1.0588 - 1] \times 100$$
$$= .0588 \times 100$$
$$= 5.88 \text{ percent (a bit less than the intuitive 6 percent calculated previously)}$$

(See Appendix C for further discussion of the logic of the inflation-adjusted rate of return.)

The Rule of 72

There are times when a financial planner or investor is interested in knowing roughly how long it will take for a single sum to double in value or, alternatively, the interest rate required for an investment to double within a specific number of years. Rather than using the financial function calculator, a simple guideline can be employed to estimate these values. To calculate the number of years required for an investment to double in value, divide 72 by the annual interest rate. For example, if the objective is to double a $1,000 investment to $2,000 where the original investment is earning an annual compound rate of nine percent, it will take approximately eight years for this to happen (72 ÷ 9 = 8).

To calculate the interest rate required for an investment to double in value, divide 72 by the number of years. If, for example, an investor wants to double his original investment in ten years, it will require an approximate annual interest rate of 7.2 percent (72 ÷ 10 = 7.2).

VARIATIONS ON THE THEME

As noted, once the basics of present and future value concepts have been mastered, it is then possible to solve calculations that involve additional variations. This section of this chapter presents several of these variations that financial planners need to understand. The last of these variations (Examples 5–8) involve the consideration of inflation and an inflation-adjusted interest rate calculation. This is particularly useful when computing life insurance needs and when performing a retirement savings analysis. As before, all computations are done with the assistance of a financial function calculator—in this case, the HP 10BII. (Please consult the owner's manual for the calculator you are using if it is not the HP 10BII).

Remember, when performing time value of money calculations, ALWAYS clear the calculator's memory after each problem. On the HP 10BII, press the SHIFT key and C ALL key.

Examples

1. Number of Years for a Present Value to Grow to a Future Value

Description: The number of years it takes for a given sum to increase to another specified sum in the future.

Facts and Question: George has an IRA with a current balance of $4,000. How long will it take for this account to grow to $20,000 at a 12 percent annual rate of return?

Answer: 14.2 years

Keystrokes:

- 4000 +/– PV
- 20000 FV
- 12 I/YR
- Solve for N

2. Number of Years for Payments to Grow to a Future Value

Description: The number of years for payments to accumulate to a future value.

Facts and Question: The Barrons would like to accumulate $50,000 for a down payment on a new home. If they are able to save $500 at the end of each month and these funds earn 10 percent per year, how long will it take to accumulate the $50,000?

Answer: 6.09 years

Keystrokes:

- Set to END mode
- 12 SHIFT P/YR
- 50000 FV
- 500 +/– PMT
- 10 I/YR
- Solve for N to obtain the number of months required and then divide by 12 to convert from months to equivalent years.

3. Annuity Payments for a Future Sum, Ordinary Annuity

Description: The payment needed at the *end* of each of a series of periods to accumulate to a future value.

Facts and Question: Jack and Jane would like to save $10,000 for a down payment on a boat they would like to buy in three years. They think they can earn 14 percent on their savings.

How much will they need to save at the *end* of each year?

Answer: $2,907.31

Keystrokes:

- Set to END mode
- 1 SHIFT P/YR
- 10000 FV
- 14 I/YR
- 3 N
- Solve for PMT
- Note that the HP 10BII displays a negative number for the answer, since each year's savings amount is a cash outflow.

4. Annuity Payments for a Future Sum, Annuity Due

Description: The payment needed at the *beginning* of a period to accumulate to a future value.

Facts and Question: Joyce wants to add some money to the college education fund she has begun for her son. She wants to save an additional $40,000 over the next 10 years and believes she can earn 12 percent per year on her money. How much does she need to save at the *beginning* of each year to accumulate the $40,000?

Answer: $2,035.15

Keystrokes:

- Set to BEGIN mode
- 1 SHIFT P/YR
- 40000 FV
- 12 I/YR
- 10 N
- Solve for PMT
- Note that the HP 10BII displays a negative number for the answer, since each year's savings amount is a cash outflow.

5. Future Value of an Increasing Annuity, Annuity Due

Description: A future sum that reflects a series of payments that increase at a specified rate and earn interest at a specified rate. It results from a series of payments that are made at the beginning of each period over successive periods. Note that payments in subsequent periods include an inflation factor so as to maintain the purchasing power of the sum.

Facts and Question: Susan wants to save over the next 20 years by depositing $2,000 at the *beginning* of each year in an investment account returning her 10 percent per year. Susan expects an inflation rate of three percent and will be increasing her annual contributions by that rate. How much will she accumulate over the 20 years?

Answer: $154,672.22

Keystrokes:

- Set to BEGIN mode
- 1 P/YR
- 2000 PMT
- 20 N
- 1.10 ÷ 1.03 − 1 × 100 = I/YR (this calculation determines the inflation-adjusted rate of return for the annual investments)
- PV (this calculation determines the lump sum present value of all 20 years of inflation-adjusted payments in today's dollars; next, this PV must be compounded for 20 years at 10 percent to its future value)
- 10 I/YR (it is not necessary to reenter 20 for N, since that value is still stored in the calculator)
- 0 PMT (this replaces the previously stored value of 2000)
- Solve for FV

Note that with most other time value of money problems, there is a logical correspondence between the variables and the keystrokes. Look back at Example 4, "Annuity Payments for a Future Sum, Annuity Due." N is given as 10 years; the future value is given as $40,000; and so on. You enter each variable, press the corresponding key, and solve for the missing variable. But *increasing annuities* do not enjoy this intuitive one-to-one variable-to-keystroke relationship. Instead, because of the way financial function calculators are programmed, you have to go through a unique sequence of keystrokes, such as those given here in Example 5. The *real* math behind these increasing annuities can best be seen in Table 10.1, which shows the relationship of each $2,000 payment, inflation, and the corresponding future value over time for Example 5.

Table 10.1: Future Value of An Increasing Annuity, Annuity Due

Year	Payment Growing at 3% Per Year	Compounded Value at 10%	Years of Compounding
1	$ 2,000.00	$ 13,455.01	20
2	2,060.00	12,598.78	19
3	2,121.80	11,797.03	18
4	2,185.45	11,046.31	17
5	2,251.02	10,343.37	16
6	2,318.55	9,685.15	15
7	2,388.10	9,068.82	14
8	2,459.75	8,491.72	13
9	2,533.54	7,951.33	12
10	2,609.55	7,445.34	11
11	2,687.83	6,971.55	10
12	2,768.47	6,527.90	9
13	2,851.52	6,112.49	8
14	2,937.07	5,723.51	7
15	3,025.18	5,359.29	6
16	3,115.93	5,018.24	5
17	3,209.41	4,698.90	4
18	3,305.70	4,399.88	3
19	3,404.87	4,119.89	2
20	3,507.01	3,857.71	1
	Total Future Value	$ 154,672.22	

6. Future Value of an Increasing Annuity, Ordinary Annuity

Description: A future sum that results from a series of inflation-adjusted payments made at the *end* of a period over successive periods. **Note:** As we learned earlier, you normally switch your calculator from the BEGIN mode to the END mode when switching from an annuity due to an ordinary annuity. However, **for increasing annuity calculations only, always stay in the BEGIN mode on HP calculators**. To convert an increasing annuity due to an increasing ordinary annuity, simply divide the annuity due answer by 1 + the investment (or growth) rate. Because of the way the HP calculator is programmed for increasing annuities, this simple division process effectively changes the mode within the calculator. This division process effectively reduces each periodic payment's future value by one year of growth or interest

(I/YR). In the preceding Example #5, the first $2,000 payment grew for a full 20 years (since it is an annuity due). In this example (Example #6), the first $2,000 payment grows for only 19 years, because the payment is not made until the *end* of the first year (ordinary annuity). In effect, the future value of the increasing ordinary annuity loses one year of potential growth.

Facts and Question: Assume the same fact situation as in Example #5, except that Susan makes her deposits at the *end* of each year, rather than the *beginning*. How much will Susan have accumulated on an inflation-adjusted basis after 20 years?

Answer: $140,611.11

Keystrokes: (same as Example 5 except for the last step)

- Set to BEGIN mode
- 1 P/YR
- 2000 PMT
- 20 N
- 1.10 ÷ 1.03 −1 × 100 = I/YR (this calculation determines the inflation-adjusted rate of return for the annual investments)
- PV (this calculation determines the lump sum present value of all 20 years of inflation-adjusted payments in today's dollars; next, this PV must be compounded for 20 years at 10 percent to its future value)
- 10 I/YR (it is not necessary to reenter 20 for N, since that value is still stored in the calculator)
- 0 PMT (this replaces the previously stored value of 2000)
- Solve for FV
- Divide the FV determined in the previous keystroke by 1.10 (which is 1 + the 10 percent growth rate on her investment; the FV is divided by 1.10 to take into account her end of the year deposits, rather than beginning of year deposits; in essence, Susan has lost one year of potential return by waiting until the end of each year to make her deposits.) Notice that on HP calculators, these keystrokes are exactly the same as those in Example #5, except that the final answer is divided by 1 + the investment rate of return to convert it to an ordinary annuity.

7. Present Value of an Increasing Annuity, Annuity Due

Description: The value today of a series of payments that are to be received in the future at the *beginning* of each period and that increase by the rate of inflation in future years.

Facts and Question: Ray wants to establish a separate fund for his daughter's college education for the next five years. Ray's daughter starts her education later this month. Ray figures that the $10,000 annual cost today will increase by six percent annually, but he can earn 12 percent on funds set aside on his daughter's behalf. How much money does Ray need to set aside today to fund his daughter's college education?

Answer: $44,922.24

Keystrokes:
- Set to BEGIN mode
- 1 P/YR
- 10000 +/– PMT
- 5 N
- 1.12 ÷ 1.06 – 1 × 100 = I/YR (this calculation determines the inflation-adjusted rate of return for the annual withdrawals required over the next five years)
- Solve for PV

8. Present Value of an Increasing Annuity, Ordinary Annuity

Description: The value today of a series of payments that are to be received in the future at the end of each period and that increase by the rate of inflation in future years.

Facts and Question: Assume the same fact situation as that of Example #7, except that Ray's daughter does not begin college until one year from now (in other words, Ray does not have to make each year's payment until the end of the year). How much will Ray need to set aside for his daughter's college education?

Answer: $40,109.14

Keystrokes: (same as Example 7 except for the last step)
- Set to BEGIN mode
- 1 P/YR
- 10000 +/– PMT
- 5 N
- 1.12 ÷ 1.06 – 1 × 100 = I/YR (this calculation determines the inflation-adjusted rate of return for the annual withdrawals required over the next five years)
- Solve for PV
- Divide the PV determined in the previous keystroke by 1.12 (which is 1 + the 12 percent growth rate on his investment; the PV is divided by 1.12 to take into account her *end* of the year deposits, rather than *beginning* of year deposits; in essence, the entire cost of his daughter's college education is less than Example #7, since Ray does not have to make each year's payment until the end of each year. Notice that on HP calculators, these keystrokes are exactly the same as those in Example #7, except that the final answer is divided by 1 + the investment rate of return to convert it to an ordinary annuity.

9. Future Value of a Lump Sum and Annuity Due Payment

Description: The future value of a series of payments added to an existing lump sum.

Facts and Question: Bill and Sue want to add $150 at the *beginning* of each month to their current $7,000 education fund for their four-year-old daughter, Megan. If they can earn eight percent per year, how much will have accumulated when Megan is ready for college at age 18?

Answer: $67,885.80

Keystrokes:

- Set to BEGIN mode
- 12 SHIFT P/YR
- 7000 +/− PV
- 150 +/− PMT
- 14 SHIFT xP/YR (top left key)
- 8 I/YR
- Solve for FV

Logic and Formulas Underlying Time Value of Money

While many students of the time value of money will be content with understanding the general concepts involved and knowing the keystrokes necessary to perform essential calculations on a financial function calculator, some students will want to explore the subject in greater depth by learning the formulas and logic that underlie the calculator keystrokes. In Appendix C of this text students who have a quantitative bent and have more than a passing interest in the theory of time value of money may explore the mathematical relationships behind many of the calculations performed in Chapters 10 and 11.

IMPORTANT CONCEPTS TO REMEMBER

Compounding

Discounting

Future Value of a Dollar

Present Value of a Dollar

Ordinary Annuity

Annuity Due

Future Value of an Ordinary Annuity and an Annuity Due

Present Value of an Ordinary Annuity and an Annuity Due

Payments Made or Received Other Than Annually

Present and Future Value of an Increasing (Inflation-Adjusted) Annuity

Combined Future Value of a Lump Sum and Annuity Payments

QUESTIONS FOR REVIEW

1. Why is a dollar owned today worth more than a dollar to be received five years from now?

2. Why is a dollar to be received five years from now worth less than a dollar owned today?

3. What are the two factors that determine the present value of a dollar to be received in the future?

4. What is the difference between an ordinary annuity and an annuity due?

5. If compounding and payments are made other than annually, what adjustment needs to be made to your financial function calculator?

6. Using a financial function calculator, how is the inflation-adjusted rate of return calculated?

7. Using a financial function calculator, how is the combined future value of an initial lump sum and periodic payments calculated?

SUGGESTIONS FOR ADDITIONAL READING

Appendix C of this text.

CHAPTER ELEVEN

More Time Value of Money Concepts and Applications

• • •

In Chapter 10, we introduced the basic time value of money concepts of present and future valuation and several variations on these themes, including inflation-adjusted payments. In this chapter, you will learn some additional practical applications of the time value of money including loan, mortgage, and lease payment calculations—as well as more advanced calculations involving unequal cash flows, net present value, and internal rate of return. A good working knowledge of these applications is essential for a financial planner's practice success.

The objectives of this chapter are:

- Analyze a given situation to compute a loan, mortgage, or lease payment.
- Explain the theory of discounted cash flow functions.
- Solve net present value and internal rate of return problems.
- Calculate sample rates of return.
- Compute a sample stock or bond valuation.

LOAN, MORTGAGE, AND LEASE PAYMENT CALCULATIONS

In this section, we will discuss the computation and application of payments that are to be made when entering into a term loan (such as when purchasing a new automobile), a mortgage loan, and when entering into a consumer lease. In paying off a loan, the borrower's monthly payments are allocated between repayment of the principal (original amount borrowed) and the interest payable on the unpaid principal balance. This process is referred to as **amortization**. Typically when a borrower enters into a mortgage loan, he or she is provided by the lender with an amortization table showing how each monthly payment will be allocated between principal repayment and interest. This becomes important when filing one's income tax return because only the portion of the payments allocable to mortgage interest paid on a loan to purchase or improve a primary residence is generally tax-deductible. This same principle is true for auto loans and other types of consumer loans, except that in these cases the interest paid on such loans is considered to be personal interest and is ordinarily not tax-deductible. Loan payments are made at the end of the period, typically on a monthly basis.

Let us look at some examples:

1. **Loan Example and Application:** Charles finances the purchase of a new car valued at $24,000 with a down payment of $4,800 and by taking out a four-year loan at 9.9 percent annual interest. What is the amount of his monthly payment on this loan?

   Answer: $486.04

   Keystrokes:
   - Set to END mode
   - 12 SHIFT P/YR
   - 24000 – 4800 = 19200 PV
   - 4 SHIFT xP/YR
   - 9.9 I/YR
   - Solve for PMT. Note: The HP calculators display the answer as a negative number, since each month's payment amount is a cash outflow.

2. **Mortgage Amortization Example and Application:** John and Susan have recently financed the purchase of a new home with a $200,000 mortgage note at 7.75 percent annual interest over 30 years.

   (a) What is the amount of their monthly payment?

   Answer: $ 1,432.82

   Keystrokes:
   - Set to END mode
   - 12 SHIFT P/YR
   - 200000 PV

- 30 SHIFT xP/YR
- 7.75 I/YR
- Solve for PMT. Note: The HP calculators display the answer as a negative number, since each month's payment amount is a cash outflow. Parts (a) through (d) of this example are all part of one continuous series of calculations using the AMORT key starting in part (b). Be sure that you do *not* clear your calculator between each part.

(b) After making their 18th monthly payment, how much will they have repaid on their original mortgage balance?

Answer: $ 2,685.25

Keystrokes:
- Without clearing the calculator,
- 1 INPUT 18
- SHIFT AMORT
- =

(c) After making their 18th monthly payment, how much total interest will they have paid through that point?

Answer: $ 23,105.60

Keystrokes:
- Without clearing the calculator,
- =

(d) What will be their unpaid principal balance on this mortgage after they make the 18th payment?

Answer: $ 197,314.75

Keystrokes:
- Without clearing the calculator,
- =

3. **Maximum Purchase Price Example and Application:** George has $20,000 that he has saved for the purchase of a new home. He figures that he can afford a monthly payment of $900. Interest rates are currently 8.5 percent on a 30-year mortgage loan. What is the maximum purchase price of the home that George can currently afford? (Assume he has other funds for closing costs, property taxes and insurance.)

Answer: $137,048.28, consisting of a $117,048.28 loan plus the $20,000 down payment.

Keystrokes:
- Set to END mode
- 12 P/YR

- 30 SHIFT xP/YR
- 8.5 I/YR
- 900 +/– PMT
- Solve for PV

4. **Lease Payment Example and Application:** Jessica wishes to lease an automobile valued at $30,000 over a three-year period. The lease provides for an option to buy the auto at the end of three years for $18,000. Lease payments will be made at the beginning of each month. If the dealer needs to yield a return of 14 percent on this lease, what should be the amount of monthly payment incurred by Jessica?

Answer: $612.98

Keystrokes:

- Set to BEGIN mode
- 12 P/YR
- 14 I/YR
- 30000 PV
- 18000 +/– FV
- 3 SHIFT xP/YR
- Solve for PMT

UNEQUAL CASH FLOWS, NET PRESENT VALUE, AND INTERNAL RATE OF RETURN

In Chapter 10, we discussed the basic time value of money concepts and calculations using the simplifying assumption that cash flows occur at regular intervals and in equal amounts. We differentiated between equal payments made at the beginning of a period (an annuity due) and those made at the end of a period (an ordinary annuity). However, in the real world, particularly in the area of investments, payments may or may not occur at uniform intervals or in equal amounts. Accordingly, a financial planner needs to understand how to calculate the return on investments that have unequal cash flows. Such calculations are known as **discounted cash flow calculations**. Solving these types of problems on the HP 10BII calculator requires use of the calculator's cash flow application. But before we discuss how to perform discounted cash flow calculations, let us first discuss the concepts of Net Present Value (NPV) and Internal Rate of Return (IRR).

In the world of corporate finance, investment decisions are referred to as **capital budgeting**. The concepts used in the business world are equally applicable to personal investment planning—in both contexts the investor must determine where limited capital resources (savings) should be invested to maximize the return on those resources.

Net Present Value (NPV) is the amount determined by discounting the projected cash inflows of a proposed investment at the investor's (either an individual's or an institution's) required rate of return and subtracting the original investment (cash outflow). (**Note:** If the cash outflows do not all occur at the beginning of the investment period, they will have to be discounted at the investor's required rate of return to a present value.) If the result is a positive number, then the investor will earn a rate of return greater than his or her **required rate of return** from this particular investment and therefore should consider making the investment. Conversely, if the resulting number is negative, the investor will earn less than his or her required rate of return from this investment. If the result is zero, the investor will earn exactly his or her required rate of return. An investor's required rate of return is defined as the return that compensates the investor for his or her time, the expected rate of inflation, and the uncertainty of the return (also known as a risk premium over the nominal risk-free rate of return).

Internal Rate of Return (IRR) is that discount rate, which when applied to the cash flows of an investment, equates the net cash inflows to the net cash outflows. If the IRR calculated is equal to or greater than the investor's required rate of return, then the investor should consider making the investment, all other considerations being equal. If the IRR is less than the investor's required rate of return, the investment should not be made. The IRR is determined through trial and error—the calculator discounts the investment's cash flows at many different assumed rates until it determines the one rate that makes the cash flows equal. The resulting rate is the IRR of the investment.

Before we look at some examples of NPV and IRR problems, let us discuss the general steps for cash flow calculations on the HP 10BII:

1. Organize the cash flows on paper if possible—a cash flow diagram may be useful.

2. Clear the register.

3. Enter the amount of the initial investment as a negative number. (*Note*: As we will see, in computing Net Present Value (NPV) calculations, it is possible that this initial investment may be entered as zero and still derive the correct answer.)

4. Enter the amount of the next cash flow as a positive number. (*Note*: Cash inflows to the investor must be input as a positive number, whereas cash outflows will be input as negative. Accordingly, the initial investment number must be shown as a negative number, since it is considered an outflow to the investor.)

5. Repeat step 4 if there is more than one cash inflow.

6. In inputting the last cash inflow amount, be sure to add the amount of the final cash inflow to the ending sale price or the residual value of any initial investment.

7. To calculate Net Present Value, enter the annual interest rate and press I/YR, then press the SHIFT key followed by the NPV key.

8. To calculate Internal Rate of Return, press the SHIFT key followed by the IRR/YR key.

Now that you know the general steps to follow in performing cash flow calculations, let us consider an example of a NPV problem.

Example

An investor is considering a significant purchase in a gold mining limited partnership. It is being offered to her at a purchase price of $125,000. She expects to own the investment for at least five years and be able to sell it for $155,000 at that time. During the five-year period, she expects annual cash flows of $7,500, $8,000, $8,500, $9,000, and $10,000. If this investor has a required annual rate of return of 12 percent, should she make this purchase?

Solution: There are two methods of solving this type of problem on the calculator. As noted previously, in computing NPV, you may begin with either an initial cash outflow of zero or use the actual purchase price. We will therefore solve the problem both ways:

Method #1		Method #2	
Cash Flow	**Keystroke**	**Cash Flow**	**Keystroke**
$125,000	+/– CFj (for year 0)	-0-	CFj (for year 0)
$7,500	CFj (for year 1)	$7,500	CFj (for year 1)
$8,000	CFj (for year 2)	$8,000	CFj (for year 2)
$8,500	CFj (for year 3)	$8,500	CFj (for year 3)
$9,000	CFj (for year 4)	$9,000	CFj (for year 4)
$165,000	CFj (for year 5)	$165,000	CFj (for year 5)
12	I/YR	12	I/YR
Solve for NPV	SHIFT, NPV	Solve for NPV	SHIFT, NPV
Answer: – $6,530.79 (Since negative, do not make investment)		**Answer:** $118,469.21 (Less than $125,000 initial investment)	

Note that when entering the cash inflow for year 5 we added the $10,000 fifth year anticipated earnings to the estimated selling price of the investment of $155,000 to arrive at the total fifth year cash inflow of $165,000. Also note than when $6,530.79 is added to $118,469.21, the result is $125,000, the amount of the initial investment. In Method #1, the net present value is negative indicating that the present value of the cash inflows is less than the present value of the cash outflow. In Method #2, the present value of the cash inflows is calculated to be less than the initial investment of $125,000. While the calculations are somewhat different, the resulting decision under either method is the same (i.e., do not make the investment).

Let us now consider an example of an IRR problem. We will use the same information as we did in the foregoing NPV example but instead of calculating NPV, we will calculate IRR. Unlike the NPV calculation, there is only one method of solving for IRR on the HP 10BII calculator.

Solution: (Be sure that the calculator's memory has been cleared)

Enter	Keystroke
$125,000	+/– CFj (for year 0)
$7,500	CFj (for year 1)
$8,000	CFj (for year 2)
$8,500	CFj (for year 3)
$9,000	CFj (for year 4)
$165,000	CFj (for year 5)
Solve for IRR	SHIFT, IRR/YR
Answer: 10.66 % (This is less than the investor's required rate of return of 12%, and confirms the decision that the investment should not be made.)	

Both of these methods—NPV and IRR—lead the investor to the same decision. Which is preferable? The answer is that both of these methods may prove valuable in evaluating whether a particular investment should be pursued. However, the reader needs to understand the difference in the results that are achieved. The NPV method discounts the cash flows generated by the investment at the investor's required rate of return to determine if the net present value is positive, zero, or negative, whereas the IRR method evaluates the rate of return generated by the cash flows and compares it to the investor's required rate of return. Under the NPV method, if the NPV is positive or zero, the investment should be made; if it is negative, the investment should not be made. Under the IRR method, if the calculated IRR is equal to or greater than the investor's required rate of return, the investment should be made; if less, it should not be made.

In some instances, the IRR may artificially generate a different decision by causing an increase in the required rate of return. For example, even though an NPV calculation may indicate that the investor's required rate of return is satisfied, the IRR calculation may result in a rate of return higher than the investor's existing required rate of return. This could result in this higher rate of return becoming the revised standard for making investment decisions. In order to obtain comparable results, it is essential that the same required rate of return be used under either method.

PRELIMINARY INVESTMENT CONCEPTS AND CALCULATIONS

The previous section addressed the concept of Internal Rate of Return (IRR) in measuring the rate of return of a particular investment. IRR is a very valuable measure of investment return that takes into account the time value of money. There are, however, other measures of determining the rate of return of an investment—a skill required of a practicing financial planner. In this section, we will discuss some of these additional measures of investment return and how they are calculated on the HP 10BII calculator.

1. **Annualized Rate of Return**

   Description: The rate of return for a holding period of less than one year converted to an annual figure.

   Facts and Question: Cathy has earned an eight percent return to date on her investment. However, she has only held the investment for 120 days. What is her annual rate of return on this investment?

   Answer: 24.33%

   Calculate ROR on a daily basis and then multiply by 365 days

   Keystrokes:
   8 ÷ 120 × 365 =

2. **Holding Period Rate of Return**

   Description: A simple average rate of return over a given period of time that does not take into account the time value of money.

   Facts and Question: Harry has a mutual fund which had a balance of $10,000 at the beginning of the year. The fund paid dividends of $2,434 during the year, which Harry withdrew in cash, and the fund's balance at year-end was $13,515. What is Harry's holding period rate of return over the past year?

   Answer: 59.49%

   Increase in value plus cash received divided by the beginning balance

   Keystrokes:
   13515 − 10000 + 2434 ÷ 10000 × 100 =

3. **After-Tax Rate of Return**

   Description: A nominal rate of return accounting for federal and state income taxes, but not adjusted for inflation.

   Facts and Question: Chuck has earned a before-tax return of 14 percent on his latest investment over the past year. His federal marginal tax rate is 28% and his state marginal tax rate is 5%. What is Chuck's after-tax rate of return on this investment?

Answer: 9.58%

Use the formula: after-tax return = pre-tax return × (1-FTR) × (1-STR)

Keystrokes:
14 × .72 × .95 =

4. **Inflation-Adjusted Rate of Return (as discussed in chapter 10)**

Description: A nominal rate of return, adjusted for inflation, thereby resulting in a "real" before-tax rate of return.

Facts and Question: Bob expects to earn a nominal rate of return of 12 percent on his investment in a stock over the course of the next year. Inflation is anticipated to be four percent over this same time period. What is Bob's real rate of return on the stock?

Answer: 7.69%

Keystrokes:
1.12 ÷ 1.04 − 1 × 100 =

5. **After-Tax and Inflation-Adjusted Rate of Return**

Description: A nominal rate of return, adjusted for both taxes and inflation so that an investor can determine if he or she realized a net economic gain.

Facts and Question: Scott holds a mutual fund currently returning him 11% per year. His marginal tax rate is 28% and inflation is currently at 5% per year. What is Scott's rate of return on his mutual fund, considering the effects of both inflation and taxes?

Answer: 2.78%

Keystrokes:
(1 − .28) × .11 + 1 ÷ 1.05 − 1 × 100 =

6. **Taxable Equivalent Yield of a Tax-Exempt Security**

Description: A federally tax-free rate of return (for example, a municipal bond) converted to its taxable return equivalent so that comparisons can be made with taxable investments.

Facts and Question: Tom is purchasing a municipal bond that has a coupon rate of 5.5%. His federal marginal tax rate is currently 33%. What is the equivalent taxable rate of return of the bond?

Answer: 8.21%

Keystrokes:
5.5 ÷ .67 =

(**Note:** This can also be computed for a security that is tax-free for both federal and state income tax purposes, i.e., a double tax-exempt security. In order to compute this return, use the following formula:

$$\text{Tax equivalent yield} = \frac{\text{Tax-exempt yield}}{(1 - \text{FTR})(1 - \text{STR})}$$

Becoming familiar and proficient with the foregoing formulas/calculations is critical to a financial planner's success. Refer to Appendix C for a discussion of the formulas and logic of these investment calculations.

VALUATION OF A STOCK OR BOND

Considerations of risk and return (using time value of money principles) are the primary determinants of how much an investor should pay for a particular stock or bond. The **intrinsic value** of a stock or bond is the expected price that a share of stock or a bond should sell for in the marketplace, on a discounted cash flow basis. If the stock is currently trading below or above this price, the asset is accordingly under- or overvalued for a particular investor. As investments are not the primary focus of this text, for those interested in more in-depth information on investment valuation calculations it is recommended that they consult an investment planning textbook.

1. **Value of a Common Stock**

   Description: A common stock's intrinsic value, based on an investor's required rate of return and the stock's growth pattern. This is computed through the use of a formula known as the dividend discount or growth model.

   Facts and Question: Jane is interested in buying shares of stock in a major company. These shares currently pay an annual dividend of $3.00 that is expected to grow at a 10 percent rate. Jane has a required rate of return of 12 percent. What is the intrinsic value of the stock to Jane?

   Answer: $165.00

   Keystrokes:

   • $3.00 \times 1.10 \div .02 =$

(**Note:** the .02 that was inputted in the foregoing keystroke is the investor's required rate of return, here 12 percent, less the projected growth rate of the stock's dividend, here 10 percent.)

2. **Value of a Bond**

Description: The intrinsic value of a bond, based on a comparison to the yield of a similar bond and the investor's required rate of return.

Facts and Question: Susan is considering the purchase of a bond with an 8.5 percent coupon (or interest rate) with a ten-year maturity. The bond pays interest twice a year and will mature at a price of $1,000 in ten years. Similar bonds of this credit rating and maturity are paying 9.5 percent. What should Susan expect to pay for the bond, i.e., what is its intrinsic value?

Answer: $936.35

Keystrokes:
- Set to END mode (interest received at the **end** of every six months)
- 2 SHIFT P/YR
- 1000 FV
- 85 ÷ 2 = PMT
- 10 SHIFT xP/YR
- 9.5 I/YR
- Solve for PV

BOND YIELD CURVE

The final measure of investment return, and its consideration of inherent risk, that we will discuss is the Bond Yield Curve. Also known as the term structure of interest rates, the yield curve is a function that relates the term to maturity to the yield to maturity for a sample of bonds at a given point in time. Therefore, it represents a cross section of yields for a category of bonds that are comparable in all respects but maturity. In order for this measure to be valid, the quality of the bonds should be constant and ideally it should include bonds with similar coupons and call features within a single industry category. Yield curves can be constructed for Treasuries, government agencies, prime-grade municipals, AAA utilities, and so on. The accuracy of the yield curve will depend on the comparability of the bonds in the sample. When the yields to maturity are plotted (on the vertical axis) against the years to maturity (on the horizontal axis), a particular shape of the resulting yield curve will be observed and the behavior of the yield curve over time will be quite fluid.

The most common shape is the rising yield curve, which prevails when interest rates are at low or modest levels. This is the result of the fact that longer-term investments will tend to have higher yields since they involve greater risk. The declining yield curve tends to occur when rates are relatively high. The flat yield curve rarely exists for any significant period of time. The humped yield curve prevails when extremely high rates are expected to decline to more normal levels. Generally the slope of the yield curve tends to level off after about 15 years. The Treasury Yield Curve is published daily in financial newspapers, such as *The Wall Street Journal.* See Figure 11.1 for examples of four types of yield curves.

Figure 11.1

A **Rising Yield Curve** Is formed when the yields on short-term Issues are low and rise consistently with longer maturities and flatten out at the extremes.

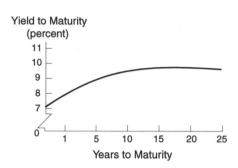

A **Declining Yield Curve** is formed when the yields on short-term issues are high and yields on subsequently longer maturities decline consistently.

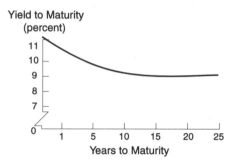

A **Flat Yield Curve** has approximately equal yields on short-term and long-term issues.

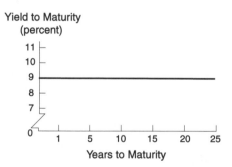

A **Humped Yield Curve** is formed when yields on intermediate-term issues are above those on short-term issues and the rates on long-term issues decline to levels below those for short-term issues and then level out.

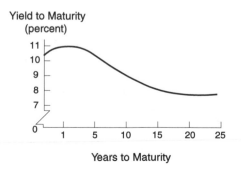

IMPORTANT CONCEPTS TO REMEMBER

Calculation of required payments on mortgage and auto loans and leases

Calculation of maximum affordable personal residence purchase price

Calculations involving unequal cash flows

Net present value

Internal rate of return

Annualized rate of return

Holding period rate of return

After-tax rate of return

Inflation-adjusted rate of return

After-tax and inflation-adjusted rate of return

Taxable equivalent yield of a tax-exempt security

Intrinsic value of a stock or bond

Bond yield curve

QUESTIONS FOR REVIEW

1. What is meant by the term loan amortization?

2. What is the process used in calculating the net present value of a proposed investment?

3. What is the internal rate of return of a proposed investment?

4. What is another name for the inflation-adjusted rate of return of an investment?

5. What is meant by the taxable equivalent yield of a tax-exempt security?

6. How is the intrinsic value of a stock or bond computed?

SUGGESTIONS FOR ADDITIONAL READING

Appendix C of this text.

CHAPTER TWELVE

Choosing the Appropriate Business Entity

• • •

Apracticing financial planner's clients very often include owners of small and/or closely held businesses. A **closely held business** is one whose stock is not publicly traded and usually is owned by only a few people. In many cases, this type of client has a significant amount of discretionary income available for financial planning and investment opportunities, making him or her a highly desirable client for the financial planner. While this type of client may be very lucrative, the financial planner must possess the requisite level of knowledge required to properly serve such a client. Very often, the financial planner will be called upon by his or her client to recommend an appropriate type of business entity, consistent with the client's goals and objectives. Such a recommendation carries with it many ramifications, both tax and non-tax, not only for the start-up period, but also for the long term.

This chapter introduces the various types of closely held business entities and their unique non-tax and tax characteristics. We will discuss some of the operational and succession problems of particular business entities as well as when a particular type of business entity may be appropriate given a client's objectives.

The objectives of this chapter are:
- State the various forms of available business entities.
- Identify the characteristics of selected types of business entities.
- Describe the unique factors involved in closely held and/or family business planning.
- Analyze a given situation to select the most appropriate form of business entity for a given client.

- Identify an aspect of financing or operating a closely held business.
- Explain a common technique used in the disposition of a closely held business.

ISSUES INVOLVED WITH CLOSELY HELD BUSINESSES

Forming, operating, selling, liquidating, transferring business interests, disposing of the business in the event of an owner's death, disability, or retirement, or retaining the business in the family are all important issues facing owners of a closely held business. Some of the many questions that must be answered in order to properly plan for such a business include:

- What type of business entity or entities should be used for the business?
- Where there are multiple owners, how will the ownership be shared and correspondingly, where will control lie?
- In the event that the business must be sold, will there be a market for it?
- How can the business provide an adequate income for the owners?
- What will be the income tax status of the business and its owners?
- What will be the effect of the value of the business on the owners' estates?
- If an owner dies prematurely or becomes disabled, will the business be able to continue and what will be the disposition of the deceased or disabled owner's business interest?
- What is the best method for selling the business to a new owner, if the owners so elect?
- What happens when an owner wishes to retire from the business?
- How can the owners gift their business interest to family members, if desired or appropriate?
- To what extent are individual owners personally liable for the debts, obligations, and tort claims of the business?

Some Common Characteristics of Closely Held Businesses

Closely held businesses share certain characteristics that differentiate them from the larger, publicly held corporations. Some of these characteristics include:

- The closely held business tends to have a small number of owners and, in many instances, these owners are also family members.
- There typically is no identifiable market for ownership interests in the business. Such ownership interests are rarely transferred in an arm's length transaction. As a result, valuation of the owners' interests in the business is quite difficult to ascertain.
- Due to the limited marketability of a business interest (and also the lack of control if the client is a minority owner), sizeable discounts may be applied for estate planning purposes in valuing such a business interest. These are known as **fractional interest discounts**.

- They can be formed as one or more of several types of business entities.
- Some of the potential business entities include **pass-through entities** in which profits and losses are not taxed at the entity level but flow through to the individual owners to whom they are either taxed or become tax deductions. Selection of a pass-through entity can avoid double taxation of corporations (once at the corporate level and again at the owner level). Most closely held businesses prefer to be taxed as pass-through entities. This is particularly true since January 1, 1997 when the so-called "check-the-box" tax regulations became effective. These regulations permit businesses to affirmatively elect either pass-through or corporate tax treatment merely by checking a box on their tax returns.
- Most owners of closely held businesses are involved in the daily management of those businesses as owner-managers. Accordingly, they often manage and control the businesses they own.
- Since owners of closely held businesses need to coordinate business planning with their financial and estate planning, it is difficult, if not impossible, to separate planning for the business from that of its owners.

In addition to these common characteristics of the closely held business, it is also important to understand those personality characteristics that set the closely held owner apart from the majority of employees today. These characteristics serve these owners well in building a business, but can also make planning for business succession very difficult.

In Depth: Some Characteristics of Closely Held Business Owners

- *A domineering personality.* Most closely held business owners have strong personalities and insist on remaining in control.
- *Self-worth tied to position within the business.* A business owner's self-esteem is often tied to being in charge. This makes it very difficult for him or her to envision the day when the business may have outgrown its founder or needs "new blood."
- *The lack of independent financial resources.* The business often represents the majority of the owner's wealth. As most closely held businesses lack both marketability and liquidity, cash flow and estate planning become very challenging.
- *An immortality complex.* Most owners believe that they can, and should, remain in charge of the business for years to come.
- *An inability to appreciate growing problems within the business.* An owner's inability to perceive problems may cause the business to decline rapidly and steadily before corrective action is taken. Even then, this action may come too late to save the operations of the business.

Because of these personal characteristics, owners of closely held businesses present a significant challenge to financial planners who seek to provide them financial planning and succession planning services.

SELECTING AN APPROPRIATE TYPE OF BUSINESS ENTITY

When forming a new business, one of the most complex and critical decisions the founder(s) need(s) to make is the appropriate legal form for the business. Decisions in this area should be guided by consultation with competent legal and tax advisors. The three key variables that will greatly influence the decision are liability, control, and taxes. Several questions must be answered before a decision may reasonably be made.

- How many owners will there be and how much control will each owner have?
- How will the risks and rewards of the business be shared by the owners?
- Do the owners wish to be insulated legally from the business's debts or claims against it?
- Which types of entities provide the most advantageous tax treatment for both the business and the individual owner(s)?
- Which legal entity is the simplest and least expensive to both establish and maintain?
- What are the long-term plans for the business?

When the answers to the foregoing questions have been determined and reconciled with each other, then it is time to select an appropriate business form. Following are the potential choices available to a business owner.

Types of Business Entities

Sole Proprietorship

If there is to be only one business owner, the sole proprietorship provides total control, maximum simplicity and flexibility but with no protection from unlimited personal liability for the debts, tort liability, and other obligations of the business. Tort liability arising out of the business may be reduced by having adequate commercial liability insurance.

The business has no existence apart from the owner. As a result, the proprietary interest ends when the owner dies. The business's assets, liabilities, and operations are an integral part of the owner's personal financial affairs. No formal documents are required to form such an entity but there may be a state requirement to register the business under the Fictitious Names Act. The sole proprietor is required to keep accurate accounting records, either on a cash or accrual basis, and file a Schedule C (Profit or Loss from a Business or Profession) as an attachment to his or her IRS Form 1040. In addition, as a general rule, a sole proprietor is liable for self-employment tax, in effect paying both the employer's and employee's shares of Social Security. However, they are not subject to unemployment tax.

For federal income tax purposes, sole proprietors can take a deduction for 100 percent of the amount paid for health insurance to cover themselves, spouses, and dependents. See Table 12.1 for a comparison of various types of business entities.

General Partnership

A partnership is an association of two or more owners to carry on a business, for a valid business purpose, for profit. The owners do not necessarily have to be individuals. Essentially any individual or entity can be a partner in a partnership. Forming a partnership can be relatively simple and informal with minimal paperwork for state and federal authorities. While not mandatory, it is advisable that there be a written agreement among the partners specifying the rights and responsibilities of each. Without a written partnership agreement, state laws will generally dictate how obligations, profits and losses, and capital are to be shared. Partnership agreements should cover how a partner joins or leaves the partnership, rights of surviving partners to purchase the interest of a departing partner and how payment will be made. In fact, the negotiation of the partnership agreement can be an effective test of the ability of the partners to work together and an indication of the partnership's long term durability.

Partners of a general partnership (unlike limited partners in a limited partnership, to be discussed next) are jointly and severally liable for the debts, tort claims, and other obligations of the partnership. Accordingly, they have unlimited personal liability for any claims against the business, including those arising from the actions of other partners or other persons when acting for the business.

Unlike sole proprietorships, partnerships do not dissolve on the death of a partner. Succession planning should provide for this eventuality through buy-sell agreements and the purchase of key person insurance. A significant advantage of the partnership form is the ease of transferring assets into and out of the business without incurring taxes. This is particularly helpful if the partners are making contributions in other than money.

General partnerships are pass-through entities for federal income tax purposes. As a result, the partnership itself pays no tax and all items of partnership income, gain, losses, deductions, and credits flow through to the partners to appear on their respective income tax returns. The partnership can be thought of as a tax-reporting entity rather than a tax-paying entity.

Since partners are not considered to be employees of a partnership, they are not eligible to receive tax-favored employee fringe benefits. However, tax-favored retirement plans are available through HR-10 plans (Keoghs) and selected other plans. In a general partnership, there are no limited partners. See Table 12.1 for a comparison of various types of business entities.

Limited Partnership

This form of partnership is defined by state law, must be registered with the state, and must include at least one general partner and one limited partner. General partners have unlimited personal liability for the obligations of the partnership, while the liability of the limited partner typically is restricted to only his or her investment in the partnership. In return for this limited liability, however, limited partners cannot take part in the active management of the partnership. If they do so, they may be treated as general partners and lose their limited liability. To limit the liability of general partners, other special-purpose corporations whose owners have limited liability may become the general partner(s).

Unlike the general partnership, a written partnership agreement is required for a limited partnership and the partnership must observe the formalities of applicable state law. This business form is frequently used as a means of raising investor capital and is the form of choice for real estate syndicates where proportional losses, if any, may be passed through to the limited partners. See Table 12.1 for a comparison of various types of business entities.

Limited Liability Partnership (LLP)

This type of partnership is available in some states under laws that permit general partners to limit their personal liability for the acts of other partners or of employees or agents of the partnership (other than those the general partner is directly supervising). In some states, general partners are also relieved of partnership contractual claims. This form is a favorite of large public accounting firms that wish to limit the liability of their general partners. An LLP is required to register under applicable state law. See Table 12.1 for a comparison of various types of business entities.

C Corporation

This type of entity is otherwise known as a regular corporation established under state corporation laws. It derives its name from Subchapter C of the Internal Revenue Code, which is the section of the Code under which it is taxed. It is subject to the corporate income tax, the corporate alternative minimum tax, the tax on unreasonable accumulation of earnings, and other levies. The owners (stockholders), which are unlimited in number and nature, are considered by law to be separate from the corporation. A C Corporation can have one or more classes of stock (including preferred stock) in its capital structure. Because a corporation is a separate entity, the personal assets of its shareholders cannot be taken in payment of corporate debts. The liability of stockholders for corporate obligations normally is limited to their investment in the corporation. One significant exception is that officers responsible for making employment-withholding tax payments to the federal government can be held personally liable for such payments.

With this type of entity, pass-through of taxable income, deductions, and credits to stockholders is not possible. There is a double taxation event on corporate income—once at corporate tax rates, and a second time to the shareholders upon payment of a declared dividend. The impact of double taxation has been reduced significantly by the taxation of dividends at capital gains rates (rather than ordinary income rates), beginning in 2003, and the simultaneous reduction of capital gains rates. While limited liability is a beneficial feature, double taxation drives most small businesses to avoid this type of organization. The strategy of C corporation stockholders is to take profits out of the corporation in ways that will be deductible by the corporation and taxable only once at the stockholder level. Unlike sole proprietors or partners, shareholder-employees of C corporations may receive many fringe benefits, such as medical coverage and group term life insurance from the corporation on a tax-advantaged basis. This may result in reducing a C corporation's taxable income to a very low level by payment of salary, bonuses, pension contributions, and benefits.

Corporations have unlimited lives with ownership passed to heirs upon the death of a shareholder. Also, corporate stock can always be sold to other investors.

Only a small percentage of American businesses are formally incorporated. Incorporation can be costly and time-consuming, including the payment of state incorporation fees and legal fees for drawing up corporate documents as well as ongoing expenses to maintain and operate a corporation. See Table 12.1 for a comparison of various types of business entities.

S Corporation

Like a C corporation, the S corporation is established under state corporation laws. The major difference is that an S corporation meets certain qualifications under Subchapter S of the Internal Revenue Code not to be taxed as a corporation for federal income tax purposes. The tax laws regarding S corporations are complex and the legal and accounting costs of starting and maintaining S status could override some of the tax advantages. In addition, state laws vary as to the taxability of an S corporation's income. Like C corporations, S corporation stockholders normally have limited liability for corporate obligations. S corporations are taxed, in most respects, like a partnership, rather than a corporation. There are usually no federal income taxes at the corporate level for S corporations. Profits or losses from S corporations flow directly through the company to the shareholders, thereby avoiding double taxation. Investors are also able to use losses from S corporations as direct tax deductions against other income, with limitations for those shareholders considered to be passive investors. Stockholders of S corporations are taxed on the net profits and gains of the corporation even if they do not receive any dividends from the corporation. In fact, since profits have already been taxed to the stockholders, dividends paid by S corporations normally are not taxable to the stockholders.

There are limits on the ownership structure of S corporations. First, only a small business corporation can elect S corporation status. To qualify, the corporation must be a domestic corporation, have no more than 75 shareholders, and have only certain classes of eligible shareholders. For instance, only individuals, estates, and certain types of trusts can be S corporation shareholders. For example, a qualified subchapter S trust (QSST) whose beneficiary chooses to be treated as owner of the S corporation stock held by the trust also may hold stock in an S corporation. Partnerships and corporations cannot be shareholders. All stockholders initially must consent to an S election. However, once made, an S election can be revoked by shareholders with more than 50 percent of the stock. Once an election is revoked or terminated, an election cannot be made again for five taxable years.

S corporations can have only one class of stock unless the only difference among the shares of multiple classes of common stock is in their voting rights. This means that an S corporation can have both voting and nonvoting common stock. S corporations must continue to meet the foregoing conditions. Otherwise, the S corporation election is terminated and the corporation is taxed as a C corporation henceforward.

Unlike C corporations, fringe benefits (including medical insurance and reimbursement plans, disability income plans, and group term life insurance) paid to shareholders owning greater than two percent of company stock are nondeductible by the corporation. Health insurance premiums can be deducted by the owner-employee in the same way that self-employed individuals can deduct these expenses. See Table 12.1 for a comparison of various types of business entities.

Limited Liability Company (LLC)

A limited liability company (LLC) is a form of unincorporated business organization, now allowed by statute in all states, which must be registered with the applicable state. It is best viewed as a partnership or sole proprietorship protected by a limited liability shield. In contrast to partnerships, all interest holders or "members" can enjoy limited personal liability for the debts of the organization. Unlike corporations, the entity can avoid "double taxation" at the corporate and shareholder levels by being qualified for flow-through treatment of income. Also, LLCs are not subject to the many restrictions imposed on S corporations, such as limits on the number of shareholders or the prohibition against corporate shareholders. An LLC with one member is treated as a sole proprietorship for tax purposes.

LLCs combine the advantages of limited liability of corporations with the pass-through treatment of partnerships. While those possessing an ownership interest are referred to as "members," LLCs can also have non-owner "managers" who manage the affairs of the business. Accordingly, an entity may be member-managed or manager-managed.

Under the "check-the-box" regulations, most LLCs elect to be taxed like a partnership. They can be flexible in their formation, structure, and operation and are relatively easy to form, usually by filing their articles of organization with the state. There is no limit on the number of members and the members can be any person or entity. They can also have more than one class of equity interest and do not have to observe many of the formalities often required of corporations under state corporation laws. See Table 12.1 for a comparison of various types of business entities.

Family Limited Partnership (FLP)

This form is established and operates like any limited partnership except that, as the name applies, it is only between family members. The entity is primarily used for estate planning purposes to permit gifting of limited partnership interests to other family members in a family business at a substantial valuation discount. The general partner in an FLP is typically the parent who manages the business and contributes property to the partnership in exchange for a partnership interest. He or she then makes gifts of limited partnership interests to children, grandchildren, or other family members. See Table 12.1 for a comparison of various types of business entities.

Table 12.1

TYPES OF BUSINESS ENTITIES

	Sole Proprietorship	General Partnership	Limited Partnership	Limited Liability Partnership	"C" Corporation	"S" Corporation	Limited Liability Company
Number of owners	One	Two or more	At least 1 general and 1 limited partner	Two or more	Unlimited	No more than 75 (and limited types)	Unlimited
Ease of formation	No formal documents required	Minimal paperwork required	Partnership agreement required	Must register under state law	Costly and time consuming	Numerous rules and regulations	Relatively easy to form; must register under state law
Liability of owners	Unlimited	Unlimited	Unlimited for general partner; limited for limited partner	Limited liability for acts of other partners, employees, and agents	Limited	Limited	Limited
Taxation concept	Individual level	Pass-through	Pass-through	Pass-through	Corporation is taxed	Pass-through	Choice of pass-through or company level
Retirement plans	Generally available	Generally available	Generally available	Generally available	Generally available	Generally available	Generally available
Other employee benefits	Employee owners have more difficulty qualifying	Employee owners have more difficulty qualifying	Employee owners have more difficulty qualifying	Employee owners have more difficulty qualifying	Employee owners typically qualify	Employee owners have more difficulty qualifying	Employee owners have more difficulty qualifying
Other issues	Ends when owner dies	Can liquidate without adverse tax consequences	Can liquidate without adverse tax consequences	Can liquidate without adverse tax consequences	Life of the corporation is not affected by death, retirement, etc. of owners	Life of the corporation is not affected by death, retirement, etc. of owners	Can liquidate without adverse tax consequences

[1] Family limited partnerships operate like limited partnerships, but they are used primarily for estate planning purposes.

Tax-Exempt Organization

A final type of entity that may be available to a client is a tax-exempt organization under Sections 501, 502 or 529 of the Internal Revenue Code (IRC). Primarily, these entities include public charities, business leagues, chambers of commerce, real estate boards, boards of trade, social and recreation clubs, fraternal beneficiary societies, orders, or associations, credit unions without capital stock, veterans' organizations, condominium and residential real estate management associations, political organizations, membership organizations, and private foundations. The most common types of tax-exempt organizations are those organized under IRC Section 501(c)(3) "exclusively for religious, charitable, scientific, testing for public safety, literary or educational purposes, or to foster national or international amateur sports competition (so long as none of its activities involve the providing of athletic facilities or equipment), or for the prevention of cruelty to children or animals, no part of the net earnings of which inures to the benefit of any private shareholder or individual, no substantial part of the activities of which is carrying on propaganda, or otherwise attempting to influence legislation, and which does not attempt to participate or intervene in any political campaign." Once they have qualified under the tax laws, these types of organizations must manage carefully their operations in order to maintain their tax-exempt status. Such organizations may be subject to income tax if they have income from the operation of a business enterprise not related to the purpose for which they received their exemption. Exempt private foundations may be subject to sanctions, primarily in the form of excise taxes, for engaging in prohibited activities or for accumulating excess income.

Factors in Choosing an Entity

Having discussed the various types of business entities, let us now turn to the factors to be considered in selecting an appropriate business entity for a client's business. Before we do so, it is important to understand that the issues involved in a choice of entity can be very complex and beyond the scope of this book; as a result, the discussion here will be only of a general nature.

In our discussion of the various types of business entities, we addressed the issue of **legal liability of the owners**. Accordingly, we will not discuss that issue further.

With regard to the **tax status of the selected entity and its owners**, there appears to be a preference for pass-through entities. However, C corporations, while potentially exposed to double taxation, can avoid or mitigate this problem through the use of various tax strategies including: (1) paying salaries, bonuses, and non-discriminatory fringe benefits to stockholder employees (subject to reasonable levels of compensation); (2) compensating family members on the payroll (also subject to reasonable levels of compensation); (3) providing discriminatory deferred compensation; (4) leasing assets from stockholders; and (5) making loans to the corporation by stockholders.

As far as **ease of formation and operation** are concerned, partnerships and LLCs are usually easier to form and operate than corporations. With regard to the **number and nature of owners,** if the business is to have only one owner, a sole proprietorship, single-member LLC, S corporation, or C corporation must be used. If more than 75 owners or particular types of owners are anticipated, an S corporation cannot be used. Regarding **transferability of ownership interests,** it is often said that stock of corporations is freely transferable. As a practical matter, the transferability of stock is often limited by a closely held corporation's bylaws. As far as continuity of life is concerned, the life of a corporation is unaffected by the death, retirement, disability, or bankruptcy of an owner. General partnerships and LLCs ordinarily are dissolved upon such events but can be continued with the agreement of the surviving owners. With regard to **ease of termination,** owners of partnerships and LLCs generally can receive liquidating distributions without current taxation. Liquidation of C and S corporations may be more problematic with possible taxable gain recognized upon liquidation and double taxation in the case of C corporations. Generally, tax law tends to favor the partnership and LLC forms by making them easier to form, operate, and terminate.

Sometimes, the **future plans for the business** will influence the choice of entity. If a business plans to go public, be sold to another firm, or kept in a family for a long period of time, a C corporation may be the entity of choice. If it is anticipated that a business will terminate or capital distributions will be taken in the near future, a partnership or LLC may be preferred.

In Depth: Other Factors in Selecting Entity Type

Other factors that should be considered in choosing the appropriate entity include the availability of:

- special allocations—the allocation of items of income, gain, loss, deductions, or credits among owners other than according to their interests in the entity are easily accomplished in partnerships and LLCs, but not in corporations.

- tax-favored employee benefits for owners—generally, owners of corporations are considered employees and can more easily qualify for employee benefits than can owners of partnerships and LLCs, who are technically not considered employees.

- qualified retirement plans—generally, such plans are available both to stockholder-employees and self-employed persons.

- health (medical expense) insurance—stockholder-employees of C corporations can receive such benefits tax-free and have them deductible by the corporation. Self-employed persons are allowed a deduction on their individual income tax returns for 100% (beginning in 2003) of the amount paid for health insurance for the self-employed person, his or her spouse, and his or her dependents. A more than two percent owner of an S corporation is treated as a self-employed person for this purpose.

- other welfare (fringe) benefits—this includes the first $50,000 of group term life insurance, disability income insurance, benefits under a cafeteria plan, and the value of certain miscellaneous fringe benefits. These are deductible to "C" corporations and tax-free to the owners. Self-employed persons and more than two percent owners of "S" corporations have to purchase these benefits with after-tax dollars since their cost is not deductible by the entity.

FINANCING AND OPERATION OF THE BUSINESS

Typically in the early years of operation, a business will rely on debt to finance its operations, with the attendant benefit that the interest paid is tax-deductible. As a result, the effective cost of borrowing funds may be much lower than the stated interest rate on the debt. Lenders to closely held businesses generally include commercial banks, corporate finance companies, and investment bankers. Such lenders look to the character of the owner(s), the business's cash flow, collateral, the extent of the owners' capital contributions, the business's debt ratios, the repayment period, and the interest rate.

TYPES OF INVESTORS

Some of the primary sources of equity financing include:

- venture capital funds
- the owner's personal or family funds or that of friends
- "angels"
- vendors
- corporate venture capitalists
- ad hoc venture pools

Investors, on the other hand, take a "piece of the action" in the form of an equity position in the business in exchange for their investment. As a result, investors will usually accept more risk.

Venture capital funds ordinarily take the form of limited partnerships, with a professional manager being the general or controlling partner who puts up as little as one percent of the fund's capital and then sells limited partnership interests to the other investors. Such organizations look for high rates of return (25-50 percent) and short-term liquidity.

Contrary to popular belief, most initial investments in closely held businesses are not made by venture capitalists but rather by the owners, their families, and friends. One of the potential drawbacks of such financing is the tendency of such investors to not conduct thorough due diligence prior to investing. This can lead to strained personal relationships if the business does not perform as expected.

Angels are informal investors willing to put their money into new businesses in exchange for relatively high expected rates of return. **Vendors** are an often-overlooked source of financing a new venture. Many times vendors may be willing to extend an additional 30 to 60 days' credit to help the business during its early period of operations. **Corporate venture capitalists** are venture capital funds set up by large companies looking to obtain new technology. On occasion, the start-up business eventually may be acquired by the large company. **Ad hoc venture pools** represent a group of private investors who have formed informal investment groups or investment pools.

Rather than resorting to outside sources, financing needs may sometimes be managed by improving business operations. For example, better inventory control can significantly improve the cash flow of a business. Similarly, stricter controls over accounts payable and receivable may minimize financing needs. Large companies regularly "extend" their trade payables by delaying payments to cooperative vendors, thus allowing the company use of funds for an extra few days. Finally, such basic strategies as scrutinizing collection activities may be used to reduce the need for external borrowing. Financial planners and other advisors should carefully analyze company financial statements for additional means of maximizing cash flow.

DISPOSITION OF THE BUSINESS

The disposition of a closely held business is a very complicated, yet interesting, subject that is beyond the scope of this book. Most of the time, the decision as to which technique to use in disposing of the business revolves around tax considerations. However, there are a number of non-tax issues that also need to be resolved. Generally, the financial planner or other advisor needs to assist the business owner in answering these four questions:

1. Should the business be sold at all or kept within the current closely held context, usually meaning in family control?
2. If the business is to be sold, who are its potential buyers?
3. If the business is kept, who should have ownership and control?
4. If the business is kept, who will manage it?

It is only after answering these questions (and remember that these may be difficult answers to obtain given the profile of the closely held business owner, discussed earlier) that transfer techniques can be selected.

Disposition or transfer techniques involving a closely held business are many and varied, but primarily break down into those involving either a sale or some form of lifetime gifting.

Sale of Business Interests

Business owners may sell, during their lifetime, their businesses or business interests to co-owners, key employees, family members, or unrelated parties. Moreover, the business itself may redeem the stock of a stockholder or liquidate the interest of a partner. The tax and economic implications will be determined by the type of business disposed of and the form of the sale.

When a sole proprietor sells his or her business, what is being sold are the underlying assets, since there is no stock. In the case of partnerships or LLCs electing to be treated as partnerships under the "check-the-box" regulations, the selling partner ordinarily will recognize capital gain (or loss) on the difference between the amount realized from the sale and his or her adjusted basis in the partnership interest. The income tax rules applicable to partnerships and LLCs electing to be taxed as partnerships can be very complex and are beyond the scope of this book.

When a corporation is sold, the seller and buyer can elect treatment as a sale of stock or, alternatively, a sale of assets. Where the transaction is treated as a sale of stock, the sellers will recognize capital gain (or loss) on the difference between the amount realized on the sale and their adjusted bases in their stock. Under this scenario, the bases of the assets inside the corporation will remain the same and the purchaser usually may not amortize the cost of any assets. In addition, the purchaser is responsible for the liabilities of the corporation.

Generally, a buyer will prefer to purchase specific business assets, which may be subject to depreciation or amortization, depending upon the nature of the asset, while sellers will prefer to sell stock to avoid continuing liability for corporate obligations. In the case of an asset sale, the selling corporation is often liquidated, pays off its liabilities, and distributes its remaining assets to its shareholders. The sale of a C corporation's assets will involve two levels of taxation—one at the corporate level and another at the shareholder level. Normally, there will be only one level of taxation upon the sale of an S corporation's assets—at the shareholder level. However, S corporations that were formerly C corporations may pay a corporate level tax (referred to as "built-in gain") on the gain from any appreciated assets owned by the corporation at the date of conversion from C to S and sold within ten years after conversion. Buyers of intangible assets, such as customer lists and goodwill, can amortize their purchase cost over 15 years.

A sale can be structured as an outright sale for cash, as a traditional installment sale over a period of years, as a private annuity (providing the seller with a lifetime income), or as a self-canceling installment note (SCIN). Structuring sales can be complex and often require professional advice.

Liquidation of Business Interests

If a business is liquidated during the owners' lifetimes, the consequences will depend upon the type of entity liquidated. In the case of a partnership (or LLC electing partnership tax treatment) ordinarily there will be no taxable gain to the partners unless cash or cash equivalents distributed exceeds the partners' bases in the partnership. Similarly to the sale of an S corporation interest, there generally will be only one level of taxation (at the shareholder level) on liquidation (other than where the "built-in gain" issue arises, as discussed earlier). As was true in the case of a sale, a C corporation liquidation will typically be taxed at both the corporate and shareholder levels.

Gifting of Business Interests

Gift transactions, unlike sales, do not result in immediate income taxation to the recipient of the gift. Rather, gifts are subject to the unified transfer tax system which includes both gift and estate taxation. Such gifts may be either outright or arranged as gifts in trust. If properly structured, some transfers can qualify for what are known as "fractional interest discounts" for a minority interest that lacks marketability. Another technique employing substantial valuation discounts, known as a grantor retained annuity trust (GRAT), is an effective method of transferring a business interest, if structured properly by a competent advisor.

Other gifting techniques include:

- an outright gift of a business interest taking advantage of the annual $11,000 (for 2004) donee gift exclusion
- a family limited partnership (or FLP), discussed earlier
- the use of a charitable remainder trust

The Buy/Sell Agreement

A buy/sell agreement is a contract among the owners of a business and/or the owners and the business entity itself to provide a market for an otherwise illiquid asset (i.e., the closely held business). One of this agreement's primary purposes is to protect the remaining owners when one owner attempts to dispose of his or her business interest to an undesirable individual or "outsider." It can also be useful in protecting an S corporation from having its stock transferred to a non-qualifying shareholder, which can terminate its S corporation election.

Buy/sell agreements provide for the situation where an owner either dies prematurely or becomes disabled for an extended period of time.

A buy/sell agreement often will have an agreed-upon price for the buyout of a business interest. Sometimes, this price is stated as a formula, such as a multiple of earnings or a percentage of "book" or balance sheet value. Typically, if such an agreement is entered into between unrelated parties, it will be viewed as fair and representative of the actual value of the business. The problem arises in the context of a family business where there is not an "arm's length" business relationship. If a business owner can demonstrate that an agreement price entered into with a family member is similar to a price negotiated with an unrelated party, this price will be respected for tax purposes. In recent years, tax rules have made it more difficult to meet this burden of proof. It is here that the professional advisor may play an important role in assisting to draft and negotiate a recognized agreement.

IMPORTANT CONCEPTS TO REMEMBER

Definition of a closely held business

Issues typically involved with closely held businesses

Common characteristics of closely held businesses

Characteristics of closely held business owners

Factors and considerations in selecting an appropriate type of business entity

Various types of business entities

Financing a closely held business

Disposition of a closely held business

QUESTIONS FOR REVIEW

1. In starting up a closely held business, what are some of the questions that must be answered in order to properly plan for its start-up?

2. What are some of the common characteristics of closely held businesses?

3. What typical characteristics of owners of closely held businesses make them a challenge for the financial planner in providing financial and succession planning?

4. What questions is it necessary to answer before selecting an appropriate type of business entity for a closely held business?

5. In what ways are the various types of business entities similar and in what ways do they differ?

6. What are some of the factors to be considered in selecting an appropriate business entity for a client's business?

7. What are the two general sources of outside financing for a closely held business?

8. Discuss some of the primary sources of equity financing for closely held businesses?

9. Discuss some of the ways to dispose of a closely held business and the related tax and non-tax implications of each?

SUGGESTIONS FOR ADDITIONAL READING

Personal Financial Planning, 10th edition, by Lawrence J. Gitman and Michael D. Joehnk, South-Western/Thomson, 2004.

Personal Financial Planning, 7th edition, by G. Victor Hallman and Jerry S. Rosenbloom, McGraw-Hill, Inc., New York, 2003.

CHAPTER THIRTEEN

Business Law as it Relates to Financial Planning

• • •

The purpose of this chapter is to provide the reader with a basic working knowledge of business law and those legal concepts that may impact a financial planner in providing personal financial planning or related services to clients. The main topics covered are contract law, the law of torts, agency law, the law of negotiable instruments, professional liability, fiduciary liability, and forms of alternative dispute resolution: negotiation, mediation, and arbitration. In order to provide effective and competent financial planning services, a financial planner must be generally familiar with business law and certain legal concepts involved in providing those services. While it is important that a financial planner not engage in the unauthorized practice of law, it is equally important that he or she possess an informed awareness of the potential implications of legal issues that may require advice from legal professionals.

The objectives of this chapter are:

- Identify the essential elements of a contract and additional elements that may render a contract unenforceable.
- Identify the various types of contracts categorized by how they are formed, how they are enforced, and how they will be performed.
- Identify the requirements of an offer.
- Describe the three ways in which a contract can be terminated.
- Describe the three elements of consideration.
- Explain the basic requirements of the Statute of Frauds.
- Describe the most common remedies for breach of contract.

- Identify the most common intentional torts against persons and business relationships.
- Describe the intentional torts against property.
- Describe the elements that a plaintiff must prove in a negligence suit.
- Identify the duties of an agent to a principal and the duties of a principal to an agent.
- Describe the ways in which an agency relationship may be terminated.
- Identify the four types of negotiable instruments.
- Describe the requirements for negotiability of an instrument.
- Explain how a holder of a negotiable instrument differs from a holder in due course.
- Discuss the concept of duty of care owed by a professional to a client.
- Identify the three main methods of alternative dispute resolution.

LAW OF CONTRACTS

One of the basic underpinnings of an ordered society is a party's expectation that another party will do what he or she promises to do. Without this expectation, one can only imagine the unsettling effect on everyday commerce. What we are talking about here is the concept of a promise, and it is important that we distinguish between the type of promise that is in the nature of a moral obligation, and one that constitutes a legal obligation. Contract law deals with the latter type of promise and how such promises are created and enforced.

But first we must determine what constitutes a contract. According to the Second Edition of the Restatement of the Law of Contracts, which is a nonstatutory, authoritative exposition of the common law of contracts originally compiled by the American Law Institute in 1932, a **contract** is "a promise or a set of promises for the breach of which the law gives a remedy, or the performance of which the law in some way recognizes as a duty." In layman's terms, it is an agreement that can be enforced in court. Contracts help provide a stable and predictable environment within which commercial transactions can take place.

Required Elements of a Valid Contract

The following four basic elements are needed to form a legally enforceable contract:

1. **Agreement**, which includes an **offer** by one of the contract parties and an **acceptance** by the other party. To be considered a valid offer, the person making the offer (the offeror) must have intended to form a contract, the offer's terms must be clearly stated or easily determinable on its face, and the person to whom the offer was made (the offeree) must be aware of the offer.

Once a valid offer is made, it can be withdrawn by the offeror through what is known as **revocation.** If the offer is not withdrawn, it can be accepted by the offeree only if accepted exactly as made and if such acceptance is properly communicated to the offeror. Alternatively, the offeree can reject the offer. A third option is for the offeree to make a **counteroffer.** Technically, making a counteroffer constitutes rejecting the offer as originally made and making an alternative offer to the original offeror. If the offeree simply remains silent, he or she is not considered to have accepted the offer unless the offeree realized some benefit from the contracted services, was in a position to reject those services, and knew that the offeror expected to receive payment for them. Also, an offer has a limited life. It expires at the time limit specified in the offer or after a reasonable period of time. Other ways in which an offer can be terminated are (1) if the subject of the proposed contract is destroyed; (2) if the offeror or offeree dies or becomes incompetent; and (3) if the subject of the proposed contract becomes illegal.

2. **Consideration**, which is anything of meaningful value provided or promised to be provided. Consideration must meet three requirements. First, it must have what is known as legal value, which is not necessarily money but instead could be an act, a promise, or an agreement *not* to do something. Second, there must be a "bargained-for-exchange", which is just an acknowledgement by both parties that they will each derive equal value from the contract. Third, consideration must be of legal sufficiency such as doing something, promising to do something, refraining from doing something, or promising not to something that the promissor is otherwise entitled to do. For example, if a party to the contract promises to do something that he or she is already required to do or that has already been accomplished, such a promise would not constitute sufficient consideration.

3. **Contractual capacity**, which means both parties are considered legally competent. For example, a minor, drunk, or mentally incompetent (not as determined by a court) is deemed to have limited competence and can therefore avoid liability under a contract. In almost every state the age of majority is 18. However, in some states, a minor is considered to have reached majority when he or she marries or is "emancipated" by his or her parents. If a minor wishes to avoid liability on a contract, the minor must disaffirm the entire contract. Usually the minor can simply return the goods unless he or she has damaged them, in which case restitution is required. One case in which a minor may not be able to disaffirm a contract is where he or she has misrepresented his or her age. Also, if a minor contracts for what are referred to as "necessaries" (e.g., food, clothing, shelter, medical services), the minor may disaffirm the contract but will be responsible for the value of such items.

If it can be demonstrated that a person was drunk at the time he or she entered into a contract and as a result did not understand what he or she was doing, that person can avoid the contract. But if there is not a demonstration of diminished judgment and reasoning ability affecting the intoxicated person's understanding of the legal significance of forming a contract, the contract will be binding. When minors reach majority and drunks become sober they may ratify a contract entered into as minors or while intoxicated.

Where a court has ruled a person to be mentally incompetent and has appointed a guardian for such person, any contract entered into by that person is void, rather than voidable.

4. **Legality**, referring to the fact that the subject of the contract must be both legal and not in violation of public policy. A contract created for either of these purposes is considered void and unenforceable from the moment of its creation. For example, a contract to hire a "hit man" to murder someone is both void and unenforceable.

Even where each of these four basic elements of a contract is present, a contract may still not be enforceable if there is not what is called **genuineness of assent**. This would be the case if there was a mistake of some material fact, if one or both parties misrepresented important information, or if one of the parties was coerced by the other party to enter into the contract. Moreover, certain types of contracts are required by what is known as the **Statute of Frauds** [see **In Depth: The Statute of Frauds**] to be in **proper legal form**, for example in writing.

NEED TO KNOW: PARENTAL RESPONSIBILITY

Generally, parents are not liable for contracts made by minor children acting without the parents' knowledge and consent. That is why businesses usually require parents to cosign a contract made with a minor. Also, minors are generally personally liable for their own torts (discussed later in this chapter). However, some states hold the parent legally responsible for failing to exercise proper control over the minor, based on the parent's knowledge of the child's history, and that by failing to exercise control, the parent placed others in peril.

The Parol Evidence Rule

Often parties to a contract had certain understandings of the terms of a contract before it was reduced to writing. If these understandings do not end up in the written contract, a court will try to determine whether the parties intended the written contract to represent their total and final agreement. If the court so finds, neither party may then introduce in court oral (also known as parol) evidence of any oral understandings that preceded the written contract.

Types of Contracts

Contracts are categorized by how they are created, how they are enforced, and how they will be performed.

Bilateral and Unilateral

Two types of contracts categorized by how they are created include **bilateral** and **unilateral contracts**. A bilateral contract, as its name implies, is a two-way agreement characterized by promises running in both directions. In a unilateral contract, only one party makes a promise in exchange for an act performed by the other party, rather than a promise for a promise as is the case in a bilateral contract. If the party to whom the promise is made fails to perform the act called for under the contract, there are no legal consequences. An example of a unilateral contract is a life insurance policy in which the insurer promises to pay a death benefit to the insured's beneficiary in exchange for the payment of insurance premiums. However, if the insured elects not to pay the required premiums, the policy is simply cancelled and the contract ends without any continuing legal obligation to either party.

In Depth: The Statute of Frauds

As discussed earlier, certain types of contracts must be in proper form. For example, certain types of contracts are required to be in writing. Nearly every state has a statute patterned on the English Statute of Frauds, which spells out which contracts must be in writing. Some of the more significant types of such contracts include (1) contracts involving interests in real estate; (2) contracts that will take more than one year to be performed; (3) prenuptial agreements; and (4) under the Uniform Commercial Code (UCC), contracts for the sale of goods priced at $500 or more.

Real property includes land and all physical objects permanently attached to the soil, such as buildings, fences, trees, and the soil itself. The Statute of Frauds also requires all contracts for the transfer of mortgages and leases to be in writing.3.

Express and Implied

Those contracts categorized by how they are formed include **express** and **implied contracts**. An express contract is one in which the terms are explicitly spelled out either orally or in writing. An **implied-in-fact or implied contract** is created by the actions of the parties, rather than by explicit oral or written words. Accordingly, if one party supplied a service or good expecting payment from the other party and the other party either knew or should have known that payment was expected and did not reject the service or good, then an implied contract is considered to exist. For example, a person drives his or her car into a self-service gas station, fills the car's fuel tank with gasoline, and then leaves without making payment. The gas station had made the gasoline available to the motorist at a specific price and the motorist, being aware of the price and having the option available to not take the fuel, had pumped the fuel into his or her auto. Therefore, it was the actions of the parties that created an implied contract and legally obligated the motorist to pay for the fuel.

There is an additional type of contract in this second category—that of a **quasi contract**. A quasi contract is imposed on parties by law to achieve a degree of fairness. It cannot coexist with either an express or implied contract. For example, consider a case where a motorist loses control of his auto, causing it to roll down an embankment resulting in serious injury to the motorist and rendering him unconscious and under threat of death without prompt medical attention. If the motorist is then rescued by emergency medical personnel and another passing motorist and is taken to the emergency room of a nearby hospital thereby saving his life, he cannot refuse to make payment to the hospital because he never authorized its services. He obtained a valuable service, and a quasi contract is said to have been created between the motorist and the hospital.

Executed and Executory

Other contracts are classified according to the degree to which they have been performed. They include executed and executory contracts. **Executed contracts** are those that have been fully performed by both parties. Those not yet fully performed by both parties are referred to as **executory contracts**. If only one party has fully performed but the other has not, the contract is said to be executed on the one side and executory on the other side, but the overall contract is considered to be executory.

Valid, Void, Voidable, and Unenforceable

A final category of contracts is those contracts classified by their enforceability—that of **valid, void, voidable, and unenforceable contracts**. A **valid contract** contains the four basic elements of a contract (discussed earlier) that render it enforceable, including (1) an agreement (offer and acceptance); (2) consideration; (3) competent parties; and (4) a legal purpose. A **void contract**, such as one drawn for an illegal purpose, is a noncontract that does not impose legal obligations on the parties thereto. A **voidable contract** is a valid contract that can be avoided at the option of one or both of the parties, such as a contract made by a minor or a contract entered into under fraudulent conditions, duress, or undue influence. Finally, an **unenforceable contract** is a valid contract that cannot be enforced because it does not meet certain statutory or legal requirements, such as the requirement that the document be in writing.

Transfer of Contractual Rights

If a person wishes to transfer his or her rights or duties under a contract to a third party, this can be accomplished in one of two ways. First, the contract holder can make an unconditional transfer of contractual *rights*, known as an **assignment**. By employing this option, the person making the assignment (the assignor) gives up his or her rights in the contract, and the person to whom the contract was assigned (the assignee) can enforce it against the remaining original party to the contract. Assignments are commonly used in business financing, such as in the assignment of accounts receivable for immediate cash.

In order to transfer his or her *duties* under a contract, rather than his or her *rights* under the contract, a contract holder can make a **delegation**, rather than an *assignment*. Duties cannot be assigned—they must be delegated. One of the major differences between an assignment and a delegation is that under a delegation, the person making the delegation (the delegator) continues to be legally obligated to perform his or her contract duties if the person to whom those duties were delegated (the delegatee) fails to perform those duties. There are a few cases where duties cannot be delegated, including the following:

1) when one of the parties to the contract has placed special trust in the other party to the contract (such as may exist in a contract for personal services [e.g., attorney, financial planner, tax advisor]).

2) when the person contracted to perform possesses unique personal skill or talents such as exists in a contract to create a work of art.

3) when delegating the contract to a third party will result in significantly different performance than that required under the contract.

4) when the contract contains a provision that delegation is not permitted.

Where an enforceable delegation has been made, the remaining party under the contract to whom performance is owed must accept performance from the party to whom the duties were delegated.

Contract Performance and Discharge

When both parties to a contract have either performed or tendered their performance under the contract, a contract is said to be terminated. Examples of tendering performance under a contract include placing goods at a buyer's disposal or offering to pay for goods. A tender of performance constitutes performance under the contract.

Types of Contract Performance

There are two basic types of performance—**complete performance** and **substantial performance**. Performing exactly as required by the contract is considered complete performance. If, on the other hand, a party acting in good faith performs essentially all of his or her obligations under a contract, that party is considered to have substantially performed and accordingly can enforce the contract. Of course, if the party purposefully failed to complete all of his or her obligations under the contract, it is not considered substantial performance but rather breach of contract. The determination of the point at which performance is considered substantial depends on the facts and circumstances of each case. Where performance is considered to be substantial, the party receiving less than full performance is entitled to damages for the performance shortfall under the contract. In the next section you will learn why it is important to determine whether performance has been substantial.

Material Breach of Contract

Failure to perform under a contract exactly as agreed constitutes a breach of contract. But if it is determined that there has not been substantial performance (as discussed in the previous section), then the breach is considered "material." A material breach of contract permits the nonbreaching party to sue for damages caused by the breach and to not have to perform under the contract. This is not the case when the breach is minor (not material); the nonbreaching party may be able to defer his or her performance until the breach has been remedied, but he or she cannot completely avoid his or her contractual duties.

Time for Contract Performance

Normally, contract parties must perform in accordance within the time limit established in the contract. If the contract is silent on when performance is required, it must be completed within a "reasonable time." Even where the contract includes a specific time for performance, late performance will not affect the right of the performing party to receive payment. In some contracts, the timing of performance under the contract is critical. In these cases, it is important to include in the contract the phrase "time is of the essence." Such language makes the timing of performance a contract condition.

Contract Discharge by Agreement

There are three basic methods to cancel or terminate a contract. A contract that has not yet been performed by both parties (an executory contract) can be cancelled or terminated by mutual agreement and the creation of a new contract to replace the old one, referred to as **rescission**. Rescission places both parties in the same position they were in before entering into the contract, just as if the contract never existed. In the situation where one of the parties has performed under the contract, that party must be compensated for agreeing to rescind the contract.

A contract also may be discharged through **novation**, where a third party is substituted for one of the original parties. In order for a novation to be effective, the contract being cancelled must have been valid to start with, all three parties must agree to the creation of a new contract, the previous contract must be considered null and void with discharge of the prior party, and a valid new contract must be created.

The third basic method of discharging a contract is by **accord and satisfaction**, where the parties agree to accept performance that varies from that included in the original contract.

Contract Discharge by Operation of Law

Rather than the parties agreeing to discharge a contract under rescission, novation, or accord and satisfaction as discussed in the previous section, the law may operate to terminate a contract. For example, if (1) one party has made significant revisions to a written contract without the other party's permission, (2) an applicable statute of limitations has expired, (3) one of the parties has become bankrupt, or (4) the contract either cannot be performed or is impractical to perform, the contract will be terminated by operation of law.

Breach of Contract and Remedies

When one of the parties fails to perform under a contract, he or she is said to have breached the contract. In this situation, the law provides to the other party some type or types of satisfaction known as **remedies** to either obtain his or her rights under the contract or to be compensated in some other manner. The most common types of remedies are **damages**, **rescission** and **restitution**, **specific performance**, and **reformation;** all of which are explained in **In Depth: Remedies for Breach of Contract.**

In Depth: Remedies for Breach of Contract

Damages are designed to compensate a party for the unfavorable effects resulting from the other contract party's breach. There are four broad categories of damages:

1) **Compensatory damages** provide compensation for damages actually incurred as a direct result of the breach of the contract by the other party. They are intended to reimburse the injured party for any losses resulting from the wrong or damage. Additional out-of-pocket expenses resulting directly from a contract breach are known as **incidental damages**.

2) **Consequential (or special) damages**, unlike compensatory damages, are the result of extra-contractual circumstances. They are applicable only where the breaching party knew, or should have known, that such circumstances would cause the other party to suffer losses in addition to those directly arising from the contract.

3) **Punitive (or exemplary) damages** are designed to punish a guilty party and to act as a deterrent against similar future actions.

4) **Nominal damages**, perhaps only one dollar, may be awarded when the nonbreaching party has not sustained a monetary loss but the court wishes to establish the breaching party's wrongdoing.

Some contracts provide for what are known as **liquidated damages,** which require a breaching party to pay a specific amount to compensate for such breach.

Rescission

As discussed earlier, **rescission** is essentially the cancellation of a contract as if it never existed.

Restitution

When a contract is rescinded, each party must compensate the other by returning the goods, property, or money already transferred. This is known as **restitution**. If the goods or property are no longer in existence or for some other reason cannot be returned, restitution must be made in an equivalent amount of money.

Specific Performance

Under the remedy of **specific performance**, the nonbreaching party demands performance under the terms of the contract. This can be beneficial to the nonbreaching party because it is often more valuable to have the breaching party perform under the contract than to have to seek money damages or an alternative contract.

Reformation is a remedy used to clarify the terms of a contract that was not well drafted at the outset in that it may not have expressed the true intentions of the parties. Reformation involves redrafting the contract to reflect the true intentions of the parties.

Relevance of the Law of Contracts to Financial Planning

It is nearly impossible to function either in the business world or in one's personal life without entering into contracts, whether written or oral. A financial planner enters into a contract with his or her client for the provision of personal financial planning services, for portfolio management, for securities brokerage, for the purchase and sale of insurance products, or for any one of several other services. Contracts may be required for services and products received by a financial planning practice, such as with a broker/dealer firm, an insurance company or agency, or with another investment advisory firm. For these reasons, financial planners must have a working knowledge of the law surrounding the creation, performance, termination, assignment, or breach of contracts.

LAW OF TORTS

In today's society, businesses and individuals are increasingly subjected to the risk of being sued. One of the most common sources of such lawsuits is the alleged wrongful conduct of a person resulting in injury to others, known in the law as a **tort action**. In a tort action, one party brings a civil suit against another to obtain compensation (money damages) or some other form of relief for the harm he or she has experienced. Where the alleged wrong is so serious as to constitute a wrong against society in general (rather than just a wrong against one party), it is referred to as a **crime**, and the offender is prosecuted and punished by the state. The law of torts was designed to protect certain vital interests of individuals and businesses such as their physical security, their right to come and go as they please, the security of their property, their personal privacy, their family relations, their reputation, and their dignity. Tort law provides remedies against those who invade these interests.

Some of the torts discussed in the previous paragraph are considered **business torts**. These include wrongfully interfering with the rights of a business through the use of unfair competitive practices or by intruding upon its established business relationships.

Intentional Torts Against Persons and Business Relationships

As the name implies, an **intentional tort** is one where the person committing the tort did so on purpose, not accidentally or through negligence. Some of the most common intentional torts against persons and business relationships include assault and battery, false imprisonment, infliction of emotional distress, defamation, invasion of one's privacy, appropriation, misrepresentation, and wrongful interference. We will discuss each of these torts briefly in the following sections.

Assault and Battery

Assault is an intentional act that, because of its character, causes another person to justifiably fear being physically attacked or harassed. Such an act can take the form of a threat to commit another tort known as battery. **Battery** is the intentional carrying out of such a threat or following through with the act that caused fear in the other person, provided it results in harm to the plaintiff.

False Imprisonment

Intentional and non-justifiable interference with a person's right to move without restriction is known as **false imprisonment**. This would be the case where the perpetrator uses some form of physical restraint or threatens physical violence.

Infliction of Emotional Distress

When one intentionally performs an act that is so extreme and outrageous that it results in severe emotional distress to another, the person performing such an act has committed the tort of **intentional infliction of emotional distress.** It is essential that the victim's severe emotional distress can be demonstrated in some manner or documented by an appropriate healthcare professional. The fact that such an act is simply annoying or insulting is generally not adequate to support a lawsuit for infliction of emotional distress.

Defamation

Every person has a legal duty to not disparage another's good reputation. If a person breaches this duty by making untrue, derogatory oral statements about another person, he or she has committed **slander**. If a person does so in writing, it is referred to as **libel**. In order to constitute slander or libel, such statements must be addressed to third parties rather than to the person being defamed. In order to support a case for slander, it must be demonstrated that the plaintiff actually incurred financial losses as a result of the alleged slanderous statements. The plaintiff's burden of proof is not as high in the case of libel, in which it is not necessary to demonstrate the infliction of injury by the libelous statements. If it is determined that a statement made about a plaintiff is true, generally no tort will be deemed to have occurred. Speech by certain individuals in a particular context is considered privileged, such as that of judges and attorneys in a courtroom during a trial. As a result, such individuals may not be sued for such statements. Also, statements against public figures are privileged unless made with what is known as "actual malice" (knowledge of the statement's falsity or a reckless disregard of the truth).

Invasion of Privacy

Performing any of the following four acts constitutes **invasion of privacy**:

1) Unauthorized commercial use of a person's name, picture, or other likeness. (See Appropriation in the next section.)

2) Unauthorized entry into another person's residence, inspection of someone's private property without legal authority to do so, or listening in on another person's telephone conversations by electronic means.

3) Dissemination of untrue information that portrays an inaccurate picture of a person, such as information about ideas allegedly held by a person or acts allegedly committed by that person.

4) Public disclosure of private, intimate details about a private citizen (not a public figure) that the average person would consider offensive.

Other Intentional Torts Against Persons and Business Relationships

Other intentional torts against persons and business relationships include the following:

- **Appropriation**—unauthorized use of another person's name or likeness for the purpose of enriching the user.

- **Misrepresentation**—purposefully misleading another person for one's own enrichment. The burden of proof for misrepresentation is daunting. Five factors must be present for misrepresentation to be sustained: (1) knowing misrepresentation of material facts or conditions; (2) intent to have the other party place reliance on such misrepresentation; (3) reliance by the other party on the misrepresentation; (4) damages resulting from such reliance; and (5) the damages being the direct result of the misrepresentation. The person committing this tort must know that the statements made are false.

- **Wrongful interference**—interfering with either a contractual or business relationship. In the case of a contractual relationship, the defendant must have known that there was an existing contract and must have persuaded one of the contract parties to breach the contract for the economic benefit of the defendant. Wrongful interference with a business relationship involves gaining entrance to a particular market through the use of unfair trade practices (as contrasted to aggressive, successful promotional activities). A person claiming wrongful interference with a business relationship is required to demonstrate not only that there was a preexisting business relationship, but that the defendant brought about the relationship's end by using unfair trade practices and that damages were incurred by the plaintiff from such practices.

Intentional Torts Against Property

There are three types of intentional torts against property: trespass to land, trespass to personal property, and conversion.

Trespass to Land

A landowner is entitled to the **right of exclusive possession**. If someone enters upon the owner's land, places something on the land, continues to stay on the land or allows anything to remain on the land without the owner's permission, the intruder has committed the act of

trespass to land. It does not matter whether the intruder harmed the land. Of course, one of the difficulties is in sorting out who is in fact a trespasser. Clearly, someone who pays no attention to posted "no trespassing" signs or comes on the property with the purpose of doing something against the law is considered to be a trespasser. A guest in one's home only becomes a trespasser at such time as he or she is requested to leave and declines to do so. A person who purchases a ticket to a theater performance and during the performance engages in obnoxious conduct and is asked to leave by the management but refuses to do so is also considered a trespasser.

Generally, if a trespasser sustains injuries while trespassing, he or she has no legal redress against the landowner. On the other hand, if a young child enters one's land because of what is known as an "attractive nuisance" (the classic case is a swimming pool), and is injured while on the land, the child's parents may bring legal action against the landowner. A landowner may either remove a trespasser from the property or use reasonable force to keep him or her on the premises for a reasonable period of time without being deemed to have committed assault and battery or false imprisonment (discussed earlier).

Trespass to Personal Property

Like a landowner, the owner of personal property enjoys a right of exclusive possession and enjoyment of that property. When another person brings harm to that property without the owner's permission or in any way interferes with the aforesaid right of the owner, he or she has engaged in **trespass to personal property.**

Conversion

Conversion is any act that deprives an owner of personal property without his or her permission and without a valid reason. A thief, for instance, commits both the crime of theft and the tort of conversion. Even a buyer of stolen goods unaware that the goods were stolen has committed the tort of conversion.

Negligence

While the foregoing discussion dealt with the topic of intentional torts, in this section we will discuss **unintentional torts.** Here the person committing the tort does not intend to bring harm to another and does not reasonably foresee that result. Probably the best-known unintentional tort is that of negligence.

In a negligence suit, a plaintiff must prove (1) that the defendant owed what is known as a duty of care to the plaintiff; (2) that the defendant failed to honor that duty; (3) that the plaintiff was harmed (as that term is defined in the law); and (4) that the defendant's failure to honor his or her duty of care directly resulted in the plaintiff's injury. If there is no harm or injury resulting from a negligent action, there is no need to compensate the plaintiff and as a result, there is no tort. If the plaintiff can demonstrate a harm or injury, he or she must next prove that it was the direct result of the defendant's negligence. Courts will not impose liability on a defendant unless there is what is referred to as **proximate cause**, meaning that there is a causal relationship between the defendant's act and the plaintiff's injury. If, on the other hand, the defendant could have reasonably foreseen that such an injury was the likely result of the defendant's act, courts will hold the defendant liable for damages.

A duty of care is determined under the **reasonable person standard**. In other words, what would a reasonable person have done in the same situation, recognizing that each situation is unique? Because of the distinctive facts and circumstances of each situation, the duty of care owed in a particular situation can vary significantly depending on many factors. In the case of professionals, including financial planners, they are required to have a minimum level of special knowledge and ability and to use it effectively in providing client services.

Defenses to Negligence

A defendant sued for negligence can raise any of three basic defenses: (1) **assumption of risk**, meaning that the plaintiff made a voluntary choice to engage in a risky activity; (2) **superseding cause,** where it is demonstrated that an act (other than that of the defendant), which could not reasonably have been foreseen, is the real cause of the plaintiff's injury; and (3) **contributory negligence**, now recognized in only a handful of states. Most states compare the relative negligence of both parties and apportion damages on that basis under the doctrine of **comparative negligence.**

Special Negligence Doctrines and Statutes

There are several special doctrines and statutes that are applicable to negligence. The doctrine of **res ipsa loquitur** (Latin for "the facts speak for themselves") comes into play when the event creating the damage or injury could only have occurred as a result of negligence. Under this doctrine, negligence is presumed to have occurred and accordingly the defendant takes on the burden of proof. Of course, the defendant must have been able to exercise control over the event that caused the damage or injury, and the plaintiff must not have voluntarily contributed to it.

Under the doctrine of **negligence per se** ("in or of itself"), if a person causes injury to another in the process of committing a crime, the perpetrator is considered negligent per se.

In many states, **Good Samaritan statutes** have been enacted to protect medical service personnel who voluntarily come to the aid of persons injured in emergency situations. Under the **dram shop acts** of many states, a tavern owner or bartender can be held liable for injuries caused by a person who was served alcohol at the bar until intoxicated or who was already intoxicated when served by the bartender. Some states have enacted **social host statutes** that hold social hosts liable when their guests become intoxicated and cause injuries to others.

Strict Liability

Sometimes, a person chooses to conduct what the law considers an "abnormally dangerous activity" in an area where such activities are normally not conducted. For instance, if a person living in a semi-rural neighborhood near other homes were to raise dangerous, wild animals such as lions or tigers, and one or more of these animals was to escape and cause injury or kill a neighbor, the animal owner would be held to what is known as **strict liability**. In this situation, the law would hold the animal owner *prima facie* (at first sight; on the face of it) legally responsible for any damages resulting from the escape of the animals, simply because they elected to engage in such activity. An activity is deemed to be abnormally dangerous if the activity: (1) has the potential of causing serious harm to persons or property; (2) is very risky even if the owner were to exercise reasonable care; and (3) is typically not engaged in by others in the area.

Product Liability

A product manufacturer is required to exercise "due care" to make its product(s) safe. A manufacturer failing to do so by producing a defective product may be sued for negligence by any person whose injury was proximately caused by the manufacturer's product.

Relevance of Tort Law to Financial Planning

Most people are aware that we live in a litigious society. In providing personal financial planning services, financial planners need to operate their practices in a manner that does not violate the rights of others. Conversely, they should know what rights they possess and when those rights may have been violated. This requires knowledge of what constitutes a tort—both intentional and unintentional. Tort law provides remedies for the invasion of various "protected interests," such as physical security, freedom of movement, property, personal privacy, family relations, reputation, and dignity. Professionals, including financial planners, who fail to understand the basics of tort law can inadvertently expose themselves and their businesses to significant legal liability.

THE LAW OF AGENCY

In the modern business world, financial planners often act as an agent. As a result, they must have at least a general understanding of the law of agency. In an agency relationship, one party, the **agent**, is engaged to represent or act for the other party, the **principal**. In agency matters, the agent's conduct is under the direction of the principal. Corporate officers and employees who deal with third parties are normally considered to be agents for their corporate employer. Later in this chapter, we will discuss what constitutes a fiduciary relationship. An agent and principal have such a relationship; accordingly an agent must work primarily for the benefit of the principal in matters related to the agency.

Formation of the Agency Relationship

In order to create an agency relationship, the two parties need simply to agree to do so. In fact, it is not even necessary to reduce such an agreement to writing nor does consideration have to be provided. While a principal must have legal capacity, an agent, even one who is legally incompetent, does not have to. Since an agency is a contractual relationship, it must be formed for a legal purpose. In addition to the agent and principal simply agreeing to form an agency relationship, a person acting without express authority from a principal may perform certain acts on behalf of the principal that the principal subsequently approves. This is known as ratification. Also, if a principal leads a third party to believe that another person is the principal's agent and the third party places reasonable reliance on that belief, then the principal is estopped from claiming that no agency exists. Finally, courts may create an agency relationship in the interest of public policy, as would be the case if a spouse purchased food and clothing on credit and the other spouse refused to pay for such items. In this situation, a court might rule that the other spouse is required by law to supply necessaries to one's family members.

NEED TO KNOW: DUTIES OF AN AGENT TO THE PRINCIPAL

In an agency relationship, the agent owes the principal five duties: (1) performance; (2) notification; (3) loyalty; (4) obedience; and (5) accounting. An agent is obligated to employ reasonable diligence and skill in performing his or her agency duties and to keep the principal informed of agency matters. Under the law, the principal is charged with knowledge of such matters, even if the agent fails to communicate it to the principal. Since an agency relationship is a fiduciary relationship, loyalty to one's principal is a clearly understood requirement. Moreover, an agent must obey the principal's instructions, provided they do not violate the law and are reasonably understandable, except in an emergency when the principal is not available. Finally, an agent is obligated to keep current, accurate records of all property and money collected and disbursed on behalf of the principal and to make those records available to the principal. Agency funds must not be commingled with the agent's personal funds.

Remedies and Rights of Agents and Principals

In those cases where disputes arise between agents and principals as a result of misrepresentation, negligence, fraud, deceit, libel, slander, or trespass committed by the agent, both parties may seek monetary damages, termination of the agency relationship, injunction, and required accounting under both contract and tort law.

Types of Agent Authority

If an agent is said to have actual authority, it must be either express or implied. **Express authority** is that given by a principal either orally or in writing. If the subject matter of the agency requires the agent to enter into, on behalf of the principal, one of the kinds of contracts that the law requires to be in written form, then the agency agreement must also be in writing. Failure to observe this formality can render the contract voidable by the principal.

If it is customary for an agent who performs a particular function to have a certain amount of authority or if the agent is unable to perform under an express agency agreement without having a reasonable amount of authority, then the agent is considered to have **implied authority**. For example, an insurance agent, simply by virtue of being an insurance agent, customarily has the authority to accept premium payments on behalf of the insurer, even if such authority is not included in his or her express authority.

As discussed earlier, if a principal leads a third party to believe that a person is empowered to perform certain acts and the third party relies on such a representation (even if the person has neither express nor implied authority), then the agent is said to possess **apparent authority.** In this situation, the principal cannot then claim that the agent has no authority.

NEED TO KNOW: DUTIES OF A PRINCIPAL TO AN AGENT

In an agency relationship, the principal owes four principal duties to the agent including (1) compensation; (2) reimbursement and indemnification; (3) cooperation; and (4) safe working conditions. Clearly when a principal enters into an agency agreement, the principal is obligated to pay the agent the agreed-upon compensation at the time required by the agreement and to reimburse the agent for cash disbursements made for the principal and for any reasonably necessary agency expenses. In addition, a principal must not only cooperate with the agent to facilitate the performance of the agent's duties, but must refrain from impeding the agent's performance. Finally, common law requires the principal to provide safe working conditions for the agent.

Liability for Agent's Torts

A principal is not liable for torts committed by his or her agent, unless authorized by the principal, connected to the commission of a tort or torts by the principal, or constitutes an unauthorized misrepresentation made in connection with the agency agreement. If you remember that the act of an agent is considered the act of the principal, a principal is legally responsible for acts committed by the agent that the principal authorized. Moreover, a principal is liable to third parties for an agent's misrepresentation of the principal's product or service if the agent was authorized to provide information about the principal's product or service.

Liability for Agent's Crimes

Just as is the case with torts, an agent is responsible for his or her own crimes. Even if an agent commits a crime pursuant to the agency agreement, the principal has no liability unless he or she participated or conspired with the agent to commit the tort.

Termination of an Agency

Just like a contract, it is possible to terminate an agency either by an act of the parties or by operation of law. If an agency is terminated by the parties, it is necessary that third parties be so informed so that the principal will be relieved of liability for the future acts of the agent under his or her apparent authority.

In Depth: Termination of an Agency

Termination by Act of the Parties

1) Lapse of time—at the date established in the agency agreement, after a reasonable time (depending upon the specifics of the agency relationship), or at will by either party.

2) Purpose achieved—the agency's objective has been accomplished.

3) Occurrence of a specific event—e.g. the principal has become legally incompetent.

4) Mutual agreement—each party advises the other of his or her desire to end the relationship.

5) Termination by one party—generally, either party can end the relationship simply by providing reasonable notice to the other party.

6) Notice of termination—the principal must inform any third parties who were aware of the agency relationship of its termination.

Termination by Operation of Law

1) Death or insanity—after the principal's death, the agent is no longer able to bind the principal's estate, even if the agent was not aware of the principal's death.

2) Impossibility—when the objective of an agency can no longer be accomplished because of the destruction or loss of the agency's subject matter.

3) Changed circumstances—if a subsequent event in effect obviates the reason for creating the agency and the agent is justified in assuming that the principal will not want to continue the agency under the revised conditions, the agency terminates. For example, where the value of a product or service changes substantially due to an event taking place after the agency was formed, the agency will be terminated.

4) Bankruptcy—if either the principal or agent files for bankruptcy, ordinarily the agency is terminated, unless the financial status of the parties has no bearing on the purpose of the agency.

5) War—when the principal's country and the agent's country are at war with each other, the agency is terminated.

Relevance of Agency Law to Financial Planning

Financial planners constantly function as agents for their clients, for their securities broker/dealer firm, for insurance companies, for their investment advisory firm, and for their employers, among others. Understanding the law of agency is essential to their efficient and successful delivery of personal financial planning services.

NEGOTIABLE INSTRUMENTS

Negotiable instruments make up a large portion of daily commercial transactions. A negotiable instrument is a document signed by one party who either makes an unconditional promise (or directs another party) to pay an exact sum of money, either upon demand or at a determinable time in the future. The classic example is a personal check, which can serve as a substitute for cash. A negotiable instrument can also take the form of a loan document (a promissory note). What makes negotiable instruments so useful in the world of commerce is the ease with which they can be transferred.

The law related to negotiable instruments was originally the Uniform Negotiable Instruments Law most of which was incorporated in Article 3 of the Uniform Commercial Code (UCC), revised in 1990, and subsequently adopted by almost all of the states.

Types of Negotiable Instruments

Under the UCC, there are four basic types of negotiable instruments: drafts, checks, notes, and certificates of deposit. Drafts and checks are considered "orders to pay," while promissory notes and CDs are "promises to pay." Negotiable instruments are further classified as **demand** or **time instruments**. As its name implies, a demand instrument, such as a check, is payable on demand (if it states that it is payable on demand, at the will of the holder, or does not include a specific payment date) or at sight. Checks are actually a type of **draft** (bill of exchange) involving three separate parties, including the **drawer** who creates the draft, the **drawee** against whom the draft is drawn, and the **payee**, the party to whom the proceeds are payable. Usually the three parties to a check are separate parties, except in the case of a cashier's check, where the bank is both the drawer and the drawee. In this case, the bank customer deposits with his or her bank the amount needed to honor the check and then fills in the name of the payee.

A draft can take one of three forms—a sight draft payable on sight or on demand, a time draft payable at a specific time in the future, or a combination of both payable at a certain time after sight. Some drafts are payable upon **acceptance**. The act of accepting a draft by signing it in the appropriate location on the draft constitutes the acceptor's promise to pay the draft on its due date.

Where goods are sold on credit, the parties may finance the purchase through the use of what is known as a **trade acceptance.** Under this type of instrument, the seller draws a draft on the buyer payable to the seller for the value of the goods purchased and dates the draft for an agreed-upon future date (such as 90 days from shipment). Then the draft is sent to the buyer for his or her acceptance, evidenced by signing and dating the draft on its face. After acceptance by the buyer, the draft is returned to the seller who maintains possession of the draft until the due date. If instead of drawing the draft directly on the buyer, the draft is drawn on the buyer's bank for acceptance, it becomes a **banker's acceptance**, used to a greater extent in international trade.

A **promissory note** is a written document evidencing one party's indebtedness to another. The debtor who signs the note is referred to as the **maker** and the party to whom the debt is payable is known as the **payee**. However, a note may be made payable to bearer, discussed later in this chapter. Promissory notes are payable either on demand or at a specific date. There are various types of promissory notes, depending on the type of loan involved. For instance, a **collateral note** is one in which some sort of collateral has been pledged to secure the payment of the note, such as an auto loan. Where the indebtedness is to extend over several months or years and requires monthly payments, the note is known as an **installment note**.

In the situation where a bank customer deposits a certain sum of money with the bank with the understanding that the sum will be repaid to the customer plus interest at a specific future date, the resulting promissory note is known as a **certificate of deposit** (CD). Unlike a promissory note evidencing a loan by a bank to a bank customer, in which the customer is the maker and the bank is the payee, with a CD the bank is the maker and the customer is the payee. CDs are sold by savings and loan associations, savings banks, credit unions, and commercial banks.

Requirements for Negotiability

There are certain basic requirements that an instrument must meet before it will be considered negotiable. It must:

1. Be in writing.
2. Be signed by the maker or the drawer.
3. Be an unconditional promise or order to pay.
4. State a fixed amount of money.
5. Be payable on demand or at a definite time.
6. Be payable to order or to bearer, unless it is a check.

To provide certainty, negotiable instruments must be written.

Instead of appending his or her signature to a negotiable instrument, a maker or drawer may use a symbol adopted by him or her for the purpose of authenticating a written document. However, an unusual signature or symbol may create uncertainty and thereby decrease the marketability of an instrument.

Negotiable instruments cannot be conditioned on the occurrence or nonoccurrence of some other event or agreement—they must be unconditional promises to pay rather than just an acknowledgment of the debt.

A **fixed amount** refers to an amount that can be determined from the face of the instrument.

The value of a negotiable instrument will vary depending upon when the party required to pay under the instrument is required to make payment, since this date or dates will determine the period of time during which interest will accrue. If an instrument is not payable on demand, a definite time of payment is required. A definite time is defined as (1) payable on a specific date; (2) payable within a definite period of time after sight or acceptance; or (3) payable on a date or time that can be readily determined at the time the instrument was created.

Some instruments include what is known as an **acceleration clause**, which requires full payment of the unpaid balance plus interest if the payor fails to make a required payment at the time specified in the instrument.

In creating an instrument, the maker has two choices—"payable to order" or "payable to bearer." If one of these two options is not selected, the instrument will not be negotiable. Making an instrument "payable to order" means making it payable to the order of a specific person or, alternatively, to a specific person or that person's order. To make an instrument "payable to bearer" simply means to not indicate a specific payee. A "bearer" is a person in possession of an instrument that is payable to bearer or one that has been endorsed in blank (with a signature only). By making an instrument payable to bearer, the maker is promising to pay anyone who presents the instrument for payment. A bearer instrument can be identified by whether it contains any of the following terms:

1. "Payable to the order of bearer."
2. "Payable to John Jones or bearer."
3. "Payable to bearer."
4. "Pay cash."
5. "Pay to the order of cash."

Failing to include a date on an instrument does not render it nonnegotiable unless the date is required in order to determine its due date.

Transferability

There are two ways to transfer negotiable instruments to others: **assignment** and **negotiation**. A person receiving an instrument by assignment is referred to as an assignee and obtains only those rights that the assignor originally had. On the other hand, when an instrument is transferred by negotiation, the transferee becomes a holder, rather than an assignee. A certain type of holder, known as a **holder in due course,** receives more rights than those held by the prior possessor. We will discuss holders and holders in due course later in this chapter.

A possessor of an instrument payable to order wishing to negotiate the instrument must deliver it with any necessary endorsements affixed to the instrument. For example, if a check is payable "to the order of John Smith," and John Smith wants to negotiate it, he need only sign his name on the back and deliver it to another party in exchange for cash or credit to his account, if delivered to a financial institution. To negotiate a bearer instrument, no endorsement is required; the possessor need only deliver the instrument to another. Consequently, the use of bearer instruments involves a greater amount of risk. While a thief has no rights in a stolen bearer instrument, the thief can obtain such rights by merely delivering the instrument to an innocent third party.

An order instrument can be converted to a bearer instrument just as a bearer instrument can be converted to an order instrument. An example of converting an order instrument to a bearer instrument is where a check is originally made out to "John Smith" and John Smith simply signs his name on the reverse side of the check. An example of a conversion running in the opposite direction is one where a check originally made payable to "cash" is subsequently endorsed with the words "Pay to John Smith" or "Pay to the order of John Smith." The check must now be negotiated only as an order instrument, even though it started out as a bearer instrument.

Endorsements

As mentioned previously, an order instrument can only be negotiated by endorsing it. An endorsement is a signature with or without additional words or statements. A person who transfers a note or a draft by signing (endorsing) it and delivering it to another person is an endorser.

There are basically four types of endorsements—**blank, special, qualified, and restrictive**. A blank endorsement is simply a signature on the document without mentioning a specific endorsee. The effect is to convert an order instrument into a bearer instrument. A special endorsement names a specific party to whom the endorser desires to make the instrument payable, thereby converting the instrument to an order instrument. It is important to realize that someone who endorses a negotiable instrument assumes the obligation to make payment under the instrument to the holder (or subsequent endorser) if the drawer (or maker) defaults under the instrument. One way to avoid such liability is for the endorser to use a qualified endorsement which means adding the notation "without recourse." Restrictive endorsements include conditional, trust, and for deposit or collection endorsements.

Holder versus Holder in Due Course

As discussed previously, a holder is a person who has possession of an instrument if the instrument is either payable to bearer or to the person in possession. An ordinary holder, just as an assignee, acquires from the transferor only those rights that the transferor had in the instrument. However, a holder in due course (HDC) obtains greater rights than the transferor possessed. To qualify as a holder in due course and therefore obtain these greater rights, a holder must take the instrument (1) for value; (2) in good faith; and (3) without notice that the instrument is overdue, that it has been dishonored, that anyone has a defense against it or a claim to it, or that the instrument contains either forged signatures or has been altered, or that its authenticity is suspect. Because a holder in due course has met these acquisition requirements, he or she takes the instrument free of most of the defenses and claims to which the transferor may have been subject. As a result, a holder in due course has more protection than an ordinary holder against any defenses or claims against the instrument.

With regard to the "for value" requirement, a person receiving an instrument as a gift or inheritance becomes an ordinary holder, but not a HDC, since he or she did not give anything of value to obtain it.

The holder of an instrument, in order to meet the "good faith" requirement to become a HDC has to demonstrate "honesty in fact and the observance of reasonable commercial standards of fair dealing" as specified in the UCC. This requirement is not applicable to the transferor. As a result, it is possible for a person to take a negotiable instrument in good faith from a thief and thereby become a HDC.

The third requirement to qualify as a HDC, as discussed previously, is that the person must not have known or had reason to know (had guilty knowledge) that the following conditions were present:

1) The instrument is overdue.

2) The instrument has been dishonored.

3) There is an uncorrected default with respect to another instrument issued as part of the same series of instruments.

4) The instrument contains an unauthorized signature or has been altered.

5) There is a defense against the instrument or a claim to the instrument.

6) The instrument is so irregular or incomplete as to call into question its authenticity.

Holder through a HDC

Someone who fails to meet the requirements of a HDC, but who nevertheless obtained in good faith an instrument from a HDC, acquires the rights and privileges of a HDC.

Relevance of Negotiable Instruments Law to Financial Planning

It is through negotiable instruments that the world's daily business is transacted. Any business person, including a financial planner, must be familiar with the basic types of negotiable instruments, their proper transfer, the responsibilities of the parties to such instruments, and factors that may affect their value. In dealing effectively with clients, a financial planner must understand the law surrounding such everyday instruments as checks, promissory notes, certificates of deposit, and both trade and banker's acceptances.

PROFESSIONAL LIABILITY

The most common ways in which professionals may incur legal liability to clients is through breach of contract, negligence, or fraud. A professional owes a duty to his or her client to fulfill the obligations imposed on the professional by their contract, including timely performance. In fact, a professional may be required to reimburse a client for expenses or losses incurred as a direct result of the professional's breach of contract.

A professional is charged with the possession of special knowledge, skill, or intelligence not possessed by an ordinary person, and as a result, the professional must act accordingly. Most professionals, such as physicians, dentists, psychiatrists, architects, engineers, accountants, lawyers, and financial planners, are required by their respective professions to have a standard minimum level of special knowledge and ability and to abide by the applicable professional standards of care. Accordingly, a financial planner cannot defend against a lawsuit for negligence by stating, "But I was not familiar with that financial planning practice standard."

The event that can trigger legal liability for a professional is the violation of his or her duty of care to a client. In order to establish negligence, a client has a difficult burden of proof, including (1) that a duty of care existed; (2) that the duty of care was breached; (3) that the client suffered an injury; and (4) that the injury was the direct result of the professional's breach of the duty of care.

Just as with a suit for negligence, a client bringing a suit against a professional for fraud must prove (1) that misrepresentation of a material fact has occurred; (2) that the professional intended to deceive the client; (3) that the client reasonably relied on the misrepresentation; and (4) that the client incurred damages.

Professionals may be able to limit their liability for the misconduct of other professionals with whom they work by organizing the business as a professional corporation (P.C.) or a limited liability partnership (LLP). In most cases, a disclaimer of liability by the professional will not be effective.

Relevance of Professional Liability to Financial Planning

Financial planners, just as other professionals, normally owe a duty of care to their clients. If this duty is violated, a client incurs damages, and the violation of the financial planner's duty is the proximate cause of such damages, then the client may be in a position to bring legal action against the financial planner. Accordingly, financial planners must be familiar with the duty of care owed to their clients and understand what constitutes a violation of that duty. Financial planners may attempt to reduce their risk of legal liability by fully complying with financial planning practice standards, by insuring against such risks (if possible), or by using the appropriate business entity to conduct their professional pursuits.

FIDUCIARY LIABILITY

A **fiduciary** is a person having a duty arising from the nature of his or her relationship with a client (e.g., a financial planning relationship) to act primarily for the client's benefit in matters connected with the client relationship. The relationship created is one of trust and confidence. In Chapter 6, we discussed the requirement of a registered investment adviser to function as a fiduciary on behalf of his or her client. In a fiduciary relationship, such as between a financial planner and a client, the dominant party (the financial planner) is required to act with extreme or utmost good faith in dealing with the client.

Fiduciary duties are among the highest duties owed by professionals to their clients. Violation of these duties can give rise to significant legal liability for the professional, including financial planners.

ALTERNATIVE DISPUTE RESOLUTION

Alternative dispute resolution (ADR) is a general method of settling disputes without resorting to the courts. Since 95 percent of civil lawsuits are resolved through pre-trial settlements, thus saving the litigants significant time and money, clients are usually advised to settle such disputes outside of the court system. ADR offers the advantages of (1) significant cost savings; (2) flexibility; (3) speed in resolution; and (4) greater privacy. Many state and federal court systems now either encourage or require some form of pre-trial ADR. There are three basic types of ADR—negotiation, mediation, and arbitration.

Negotiation

Realizing the potential toll of a court proceeding in terms of money, time, and psychological stress, adversarial parties often attempt to settle their dispute informally by direct contact, by use of a neutral third party, or through their attorneys. As mentioned previously, some courts will not hear a lawsuit until the parties can demonstrate that they have made a serious attempt to negotiate a settlement beforehand.

Mediation

Under **mediation**, the parties attempt to negotiate a settlement of their issues through the use of a paid mediator, who is a neutral third party, not necessarily an attorney. Mediation fees are usually shared equally by the parties involved. A trained mediator is invaluable in terms of his or her ability to summarize areas of agreement and disagreement on the issues of the dispute. Particularly helpful is the mediator's skill at digging beneath the surface to find out where both parties are coming from and helping them evaluate their positions and determining their true interests. The mediator normally reserves the right to separate the parties in order to extract important information not being shared in the joint sessions. Usually, at the conclusion of the mediation sessions, the mediator will propose one or several options to the parties with an analysis of what each will have to relinquish to arrive at an agreement. Unlike negotiation, mediation is, in theory, non-adversarial. In fact, a precondition for successful mediation is that both parties are able to deal reasonably with each other. Where the parties need to maintain a reasonable working relationship in the future, mediation can be particularly useful in that it helps to build a basis for continued communication.

Arbitration

Arbitration is conducted through the use of an arbitrator, which can be a neutral third party (as in either negotiation or mediation) or a panel of experts in the area under dispute. Often the parties agree in advance that the decision of the arbitrator will be final and legally binding on both parties. In those cases where a court has required that disputes be arbitrated before trial, the decision of the arbitrator usually does not bind the parties.

While the procedural rules of arbitration are more formal than those of mediation, they are not as rigorous as those employed in a court of law. Similar to a court proceeding, the arbitrator hears opening arguments, examines evidence, and hears witnesses (with an opportunity for each side to question witnesses), and then renders his/its decision, known as an award. As mentioned previously, the arbitrator's award is normally the final word on the matter. Normally, courts will uphold the arbitrator's award unless it can be demonstrated that the arbitrator was in error or acted inappropriately.

It has become normal procedure to include an arbitration clause in commercial contracts requiring arbitration of disputes rather than the filing of lawsuits. Absent such a clause in a contract, parties can also agree to arbitrate a dispute when it occurs.

ADR services are available from the nonprofit American Arbitration Association (AAA), whose membership is composed of major U.S. law firms. There are also governmental and private options available.

Financial planners should be familiar with the alternative dispute resolution techniques discussed earlier both with regard to their relationship with their clients but also with regard to advising their clients about their clients' relationships with their customers/clients, employers, providers of services, and others.

IMPORTANT CONCEPTS TO REMEMBER

Required elements of a contract

Bilateral versus unilateral contracts

Express versus implied contracts

Quasi contract

Executed versus executory contracts

Valid, void, voidable, and unenforceable contracts

Requirements of an offer

Various ways to terminate an offer

Acceptance of an offer

Three elements of consideration

Statute of Frauds

Parol evidence rule

Remedies for breach of contract

Intentional torts against persons and business relationships

Intentional torts against property

Negligence and defenses to negligence

Duty of care

Duties of agents and principals to each other

Termination of an agency relationship

Orders to pay versus promises to pay

Demand versus time instruments

Requirements for negotiability of an instrument

Holder versus holder in due course

Professional liability

Fiduciary liability

Negotiation, mediation, and arbitration

QUESTIONS FOR REVIEW

1. What is the primary purpose of contract law?

2. What are the required elements of a contract and the two additional elements which, if not satisfied, may render a contract unenforceable?

3. What is the difference between a void and a voidable contract?

4. Under the common law, what are the three elements necessary for an offer to be effective?

5. How can an offer be terminated by the action of the parties?

6. What are the three elements of consideration?

7. What are the basic provisions of the Statute of Frauds?

8. What is the parol evidence rule?

9. In what ways may contractual rights be transferred?

10. What are the most common remedies for breach of contract?

11. What are the most common intentional torts against persons and business relationships?

12. What are the three main types of intentional torts against property?

13. What must a plaintiff prove in a negligence suit?

14. What is the difference between contributory negligence and comparative negligence?

15. What are the duties owed by an agent to a principal and vice versa?

16. What are the main ways in which an agency relationship may be terminated?

17. What is the most widely used example of a negotiable instrument?

18. What requirements must a document meet in order to be negotiable?

19. What is the difference between a holder and a holder in due course of a negotiable instrument?

20. What are the three main forms of alternative dispute resolution and how do they differ?

SUGGESTIONS FOR ADDITIONAL READINGS

West's Business Law, 9th edition, by Kenneth W. Clarkson, Roger LeRoy Miller, Gaylord A. Jentz, & Frank B. Cross, West Legal Studies in Business, a division of Thomson Learning, 2004.

CHAPTER FOURTEEN

The Implications of Property Titling

• • •

How various types of property are owned by individuals can have a significant effect on how it is taxed both during their lifetime and at their death; on its ownership in the event of legal separation or divorce and death; and on the ability to transfer it to others. It is a topic of great importance that is too often ignored or not given adequate attention by financial planners and others. Even when its significance is understood, appreciated, and reflected in financial planning recommendations developed for clients, such recommendations often are not implemented or are implemented ineffectively. In these cases, certain legal documents drafted by the client's attorney can be rendered ineffective because of a failure to re-title property in the recommended manner.

In this chapter we will discuss the various types of property, how property may be owned, and the implications and effects of ownership in particular forms.

The objectives of this chapter are:

- Identify the various classifications of property and ownership interests.
- Describe how property is owned by the parties to a trust.
- Distinguish between the characteristics of a trust and those of a custodial account.
- Explain what is meant by an undivided ownership interest in property that is owned concurrently.
- Distinguish among the three forms of joint or concurrent ownership in common law property states.

- Identify the basic characteristics of property ownership by married couples in community property states.
- Discuss how it is possible for married couples living in common law states to have community property.
- Describe some of the similarities and differences between owning property as joint tenants with right of survivorship (JTWROS) and owning community property.

CLASSIFICATIONS AND TYPES OF PROPERTY AND OWNERSHIP INTERESTS

Property consists of the rights and interests a person holds in anything of value that is capable of being owned. If the law did not protect a person's right to use, sell or otherwise dispose of, or exclusively possess and enjoy property, such property would be of little value.

Property ownership can be viewed as a "bundle of rights" including the right to possess it and to dispose of it by sale, gift, rental, lease, etc.

Property interests are classified in several ways. One of the most meaningful distinctions is between real property and personal property. **Real property** (also called realty or real estate) means land and everything permanently attached to it, such as buildings, fences, pavement, sidewalks, storm drains, and trees. Basically, everything else is **personal property** (also called personalty or chattel). Personal property can then be classified as tangible or intangible. **Tangible personal property** has physical existence and accordingly is capable of being touched. Examples include a television set, heavy construction equipment, an automobile, etc. **Intangible personal property** represents a set of rights and interests, but has no physical existence. Stocks and bonds, patents, trademarks, purchased goodwill, promissory notes and copyrights are all examples of intangible personal property.

In addition, property interests are classified by the extent of ownership interest. A person who holds the entire bundle of rights is called an **owner in fee simple**. Such an owner can use, possess, and dispose of the property as he or she chooses during his or her lifetime. At death, the owner's property interest passes to his or her heirs. In some cases, a person has only what is referred to as a **life estate**. It is a powerful form of ownership but the interest ceases upon the death of either the owner or another person. An estate for years is a right to possession and use of property for a specified time, even if the fixed period is something other than a certain number of years. A common example is a leasehold, which permits the lessee to possess and use the property for a specified time, usually in exchange for a fixed series of payments. Such an interest may have value if the required fixed payments are below current market rate and the lessee has the right to "sublet" the property.

Other classifications of property interests include a legal versus a beneficial interest. For instance, the trustee of a trust holds legal title to the property in the trust while a beneficiary of a trust does not hold legal title, but rather enjoys a beneficial or equitable interest resulting from his or her right to receive income and/or principal from the trust. Moreover, property interests are divided into present versus future interests. Using the same example of a trust beneficiary, if the beneficiary has an income interest in a trust, he or she is said to enjoy a present interest. On the other hand, if the beneficiary has only a remainder interest, which takes effect only at the end of another beneficiary's life interest, the remainder interest is considered a future interest. Finally, there are vested versus contingent interests. For example, a participant in a qualified retirement plan, to which the participant's employer makes matching contributions, may not vest in the employer's contributions until completing a certain number of years' participation in the plan. Prior to the completion of the prescribed number of years' participation, the participant has only a contingent interest in the employer's contributions, which only becomes a vested interest when the required number of years have elapsed.

OTHER FORMS OF PROPERTY OWNERSHIP

Two other forms of property ownership, frequently used in the titling of personal assets, are important for a financial planner to understand—trust and custodial account ownership.

Trusts

As discussed briefly earlier in this chapter, ownership of property in trust separates what is called one's legal interest in property from that of his or her "beneficial" or "equitable" interest. A **trust** is an arrangement under which one individual or institution holds title to property for the benefit of another, usually under the terms of a written agreement specifying the rights and responsibilities of all parties involved. Legal title resides in one party, known as the trustee, while beneficial or equitable title remains in the individual for whose benefit the trust was established, known as the beneficiary. The trustee is required by law to act for the sole and exclusive benefit of the beneficiary and has an overriding fiduciary duty to do so.

There are many different kinds of trusts, but generally they are delineated by how the trust is recognized for tax purposes. In this regard, trusts can either be revocable (not recognized as a separate taxable entity) or irrevocable (a separate entity is recognized). Inasmuch as this book deals only with the fundamentals of personal financial planning, it is important for the reader to recognize only that a trust is another common form of property ownership and to understand the concept of separating a legal interest from an equitable or beneficial interest.

Custodial Accounts

A **custodial account** is similar to a trust, in that one party holds property on behalf of another (usually a parent on behalf of a minor child); however, the legal and equitable interests are not separated. In a custodial account, both the legal and equitable interest are maintained by the donee (the individual to whom the property is gifted or transferred), but the donee's right to manage and control the property is restricted, at least for some period of time. Custodial accounts are frequently used in the education funding process (discussed in Chapters 15 and 16 of this book), but also may be used in cases of physical or legal disability generally (discussed in Chapter 17). The Uniform Gifts (or Transfers) to Minors Act account is a common example of a custodial account found in all 50 states.

COMPARISON OF THE PRINCIPAL FORMS OF PROPERTY OWNERSHIP

The following table summarizes the principal types of property ownership and their respective characteristics that a financial planner is likely to encounter.

Table 14-1 Principal Types of Property Ownership and Their Characteristics

Types of Ownership	Property Rights during Lifetime	Property Disposition at Death	Income Rights	Will or Law Controls
Sole or individual (outright)	Absolute (can sell, mortgage, or gift)	Absolute (right to leave to anyone)	100% of income to sole owner	Will is required
JTWROS* between spouses	Spousal consent to act sometimes required	No right of disposition	Split half to each spouse	Transfers automatically by operation of law
JTWROS* among non-spouses	Absolute for joint tenant's own interest	No right of disposition	Split equally among tenants	Transfers automatically by operation of law
Tenancy by the entirety**	Consent of other spouse to act always required	No right of disposition	Split half to each spouse	Transfers automatically by operation of law
Tenancy in common	Absolute, over tenant's fraction	Absolute, over tenant's fraction	Split based upon fractional shares	Will is required
Community property***	Absolute for each half	Absolute for decedent's half	Split half to each spouse	Will is required

* JTWROS = Joint tenancy with right of survivorship
** Only recognized between spouses in some states (according to state statute)
*** Only between spouses in AZ, CA, ID, LA, NM, NV, TX, WA, WI

Concurrent Ownership

In the foregoing discussion, there has been an implicit assumption that we are talking about property ownership by one person. In fact, a large portion of property is owned by more than one person concurrently. It is critical to understand the various forms of concurrent ownership and the rights and privileges that pertain to each form. Forty-one of the 50 states use what is known as the common law property system. The remaining nine states use the community property system or an equivalent system. Which system applies to a client's property depends on the laws of the state where the client lives (or the state in which the property was acquired). The concept of concurrent ownership applies most importantly among married couples. In a common law state, a husband or wife can title property separately in his or her own name to the legal exclusion of the other spouse. This does not mean, however, that a married individual in a common law state can totally disinherit or otherwise convey property to the detriment of the other spouse. Indeed, in such an event, the spouse's inchoate or expectancy rights in the property may be enforced (for example, in the case of an equitable distribution settlement upon divorce).

A common characteristic of all types of concurrent ownership is the *undivided* right to use the entire property, not just a physically identifiable portion. Also, the co-owners usually each have the right, in the event of a dispute, to have the property physically divided (partitioned), at which time concurrent ownership ceases to exist. Certain types of property do not lend themselves to partitioning, in which case a court may order it sold and the proceeds divided among the owners according to their respective shares.

Concurrent Property Ownership in Common Law States

There are three forms of joint or concurrent ownership in common law property states:

1) Joint tenancy with right of survivorship
2) Tenancy in common
3) Tenancy by the entirety (recognized in a few states)

It is critical that a financial planner understand the various forms of joint ownership and their various rights and privileges, particularly what is meant by the term "joint tenancy." The three forms of joint ownership listed above are primarily distinguished by the presence or lack of survivorship rights in the property, but also by the varying rights of lifetime disposition or transfer that the owners possess. When a client informs a financial planner that he and his spouse hold property "jointly" in a common law state, the financial planner will need to determine whether this characterization means they hold property as joint tenants with right of survivorship, as tenants by the entirety, or as tenants in common, which does not carry survivorship rights. Following are descriptions of the three forms of concurrent ownership:

1. Joint tenancy with right of survivorship (JTWROS)

The distinguishing characteristic of this form of ownership is that if one of the joint owners dies, all ownership in the property passes automatically or by operation of law to the other joint owner. This is the definition of "with right of survivorship." In practical terms, this feature means that a joint owner (usually a spouse) does not have to execute a will to leave his or her interest in JTWROS property to the surviving joint tenant. Indeed, if a joint tenant writes a will and leaves his or her interest in JTWROS property to another person, the provisions of the will must be ignored. The automatic right of survivorship prevails over transfer by will or otherwise. While the law recognizes the transfer of title as immediate on the cotenant's death without any action required by the survivors, as a practical matter, some authorities, such as banks and title companies, will require document revision in order to transact further business or to obtain title insurance upon transfer of title to another party.

During the lifetime of the joint tenants, the survivorship aspect of the property can be destroyed by a sale or gift of an interest in the property by one of the parties to a third party, in which case the two remaining parties now hold title as tenants in common.

Also, the owners' respective shares are required to be equal and, accordingly, those shares should not be stated as part of the title. If a specific percentage is mentioned for each owner, it may result in a claim by the heirs of a deceased co-owner that tenants in common was actually intended and that the stated percentage interest belongs to them and not to the surviving co-owner(s).

2. Tenancy in Common

Under this form of co-ownership, each of two or more persons owns an undivided interest in the property. The interest is considered undivided because each tenant has rights in the *whole* property. In this form of ownership, the owners do not have the right of survivorship. Accordingly, in contrast to JTWROS, property held as tenants in common does not pass automatically to the other owner(s) at the death of the first tenant to die. Rather, a will is necessary to leave an interest in the property. If there is no will, the property interest will pass by the laws of intestate succession, which is beyond the scope of this book. During lifetime, this form of ownership is similar to that of a married spouse in a community property state (to be discussed later); that is, the owner has an absolute right of ownership in one half of the property so titled that generally can be used in any manner he or she chooses. However, unlike married owners of community property, tenancy in common may be held in any proportionate interest in the property and not just one half.

3. Tenancy by the Entirety

This is a form of concurrent ownership that exists only in some states—and then, only between spouses. It is similar to JTWROS, but cannot exist among non-spouses and a spouse's interest cannot be transferred separately during his or her lifetime without the consent of the other spouse. Tenancy by the entirety is terminated only upon divorce, either spouse's death, or mutual agreement. It does carry survivorship rights and is treated the same as JTWROS for purposes of passing property—that is, a will that provides for disposition of the property to other than the surviving spouse will not be recognized. This form of joint ownership between spouses is less common today than it once was.

Concurrent Property Ownership in Community Property States

Eight states (Arizona, California, Idaho, Louisiana, Nevada, New Mexico, Texas, and Washington) have adopted community property laws. In addition, Wisconsin has adopted marital property, an equivalent legal form of property granting community property rights. In the state of Alaska, married couples are permitted to elect to treat some assets as marital property. The laws of each community property (or equivalent) state are not uniform; however, in all of these states, it is accepted that husband and wife can own both community and separate property. Community property generally consists of property acquired by the efforts of either spouse during their marriage while living in a community property or marital property state, and other property which by the agreement of the spouses is converted from separate property into community property. Each spouse has an undivided one-half interest in community property, which is the same as sole or outright ownership in a common law state. Generally, both spouses must consent to a gift of community property. At death, each spouse can dispose of his or her half in the community by will.

Community property treatment generally does not apply to property acquired prior to the marriage or to property acquired by gift or inheritance during the marriage. After a divorce, community property is divided equally in some states and according to the discretion of the court in other states.

Separate property is all other property owned by the spouses which was acquired by only one of the spouses by gift, devise, bequest, or inheritance, or by a spouse domiciled in a common law state, or acquired by either spouse prior to their marriage. This type of property remains separate, and the owner-spouse can deal with it as he or she sees fit. The treatment of income from both separate and community property depends on state law.

Community property laws generally presume that all property owned by a married couple while residing in a community property state is community property regardless of how titled. This presumption can be overcome by:

- a written agreement to the contrary between the spouses
- proof that the property is otherwise separate property (e.g., owned prior to the marriage or acquired by inheritance)

It is because of this presumption of community property that it is critical that spouses in a community property state maintain good records. By so doing, they may prove that property is other than community property. In the absence of adequate records, and if separate and community property are commingled, the presumption of "community first" will result in all the commingled property being treated as community property, not separate.

It is possible that even those living in common law states may have community property and not realize it. This is because property acquired in a common law state does not lose its community property "taint" if the funds used to purchase it may be traced back to the sale of community property. This happens frequently in situations where a homeowner couple has moved from a community property state, such as California, to a non-community property (common law) state, such as Oregon, and purchases a home in Oregon using the sale proceeds of their former home in California. In this instance, the Oregon home really belongs to "the community," and each spouse has an undivided one-half interest regardless of titling in some other manner.

It is important to note, however, that property acquired by spouses while residing in a common law state does not generally become community property when the couple moves to a community property state. The only exception to this is those community property states that recognize the "legal fiction" of *quasi-community property*. This will depend upon the laws of the particular community property state involved.

Comparison of Joint Tenancy and Community Property

What are some of the similarities between joint tenancy (JT) and community property (CP)? First, both involve ownership by more than one person. Second, the owners have equal ownership rights and equal rights to use the entire property. Their interests are undivided. Finally, any owner may demand a division of the property into separate, equal shares.

What, then, are some of the differences between JT and CP? First, CP exists only between spouses. JT can exist between any two or more persons. Second, CP rights arise automatically, by operation of law under state statute, even if title or possession is taken by just one of the spouses. Hence, CP is created immediately on acquisition of the property. JT rights, on the other hand, are usually created by an agreement of the parties (e.g., they direct a stock broker to issue stock in their names as joint tenants) and are not imposed by operation of law. JT includes an automatic right of succession to ownership (right of survivorship) by surviving joint owners. As discussed earlier, this right takes priority over any will. In contrast, CP includes no automatic succession to ownership of the decedent's share by the surviving spouse. Therefore, at death, a spouse can transfer his or her share of CP, by will, to someone other than the spouse. However, if a spouse dies without a will, most state laws of intestate succession will pass ownership to the surviving spouse. A final difference between JT and CP is that property held in JT will not be subject to the probate process, which can be expensive and makes all information public. Some CP states no longer require probate if the property is left to the surviving spouse or if, in those cases where there is no will, the surviving spouse will inherit the property by the laws of intestate succession.

IMPORTANT CONCEPTS TO REMEMBER

Real property versus personal property

Tangible versus intangible property

Fee simple ownership

Life estate

Estate for years

Legal versus beneficial or equitable interest

Present versus future interest

Vested versus contingent interest

Trust ownership

Custodial account ownership

Joint Tenancy with Right of Survivorship

Tenancy in common

Tenancy by the entirety

Community property

Separate property

JTWROS versus Community Property Ownership

QUESTIONS FOR REVIEW

1. Why is it critical that financial planners understand the implications of property titling in providing personal financial planning services?

2. What are some examples of tangible and intangible property?

3. How does fee simple property ownership differ from a life estate in property?

4. What is meant by a beneficial or equitable property interest?

5. How does trust ownership differ from custodial account ownership?

6. In which types of property interests does a decedent owner's interest pass automatically by operation of law and in which interests is a will required?

7. How does joint tenancy with right of survivorship differ from tenancy in common?

8. What is meant by an undivided interest in the whole property?

9. How does separate property differ from community property?

10. What are some of the similarities and differences between JTWROS and community property ownership?

SUGGESTIONS FOR ADDITIONAL READING

West's Business Law, 9th edition, by Kenneth W. Clarkson, Roger LeRoy Miller, Gaylord A. Jentz, & Frank B. Cross, West Legal Studies in Business, a division of Thomson Learning, 2004.

Estate Planning and Taxation, 2003-2004 edition, by John C. Bost, Kendall/Hunt Publishing Company, 2002.

Personal Financial Planning, 7th edition, by G. Victor Hallman & Jerry S. Rosenbloom, McGraw-Hill, Inc., 2003.

Personal Financial Planning, 10th edition, by Lawrence J. Gitman & Michael D. Joehnk, South-Western/Thomson, 2004.

CHAPTER FIFTEEN

Introduction to Education Funding

• • •

One of the most significant costs that many clients will incur is the cost of educating their children or themselves. According to the College Board, over the ten-year period ending in 2001-2002, tuition at public four-year institutions rose an average of 6.4 percent a year nationally, ranging from a 3.5 percent increase in 1999-2000 to a 10.8 percent increase in 1992-1993. Most people tend to confine their thinking to putting their children through four years of undergraduate education at a college or university. In many cases, that may be the only education cost involved for a particular family. However, in today's job market, more and more parents are finding the need to obtain additional education for themselves in order to enhance their earning potential. Education costs may include the cost of private elementary and/or secondary school, two years at a community college to obtain an associate's degree, four or more years at either a private or state-supported college or university to obtain an undergraduate degree, additional graduate study at a college or university to obtain a master's and/or doctorate degree, the costs of non-degree specialized training leading to a trade, profession, or professional designation or certification required for changing careers, career maintenance, or career advancement.

Recent income tax law revisions have made the subject of education funding very complex. For this reason, clients rely on financial planners to advise them in this complicated area. As a result, financial planners need to have more than a passing familiarity with this subject. In this chapter, we will explore some of the basics including calculating the education cost need, qualifying and applying for financial aid, and the various loan programs available for this purpose. In Chapter 16, we will discuss the programs available to save for education costs, including the tax and other incentives to do so, some of the investment vehicles available for saving for education costs, the tax and other incentives to spend money on education costs, and the coordination provisions that limit the ability to simultaneously take advantage of multiple education cost incentives.

The objectives of this chapter are:

• Calculate a client's education cost need based upon given client information.

• Identify the four calculations required to determine a client's Expected Family Contribution to education costs for the purposes of financial aid.

• Distinguish between the Federal Methodology and the Institutional Methodology in determining the extent of financial assistance required for a family's education costs.

• Describe the main elements of a financial aid package.

• Identify the various types of loans available for education costs.

• Discuss the advantages and disadvantages of certain types of loans used to finance education costs.

DETERMINING THE EDUCATION COST NEED

Of the many calculations that a financial planner needs to know how to perform, the education cost need calculation may be the most difficult, from the standpoint that every piece of information required is an unknown at the time the calculation is completed. For instance, where will the student attend school? Will it be a private elementary or secondary school, a private or state-supported college or university, a local community college, a graduate program at a private or state-supported college or university, or specialized training at a trade or professional school? Will the student live on campus or commute from home? Depending upon the answer to these questions, the annual cost might run from as little as $1,000 to as much as $35,000. In addition, how much will the annual costs for the education selected increase between now and when the student starts school, and during the years that he or she attends school? Depending upon the area of study, what will be the cost of books and other required equipment and supplies? It should be clear by now that, unless a student knows with a high degree of specificity what school and educational program he or she will attend and when, almost every item of cost input is an estimate, making the calculation subject to a wide range of outcomes. This is what makes the determination of the education cost need so difficult. Combine this with a client simultaneously saving for other goals, and it is easy to understand why clients find saving for education so daunting.

During our discussion of the time value of money in Chapters 10 and 11, we emphasized the importance of starting early in funding a goal, such as education costs. Clearly, the greater the time period until a student enters college, the greater the opportunity to take advantage of compounding. By putting aside in an education fund even $2,000 to $3,000 at the birth of a child, parents can go a long way toward helping fund their child's education costs eighteen years or so hence. At seven percent per year, these original investments would grow to over

$6,700 and over $10,000 respectively in eighteen years. In addition, or alternatively, if the parents were to begin a regular monthly savings plan starting at or soon after the birth of a child, they would have the opportunity to accumulate a significant sum of money by the child's eighteenth birthday. For instance, investing as little as $200 at the beginning of each month over a period of eighteen years at an annual interest rate of only seven percent can result in a sum of more than $86,000. Some parents may have no choice but to wait to begin their monthly savings plan until their child enters public elementary school, when child-care costs usually decline and the spouse who previously stayed at home may be able to enter (or return to) the workforce. Certainly, by starting later, parents will have to invest a much larger initial sum and/or save much more per month to meet their goal. In fact, in our previous example, parents would need to save nearly $340 per month rather than $200 starting at birth. This just further illustrates the advantage of starting early.

How to do an Education Cost Needs Analysis

To project what college costs will be when the student starts school, the first step is to determine what these costs are today for the specific school or type of school he or she is expected to attend. This information is available from any of the schools that the student may attend. Many schools will even project today's costs to the time when the student will begin school.

The next step is to be certain that you have accounted for *all* the costs of attending the school. In addition to tuition, room and board, books, equipment, supplies, and any other costs indicated by the school, there are the costs of travel, telephone, and spending money. Once you have a reasonably accurate and complete estimate of the total costs of attending a school, the next consideration is the inflation rate between now and the time the student will begin his or her education. It should be recognized that the inflation rate for college or other school costs may be higher than the general inflation rate. A general rule of thumb is to add two percentage points to the projected general inflation rate to estimate the inflation rate for education costs.

When a reasonably accurate estimate of education costs has been determined, the client's net annual cash flow position should be projected through the student's college years to determine how much of the projected costs need to be funded. If a client will be able to pay for a portion of the projected education costs from net cash flow during the education period, then only the balance will need to be funded.

Using the methodology and calculator keystrokes we discussed in Chapters 10 and 11, we are now in a position to perform the required calculations to determine a client's education cost need. Assume that Ruth Givens' only son, Tommy, is seven years old. He will attend college in eleven years, and Ruth wants to start saving now for this goal. Ruth has contacted the college she expects Tommy to attend and determined that the current annual cost of attending this school is $20,000. Ruth assumes that general inflation will average four percent per year until

Tommy enters college. Accordingly, she adds an additional two percent to arrive at the anticipated college cost inflation rate of six percent per year. Ruth also assumes that the college costs will continue to increase at six percent per year while Tommy attends college for four years. Ruth would like to establish an automatic monthly investment program into a balanced mutual fund currently paying an annual return of seven percent compounded monthly. She wants to stop saving when Tommy enters college and use the funds accumulated to pay for his college education. How much will Ruth need to deposit at the beginning of each month into this account, starting today, in order to fund Tommy's four-year college education?

Step 1—Calculate the Cost of the First Year of College

An education cost needs analysis, including a periodic savings calculation, usually involves a three-step process. Since Ruth wants to stop saving when Tommy begins college, she will need a lump sum of money at that time to pay for four years of college costs projected to increase by six percent per year. How much will this lump sum need to be? First, we need to calculate what the first year of college will cost in future dollars eleven years from now. Since Ruth will need to pay for college at the beginning, rather than at the end, of each year, we must set the HP 10BII calculator to the BEGIN mode and to 1 P/YR. Then we enter 11 N; 20000 +/- PV; and 6 I/YR to reflect the eleven years until Tommy enters college, the current annual cost of $20,000, and the estimated six percent inflation in college costs. Then solving for FV, we determine that the cost of the first year of college for Tommy when he starts school in eleven years will be $37,965.97.

Step 2—Determine the Total Sum Required

The second step is to determine the amount that must be in place when Tommy is 18 and starts college, which is eleven years from now. Without clearing the calculator from the first step, enter SHIFT STO 1 to store the previously calculated first year college cost of $37,965.97 in register 1 of the calculator. Next, we must clear the $37,965.97 from the FV register by entering 0 FV. Then we enter RCL 1 +/- PMT to make the previous future value of $37,965.97 the first in a series of four payments while Tommy is in school. Then we enter 4 N for the number of years that Tommy will need funds. Next, we need to calculate and enter the inflation-adjusted annual rate of return on funds invested. To do this we enter 1.07 ÷ 1.06 –1 x 100 = 0.9434 I/YR. The funds are assumed to be invested at a seven percent annual rate and the education costs are assumed to increase at an annual rate of six percent. Then we solve for PV obtaining an answer of $149,748.19 for the amount that must be in place when Tommy is 18 and ready for college (11 years from now).

Step 3—Determine Required Savings Payments

The third step is to determine how much Ruth needs to save at the beginning of each month starting now to fund Tommy's four years of college. First, without clearing the calculator, we enter SHIFT STO 1 to store the $149,748.19 calculated in the second step. Then we enter 12 SHIFT P/YR to set the calculator to twelve payments per year (or monthly payments). Next, we enter 7 I/YR since the funds will earn seven percent per year and 0 PV to replace any number that may be in the PV register with zero. Next, we enter 11 SHIFT xP/YR to multiply the eleven years until Tommy enters college by the number of payments per year (12) arriving at 132 monthly payments for the value of N. [Note: Do not enter the 132 as N. The calculator does this automatically.] Next, we enter RCL 1 +/- FV to establish that the goal is to have $149,748.19 at the end of the accumulation period. Then we solve for PMT obtaining an answer of $751.96, which is the amount that Ruth will need to save at the beginning of each month for the next eleven years to be able to fund Tommy's college education costs.

APPLYING FOR FINANCIAL AID

Now that we have discussed how to determine the education funding need, let us turn to the subject of obtaining financial aid. According to the College Board, nearly 60 percent of the students currently enrolled in colleges and universities are receiving some financial aid. Many clients assume that their income is too high to qualify for financial aid, and in many cases that may be correct. However, even if it appears intuitively that a client's family income is too high to qualify for financial aid, applications for financial aid should still be submitted due to the methodology used in evaluating other assets and liabilities, and the total number of children attending college simultaneously.

Many years ago it was recognized by the federal government that a college education is too expensive for many families and that the federal government had a special role in financing education, to make it available to all, regardless of resources. As a result, over the years, a number of programs have been developed to provide general assistance. Financial assistance is now well entrenched in the nation's college funding system. While some feel reluctant to apply for financial aid, it should be remembered that it is funded by income taxes paid by many of those same persons.

All applicants for federal student aid must complete the **Free Application for Federal Student Aid (FAFSA)** and file it with the College Scholarship Service (CSS). Depending upon the college or colleges at which application for admission is being made, the FAFSA may be the only form a client needs to complete. However in order to apply for state scholarship or grant programs, and for aid at many other colleges and most private scholarship programs, other forms may have to be filed. Many colleges and universities, for purposes of awarding their own private funds, require the **CSS/Financial Aid PROFILE**.

Within a few weeks of filing a FAFSA, the applicant will receive a **Student Aid Report (SAR)**. This form should be carefully reviewed and corrections made as necessary in order to obtain a revised SAR. If a PROFILE form is filed, the applicant will receive an Acknowledgment and a Data Confirmation Report. As with the SAR, the applicant should carefully review the information and make corrections as required.

How Financial Need is Determined

The presumption made in determining a family's need for financial aid is that the family is considered the primary source of funds for college and is expected to pay its fair share of the cost of a college education. How, then, is a family's college education financial need determined? First, there are three factors:

- The amount that the family is judged capable of contributing to the student's college education costs
- The cost of attending a particular college or university
- The resulting difference, if any, or the amount of need

To determine the extent of the assistance required, financial aid administrators use a formula determined by the federal government, better known as the **Federal Methodology**. It takes into consideration earned income, unearned income, assets, expenses, family size, age, and other factors. It does *not* consider the value of a family's home in arriving at a family's total assets nor does it consider the income of a divorced, noncustodial parent in determining total income.

Need to Know: Expected Family Contribution

The amount of money that a family must contribute to the cost of a student's education is referred to as the **Expected Family Contribution (EFC)**. In determining EFC for a dependent student (i.e., one that is dependent on his or her parents for financial support) under the Federal Methodology, there are four separate calculations made, the total of which constitutes EFC.

The first calculation is that of **parental income**. This includes taxable and nontaxable income from the year preceding the award year and is reduced by a specified income protection allowance based upon income, as well as federal income taxes and Social Security taxes, and an employment expense allowance. The amount remaining is referred to as available income.

The second calculation is that of **parental assets**, which includes almost everything owned by the parents, with the notable exceptions of the equity in the family home (as discussed previously), cash value in a life insurance policy, and assets in (as opposed to contributions to) a retirement plan. Next, a specified asset protection allowance is subtracted and the remainder is multiplied by 12 percent to determine parental contribution from assets. Parental available income and the parental contribution from assets are then totaled, and a specified percentage ranging from 22 to 47 percent is applied to that total. At this point, a "number in college adjustment" is applied to determine the parental contribution per student.

Third, is the calculation of **student income**, which includes both taxable and nontaxable income from the year preceding the award year minus an income protection allowance and taxes. The balance remaining is multiplied by 50 percent to determine the student's expected contribution.

Finally, **student assets** are determined by adding the value of everything the student owns or that has been saved in his or her name and on his or her behalf. No asset protection allowance is deducted and the student is expected to contribute 35 percent of the total student assets.

Institutional Methodology

If an educational institution requires the CSS/Financial Aid PROFILE to be filed, as do many private institutions, then the Expected Family Contribution determined by completing the FAFSA is not a good indicator of how much aid that school may offer. Such a school will then use its own formula to compute an "institutional" EFC that determines how much need-based aid will be awarded. The following are some of the differences between the Federal and Institutional Methodologies:

- Home equity is added back in the Institutional Methodology (IM), often increasing EFC significantly. (An available planning opportunity is to convert credit card debt to home equity debt to decrease the amount of home equity).

- The IM eliminates the standard asset protection allowance and institutes an emergency reserve allowance based on family size.

- The IM includes siblings' assets and the value of prepaid tuition plans with parental assets.

- The IM implements an educational savings allowance for other children in the family, and it lowers the assessment rate on student assets from 35 percent to 25 percent.

- The IM has no simplified needs tests—no matter what the family's income, the family members' assets are always used as a factor in measuring their ability to pay.

- The IM adds business, farm, and capital losses back into adjusted gross income. It gives families an annual savings allowance for each of their pre-college age children.

- The IM provides an allowance for non-reimbursed medical expenses, and it institutes a minimum expected contribution level from student income.

- Information about the income of a noncustodial parent must be reported in the Institutional Methodology.

- Under the IM, parents must report how much has been contributed to flexible spending accounts (FSAs) for child care and medical expenses.

- Unlike the information requested on the FAFSA, PROFILE requires the *expected* income of the parents. Also, students must provide information regarding outside scholarships that are expected, employer-provided tuition benefits, and contributions from relatives. These additional items may reduce any financial aid package awarded.

It should be apparent that it is more difficult to qualify for financial aid under the Institutional Methodology than it is under the Federal Methodology. But while use of the Institutional Methodology is likely to diminish aid eligibility, under the federal formula there is little college discretion in the amount of the award. The institutional approach gives a college wider discretion, and the first offer of assistance is not necessarily the last and/or optimum offer.

Elements of the Financial Aid Package

At each school, there is typically a Financial Aid Administrator (or FAA) who analyzes the information provided on the FAFSA or PROFILE application. The first step that the FAA takes is to compare the student's cost of attendance at the school with the EFC to determine the family's need. Then, the FAA can develop an applicable financial aid package or a combination of grants, loans, work-study, and possibly some special scholarship assistance to satisfy the financial need. It is important to understand that while the FAA also considers private scholarships received by the student, scholarship awards do not reduce the EFC. Rather, in these cases, the school usually takes the scholarship amount and includes it as part of the family's available resources. See Figure 15.1 for a summary of federal student aid programs.

Need to Know: Special Situations

There are special situations that need to be mentioned that commonly arise in both of the foregoing methodologies.

First, in computing the EFC for parents who are divorced or separated, the student must use the income and assets of the parent with whom he or she lived for the greater part of the twelve months preceding the date of the financial aid application. If that parent has remarried, the stepparent's income and assets must also be included—just as if he or she was indeed the natural parent.

Second, if there is more than one family member in college at the same time, the parental contribution to the cost of college may be divided by the number of family members who are in college at least half time. Since the definition of family member also includes a parent, an older generation family member who has not yet completed his or her college degree may now take the opportunity of doing so and thereby reduce the amount of expected family contribution (EFC). A parent in college only counts as a "college student" when the parent files his or her own FAFSA. Parents cannot count themselves as students on their child's FAFSA—the instructions specifically say not to include parents. If a parent in college files a FAFSA, he or she can count him- or herself as well as his or her children that are in college at least half time.

Federal Student Aid at a Glance for 2003-2004

The following is a summary of Federal Student Aid Programs that will help pay for school. Note that not all schools participate in all programs. Check with the applicable school to find out which programs it participates in.

Table 15.1

Federal Student Aid Program	Type of Aid	Other Information	Annual Award Limits	Disbursement
Federal Pell Grant	Grant: does not have to be paid back	Available to undergraduates only	Up to $4,000 for 2003–2004	School acts as the U.S. Department of Education's agent
Campus-Based Aid Programs				
FSEOG	Grant: does not have to be paid back	Not all schools participate in all Campus-Based programs. For undergraduates only	Up to $4,000	School disburses funds to students
Federal Work Study	Money is earned, does not have to be repaid	Not all schools participate in all Campus-Based programs. For undergraduate and graduate students	No annual maximum	School disburses earned funds to students
Federal Perkins Loan	Loan: must be repaid	Not all schools participate in all Campus-Based Programs. For undergraduate and graduate students	$4,000 for undergraduate students: $6,000 for graduate students	School disburses funds to students
Federal Direct Student Loan (FDSL) and Federal Family Education Loan (FFEL) Programs				
Subsidized Stafford Loan	Loan: must be repaid	Subsidized: The Department of Education pays interest while the student is in school and during grace and deferment periods. Must demonstrate need.	$4,000 for undergraduate students: $6,000 for graduate students	Direct Student Loans: the federal government provides funds to schools to disburse to students. FFEL: private lenders provide funds to schools to disburse to students.
Unsubsidized Stafford Loans	Loan: must be repaid	Unsubsidized: The borrower is responsible for interest during the life of the loan. It is not neccessary to demonstrate need.	$2,625 to $5,500 per year depending on grade level. $23,000 maximum undergraduate loan amount. Also available to graduate students.	Same as above
PLUS Loan	Loan: must be repaid	Available to parents of dependent undergraduate students. Not need-based.	Cost of attendance minus any other financial aid received	Same as above

Need-Based Government Grants

There are several layers or building blocks to any financial aid package. The first layer consists of federal Pell Grants and scholarships awarded by the applicable school. This layer is the most preferable type of aid because it is a gift and does not have to be repaid. An undergraduate student is eligible for a Pell Grant if the family's EFC does not exceed a specified amount as determined annually. Scholarship awards do not affect eligibility for grants, although as noted earlier, they do impact eligibility for other types of need-based aid. Scholarships may be awarded for academic excellence, art, music/drama, ROTC, athletics, and many other reasons.

In several states (such as Georgia and Florida), the opportunity to receive a state grant to attend an in-state college is significant and should not be overlooked. The proliferation of these grants is an outgrowth of states' attempts to ensure that students, once educated in the states' public elementary and secondary school system, remain "home" to complete higher education as well.

The FAA then usually delves into the next layer of the financial aid package—those funds which the federal government gives to the schools directly to distribute (with the schools determining who gets these funds). This is known as so-called "campus-based aid" and consists of three programs for students with financial need:

- Federal Supplemental Educational Opportunity Grants (SEOGs) with priority given to those undergraduate students who also received Pell Grants.
- Federal Work-Study programs that provide students with part-time jobs while attending college.
- One of various types of loans which, because they are loans, must be repaid. We will discuss in the next section the various loan programs available.

Finally, after the FAA has investigated and utilized all external sources for financial aid (principally the federal government), he or she will then look to the college's own pool of funds. These may include academic, band, or athletic scholarships or awards. Nevertheless, before doing this, the FAA will probably once again look at the FAFSA filed by the student's family and make any additional adjustments that may impact the EFC positively or negatively. This speaks to a fundamental rule in the financial aid process: *any financial aid package awarded is probably not final and, for those families with financial need, it probably means that some negotiation can occur*. It is here where the assistance of a professional college or financial aid counselor may well prove to be advisable.

EDUCATION LOAN PROGRAMS

In the event that there are insufficient education savings available and/or financial need has not been demonstrated in the process of applying for financial aid, parents and students have only two choices. One is to finance the student's college education from current income. The other is to borrow from private or governmental sources to meet the need. According to the College Board, more than 60 percent of all financial aid is in the form of loans. There are a large number of loan options available for funding education needs.

Federal Perkins Loans

These are direct student loans administered by local colleges and, as loans, accordingly must be repaid, but at relatively low interest rates. The program gives priority to students with exceptional need, and the student's family must pass a needs test. A student must be enrolled at least half time to be eligible. The actual amount of the loan is determined by the college, within federally set limits. This type of loan is the least expensive of all federally sponsored loans, with the federal government paying the interest on the loan while the student is in school and for a grace period thereafter (typically nine months after graduation). It may be possible to defer these loans for up to three years for service in the military, the Peace Corps, or approved comparable organizations, or if study is resumed on at least a half time basis.

Federal Stafford Loans

Formerly called the Guaranteed Student Loan, Stafford loans permit students to borrow funds for educational expenses from private sources such as banks, credit unions, savings and loan associations, and educational organizations. These loans are available in "subsidized" and "unsubsidized" versions. Eligibility for subsidized loans depends on demonstrated financial need while unsubsidized loans are available without proving financial need. The loan limits and terms are identical for both types of loans, but the federal government pays the interest due on subsidized loans while the student is still in school. Repayment of subsidized Stafford loans is deferred until six months after the student's graduation. Unsubsidized loans require interest payments while the student is still in school. If an unsubsidized borrower so elects, he or she may defer interest payments until after graduation, with the cumulative interest, while the student is still in school and after graduation, added to the principal of the loan.

Currently, financially dependent college freshmen may borrow up to $2,625, sophomores may borrow up to $3,500, juniors and seniors can borrow up to $5,500 annually, and graduate students can borrow up to $18,500 per year. These loans are subject to the payment of an origination fee and, in some cases, an insurance premium. Financially independent students can borrow more.

Student Loan Marketing Association (Sallie Mae) PLUS Loans

Sallie Mae offers the federal Parent Loan for Undergraduate Students (PLUS) to parents regardless of financial need. The interest rate charged is variable (based on the 91-day Treasury bill rate plus 3.1 percent and a one-time repayment fee of three percent, subject to a 9 percent cap). The annual limit on loans is calculated on the student's "cost of education" less other financial aid to be received for the school year. Repayment must begin within 45–60 days of loan disbursement and may not be deferred, though some lenders may allow borrowers to make interest-only payments while the student is enrolled in college. There are no restrictions on the loan's use. Some parents borrow under the program to meet all or part of the expected parental contribution, while others borrow to make up the difference between costs and their contribution plus available financial aid.

ExtraCredit Loans

These are privately sponsored loans for creditworthy borrowers who need more help than is available through financial aid programs and government-sponsored loan programs, such as PLUS. These are signature loans with no requirement to demonstrate financial need or collateral, but a credit check is required to prove good credit. These loans are used primarily by parents of students rather than students themselves.

Educational Resources Institute (TERI) Loans

This type of loan is available through local designated banks. Loan amounts begin at $2,000 per year and can be as high as the total cost of education determined by the school. The interest rate is variable and is generally prime rate plus 1.5 to 2.0 percent. The borrower may elect to defer repayment of principal, but interest payments are required currently and total repayment is required within 25 years.

College Board Loan Programs

The College Board sponsors two private supplemental loans as part of its CollegeCredit program, in partnership with Sallie Mae. The Student Signature Education loan offers low interest rates, deferred repayment while in school, and a 1/4 percentage point interest rate reduction for electronic repayment through Sallie Mae's Direct Repay Plan. Borrowers have up to 25 years to repay and can borrow up to $25,000.

The CollegeCredit Private Parent Loan allows parents to borrow up to the full cost of their child's education with up to 15 years to repay, and the loan also covers students who are enrolled part-time or in non-degree programs.

State Education Loans

Every state has some agency or department that administers the state's program for higher education. These agencies will list and provide free information on all the special loans available within the state, such as loans to veterans or health-profession students. This can be a valuable resource for students or parents needing to borrow education funds.

Defined Contribution Retirement Plan Loans

Generally, parents (or students) who have funds invested in defined contribution retirement plans, such as 401(k) or 403(b) plans, may be able to borrow from their vested balance in such plans, assuming the plan has such loan provisions. Many 401(k) plans allow plan participants to borrow a portion of their vested balance in the plan for the purpose of paying college tuition. The interest paid on such loans is credited to the participant's account so that he or she is, in effect, paying interest to him- or herself. The interest on such loans is not tax deductible, as it is considered personal interest. It is important that the plan sponsor and the participant fully comply with the terms of the plan's loan provision in order to avoid unfavorable tax treatment.

Home Equity Loans

As discussed in Chapter 5, home equity loans are a very efficient way to incur debt in that the interest rate is reasonably low (due to the fact that the lending institution has a secured interest in the lender's residence) and the interest paid is tax deductible as long as the total home equity indebtedness does not exceed $100,000.

Life Insurance Loans

In those cases where a parent or a student has a significant cash surrender value in an existing life insurance policy, he or she may borrow against this balance. Like a 401(k) loan, the interest is not tax deductible and there is no taxable income as a result of taking out the loan. Alternatively, the parent or student policyholder may prefer to cancel the policy at the time that funds are needed for college, but this may result in taxable income to the extent of the difference between the amount received in exchange for the policy and the total amount of premiums paid into the policy.

Securities Margin Loans

If a parent or student owns marginable securities that are on deposit with a broker/dealer firm, he or she may borrow a percentage of the current market value of the securities owned at a favorable interest rate (one or two percent above the rate paid by the broker to borrow from banks) with the ability to deduct the interest to the extent of his or her "net investment income." Net investment income is the excess of investment income over investment expenses (other than interest paid). Any disallowed investment interest can be carried over to a succeeding tax year.

The advantages include the fact that there are no loan papers involved, no eligibility or needs test, and no credit checks. One down side of this type of loan is that if the particular securities are subject to wide swings in market value, they may result in the borrower having to deposit either additional cash or securities to meet maintenance margin requirements. If the margin call is not met, the broker may be forced to sell some or all of the securities to cover the debt. Consequently, a reasonably conservative portfolio is the best candidate for this type of financing.

OTHER EDUCATION COST FUNDING TECHNIQUES

AmeriCorps

Rather than a loan program, this is a service program administered by the Corporation for National and Community Service that allows people of all ages and backgrounds to earn help paying for education in exchange for a year of national service. This may involve service in schools, national parks, auxiliary police, and other public service sectors. The program currently provides a minimum wage stipend of up to $9,300 plus up to $4,725 in education benefits for each full-time one-year term of service (1,700 hours) completed. A volunteer can earn up to two education awards, or a total of $9,450 by serving two full-time one-year terms. The education award may be applied to existing student loans or to current or future education costs. Furthermore, the money does not affect their eligibility for other federal student aid. Students delaying their entry into the workforce and those attracted to public service may find this program of value. Unlike a grant or scholarship, these education awards constitute federal taxable income.

Veteran Educational Benefits

The U.S. Armed Forces also offer financial aid opportunities. For example, all branches of the U.S. Armed Forces offer the Reserve Officers Training Corps (ROTC) Program, which is a federal merit-based scholarship program that will pay an eligible student's tuition, fees, and books and provide a monthly allowance. The U.S. Army also offers a student loan repayment enlistment incentive through the Army's student loan repayment program for new recruits who have already attended college and accumulated debt. In return for a three-year enlistment, the Army will repay up to $65,000 (currently) on specific federally guaranteed loans to qualified applicants. For a complete list of recruitment incentives offered by the U.S. Armed Forces, visit the U.S. Department of Defense (DOD) DefenseLINK Web site at www.defenselink.mil/sites/r.html#recruiting or www.myfuture.com.

Also, veterans or dependents of veterans may be eligible for veterans' educational benefits. Information is available through the U.S. Department of Veterans Affairs local office. Information is also available through the Internet at www.gibill.va.gov.

Employer-Provided Educational Assistance

If the student is employed by an organization that has an educational assistance program, he or she may currently receive up to $5,250 tax-free for tuition, fees, books, supplies, etc. (not meals, lodging, or transportation), if certain requirements are met. Generally, the employer will obtain a tax deduction for the amount of qualifying education expenses paid to or on behalf of the employee. The Economic Growth and Tax Relief Reconciliation Act of 2001 (EGTRA) extended the deduction and corresponding exclusion to graduate courses and made the exclusion for both undergraduate and graduate courses permanent, effective for courses starting in 2002. Prior to the enactment of EGTRA, the exclusion was scheduled to expire with respect to undergraduate courses starting after December 31, 2001.

IMPORTANT CONCEPTS TO REMEMBER

Education cost needs analysis

Free Application for Federal Student Aid (FAFSA)

CSS/Financial Aid PROFILE

Student Aid Report (SAR)

Expected Family Contribution

Federal Methodology

Institutional Methodology

Financial Aid Administrator (FAA)

Pell Grant

Supplemental Educational Opportunity Grants (SEOG)

Perkins Loan

Stafford Loan

Sallie Mae

Parent Loan for Undergraduate Students (PLUS Loan)

Educational Resources Institute (TERI Loan)

Direct Student Loan Program

QUESTIONS FOR REVIEW

1. Why is the education cost needs analysis such a difficult calculation to perform?

2. What are the three steps in the process of performing an education cost needs analysis?

3. For purposes of awarding their own private funds, many colleges and universities require the submission of what form?

4. When establishing one's eligibility for federal student aid programs, what form must be filed?

5. How does the Federal Methodology differ from the Institutional Methodology in determining the extent of financial assistance required?

6. What are the four components that must be calculated in order to determine a family's Expected Family Contribution?

7. How does a Pell Grant differ from a SEOG?

8. How does a Perkins Loan compare to a Stafford Loan?

9. What types of loans, other than those available through federal and state loan programs, are available to finance education costs?

10. How can a volunteer participant in AmeriCorps qualify for an education award?

SUGGESTIONS FOR ADDITIONAL READING

College Cost & Financial Aid Handbook 2004, 24th edition, published by College Entrance Examination Board, 2003.

Don't Miss Out, 28th edition, by Anna & Robert Leider, Octameron Associates, 2003.

The Student Guide: Financial Aid 2003-2004 published by U.S. Department of Education, available at http://studentaid.ed.gov/students/publications/student_guide/index.html.

Federal Student Aid Information Center, P.O. Box 84, Washington, DC 20044-0084; 1-800-433-3243.

Meeting College Costs: What You Need to Know Before Your Child and Your Money Leave Home, 2004 edition, published by College Board Publications, 2003.

The Parent's Guide to Paying for College published by College Board Publications, 2003.

College Savings Rx, 3rd edition, by David G. Speck, Octameron Associates, 2002.

Loans and Grants From Uncle Sam: Am I Eligible and for How Much?, 11th edition, 2004–2005, by Anna Leider, Octameron Associates, 2003.

Guide to College Savings 2002-2003 by Joseph F. Hurley CPA, LLC, 2002, available at http://www.SavingforCollege.com.

Year End Planning for Education Tax Benefits 2003 by Kaye A. Thomas, Esq. & Joseph F. Hurley CPA, CCPS, LLC, 2003, available at http://www.SavingforCollege.com.

More Education Funding Techniques and Tax Incentives

• • •

In Chapter 15, we discussed the calculation of an education cost needs analysis, financial aid, various education loan options, and other education cost funding techniques. Clearly, if a client cannot qualify for financial aid and cannot fund education costs as incurred from current cash flow, the only remaining options are to either borrow the necessary funds or begin to save preferably well in advance of the education cost need. In this chapter, we will discuss the various methods of saving for future education costs, appropriate investment vehicles for such savings, the income tax incentives for both saving for and spending money on education costs, and the coordination provisions that limit the ability to obtain tax benefits from multiple education cost tax incentive programs.

The objectives of this chapter are:
- Identify the principal methods of saving for education costs.
- Differentiate between a Section 529 Qualified Tuition Plan and a Section 529 State Savings Plan.
- Describe the income tax treatment of the principal methods of saving for education costs.
- Identify appropriate investment vehicles for saving for education costs.
- Describe the income tax incentives for spending money on education costs.
- Discuss the coordination provisions that limit the ability to obtain simultaneous income tax advantages from multiple education cost tax incentives.

EDUCATION INCENTIVES

When planning for and financing education, there are many government incentives for saving (before the student enters school) as well as for spending (when the student is attending school). In the subsequent sections, we will discuss these incentives as well as other education cost saving techniques and attempt to show how they can work together, as well as how they might conflict.

Incentives to Save

Planning for education arises because of the realization that it will require a considerable amount of money, and the sooner one begins to prepare, the better. The numbers may seem daunting, but whatever a family can do to prepare is much better than not preparing at all. It may be reasonable to presume that clients who hire a financial planner are not likely to be in the position of having so little that a substantial portion of the education need will be provided through financial aid. This does not mean, however, that they will be able to afford the cost of an education from current income or will have otherwise adequately planned for what could be four or more years of college and possibly private secondary school. As a result, it is reasonable to assume that a substantial portion of financial planning clients will need to save for education costs through various savings programs and techniques.

Internal Revenue Code Section 529 Plans

Since the enactment of the Economic Growth and Tax Relief Reconciliation Act of 2001 (EGTRA), Section 529 of the Internal Revenue Code now includes two basic types of programs designed to encourage either the prepayment of or systematic savings for education costs—qualified prepaid tuition programs and state savings plans.

Section 529 State or Private Qualified Tuition Programs

One type of Section 529 plan is the qualified state prepaid tuition program (or QTP) that has been in existence in some eighteen or so states for some period of time. These programs, which also may now be offered by eligible public or private educational institutions, permit contributors (usually parents) to pay a specified present amount for tuition credits or certificates that provide a guarantee that future college tuition will either be waived or paid for a designated beneficiary (usually their child) if he or she goes to any state college or university. If the child goes out of state or to a private school, provisions are made to pay a sum for that purpose, although it will not likely be an equivalent amount. Prepaid tuition plans generally may be used to pay not only for tuition expenses but also for room, board, books, or supplies at an eligible educational institution. Contributions limitations vary from around $100,000 to $250,000, depending upon the state involved.

These types of plans offer significant income tax benefits including the ability to make contributions regardless of the contributor's income, tax-free earnings growth, and tax-free withdrawals to the extent used to pay qualified higher education expenses. [This tax exemption for 529 plan distributions will expire after the year 2010 absent Congressional renewal]. If withdrawals are not used to pay qualified higher education expenses, the income portion is included in the gross income of the beneficiary and subject to a 10 percent penalty tax, except in the case of the beneficiary's death, disability, or receipt of a scholarship. Taxable income attributable to these withdrawals is taxed at the designated beneficiary's tax rate rather than that of the account owner.

Distributions from QTPs established and maintained by an entity other than a state will be tax-free beginning in the year 2004. In addition, many states allow contributors to claim state income tax deductions for all or part of their contributions. Federal gift tax rules are also quite beneficial permitting a contributor to spread a contribution/gift over five years, currently permitting a contribution of $55,000 ($110,000 for joint spousal gifts) for the benefit of a single beneficiary without incurring gift tax. Contributions are correspondingly removed from the contributor's estate. Also, the contributor is treated as the account owner, with the right to control distributions, change beneficiaries, and name successor account owners.

Moreover, most states permit any adult individual to own a Section 529 account. Many permit any individual—regardless of age and including the account owner—to be a beneficiary. Multiple accounts may be established for multiple beneficiaries, subject to a per-beneficiary account limit of $100,000 to $250,000 in most states. Contributors may open accounts in multiple states (subject to state residency requirements). Furthermore, at least eleven states currently provide some form of explicit creditor protection for plan assets, which could prove useful as part of an asset protection strategy.

These plans permit tax-free rollovers once per year if made within 60 days to a member of the beneficiary's family (including parents, grandparents, siblings and first cousins), or to another Section 529 plan for the benefit of the same designated beneficiary. They have proven to be extremely attractive investments that may be used in some states for retirement and other nonqualified purposes in addition to education cost needs. While the national prepaid tuition plan return of 6.3 percent over the last ten years is comparable to that of municipal bonds (6.6 percent), the prepaid tuition plan involves 40 percent less risk (measured by standard deviation). While their return has been only half that of the S&P 500 index for the same period of time, their level of risk has been only 1/6th of that of the S&P 500 index. The rate of return of these plans is tied to the inflation rate for education costs that not only shows no signs of abating, but continues to exceed the general inflation rate.

In contrast to Section 529 state savings plans, discussed next, QTPs generally do not invest in the stock market and, in fact, are not really investment vehicles. Instead they lock in college costs for parents so that tuition inflation does not outpace the growth of their savings.

With regard to the effect of such plans on federal financial aid, it is generally agreed that QTP balances are treated as a student resource. As a result, the net effect is a dollar-for-dollar reduction in eligibility for financial aid.

Section 529 State Savings Plans

This type of education cost funding plan may be offered only by states or state-sponsored organizations. Section 529 savings plans allow contributors to select among various traditional investment options such as equity mutual funds. Unfortunately, in using a state-based savings plan, an investor relinquishes control of his or her money. While he or she may be able to choose from among a handful of investment options, if the investor is unhappy with the selected fund's performance, there are only a few options available: (1) roll the account over to a different plan; (2) stop adding to the account; and (3) withdraw the money and pay a 10 percent penalty.

Just as with QTPs, contributions can be made regardless of the contributor's income, earnings grow tax-free, and withdrawals are exempt from federal income tax to the extent used to pay "qualified higher education expenses" (i.e., beyond high school). Such expenses include tuition, fees, books, supplies, equipment required for the enrollment or attendance at an eligible educational institution, expenses for special needs services, and reasonable costs for room and board, subject to the greater of actual expenses or an allowance for room and board as determined by the institution. Contributors to these plans have no control over how funds are invested. Investment decisions are made by the organization/institution offering the account (usually an open-ended investment company or mutual fund). However, the account owner may change the account investment selection among the options offered both annually and upon a change in the designated beneficiary. Also, the owner of the funds can move the money from one plan to another. These rollovers, as mentioned earlier, can only be done once every 12 months with the measurable period beginning when the rollover is actually completed.

Section 529 savings plans are run like mutual fund portfolios by firms such as Fidelity Investments, Vanguard Group, T. Rowe Price Associates, Putnam Investments and Alliance Capital. They invest in stocks, bonds, money market funds or some combination of the three. Some options automatically adjust asset allocation as the child nears college age. Others are more aggressive and have the potential for both higher appreciation and loss of value.

With regard to the effect of such plans on federal financial aid, the account owner is required to report the balance in a savings plan as an asset. This treatment is more favorable than having the balance reported as an asset by the student, because of the weighting factor used in the Federal Methodology. As a result, only 5.6 percent of its value will be assessed for college. It is still unclear how needs analysis will treat annual distributions (i.e., as student or parental income).

Coverdell Education Savings Accounts (CESAs)

These accounts were previously called Education IRAs and were of limited value in saving for education costs because the annual contribution was limited to only $500 and the income phaseout ranges were $95,000 to $110,000 for single filers and $150,000 to $160,000 for joint filers. EGTRA increased the allowable annual contribution to $2,000 and the income phaseout ranges to $190,000 to $220,000 for joint filers (the phaseout ranges were unchanged for single filers). These limits are indexed annually for inflation. The beneficiary of a CESA must be under age 18 in those years when contributions are made to the account and amounts remaining in the account must be distributed within 30 days after the beneficiary reaches age 30 or dies. Alternatively, the funds can be rolled into a younger family member's account. The beneficiary of a CESA may accept only $2,000 annually no matter how many contributions are involved. Qualified expenses include public, private and religious elementary and secondary school expenses and the age limit does not apply to beneficiaries with special needs. This provision makes the CESA very attractive for parents and grandparents who intend to send their children or grandchildren to private grade schools.

Amounts held in a CESA may be distributed and put into a CESA for a member of the beneficiary's family. Such rollovers will be tax-free to the distributee as long as the rollover occurs within 60 days of the distribution. Likewise, amounts held in a CESA may be rolled over into another CESA for the benefit of the same beneficiary.

With regard to tax treatment, contributions are not tax deductible but earnings are tax-deferred and distributions are excludable from gross income to the extent that the distribution does not exceed the qualified higher education expenses incurred by the beneficiary during the year in which the distribution is made. In addition, withdrawals from a CESA can be used for elementary and secondary education expenses as well as for higher education. The income portion of distributions not used for education expenses is taxable and subject to a 10% penalty. Contributions to a CESA are treated as a gift from the contributor to the beneficiary at the time of the contribution and are subject to the current $11,000 annual gift tax exclusion.

CESAs offer much greater investment flexibility, with investors able to invest in the funds of their choice, including individual stocks and bonds.

With regard to the effect of a CESA on qualification for federal financial aid, it is considered the child's asset and accordingly is assessed a higher value in determining expected family contribution. The beneficiary of a CESA may assume control of the account at the age of majority, which is 18 or 21 in most states.

Other Education Cost Savings Techniques

There are additional ways to save for education costs that are somewhat less restrictive but may not offer income tax advantages comparable to those of Section 529 plans and CESAs. We will discuss some of these additional options.

UGMA or UTMA Custodial Account

These accounts operate under either the Uniform Gift to Minors Acts (UGMA) or Uniform Transfer to Minors Acts (UTMA) of the various states. Generally, they are established by parents for their children through any bank, brokerage, or mutual fund company, with the parents acting in the capacity of a fiduciary. They offer the advantages of an unlimited contribution, control over the investments, and the ability to withdraw the funds at any time for the benefit of the child. However, for children under age 14, the first $750 (currently) of income earned by the account is tax-exempt and the next $750 (currently) is taxed at the child's rate. Any amount in excess of $1,500 (currently) is taxable at the parent's rate. Children 14 and older are taxed at their own rate. Other disadvantages are that the funds constitute the child's asset for financial aid purposes and at the state's age of consent (usually 18 or 21), the child takes control of the assets and can spend them as he or she sees fit. The balance in an UTMA or UGMA account may be spent in any manner desired and does not have to be spent on qualified educational expenses.

Individual Retirement Accounts (IRAs)

While these accounts are primarily intended to provide for one's retirement, they offer tax advantages if early withdrawals (prior to the owner reaching age 59 1/2) from traditional IRAs are used to pay for "qualified higher education expenses" for the owner, the owner's spouse, child, or grandchild of the owner or of the owner's spouse. Qualified expenses include tuition at a post secondary educational institution, room and board, fees, supplies and equipment. Limits on contributions to traditional and Roth IRAs will increase over the next several years from $3,000 in 2003 to $5,000 in 2008. Individuals who are age 50 or over may make additional annual catch-up contributions of $500 for 2003 through 2005 and $1,000 thereafter. Contributions to traditional IRAs are tax-deductible if certain income and plan participation requirements are met. The application of the contribution and deduction limitations are different for spouses filing joint returns than for other individuals. If the requirements for tax deduction of contributions to traditional IRAs are not met, nondeductible contributions may still be possible. When funds are withdrawn from a traditional IRA, the distribution is 100 percent taxable to the owner unless he or she has a cost basis in the plan (usually from making nondeductible contributions) to offset against the gross distribution. However, if the owner has not attained the age of 59 1/2, withdrawals are also subject to a 10 percent penalty for early withdrawal, unless certain exceptions apply to the withdrawal. One of those exceptions is if the withdrawn funds are used to pay for qualified higher education expenses as indicated earlier.

As a result, the owner of the IRA may qualify for tax-deductible contributions during the accumulation stage of IRA ownership and then upon early withdrawal of either the entire balance or a portion of the balance to pay for qualified higher education expenses for the owner, the owner's spouse, child or grandchild of the owner or of the owner's spouse, the owner can avoid paying the 10 percent penalty but will have to pay the income tax applicable to the taxable portion of the distribution. While the IRA is accumulating, the earnings grow on a tax-deferred basis.

In the case of a Roth IRA, "qualified" distributions are not included in the individual's gross income and are not subject to the additional 10 percent penalty for early withdrawals. A qualified distribution is one that satisfies a five-year holding period and meets one of four other requirements (after age 59 1/2; made to a beneficiary or the owner's estate after the owner's death; attributable to the owner being disabled; a distribution to pay for "qualified first-time homebuyer expenses"). As a result of the five-year requirement, no qualified Roth IRA distributions could have occurred before tax years beginning in 2003. Even if the Roth IRA distribution is not "qualified", one can withdraw all contributions without paying taxes. Income taxes will be triggered only when nonqualified withdrawals exceed the amount of all contributions. In addition a nonqualified withdrawal may escape the usual 10 percent early withdrawal penalty if it satisfies one of the exceptions for traditional IRAs, including the educational expense exception described earlier. While earnings grow tax-free, contributions to a Roth IRA are not tax-deductible. Contribution limits for Roth IRAs are the same as for traditional IRAs. They are also subject to income limitations on the account owner.

Series EE and Inflation-Adjusted Series I U.S. Savings Bonds

An individual who redeems any qualified U.S. savings bond in a year in which qualified higher education expenses are paid may exclude from income amounts received under such redemption, provided certain requirements are met. A "qualified" U.S. savings bond is any such bond issued after 1989 to an individual who has reached age 24 before the date of issuance and which was issued at a discount (such as Series EE bonds). Qualified higher education expenses include tuition and fees required for enrollment or attendance at any eligible educational institution of either a taxpayer, the taxpayer's spouse, or any dependent of the taxpayer for whom the taxpayer is allowed a dependency deduction. Taxpayers are also entitled to the exclusion if the redemption proceeds are contributed to a qualified tuition program (QTP).

The amount that may be excluded is limited if the redemption proceeds during a tax year exceed the qualified higher education expenses paid during that year. Also, qualified higher education expenses must be reduced by the sum of the amounts received with respect to an individual for a tax year as a tax-exempt scholarship; as an educational assistance allowance; as a payment, waiver, or reimbursement under a qualified tuition program; by expenses taken into account for the Hope or Lifetime Learning credits; and amounts taken into account in determining the exclusion for distributions from a QTP or the exclusion for distributions from a CESA.

In addition, the exclusion is subject to a phaseout in the years in which the bonds are cashed and the tuition is paid. For 2003, the joint return phaseout begins at $87,750 and ends at $117,750; for other returns, the phaseout begins at $58,500 and ends at $73,500. Below these phaseout ranges, taxpayers may exclude from gross income bond interest up to the amount of qualified higher education expenses. Above these ranges, no exclusion is allowed. For those falling within the ranges, the amount of interest excludable from income is reduced, depending on the taxpayer's modified adjusted gross income. [Note: This exclusion is not available to married individuals who file separate returns.] Cash basis taxpayers who anticipate qualifying for this interest income tax exclusion in the year of redemption and payment of qualified higher education expenses should not make the election to treat the annual increase in value of Series EE and Series I bonds as income in each year.

Minors Trust (IRC Section 2503(c) Trust)

This is a formal legal entity created by an attorney drafting the necessary trust document, the parent or grantor making a gift of funds to the trustee of the trust and naming a child (or children) as beneficiary. Additional funds can be added in subsequent years. The trustee is charged with all the investment decisions, fulfilling the terms of the trust, and distributing income from the trust to the child. As a rule, the parent should not be the trustee, and the trust instrument should specifically state that the parent may not benefit from the funds in any way, nor use them to satisfy any parental obligations of support. Should the donor exercise any control of the trust property, income from the assets will be taxed to the donor.

The purpose of this Minors trust, as with most trusts, is to shift income from a high tax bracket to a low one and to extend control over the money beyond the age of 18, which is the usual age of majority under an UGMA or UTMA account. Under the 2503(c) trust, income from the trust property can accumulate in the trust and is taxed at the parent's tax rate to the extent it exceeds $1,500 (currently) until the child reaches the age of 14. The trust is not taxed on the income that it disburses during the course of the year. After the child reaches age 14, the income is taxed at the child's rate.

This type of trust can distribute only interest income during the years preceding age 21—in other words, during the usual college years the recipient would receive only interest income from the trust. When the beneficiary reaches 21 years of age, there are three possibilities:

- The trust is terminated and the child receives all the remaining assets.
- The trust is terminated and the principal is returned to the parents or grantors.
- The principal may remain in trust for the child after 21 if he or she chooses to leave the trust intact. After the child reaches 21, the beneficiary has 60 days to withdraw the funds. If they are not withdrawn, they will be kept in trust.

The main reason for establishing such a trust is to maintain control of the funds beyond the time the beneficiary reaches age 18. If the parents or grantors are in a position to place income-producing property generating a meaningful amount of income during the student's college years into trust for the benefit of their child, this type of vehicle can be effective in financing the child's college education. It also provides the potential for the parent or grantor to pass the trust principal to the child at age 21.

Appropriate Investment Vehicles for Saving for Education Costs

If instead of using some of the foregoing savings vehicles, an individual elects to create a taxable portfolio to fund a student's education, what are appropriate investment vehicles for this purpose?

Federally-Insured Accounts

Starting with the most conservative investments, which also earn the lowest rate of interest, there are cash-equivalent accounts such as savings accounts, NOW and Super-NOW accounts, and money market accounts. These accounts are generally federally-insured up to $100,000 and not subject to downside risk, but as mentioned, they bear a very low rate of interest. For students within a year or so of entering college, they may make some sense. Certificates of deposit (CDs) are also insured by the FDIC up to $100,000. However, not all banks and thrifts are so insured, which makes their debt paper risky. CDs are definitely not liquid instruments. In return for their higher yield compared to money-market deposit accounts, depositories insist upon penalties if the CDs are cashed in prematurely. They can be designed to mature in 6 to 60 months, or sometimes even longer periods. The maturities can be laddered to correspond with tuition due dates. For example, one might structure their CDs to mature systematically at the times tuition and fees are due each semester.

Money Market Funds

Money market funds, unlike the cash-equivalent accounts discussed earlier, are not all insured by the FDIC. A few have private insurance, but the majority do not. Others invest only in U.S. government paper, which in effect provides a government guarantee. Most such funds have check-writing privileges, but may have minimum deposit and withdrawal requirements. Again, if a student is very close to beginning college, this type of investment makes a lot of sense and also as a component of a larger portfolio for a student who is several years from entering college.

U.S. Government Securities

U.S. savings bonds were discussed earlier from the standpoint of the interest income being tax-free for certain taxpayers if used to pay for qualified higher education expenses. It should be mentioned here that they involve essentially no credit risk but are subject to interest rate risk since very high rates of inflation would reduce the purchasing power of the redeemed bonds. A person may purchase only $30,000 per year of Series I and $15,000 per year of Series EE bonds.

Rather than purchasing money market funds that invest only in government securities, one might consider purchasing U.S. Treasury bills, notes, and bonds directly. Treasury bills are short term (i.e., 90, 180, or 360 days). Notes are 1 to 10 years in duration, while bonds are 10 years or more. Treasury bills are discounted from their face value, $1,000, and redeemed at maturity at full face value. How long they are held and how deep the discount determine the yield to the investor. Notes (in $1,000 or $5,000 denominations) and bonds (in $1,000 denominations) are interest bearing, paying interest semi-annually. Since there is such a large secondary market in government securities, they can be turned into cash at a moment's notice. With such a wide variety of maturity dates, from a few days to many years, it is possible to customize purchases to fit with college tuition needs. One downside is the possibility of incurring a substantial loss on a premature or forced sale of these obligations, since their value can fluctuate quite widely. The interest on such obligations is tax-free for state and local income tax purposes.

Government Agency and Quasi-Governmental Agency Securities

In addition to direct obligations of the federal government, there are government agencies and government-guaranteed or –sponsored organizations of a quasi-official nature that issue debt instruments. Some of the more common ones are Federal National Mortgage Association (FNMA); Bank for Cooperatives; Federal Farm Credit; Student Loan Marketing; Federal Home Loan Bank; World Bank; and Inter-American Development Bank. They usually offer yields that are 1/2 to one percent higher than Treasury securities of comparable maturity. While there may not be a legal pledge for the federal government to make good on these obligations, there is clearly an implicit one. It is doubtful that the government would permit any of these agencies to face a liquidity crisis or to default. The interest received on some of these obligations is free of state and local income taxes.

Mortgage-Backed Securities

Another option is mortgage-backed securities, based upon a pool of residential mortgage loans. They are known as pass-throughs since the public agencies (Ginnie Mae, Freddie Mac, and Fannie Mae) and private companies that sponsor them are simply transferring interest and principal to the investors, usually on a monthly basis. These are very safe investments usually held for the long term (average life of 12 years). They offer some of the highest yields among federal guaranteed obligations, but their appeal is primarily to investors who wish not only higher yields but also monthly income. Receiving monthly income is not advantageous for the long-term saver since part of each monthly payment contains repayment of principal as well as interest. Unless it is immediately reinvested, there is the danger that the monies will be gradually dissipated. Some investors deposit the monthly income in money market accounts when received. Since a large secondary market exists for these securities, it is easy to sell certificates before they mature.

Zero-Coupon U.S. Treasury Securities

Zero-coupon U.S. Treasury bonds offer virtually no risk, high yields compared to other interest-bearing securities, availability in small amounts, and rates that are locked in. They are deeply discounted bonds that do not pay semi-annual interest but produce earnings by rising to the face value of $1,000 over a series of years. The Treasury issues Separate Trading of Registered Interest and Principal of Securities (STRIPS), but many zero-coupon bonds are created by investment banking houses, which take the basic Treasury securities and deposit them with a custodial bank, which in turn separate the corpus and the interest coupons. The investment banker then issues certificates or receipts based on the underlying Treasury paper referred to as Certificates of

Accrual on Treasury Securities (CATS) and Treasury Investment Growth Receipts (TIGRS), among others. Zero-coupon bonds are long-term investments, but a secondary market exists should it become necessary to terminate the holding before maturity. Due to the lack of interest payments, these investments tend to be volatile, depending on interest rates. Income taxes, if any, on imputed interest must be paid by the parents until the child is 14 years old.

Zero-Coupon Municipal and Corporate Bonds

Zero-coupon municipal and corporate bonds are very similar to Treasury zeros except that municipals are tax-free for federal purposes and can be tax-free for state and local purposes. Corporate zeros are a better bet for accumulating funds for education since their yields are higher than Treasuries or municipals. In the case of municipals, issues of small towns or special issuing authorities may be subject to higher risk than those of larger entities. Even blue-chip corporate issues may be subject to some market risk, virtually unknown in Treasury securities. Funds of corporate zeros tend to diversify this risk. While these issues are highly liquid, their value fluctuates with interest rate changes.

Municipal Bonds

Another investment alternative is municipal bonds other than zeros. These can take the form of general obligation bonds, based on the taxing powers of local government, and revenue bonds which rely on fees, tolls, and charges of waterworks, terminals, airports, or turnpikes. Munis often have call provisions, which can be avoided (or their effect much reduced) by buying shares of a closed-end unit trust or an open-end mutual fund. These investments make sense for high-income parents wishing to maintain control and ownership over their education savings, but this advantage is somewhat offset by the generally low rates of return.

Corporate Bonds

Corporate bonds (other than zeros) are sold in $1,000 denominations with fixed interest coupons. Debentures are perhaps the most common form of bond, relying on the issuer's name and its ability to repay. Mortgage bonds are somewhat more secure since they have specific assets pledged to pay them off. Parents investing for college should generally avoid bonds with speculative ratings (junk bonds), though academic studies have demonstrated that they do not carry much more risk than investment grade bonds. Corporate bonds have the advantage that issuers generally establish a sinking fund to put aside the interest and principal due the bondholders. Good quality corporate bonds make an excellent vehicle for accumulating college funds especially if the student is age 14 or older, since they offer returns considerably higher than money-market deposit accounts or Treasury paper. For college savers, intermediate-term bonds with maturity dates ranging between 7 and 10 years will offer close to the highest returns for fixed-interest securities.

Common Stocks

Common stocks are subject to substantial company risk and therefore should be supplemented by other savings and investments that are not subject to the vagaries of the marketplace. An efficient way to purchase common stocks is by the use of dollar cost averaging (buying a fixed dollar amount at regular intervals over a long period of time). Investments in common stocks should be well diversified across specific industries and across blue chips, growth stocks, and speculative stocks. Common stocks offer the potential for a rate of return far in excess of most savings vehicles but at a significant amount of risk. While capital appreciation can be significant, there is no guarantee that share prices will increase in value. Only a portion of one's total education funds should be invested in common stocks.

Mutual Funds

Finally, investing in mutual funds offers diversification (increased safety)—the ability to purchase a fractional interest in hundreds of companies with a fairly nominal investment. Mutual funds are subject to sales charges (other than no-load funds), management fees, and year-end capital gains distributions, but are very liquid. If one accepts the proposition that three out of four professional money managers underperform the major stock market indices, index funds may have a lot of appeal since the owner is guaranteed to do as well as the market and he or she avoids annual capital gain distributions.

Income Tax Incentives to Spend Money on Education Costs

In addition to the various incentives to *save* money for education costs, Congress has enacted a number of incentives to encourage individuals to *spend* money on education costs and to make it easier to afford. Some of the principal incentives are discussed here.

Deduction of Student Loan Interest

In Chapter 15, we discussed many of the various education loans available. The interest paid by individuals during the tax year on any qualified education loan is deductible from gross income in arriving at adjusted gross income to a maximum of $2,500 per year (subject to an income phaseout). The income phaseout range is $50,000 to $65,000 for single filers and $100,000 to $130,000 for joint filers. The debt must be incurred by the taxpayer solely to pay qualified higher education expenses at an eligible institution. Interest paid after the inception of mandatory repayment status on the loan until the loan is paid off is deductible up to the $2,500 annual limitation.

Qualified Higher Education Tuition Deduction

An above-the-line income tax deduction from gross income is allowed for qualified tuition and related expenses associated with higher education of the taxpayer, the taxpayer's spouse, or dependents. The maximum tuition allowable for the deduction is $3,000 for 2003. For tax years 2004 and 2005, the allowable deduction increases to $4,000, with a lower $2,000 limit applicable to taxpayers with greater modified adjusted gross income (AGI).

For 2003, the $3,000 deduction is permitted for single and head of household filers whose modified AGI does not exceed $65,000, and for joint filers whose modified AGI does not exceed $130,000. The same AGI limits apply for the $4,000 limit applicable to the years 2004 and 2005, except that a lower tier $2,000 deduction is permitted as modified AGI for single and head of household filers increases to $80,000, and as joint modified AGI increases to $160,000. The income limit applicable to the tuition deduction is not a phase-out, as occurs with other provisions in the tax law. Rather, it represents a cliff, where $1 of income in excess of the limit causes a taxpayer to lose the entire deduction.

A taxpayer is not allowed to claim this deduction in the same year as a Hope or Lifetime Learning credit (to be discussed later) is claimed for the same student. As a result, parents with two students in college could claim up to the annual maximum of combined tuition for both students, but no Hope or Lifetime Learning credits for either. However, if a Hope or Lifetime Learning credit was claimed for one student, a deduction of up to the maximum limit of tuition for the other student is allowable. Also, to the extent amounts are withdrawn from a CESA, or to the extent of the tax-free income portion of a Section 529 tuition plan withdrawal, the higher education deduction is not permitted. In a later section, we will discuss the so-called coordination provisions that specify which education incentives may be used in the same year and for which students.

Finally, the above-the-line higher education tuition deduction cannot be taken by an individual who is claimed as a dependent by someone else for the year.

Credits for Higher Education Tuition

There are two education-related credits: the Hope scholarship credit and the Lifetime Learning credit. These credits may be claimed by the taxpayer, the taxpayer's spouse, or the taxpayer's dependent for tuition and related expenses incurred by students pursuing college or graduate degrees or vocational training at an eligible educational institution. The Hope and Lifetime Learning credits cannot both be claimed for the same student's expenses in the same tax year. However, the Hope credit can be claimed for one or more qualifying students in a family while the Lifetime Learning credit is claimed for another student in the same family. The Hope Credit is not allowed for any academic period if the student has been convicted of a federal or state felony drug offense consisting of the possession or distribution of a controlled substance, before the end of the taxable year with or within which such academic period ends.

Moreover, if a third party (someone other than the taxpayer, taxpayer's spouse, or a claimed dependent) makes a payment directly to the educational institution to pay tuition, the tuition is treated as paid by the student for purposes of the credits. If the expenses relate to a dependent, they are in turn considered, for purposes of the college credits, as paid by the taxpayer on whose return the dependent is claimed (usually the parent).

Qualified tuition and related expenses must be reduced by scholarships excludable from gross income when computing eligibility for an education credit. Qualified tuition and related expenses does not include room and board, books, student health fees, or transportation. Taxpayers claiming students as dependents may find it advantageous for the student to include scholarship amounts in gross income (presumably at a lower tax bracket), while using other funds to pay tuition and related expenses.

Hope Scholarship Credit

This credit is aimed at helping families pay for the first two years of college for their children. The family's income tax is reduced by a credit equal to 100 percent of the first $1,000 of qualified expenses and 50 percent of the next $1,000 of qualified expenses incurred for the first two years of college. What this means is that if a family is otherwise paying at least $1,500 in income taxes, and pays $2,000 or more in qualified education expenses, its federal income tax bill will be reduced by $1,500. The $1,500 maximum Hope credit is allowed per student and no double benefit is permitted (i.e., the credit is not permitted to more than one taxpayer in the same year). In addition, the credit cannot be claimed for the same expenses for which another tax benefit is also received. This credit is subject to income limitations (see the description of these limitations under "Lifetime Learning Credit").

In order to qualify for the Hope credit, the student must be enrolled in a program leading to a degree, a certificate, or other recognized educational credentials with a course-load commitment of at least half of a normal full-time workload. Also, if a parent claims a student's dependency exemption, the student is not allowed to claim the Hope credit.

Lifetime Learning Credit

The Lifetime Learning credit allows a credit of 20 percent of the first $10,000 of qualified tuition expenses paid by the taxpayer for any year the Hope credit is not claimed. This results in a maximum nonrefundable credit of $2,000.

The amount of both the Hope scholarship credit and the Lifetime Learning credit are reduced for taxpayers who have modified adjusted gross income above certain amounts. For 2003, the phaseout of the credits begins for most taxpayers when modified AGI reaches $41,000; the credits are completely phased out when modified AGI reaches $51,000. For joint filers, the phaseout range is $83,000 to $103,000 for 2003. These phaseout limits are projected to increase to $42,000 to $52,000 and $85,000 to $105,000 respectively in 2004. The Hope credit and the Lifetime Learning credit are not available to married taxpayers who file separate returns.

For any tax year, a taxpayer is permitted to elect only one of the following with respect to one student:

- the Hope credit
- the Lifetime Learning credit
- the exclusion for distributions from a CESA used to pay higher education costs

In addition, the amount of qualified higher education expenses, otherwise taken into account in determining the Series EE U.S. savings bond interest exclusion, is reduced by the amount taken into account in computing either the Hope or Lifetime Learning credit.

There is no requirement of enrollment in a degree program and enrollment for at least half of a normal full-time workload, as is the case with the Hope credit. Also, if a parent claims a student's dependency exemption, the student is not allowed to claim the Lifetime Learning credit.

New 10 Percent Federal Income Tax Bracket

While not a specific education provision of EGTRA, the 2001 tax revisions carve a 10 percent federal income tax bracket out of the existing 15 percent bracket. For a single student, the 10 percent rate will apply to the first $7,000 in taxable income. The reduced rate provides an increased incentive to shift income to the college student, including withdrawals from Section 529 plans that remain taxable to the beneficiary because the parent claims a Hope or Lifetime Learning credit.

Coordination Provisions

One of the most confusing parts of EGTRA is the so-called "coordination provisions" which limit the ability of taxpayers to claim multiple tax benefits in the same tax year either for the same or different students. Rather than attempt to describe each and every mutually-exclusive situation under these provisions, the following table and related footnotes are provided to help clarify these provisions.

Table 16.1

Education Incentives Available in the Same Year							
To Save				**To Spend**			
	Sec. 529 QTP tax-free withdrawals (1)(2)(3)	Sec. 529 Savings Plan tax-free withdrawals (1)(2)(3)	Coverdell Education Savings Account withdrawals (2)	Series EE & I Savings Bonds tax-free redemption	Student Loan Interest Deduction	Tuition Deduction	Hope Credit (5)	Lifetime Learning Credit (5)
Sec, 529 QTP tax-free withdrawals (1)(2)(3)		not for the same expenses	Qualified higher ed expenses allocated between programs (4)	not for the same expenses	yes	not with income portion of withdrawal	not for the same expenses	not for the same expenses
Sec. 529 Savings Plan tax-free withdrawals (1)(2)(3)	not for the same expenses		Qualified higher ed expenses allocated between programs (4)	not for the same expenses	yes	not with income portion of withdrawal	not for the same education expenses	not for the same education expenses
Coverdell Education Savings Account withdrawals (2)	Qualified higher ed expenses allocated between programs (4)	Qualified higher ed expenses allocated between programs (4)		not for the same expenses	yes	not with same funds	not for the same expenses; not for same student	not for the same expenses; not for same student
Series EE & I Savings Bonds tax-free redemption	not for the same expenses	not for the same expenses	not for the same expenses		yes	not with same funds	not for the same expenses	not for the same expenses
Student Loan Interest Deduction	yes	yes	yes	yes		yes	yes	yes
Tuition Deduction	not with income portion of withdrawal	not with income portion of withdrawal	not with same funds	not with same funds	yes		not in same year for same student	not in same year for same student
Hope Credit (5)	not for the same education expenses	not for the same education expenses	not for the same expenses and same student	not for the same expenses	yes	not in same year for same student		not in same year for same student
Lifetime Learning Credit (5)	not for the same expenses	not for the same expenses	not for the same expenses and same student	not for the same expenses	yes	not in same year for same student	not in same year for same student	

Footnotes to Table 16.1

(1) It would appear that an individual can make a contribution to both a Section 529 QTP and a Section 529 state savings plan in the same year for the same beneficiary within the limits of the particular plans and subject to gift tax, if applicable.

(2) An individual meeting the income and annual contribution limits can make contributions to both a Section 529 plan and a Coverdell Education Savings Account (CESA) in the same year for the same beneficiary, without giving rise to an excise tax on "excess" contributions as was the case under prior law. Of course, such contributions may be subject to gift tax. Five-year gift tax averaging is only available for contributions to a Sec. 529 plan, not for a CESA.

(3) Withdrawals from a Section 529 QTP and a Section 529 state savings plan in the same year for the same beneficiary can both receive tax-free treatment only if the total of both withdrawals does not exceed the total amount of qualified higher education expenses paid in that same year.

(4) Qualified higher education expenses (as reduced by Hope and Lifetime Learning credit expenses) must be allocated between a withdrawal from a Section 529 plan and a withdrawal from a CESA made in the same year for the same beneficiary. The method to be used in making this allocation is not specified. If the total withdrawals from both accounts exceed the total qualified higher education expenses, then a portion of the total withdrawals will be taxable. Clearly, the taxpayer will want to allocate as much as possible to the withdrawal that contains the highest percentage of earnings so that as much as possible will be received tax-free. Presumably final IRS rules will clarify how this allocation is to be made.

(5) Taxpayers may waive the Hope or Lifetime Learning credit even when they qualify for one of the credits. This may be the case if the tax savings resulting from the credit is less than the savings from the tuition deduction (they are mutually exclusive), or is less than the savings from tax-free and penalty-free treatment of Section 529 plan withdrawals and CESA withdrawals. (Expenses used in computing the credit reduce the amount of expense that can be used in computing tax-free Section 529 and CESA withdrawals.)

IMPORTANT CONCEPTS TO REMEMBER

Section 529 Qualified Tuition Plan

Section 529 State Savings Plan

Coverdell Education Savings Account

UGMA or UTMA custodial account

Series EE and Inflation-Adjusted Series I
U.S. Savings Bond Interest (used to pay
qualified higher education expenses)

Section 2503(c) Trust

Zero-coupon bonds

Student loan interest

Qualified higher education tuition
deduction

Hope and Lifetime Learning credits

Coordination provisions

QUESTIONS FOR REVIEW

1. In what ways is a Section 529 Qualified Tuition Plan similar to and in what ways does it differ from a Section 529 State Savings Plan?

2. What primary advantage is offered by a Coverdell Education Savings Account as compared to a Section 529 plan in saving for education costs?

3. What benefit afforded by a Section 2503(c) trust is not offered by an UGMA or UTMA custodial account in terms of saving for education costs for children?

4. What are the primary determining factors in selecting investment vehicles for education funds?

5. What are the limitations on the deductibility of qualified student loan interest?

6. What requirements must be met to be able to claim the income tax deduction for qualified higher education tuition paid?

7. In what ways does the Hope Credit differ from the Lifetime Learning Credit?

8. What is the primary purpose of the so-called "coordination provisions" with regard to income tax incentives for education savings and spending?

SUGGESTIONS FOR ADDITIONAL READING

"Planning Strategies Under the Education Provisions of the New Tax Act" by Joseph F. Hurley CPA, *Journal of Financial Planning*, September 2001.

"Miracle Growth?" by Keith R. Davenport, Douglas Fore, & Jennifer Ma, *Investment Advisor*, September 2001.

"Section 529 Prepaid Tuition Plans: A Low Risk Investment with Surprising Applications" by Mark C. Neath, J.D., CFP, *Journal of Financial Planning*, April 2002.

The Best Way to Save for College: A Complete Guide to 529 Plans, 5th edition, 2003-2004, by Joseph F. Hurley CPA, *Savingforcollege.com*, LLC, Pittsford, New York.

IRS Publication 970, *Tax Benefits for Higher Education*, available at www.irs.gov.

"Learning Curves" by Donald Jay Korn, *Financial Planning*, March 2003.

Financial Planning for Special Circumstances

• • •

It is becoming increasingly important for a professional financial planner to be conversant in planning for special situations, such as the disability or incapacity of a client. Insurance statistics indicate that it is more likely that a person will become disabled than it is that he or she will die prematurely. Also, according to the Social Security Administration and the Department of Education, somewhere between 15 and 20 percent of the total U.S. population has a disability. This group includes everyone with some type of permanent disability, including developmental disabilities (such as mental retardation, cerebral palsy, Down's syndrome and autism), acquired disabilities (such as traumatic brain injury or spinal cord injury), organic disabilities (such as multiple sclerosis, Parkinson's and Alzheimer's), and mental illness. In light of these facts, a financial planner needs to be able to assist his or her client in planning and caring for the disability or incapacity of the client or the client's dependents. In this chapter, we will discuss how a financial planner might do so.

In addition, we will discuss the special circumstances surrounding the topics of nontraditional families, job change or loss, support and/or care of adult children and aging and/or financially challenged parents, and death of one's spouse or life partner. In Chapter 18, we will discuss another common special circumstance requiring financial planning—divorce and legal separation.

The objectives of this chapter are:
- Explain the difference between incapacity and disability.
- Distinguish between a guardian and a conservator.
- Compare and contrast a revocable living trust and a durable power of attorney for property.
- Describe what is meant by a "springing" durable power of attorney.
- Discuss the design and function of a Medicaid Qualifying Trust.
- Explain the purpose of a Special Needs Trust.
- Identify the four basic types of Special Needs Trust.
- Distinguish between a living will and a durable power of attorney for health care.
- Describe the special issues affecting domestic partners, as compared to married couples.
- Identify the key issues involved in job loss or separation.
- Explain the financial and other considerations resulting from changing relationships between parents and adult children over time.
- Identify some of the more common and costly mistakes made by survivors of spouses or life partners.

PLANNING FOR INCAPACITY AND DISABILITY

The terms incapacity and disability are often used interchangeably in the personal financial planning process. However, the term "incapacity" actually is much broader than what is usually meant by the term "disability." **Incapacity** or incompetency is a legal concept taking into account both mental and physical disability. Any lack of legal capacity to act (other than that imposed by law, such as the status of a minor) must usually be determined through a medical or psychological examination. Therefore, it must be determined primarily by external sources. In contrast, **disability** usually refers to the physical inability to perform some daily life activities.

For purposes of discussion in this chapter, we will make no distinction between incapacity and disability and will consider techniques and terminology to be relevant to both cases.

Planning for Personal Care of an Incapacitated Client

There are two primary techniques employed to plan for the eventuality of having to care for the incompetent person:
- a living will
- a durable power of attorney for health care

These two documents should work in concert so that the durable power of attorney for health care, as enacted in most states, takes over where the provisions of the living will leave off.

Living Will

A **living will** provides for the suspension of medical care in the event of a terminal illness. These documents are created by individuals who do not wish to be a burden to their heirs in the event that an illness is so severe that it provides for no possibility of recovery to a reasonable quality of life. For example, a living will indicates that "heroic measures" should not be undertaken to re-start the individual's heart if he/she has no brain activity. Living wills provide documentation of the client's wishes and give the family permission to cease life support.

Durable Power of Attorney for Health Care

A **power of attorney (POA)** is a written document executed by one person, known as the **principal**, authorizing another person, known as the **attorney-in-fact** or **agent**, to perform designated acts on behalf of the principal. POA's can be either durable or nondurable. If the POA is **nondurable**, the appointment of the agent will not survive the principal's incapacity or incompetence. Therefore, such a power is impractical, as it becomes legally invalid just when it is needed most—at the onset of the principal's incapacity. To remedy this problem, all 50 states now recognize a **durable** power of attorney. While the particular powers permitted under such a power may vary according to state law, the effect of making a power of attorney durable is to cause the power to survive the principal's incapacity and thus continue to be effective.

> **NEED TO KNOW: THE DEFINITION OF "DISABILITY"**
>
> The Americans with Disabilities Act (ADA) of 1990 defines persons with disabilities as persons with:
>
> - physical or mental impairments that "substantially limit" one or more of the major life activities of such persons
>
> - a record of such impairment, or
>
> - being regarded as having such an impairment. Under ADA, determination of being disabled is made on a case-by-case basis. Generally, blindness, alcoholism, heart disease, cancer, muscular dystrophy, cerebral palsy, paraplegia, diabetes, HIV or AIDS, and morbid obesity have been considered disabilities.
>
> - Disability may also be defined by some form of contractual document or by primarily internal sources. For example, Social Security law mandates its own definition of when one is "disabled" for purposes of receiving Social Security benefits. Similarly, private disability income insurance policies provide their own definition of when one is considered disabled in qualifying for receipt of benefits.

It is important to understand the difference between an attorney and a lawyer. The terms are not synonymous. The term "attorney" refers primarily to an appointed representative. A lawyer is an attorney at law, or one who has been appointed (technically, by a court) to provide legal representation. The person to whom you entrust powers of attorney is your attorney for the purposes specified in the governing document. That does not make him or her your lawyer. If you are working with a client and any part of the discussion turns to legal representation and/or powers of attorney, precision in your language becomes quite important.

A **durable power of attorney for health care,** like its cousin, the living will, ensures that an individual's treatment preferences are considered in the event of incapacity. (Medical care providers are obligated ethically and legally to consult only the individual in need of medical treatment and no one else, unless the patient is incapacitated and a valid power of attorney document exists.) The POA for health care is much broader (and, therefore, more flexible) than a living will. A health care power of attorney (referred to in some states as a **medical proxy**) covers many more possible treatment decisions than a living will.

Planning for the Care of Dependents of an Incapacitated Client

In many instances, particularly for married individuals with minor children, an individual's goal in providing for the potential onset of disability will include more than just planning for his or her own care. Specifically, most clients will want to provide for the naming of a guardian or conservator for their children (or other loved one who requires care). As with the terms "incapacity" and "disability," there is a legal difference in meaning between the terms "guardian" and "conservator"; however, these may carry the same responsibilities, depending upon state law.

Guardian vs. Conservator

A **guardian** is usually someone responsible for the care and well being of a person (for example, caring for his or her health), while a **conservator** is responsible for this same person's property (for example, managing his or her financial accounts). Many times, the individual named should be and is the same person; however, unless provided for elsewhere, both a guardian and conservator may only be appointed subsequent to a court hearing and subject to ongoing court supervision. For example, in the case of a minor individual who has an individual appointed by the court to take care of his or her person, that individual is known as a *guardian ad litem* (a Latin term meaning "to care for").

Naming Caretakers

The method around the sometimes expensive and onerous court proceeding resulting in the appointment of a guardian or conservator is to provide for the naming of these individuals by the person involved. This is typically achieved with a legal document, such as a will or trust. If the naming of the caretaker is done in a will, it is said to have testamentary effect (that is, taking effect upon death), and is usually accomplished by the naming of a relative or close friend as the guardian or conservator of one's minor children. Another means of appointing a caretaker for one's children in a will is via the creation of a **contingent trust**. Here, certain assets are set aside for the benefit of the children (usually subsequent to the death of the surviving spouse), and left to a **trustee** responsible for the financial well-being of the children, as well as for the management of the parent's remaining assets.

Oftentimes, this trustee, guardian, and conservator are the same individual (or individuals); however, the creator of the will (known as the **testator**) should carefully consider the differences in the care of a person versus care for his or her property. Many times, the same skill set is not involved. If the naming of the guardian or conservator is done in a trust made effective during one's lifetime (known as a **living trust**), the power to change the name of these individuals is said to remain with the creator of the trust (or **trustor**) and to be revocable in nature. This is helpful, since many individuals may change their mind as to whom they want to serve as guardian or conservator of their loved ones as time passes.

Planning for Property Management of an Incapacitated Client

As with providing for one's own personal care, there are two primary techniques commonly used in planning for the management of one's property in the event of incapacity:

- a **revocable living trust**
- a **durable power of attorney for property**

A third technique, funding a special trust (known as a **Medicaid Qualifying Trust**), is frequently used in an extension of planning for disability, that of planning to take advantage of long-term care coverage afforded to qualifying individuals under Medicaid.

Living Trust

A revocable living trust has many uses, the most prevalent of which is the avoidance of probate and ancillary estate expenses. It can also continue after one's death, at which time the trust provisions become irrevocable. However, when used in planning for incapacity, the revocable living trust provides for either an original or successor trustee to take over the client's property management in the event that he or she is no longer able to do so.

Many individuals who create a revocable living trust prefer to be the trustee themselves (a "self trustee") during their lifetime, thus retaining control. Then, once they are incapacitated, a successor trustee is named. This individual (as in the case of a contingent testamentary trust for minors) is usually a relative or close friend. It can also be a professional trustee, such as a bank or trust company. The trust should include a clause providing for a private determination of incapacity, usually through the mutual agreement of at least two physicians. Accordingly, upon the event, the trust provisions and named trustee will become effective. For this reason, a revocable living trust, when used primarily for incapacity planning, is referred to as a **standby trust**. The trust "stands by" in the event that the trust creator requires its implementation.

Durable Power of Attorney for Property

The creation of a revocable living trust, while effective, can nevertheless be expensive. Accordingly, many individuals opt to plan for potential incapacity by writing a durable power of attorney for property. There are two common types of durable powers for property. The first type becomes effective as soon as it is executed. Similar to the standby revocable trust, it will become operational if and when needed. The second type, called a "springing" durable power of attorney, becomes effective only upon the principal's incapacity. There must also be some mechanism regarding how to determine when the principal is incompetent. Again, this is usually with the mutual agreement of at least two physicians. Springing durable powers of attorney are not authorized in all states: however, where permitted, their availability may provide comfort to an otherwise hesitant client. We should note that the durable power of attorney for health care is always "springing." The power to make medical decisions on another's behalf will be effective only on the cessation of an individual's ability to speak for one's self.

Medicaid Planning

The **Medicaid Qualifying Trust (MQT)** is a technique that may be used in the specialized area of Medicaid planning. Medicaid is a joint federal and state program designed to provide medical care and hospitalization for the poor. Unlike Social Security, Medicaid is not a program for most citizens; it is part of the welfare system designed to provide medical and long-term care to the financially indigent. However, in recent years, for those who require long-term and nursing home care, it has become relatively popular among Americans of all income levels. This is because Medicare pays for little or no post-hospitalization nursing home care. These limitations therefore raise the possibility that an incapacitated client will totally deplete his or her wealth accumulated during his or her lifetime. To deal with this possibility, a new area of financial planning known as Medicaid planning has arisen.

NEED TO KNOW: COMBINING POAs

While it is possible to include the legal content of a durable power of attorney for health care in a durable power of attorney for property form (and have only one document), it is not advisable. Each document is designed to cover different possibilities, and the attorneys-in-fact named in each may need to be different. Typically, the attorney-in-fact required for the health care power of attorney will be someone who knows the individual very well, including his or her most intimate wishes. Usually, this is one's spouse, but not always. In contrast, the naming of an individual to deal with the demands of property management, created either through a revocable trust or a power of attorney for property, may need to be different.

In qualifying for Medicaid, an applicant can retain a personal residence, an automobile, and a nominal amount of other assets. Thus, one strategy for qualifying for Medicaid is for the usually elderly person to bring down the total value of all of his or her other assets by spending assets to fix up his or her home or to buy an expensive new car. Assets might also be transferred to others, such as children and friends, prior to applying for Medicaid. However, a person who makes uncompensated transfers within three years (or five years, if a trust transfer is involved) prior to applying for Medicaid, faces a "penalty period" during which he or she will not qualify for Medicaid. This waiting period is derived by dividing the value of uncompensated transfers made during the "look back" period of three (or five) years by the average monthly cost of nursing home care in the region. For example, assume that Alice transfers stock worth $60,000 to her daughter so as to reduce her assets to a value less than the legal maximum. A year later, Alice applies for Medicaid to cover nursing home costs. If the average nursing home in her area charges $6,000 per month, Alice will not be eligible to receive Medicaid for ten months ($60,000 divided by $6,000).

The Medicaid Qualifying Trust, a technique frequently used in this type of planning, gives the trustee the discretionary right to take money out of the trust to provide for the benefit of the Medicaid applicant. While the client who creates such a trust and makes irrevocable gifts to it does incur some time period penalty before becoming eligible for Medicaid assistance, the trust assets are subsequently not considered among otherwise eligible resources.

Special Needs Trust

There are many individuals who are developmentally or physically disabled and who need care as adults, but who have no way to obtain it for themselves. A **Special Needs Trust (SNT)** allows individuals who meet the Social Security disability criterion to maintain eligibility for critical public benefits, including Supplemental Security Income (SSI) and Medicaid, while at the same time preserving private assets in a qualifying trust to provide for services, items, and activities not available through public programs. SSI and Medicaid are means-tested programs permitting only nominal amounts of monthly income and assets, excluding a primary residence or accessible vehicle. While the benefits available from SSI are minimal, SSI provides a gateway to Medicaid and other benefit programs often critical to the health, welfare and long-term care of an individual with a disability. In fact, Medicaid is the most comprehensive "health insurance" program available to individuals with disabilities and may be the only way to obtain lifelong-needed services.

Types of SNT

There are four types of SNT:

Settlement/Litigation SNT

The settlement/litigation SNT is established with proceeds obtained on behalf of a disabled individual from a personal injury action.

Pooled SNT

A pooled or "c" (named after 42 USC 1396p(d)(4)(c)) SNT uses "pooled" assets for investment purposes and preserves SSI and Medicaid benefits for disabled individuals over age 65 whose own assets are used to fund the trust. This type of SNT is managed through a nonprofit organization set up in each state.

NEED TO KNOW: THE "GRANNY GOES TO JAIL" LAW

From a financial planner's point of view, the use of Medicaid Qualifying Trusts and other Medicaid planning techniques creates an ethical dilemma. On one side are the individual and his or her family trying to preserve an inheritance; on the other side are the taxpayers who are being asked to pay the bill for people who have assets that could be used to pay for the needed care. In fact, in 1996 Congress passed a law effective January 1, 1997 that made it a crime for elderly Americans to transfer their assets to others, including trusts, before going into a nursing home if state Medicaid officials concluded that the transfer triggered a "penalty period." A person who violated the act was subject to a fine of up to $25,000, imprisonment for up to five years, or both. This law was soon named by elder-care professionals and others the "Granny Goes to Jail" law. In August 1997, Congress amended the law to make it a crime for attorneys to advise elderly clients to give away assets to get Medicaid coverage of nursing home costs. The penalty was a fine of up to $10,000, one year in prison, or both. This law became known as the "Granny's Lawyer Goes to Jail" law. Attorneys have claimed that it poses an ethical dilemma for them because it forces them to choose between committing a crime by giving advice and committing malpractice by not doing so. In 1998, the Justice Department stated its intent to not enforce this law

Third-Party SNT

A third-party SNT is created by interested parties to benefit a disabled individual.

Family SNT

Family special needs trusts are tools in traditional estate planning for families with disabled individuals.

In Depth: More on Special Needs Trusts

While Special Needs Trusts are often established for young adults who were disabled as children, they can apply to anyone who is in need of care but not capable of providing it. This is a highly specialized field. Not many financial planners or lawyers focus on this area, but the stakes are very high. It is important that families that need to establish these trusts are given accurate advice. Disability alone does not necessitate this type of trust. It is the inability of the individual to fully function and provide for his or her needs that dictates it. Many disabled individuals are capable of living on their own, but cannot acquire regular employment with comprehensive health benefits. Even if institutionalization is not required, these individuals generally require a lifetime of care through government programs unless their families are quite wealthy.

When disabled children reach the age of majority, their parents are not legally obligated to provide for their health and welfare. It is not an abuse of the system to permit eligible individuals to obtain government benefits to which they are entitled. However, without some family support, many of these individuals can live at no more than a mere subsistence level. A Special Needs Trust can provide quality of life assistance for individuals, such as social interaction, transportation, recreation, education, supplemental attendant care, home maintenance, job training and coaches. Other uses include paying for respite care for family caregivers, basic home furnishings, cable television, telephone service, computers, Internet access and even some vacation opportunities. Moreover, an SNT may supplement Medicaid services with additional therapy, respite or custodial care, and may provide payment for cutting-edge medical advances or therapies not covered by Medicaid. Such a trust seeks to insulate trust assets from governmental claims for reimbursement and, at the same time, retain a developmentally disabled individual's eligibility for public benefits, including Supplemental Security Income (SSI) and Medicaid.

Most SNTs require court approval and the use of a corporate trustee.

Allowable Uses

The income of these trusts must be used to supplement government benefits, not replace them. If the trust income pays for the basics, the government programs may stop. It is critical that the individual maintains a very low level of assets (for example, less than $2,000), or whatever is specified by the particular state to be eligible for public benefits. If more than this amount is in his or her name, the assets may need to be turned over to the government directly, because most government benefits will stop until the assets are essentially gone. Gifts and bequests from family and friends also should go into the trust, and not to the individual.

PLANNING FOR NONTRADITIONAL FAMILIES

Nontraditional families may have special needs. A financial planner should inquire about the client's family situation in assisting the client.

Single-Parent Households

Probably the most common type of nontraditional family situation is that of the single parent. In most cases, single parent households will incur costs similar to those of two-income families yet have only one breadwinner. This makes it even more important than for two-income families that there be a good cash flow plan, a realistic budget, an adequate contingency fund, adequate health care coverage (medical expense and disability), adequate life, homeowners, and auto insurance, and a properly executed will, including guardianship provisions, and most likely, a trust.

Most people arrive at single parenthood through either death of a spouse/partner, divorce, or breakup of a relationship. Of course, some people make a conscious decision to become a single parent by conceiving a child with a plan to raise it alone or by adopting a child. However, since most enter single parenthood through death or divorce, we will focus our discussion on the transition from two-parent families.

Often, a single parent is overwhelmed with household maintenance tasks that used to be shared. As a result, in preparing a new budget, such things as cleaning or yard services may need to be included. Single parents with young children may also need to budget for additional child care (including the effect of the dependent care credit) as well as forego extra working hours and the resulting additional income because of the trade-off with child care expenses. Then there is the issue of time off from work when children are sick and whether the children will need to be enrolled in summer camp to permit the single parent to remain at work. In addition, it makes a lot of sense for parents in a divorce situation to have life insurance on each other's lives. The resulting insurance premium needs to be budgeted along with the other extra costs discussed. Finally, single parents who can qualify for the head of household income tax filing status may be able to adjust their withholding tax to bring home more money each paycheck.

A single parent who became so as a result of the death of his or her spouse may receive life insurance proceeds. Planning will need to be undertaken to determine whether repayment of debt or investment of the proceeds makes more financial sense. Widows or widowers may be able to claim some Social Security survivor benefits for their children and perhaps for themselves. However, benefits are phased out as the widow(er)'s income increases. If the single parent's home is larger than he or she needs, consideration should be given to renting out a room or creating a rental apartment in a portion of the home.

Single parents having difficulty making ends meet may need to consider cutting back on contributions to their retirement plans. The last resort should be taking on debt. But if debt becomes necessary, borrowing against either a retirement plan or an insurance policy or taking out a home equity loan are the least expensive options. Saving for college will most likely become more difficult, but the normal reduction in household income may permit saving through Series EE U.S. Savings bonds with the resulting tax-free interest used for college expenses. Also, the reduction in household income may result in qualification for financial aid.

Domestic Partners

Another type of nontraditional family is that of domestic partners. One of the important differences between this type of relationship and that of a married couple is that many laws pertaining to married couples will not necessarily apply to unmarried partners. Just as couples about to marry often create a prenuptial agreement, it is prudent for domestic partners to have a similar written understanding. Legal advice in these matters is strongly recommended as state law varies as to the degree of enforceability of such agreements. Such agreements should address the sharing of household costs, obligations of each partner to the other, long-term plans, the effect of separation, retirement, or death, and, if children are affected by the relationship, the rights and responsibilities of the domestic partner who is not the child's parent, guardianship/custody, and payment of expenses.

With regard to financial arrangements between domestic partners, generally the law does not protect such persons as it does spouses. For instance, spouses can transfer an unlimited amount of property tax-free between each other. This is not the case with domestic partners where such transfers may be subject to gift tax, except if a domestic partner's medical bills or educational tuition costs are paid *directly* by the other partner.

In the area of retirement planning, special arrangements must be made, including the purchase of a significant amount of life insurance, to compensate for the fact that a surviving domestic partner will most likely not receive any benefits from the retirement plan of the deceased partner. With married couples, a spouse generally has a 50% interest in his or her spouse's pension plan, ordinarily entitling him or her to one half of the benefit that the deceased spouse was receiving at the time of his or her death. In light of this, domestic partners should discuss whether to fund their retirement jointly or to each be responsible for his or her own retirement.

Special consideration should be given to estate planning issues, including how property is titled and will be transferred after death, in the absence of a marital deduction. Property held jointly by domestic partners will be considered owned by the first to die, unless the survivor can prove his or her contributions (thus necessitating good record keeping). Property held by domestic partners as joint tenants with right of survivorship may not be appropriate. They may want to consider titling their property as tenants in common. The most prudent course is to consider carefully how domestic partners want to hold and distribute property and then obtain competent advice tailored to the specifics of their situation.

PLANNING FOR JOB LOSS OR SEPARATION

The loss of a job, either voluntarily or involuntarily, is a major life event to many individuals requiring significant planning for a transition into early retirement, starting a business, or providing freelance/consulting services, or job hunting. Key issues that arise in such a situation include:

- adjustments to one's living expenses, assets, and debts to take into account what could be a long period of time of little or no earned income—the financial planner should assume that the client will remain unemployed between six and nine months
- tax and financial considerations of the job separation offer and the distribution of retirement benefits
- how to invest retirement plan distributions, once received
- possible replacement or enhancement of medical expense, disability, or life insurance
- unrealistic expectations and the financial risks of starting a business

Typically, during a job transition period, a client will need to draw on his or her contingency fund (which was established partially for this reason). This period may also require shifting investments from small-cap, growth-oriented mutual funds to balanced or high-income funds. Paper gains from equities may need to be liquidated and shifted to money market funds or laddered CDs. It may even be necessary to consider selling any "luxury" assets, such as a boat, recreational vehicle, or vacation home.

Refinancing an old mortgage to obtain a lower interest rate, if possible, and to obtain cash may be necessary. Alternatively, drawing on an existing home equity line of credit or taking out a home equity loan could make sense, particularly if consumer debt, such as credit cards, auto loans, or personal loans is retired with part of the proceeds.

Another important question is whether to leave retirement funds in the former employer's plan or to take a rollover into the former employee's IRA. If such a rollover is completed, the former employee could begin to take distributions at age 59 1/2. If a distribution is taken from the former employer's retirement plan, it is subject to income tax and a 10 percent early distribution penalty if the former employee is under age 55 at separation from service. Of course, withdrawing the funds in substantially equal payments over one's life expectancy can avoid the 10 percent penalty.

Another key issue is a reevaluation of one's insurance needs at the time of job separation. Of utmost importance is the continuation of medical expense insurance coverage either through COBRA or conversion to an individual plan. Cost savings could result from increasing deductibles or converting to HMO-type coverage. Also, a former employee can take distributions from his or her IRA to pay health insurance premiums while unemployed without being subject to the 10 percent early distribution penalty. Group term life insurance may be convertible to an individual term, whole life, or universal policy. If the former employee already owns a universal policy, it may be possible to reduce the annual contribution to allow the built-up cash value to pay the premiums or to borrow against the cash value for short-term cash needs. If a former employee becomes self-employed, he or she should consider converting the former company-paid disability income insurance coverage to an individual policy.

Finally, from an income tax standpoint, the unemployed client should keep good records of job search expenses for possible tax deduction, even if the search is not successful.

PLANNING FOR PARENT/CHILD RELATIONSHIPS OVER TIME

Soon after graduation from college, young adults are generally eager to establish their financial independence. However, some fail to take control of their own finances and remain reliant on their parents for a full or partial subsidy of their living costs. Some move back into the family home, receive financial assistance in purchasing a home or in attending graduate school, or expect to be provided with monthly financial assistance. This situation can result in a financial strain on parents and indefinitely forestall the financial independence of their children. This often takes place at a time when parents should be building their retirement funds to provide for their old age. Failing to save in an adequate fashion during their peak earning years may result in a reversal of roles as the children eventually achieve financial independence and some degree of wealth. Some parents consider providing financial help for their children important, but this must be balanced with the long-term goal of helping their children become financially independent.

As children approach middle age, it is important for them to have open discussions with their parents about their respective financial situations. This is often difficult as many parents feel that their personal finances are private and they may not want to intrude on their children by making inquiries about their children's finances. As a result, each generation makes inaccurate assumptions about the financial position of the other. This mutual lack of information may manifest itself, for example, in provision (or lack of provision) for the college education of the younger generation's children.

In late middle age, children may experience a role reversal with their parents as their parents gradually become more and more dependent on them for guidance and financial support. Often, elderly parents are not aware of their estate planning options and need guidance in this area, including preparation, updating, and coordination of wills and trusts with those of the children (primarily for generation-skipping transfer tax purposes). Another important matter, as discussed in a previous section, is that of providing for asset management, health care decisions, and life support issues in the event of the parents' declining health. While the parents' medical expenses may be primarily funded through Medicare and so-called Medigap policies, custodial care, if it becomes necessary, will not be covered by these sources. As a result, planning to qualify for Medicaid or obtaining long-term care insurance coverage may need to be pursued. Otherwise, the children may have to cover this expense or provide the parents with this type of care personally.

PLANNING FOR THE DEATH OF A SPOUSE OR LIFE PARTNER

The death of a spouse, life partner, or any other close relation, while fraught with emotional trauma, also brings with it a host of financial concerns. Many survivors are ill prepared or completely unable to cope with these concerns. Countless questions confront a survivor, such as paying off the home mortgage, liquidity, selling the home, life style adjustments, college education for children or self, retirement or continued work, benefit entitlements, continuation of the decedent's employer-provided benefits, pension plan payout options, preparing a will, insurance issues, and selecting an advisor.

Normally, settling the estate of the decedent will require hiring an attorney knowledgeable and experienced in that area. The survivor also may want to consider hiring a financial planner to evaluate his or her financial situation immediately after the death of the spouse or life partner. This may include estimating the amount of income and cash flow the survivor will need, funding children's education, dealing with debt, as well as investment, insurance, and estate planning. If necessary, the financial planner may suggest the use of other professionals, such as bankers, insurance specialists, investment professionals, appraisers, etc. It is crucial that survivors soon begin to look ahead and start to determine their future expenses and the source of income to pay them.

Some of the same issues affecting single parents discussed in the section on Nontraditional Families also should be considered here.

Finally, there is the issue of income tax filing status. The survivor is permitted to file a joint return with the decedent for the year of the decedent's death and may be able to claim a similar status, qualifying widow(er), for two additional years if the survivor meets all of the following requirements:

- the couple was entitled to file a joint return the year the spouse died, whether or not the survivor elected to do so.
- the survivor's children qualify as his or her dependents, and the survivor's home is their principal residence.
- the survivor provides over half the cost of maintaining his or her household.
- the survivor has not remarried. If he or she has remarried, the survivor may file a joint return with the new spouse.

In Depth: Common Financial Mistakes Made by Survivors

Among the more common and more costly mistakes made by survivors, which financial planners should help them avoid, are the following:

- selling assets or making investment decisions too quickly without adequate consideration of market conditions and tax implications.

- failing to file, or not filing in a timely manner, the appropriate federal and state estate tax forms, even when no tax is due; such filings are essential for some title transfers and they establish a tax basis if the property is later sold.

- failing to change beneficiary designations on retirement plans and insurance policies to a living beneficiary.

- failing to segregate estate assets, liabilities, and expenses to create an additional tax entity for tax savings.

- failing to establish fair market value of assets inherited at date of death.

- failing to disclaim part of an inheritance where the deceased spouse's will does not take advantage of the estate tax unified credit equivalent.

- failing to make an adequate search for all assets and life insurance policies.

- investing life insurance proceeds or retirement plan distributions either too conservatively or too aggressively.

- failing to maintain the tax-deferred status of IRA accounts, 401(k) or 403(b) plans, Keoghs, and SEP accounts by taking distributions when not absolutely required to pay expenses.

- failing to contact the Social Security Administration immediately if the survivor or deceased is already retired, since a surviving spouse is entitled to the decedent's higher social security benefit, if applicable, at age 60, or earlier, if disabled. Others, including insurance companies, the decedent's employer, and the Veterans Administration (if applicable), also need to be notified.

DISASTER RECOVERY

In light of the terrorist attack of September 11, 2001, on New York's World Trade Center and Washington's Pentagon building as well as other natural and man-made disasters, financial planners need to be able to counsel clients in reconstructing their financial lives after such tragic events. In such situations, clients or their family members may sustain serious injuries or even lose their lives. Jobs may be disrupted, and client property may be severely damaged or totally destroyed. While dealing with the emotional and psychological aspects of these situations is more than most clients will be able to bear, they will also be confronted with the financial impact.

Clients involved in such disasters can take certain steps to mitigate the unfavorable financial effects, including the following:

- Securing one's property by removing valuables and important documents and making temporary repairs to prevent further damage. Some of the documents that may be needed in order to file insurance claims, pay bills, provide care to injured family members, or manage a loved one's estate include: (1) birth certificates; (2) death certificates; (3) marriage certificates; (4) wills; (5) powers of attorney; (6) living wills or other medical powers; (7) trust documents; (8) Social Security cards and other records; (9) military records; (10) medical records, including prescription information; (11) insurance policies, including life, health, disability, long-term care, auto, and homeowners or tenant policies; (12) bank account information; (13) retirement account records; (14) other investment statements; (15) pay stubs; (16) tax returns; (17) auto titles and registrations; (18) mortgage notes and property deeds; (19) leases; (20) credit card and other loan records; and (21) current unpaid bills.

- Notifying one's insurance company of property losses incurred, determining the extent of coverage as well as actions necessary by the insured, developing an accurate inventory of damaged or destroyed property; qualifying for tax refunds or deductions for the casualty losses incurred.

- Obtaining immediate cash through the Red Cross or the Federal Emergency Management Agency (FEMA), if in a declared major disaster area, or from one's employer, emergency fund or credit card cash advance.

- Working with a financial planner or other financial advisor to develop a financial disaster recovery plan.

- Contacting one's employer about the continuation of employee benefits, an estimated schedule for returning to work, the availability of disability, employer liability, workers' compensation benefits, and the need to care for family members under the Family and Medical Leave Act.

- Applying for Social Security disability benefits.

- Obtaining death certificates, if applicable; locating letters of instruction from deceased family members; notifying appropriate parties of the loved one's death; locating and reading the will; hiring an attorney; acting as executor(trix); filing life insurance claims; and transferring accounts in the name of the deceased or joint with the deceased to survivors.

- Obtaining temporary financing from special governmental disaster relief funds; claiming unemployment insurance benefits (if applicable); borrowing against one's retirement plan or life insurance policies; liquidating certain assets; obtaining a forbearance agreement from one's mortgage lender; maximizing tax deductions and credits; paying bills currently; considering bankruptcy if absolutely necessary.

- Initiating lawsuits as appropriate and, if successful, arranging for a lump-sum payment or a structured settlement, as discussed earlier in this chapter.

- Looking for ways to increase income, reduce expenses, or both.

IMPORTANT CONCEPTS TO REMEMBER

Incapacity vs. Disability

Guardian vs. Conservator

Durable power of attorney

Standby trust

Medicaid qualifying trust

Special needs trusts

Living will

Durable power of attorney for health care

Durable power of attorney for property

Married couples vs. domestic partners

Common and costly mistakes made by survivors

QUESTIONS FOR REVIEW

1. What is the difference between how incapacity and disability are determined?

2. What is the difference between a guardian and a conservator?

3. What are the two primary techniques commonly used in planning for the property management of an incapacitated client?

4. How is a revocable living trust used in planning for incapacity and what is another name for it?

5. What is the effect of making a power of attorney durable?

6. What is meant by a "springing" power of attorney?

7. What is meant by the "look back period" and the "penalty period" in Medicaid planning?

8. What is the function of a special needs trust?

9. What are the four types of special needs trusts?

10. What is the difference between a living will and a durable power of attorney for health care?

11. What items should be included in an agreement between domestic partners prior to cohabitation?

12. What are some of the principal issues in dealing with one's adult children and with one's parents over time?

13. What are some of the more common and costly mistakes made by survivors of spouses or domestic partners?

SUGGESTIONS FOR ADDITIONAL READING

West's Business Law, 9th edition, by Kenneth W. Clarkson, Roger LeRoy Miller, Gaylord A. Jentz, & Frank B. Cross, West Legal Studies in Business, a division of Thomson Learning, 2004.

"Special Needs Trusts: Powerful Planning Tools for Disabled Individuals" by Kate Dussault & Jeffrey R. Lauterbach, *Journal of Financial Planning*, January 2002.

"Caring for Elderly Relatives: Using the Tax Laws to Save the Most for a Family" by Randy Gardner, LLM, CPA, CFP and Julie A. Welch, CPA, CFP, *Journal of Financial Planning*, June 2003.

"Planning for Incapacity: What Every Financial Planner Should Know" by Keith Fevurly, J.D., LLM, CFP, *Journal of Financial Planning*, January 2004.

"Worst-Case Scenarios" by Donald Jay Korn, *Financial Planning*, January 2004.

"Helping Hands" by Donald Jay Korn, *Financial Planning*, April 2003.

"Adviser and Advocate" by Nadine O. Vogel, *Financial Planning*, February 2003.

Planning for Divorce and Legal Separation

• • •

While approximately one half of all marriages end in divorce, it is nevertheless a very trying experience with attendant psychological trauma for all parties involved. Adding to the mental anguish are the related financial and tax issues that are often ignored or not addressed satisfactorily. In addition, there is high cost and legal complexity. It goes without saying that one's financial situation will change significantly, usually for the worse. Most likely, both parties will experience a lower standard of living as a result of divorce or separation.

Divorce or separation is a time when personal financial planning is crucial. Both parties will need to restructure their respective lives and make certain that various aspects of their lives have been adequately addressed. Careful planning can serve to mitigate the often unfavorable financial and tax issues affecting each party. In fact, if the parties are able to suppress their strong emotions at this time, there are opportunities to cooperate in designing a divorce or separation that minimizes the negative effects on the former spouses and their children. In many cases, this is not possible because the proceedings become strongly adversarial and the former spouses are so overcome by emotion that they are unable to deal reasonably with one another. In these cases, communication often takes place only through their respective attorneys, and the process tends to deteriorate into one of unprincipled, emotionally-charged negotiation, or horse-trading.

In this chapter, we will discuss the planning issues of determining the parties' new living expenses; dividing assets and debts; structuring alimony, child support, and property divisions for maximum tax benefit; and planning for investments, retirement, insurance, and estate preservation.

The objectives of this chapter are:

- Identify the types of quantitative and qualitative information that should be collected and analyzed in a divorce or separation.
- Explain the difficulty of determining the value of a closely-held business interest in a divorce or separation.
- Describe the requirements that must be met to qualify payments to a spouse or former spouse as alimony.
- Discuss the concept of alimony frontloading and recapture.
- Explain the income tax treatment of payments characterized as alimony that are reduced based on a contingency relating to a child.
- Describe the general rule applicable to the dependency exemption, child tax credit, and child care credit in a divorce or separation and the exceptions to that rule.
- Discuss how the relative income tax brackets of the parties affect the tax planning for a divorce.
- Explain the requirements to qualify for head of household income tax filing status.
- Describe the income tax treatment of marital property settlements in a divorce.
- Discuss the rules applicable to the deduction of mortgage payments made by a departing spouse on the former marital residence occupied by his or her former spouse.
- Describe the manner in which life insurance coverage should be structured after a divorce or separation.
- Explain the purpose of a Qualified Domestic Relations Order (QDRO).

CHILD CUSTODY AND PARENTING

One of the first major decisions required in a divorce or separation is that concerning with whom the children of the marriage will live and how both spouses will parent those children. This issue is often very contentious and heavily laden with emotion, but resolution is necessary prior to initiating the financial analysis discussed in the next section. One cannot develop a meaningful estimate of future living expenses until one knows with whom children will live and what the visitation and other parenting arrangements will be.

If it is decided that one parent will have sole custody, subject to reasonable visitation rights of the other parent, the resulting cost analysis is straightforward. If, on the other hand, parents anticipate joint custody or some variation of joint custody, both parents will have to be able to provide adequate living conditions for their children in both households. This will affect the projection of living expenses for each parent.

Figure 18.1

ASSETS AND LIABILITIES AS OF_____	
ASSETS	**Personal Use Assets**

ASSETS

Liquid Assets

Checking accounts $ _____

Savings accounts _____

Money market accounts _____

Money market fund accounts _____

Certificates of deposit
(< 1 yr. to maturity) _____

Cash value of life insurance _____

Total Liquid Assets $ _____

Investments

Stocks _____

Bonds _____

Mutual funds _____

Real estate _____

Certificates of deposit
(> 1 yr. to maturity) _____

Other _____

Total Investments $ _____

Retirement Funds

Pension
(present lump-sum value) _____

IRAs and Keogh accounts _____

Employee savings plans
(e.g., 401(k), SEP, ESOP) _____

Total Retirement Funds $ _____

Personal Use Assets

Principal residence _____

Second residence _____

Collectibles/art/antiques _____

Automobiles _____

Home furnishings _____

Furs and jewelry _____

**Total Personal
Use Assets** $ _____

LIABILITIES

Charge account balances _____

Personal loans _____

Student loans _____

Auto loans _____

401(k)loans _____

Investment loans
(margin, real estate, etc.) _____

Home mortgages _____

Home equity loans _____

Life insurance policy loans _____

Projected income tax liability _____

Other liabilities _____

Total Liabilities $ _____

Net Worth $ _____

FINANCIAL ANALYSIS

In order to negotiate a divorce or separation agreement and to have the courts approve such an agreement, a significant amount of financial analysis is required to ascertain the assets, debts, and net worth of the spouses and their proposed new living expenses. See Figure 18.1 for a balance sheet worksheet to determine assets, debts, and net worth. As this worksheet is completed, the legal ownership of each item entered must be determined and indicated on the worksheet. State law may control how particular items are divided between the parties. As we discussed in Chapter 14, there are important implications in how property is titled in particular states. For instance, if the divorcing couple lives in a community property state, property may be divided differently than in common law states. And there can be significant differences among common law states in how property is divided in a divorce situation.

1. Obtain Valuations of Personal Property

Most of the information required to complete the balance sheet worksheet will come from statements provided by banks and other financial institutions, life insurance companies, securities brokerage firms, retirement plans, and employers. In the case of certain assets, expert appraisers may need to be hired to provide a current fair market value. An additional problem in inventorying assets owned by a divorcing couple is that of unequal knowledge between the spouses. One spouse may have been the primary party dealing with financial issues, while the other spouse may have little or no knowledge of the full extent of assets owned, debts owed, and income received. In fact, if one spouse has purposely kept financial information from the other spouse, this may have been a major reason for the divorce or separation. Again, forensic accountants may be needed in this situation.

Real Estate

The value of the couple's principal (and second) residence may often be determined at no cost by asking an experienced, knowledgeable real estate salesperson or broker known and respected by both spouses or by each spouse obtaining a value from separate real estate professionals. Particularly in the case where one or both residences may need to be sold, real estate professionals often will help determine the value(s) at no cost if they have the prospect of obtaining the listing(s).

High-Value Personal Belongings

Other assets that may require independent appraisal include collectibles, art, antiques, furs, jewelry, high value home furnishings, and other high value personal belongings. Ordinarily, the value of automobiles may be easily determined from publications designed for that purpose. Most liabilities may be determined from current loan statements showing the unpaid balance. One item that may involve the use of a tax professional is any projected income tax liability at the time of the divorce or separation.

Closely Held Business Interests

Determining the value of a closely held business interest is a process fraught with thorny valuation issues, and the services of a competent appraiser will be essential in this case. However, even though a professional appraisal is prepared, it is often only as good as the information used in its preparation. In many closely held business situations, the financial records of the business may reflect underreporting of income and over-reporting of business expenses for income tax purposes. This makes it difficult to know the true income of the business. The use of forensic accountants may be required in this situation to attempt to locate unreported income and assets and to ascertain the bona fides of business expenses.

A business, no matter under what form it is organized, should be valued as a whole and not subdivided into incongruent parts. This applies equally to corporations and unincorporated proprietorships. Care must be taken in using valuation methods for divorce purposes, since the exiting spouse's interest in the business may terminate as of the divorce or separation. Addressing the nonparticipating spouse's undivided interest as a minority interest may violate the "single economic entity" theory upon which the property settlement statute (IRC Section 1041) is based.

Professional Licenses

In the case of a professional license, if the license was obtained by the joint efforts of the spouses, although the license is not partitionable, its worth may be considered when partitioning other marital assets. For example, a spouse who worked to help put his or her spouse through medical school may be entitled to a portion of the value of the medical license.

2. Project Future Income and Expenses

The next step is for each spouse to prepare a projection of his or her proposed future income and living expenses. Figure 18.2 is an example of a worksheet designed for this purpose. This kind of information will need to be developed for each spouse for his or her anticipated living situation. Such information will be very important in negotiating such items as temporary support, alimony, and child support. The worksheet is designed to elicit very detailed information about a spouse's anticipated income (from whatever source, net of income taxes, payroll taxes, and other required, specified payroll deductions) and anticipated living expenses categorized as follows:

- those applicable to the spouse's household
- transportation expenses
- personal and miscellaneous expenses
- costs that are directly applicable to dependent children who, it is assumed, will live with this spouse, and
- monthly installments on debt requiring regular payments

After the information required for the worksheet has been entered on the form, gross income from all sources is reduced by income taxes, payroll taxes, and other required, specified payroll deductions to arrive at net monthly income. Next, the spouse's living expenses (before monthly debt service) are deducted from net monthly income to arrive at the difference between net monthly income and monthly living expenses. From this amount, monthly debt service is deducted to determine income available or anticipated deficit per month. If one spouse's worksheet indicates income available and the other spouse's worksheet indicates an anticipated deficit, a presumption is created that the spouse with income available will provide some sort of financial subsidy to the spouse with the anticipated deficit. Of course, this presumption is based upon both spouses having provided full, accurate information about their respective incomes and reasonable estimates of living expenses based on historical experience during their marriage or cohabitation. The natural tendency is for both spouses to overestimate their respective living expenses so that they will either receive more support or be required to pay less support. Conversely, in amicable divorces, one spouse may not want to be a financial burden on the other or may be feeling some guilt for how the relationship ended. In these cases, the dependent spouse may not receive adequate support or the payer spouse may voluntarily agree to pay more than he or she can afford. That is why it is so important to develop realistic and reasonable estimates of income and expenses so that the amount of support determined is based on true need and true ability to pay.

If the combined net monthly income of both spouses, less their combined anticipated living costs and debt service, results in an overall deficit, then the parties will need to agree on certain cost reductions and/or increases in income to bring their combined financial situation into balance and support their desired future life styles. As we discussed in Chapter 4, categorizing expenses as to those that are core (or absolutely required), those that are discretionary, and those that may be unnecessary will make the task of balancing the combined budgets much easier. Since two people living together generally live more inexpensively than two people living apart, costs will most likely increase, requiring both spouses to reduce their spending. However, many divorced spouses find that the initial increase in costs does not last indefinitely. In many cases, formerly dependent spouses start their own careers and earn an income of their own. Spouses paying support to their former spouses usually adapt as their income increases and they adjust their living situation and corresponding costs accordingly.

Once this balance has been achieved, it will become apparent which spouse will need to subsidize the other and by how much. The next important issue will be how to categorize the monthly subsidy paid by one spouse to the other.

As discussed earlier, the foregoing discussion assumes that the issue of custody of any children of the marriage has been agreed upon in advance. If this often contentious issue has not yet been resolved, it may be necessary to first reach an agreement among the parties, or alternatively to bring the issue before the applicable court for resolution. After the issue of custody has been resolved, then the worksheets discussed earlier may be completed.

Figure 18.2

Actual Monthly as of

_____

A. STATEMENT OF INCOME AND DEDUCTIONS
  1. Gross Income Per Month
     a. Salary/wages $_____
     b. Draw   _____
     c. Bonus   _____
     d. Pension   _____
     e. Annuity   _____
     f. Social Security   _____
     g. Dividends   _____
     h. Interest   _____
     i. Trusts   _____
     j. Public Aid   _____
     k. Workmen's Compensation   _____
     l. Unemployment Compensation   _____
     m. Rents   _____
     n. Disability Payments   _____
     o. Stocks   _____
     p. Bonds   _____
     q. Other (specify) _____   _____

     TOTAL GROSS MONTHLY INCOME $_____

  2. Required Deductions
     a. Taxes: Federal (based on ____ exemptions) $_____
     b. Taxes: State (based on ____ exemptions)   _____
     c. Social Security (or pension equivalent)   _____
     d. Mandatory retirement contributions required
        by law or as a condition of employment   _____
     e. Union Dues   _____
     f. Health/Hospitalization Insurance   _____
     g. Prior obligation of support actually paid
        pursuant to Court order   _____
     h. Expenditure for repayment of debts that
        represent reasonable and necessary expenses
        for the production of income   _____
     i. Medical expenditures necessary to
        preserve life or health   _____
     j. Reasonable expenditures for the benefit of
        the child and the other parent exclusive of gifts
        (for non-custodial parent only)   _____

     TOTAL REQUIRED DEDUCTIONS FROM INCOME $_____

     NET MONTHLY INCOME $_____

Actual Monthly as of

_____

B. STATEMENT OF MONTHLY LIVING EXPENSES
1. Household
   a. Mortgage or rent (specify) $_____
   b. Taxes, assessments, and insurance   _____
   c. Maintenance and repairs   _____
   d. Heat/fuel   _____
   e. Electricity   _____
   f. Telephone   _____
   g. Water and Sewer   _____
   h. Refuse removal   _____
   i. Laundry/dry cleaning   _____
   j. Maid/cleaning service   _____
   k. Furniture and appliance replacement _____
   l. Food (groceries/milk, etc.)   _____
   m. Tobacco products   _____
   n. Liquor, beer, wine, etc,   _____
   o. Other (specify) _____   _____

   SUBTOTAL HOUSEHOLD EXPENSES $_____

2. Transportation
   a. Gasoline $_____
   b. Repairs   _____
   c. Insurance/license   _____
   d. Payments/replacement   _____
   e. Alternative/replacement   _____
   f. Other (specify) _____   _____

   SUBTOTAL TRANSPORTATION EXPENSES: $_____

3. Personal:
   a. Clothing $_____
   b. Grooming   _____
   c. Medical:
      (1) Doctor   _____
      (2) Dentist   _____
      (3) Medication   _____
   d. Insurance:
      (1) Life $_____
      (2) Hospitalization   _____
   e. Other (specify) _____   _____

   SUBTOTAL PERSONAL EXPENSES: $_____

4. Miscellaneous
   a. Clubs/social obligations/entertainment $_____
   b. Newspaper, magazines and books   _____
   c. Gifts/donations   _____
   d. Vacations   _____
   e. Other(specify) _____   _____

   SUBTOTAL MISCELLANEOUS EXPENSES: $_____

Actual Monthly as of

_____

5. Dependent children:Names and date of birth:

_____

_____

_____

_____

_____

   a. Clothing $_____

   b. Grooming   _____

   c. Education:

      (1) Tuition   _____

      (2) Books/fees   _____

      (3) Lunches   _____

      (4) Transportation   _____

      (5) Activities   _____

   d. Medical:

      (1) Doctor   _____

      (2) Dentist   _____

      (3) Medication   _____

   e. Allowance   _____

   f. Child care   _____

   g. Sitters   _____

   h. Lessons   _____

   i. Clubs/summer camps   _____

   j. Entertainment   _____

   k. Other (specify) _____ _____

SUBTOTAL CHILDREN'S EXPENSES: $_____

TOTAL LIVING EXPENSES: $_____

C. Debts requiring regular payments:

CREDITOR	BALANCE	MINIMUM MONTHLY PAYMENT
_____	_____	_____
_____	_____	_____
_____	_____	_____
_____	_____	_____
_____	_____	_____
_____	_____	_____
_____	_____	_____
_____	_____	_____
_____	_____	_____
_____	_____	_____
_____	_____	_____
_____	_____	_____

SUBTOTAL MONTHLY
DEBT SERVICE: $ _____

Actual Monthly as of
_____

NET MONTHLY INCOME   _____

TOTAL MONTHLY
LIVING EXPENSES   _____

DIFFERENCE BETWEEN NET
INCOME AND EXPENSES $ _____

LESS MONTHLY DEBT SERVICE $ _____

INCOME AVAILABLE PER MONTH $ _____

3. Determine Alimony and Child Support

Alimony is an amount paid by one spouse (or former spouse) to the other marital partner (or former partner) under a divorce or separation agreement. In every state, consideration is given to the spouses' needs and their abilities to pay. Some states factor in the duration and quality of the marriage and marital fault. Over the last several decades spousal earnings have changed, resulting in many cases where no alimony is payable because of relatively equal post-divorce income levels.

Because alimony is tax-deductible by the payor as an adjustment to gross income (rather than an itemized deduction) and taxable to the payee, it is essential that the attorneys drafting the required legal documents use precise language specifically addressing the relevant Internal Revenue Code sections and expressing the intent of the parties. Payments received from a property settlement or for child support are not considered alimony and therefore are not considered income to the recipient (or deductible by the payor).

In Depth: Definition of Alimony for Income Tax Purposes

Several technical requirements must be met to qualify payments to a spouse or former spouse as alimony:

- payment must be in cash or its equivalent (includes checks and money orders)
- payment is received by or on behalf of a spouse pursuant to a divorce or written separation instrument
- the divorce instrument must not designate non-alimony treatment
- parties that are legally separated under a divorce decree or a separate maintenance decree must not be members of the same household at the time payments are made
- an agreement to make payments to a third party on behalf of the payee spouse must be in writing and the payee spouse must derive an economic benefit
- liability for payment must not continue beyond the death of the payee spouse
- a married payor and payee may not file a joint return
- payments cannot violate the excess frontloading rules

With regard to the last requirement, if payments decrease by more than a designated amount ($15,000 currently) during the first three post-separation years, the payor may be required to recapture (include in his or her gross income) some portion of alimony deducted in a prior tax year. Conversely, the payee deducts any recaptured amount from his or her income in the computation year. These rules do not apply when alimony payments end because either party dies, the spouse receiving the payments remarries before the end of the third post-separation year, or the payments are subject to fluctuation because they are tied to the payer's compensation or income from a business or property. The purpose of the special recapture rule is to prevent what are actually non-deductible property settlements from qualifying for alimony treatment (and therefore being tax-deductible). An additional benefit to the receipt of taxable alimony is that it is treated as earned income for purposes of contributing to an Individual Retirement Account (IRA).

Where divorcing spouses have children resulting from the marriage, payments between the spouses may be made for the purpose of supporting the children. These payments are characterized as **child support**. Unlike alimony, these payments are not tax-deductible by the payor and not taxable income to the payee. In the past, creative payors (or their attorneys or accountants) specified in a divorce decree or separation agreement an amount designated as alimony that is to be reduced based on a contingency relating to a child. For instance, a divorce instrument provides that alimony payments will be reduced by $100 per month when a child reaches age 18. Under these circumstances, $100 of each payment is treated from the outset of the divorce instrument as child support for income tax purposes. This is true even if the divorce instrument specifically provides for separate child support payments. Also, even if the divorce instrument does not tie a reduction of alimony to a specific child's birthday, but instead specifies a date that is within six months before of after a child reaches age 18, 21, or the local age of majority, or when two or more reductions are scheduled within one year of a child reaching an age between 18 and 24 that is designated in the agreement, the amount of the reduction will be treated as child support.

While the determination of the amount of child support required is based primarily upon the completed worksheets discussed earlier, state law will indicate a specific amount or percentage per child. In addition, certain children may require private schooling or tutoring or participate in certain vacation activities, sports, camps, and so forth. Moreover, if the child has received gifts or an inheritance, his or her own assets may affect the amount of support.

Child support amounts may need to be reduced or suspended during periods when the children are not living with the custodial parent. Payments should cease when children no longer need support (e.g., reach the age of majority, are adopted by a stepparent, or die).

In determining the optimum tax treatment of payments from one spouse to another, the relative income tax brackets of the parties must be considered. If the payor spouse expects to be in a higher income tax bracket than the payee spouse, he or she will prefer to have the payments characterized as 100 percent alimony. However, the payee spouse will want the payments to be treated as 100% child support. Generally, neither party will prevail in this situation and some sort of compromise will be necessary. Sometimes the payor spouse will offer to "gross up" the payment to cover the income taxes payable by the payee on not only the original amount expected but also on the additional alimony offered. The payor may end up with a lower out-of-pocket cost than if the payment had been treated as either child support or a property settlement.

In deciding how much of each payment to classify as alimony versus child support, there are issues other than income taxes to be considered. Alimony payments, while tax deductible, may be required to continue until the payee spouse either remarries or dies. This could potentially be a very long time. Child support payments, even though not tax deductible, ordinarily continue only until a child reaches an agreed-upon age or is emancipated. This is normally a much shorter period of time.

Financial planners, accountants, and attorneys who specialize in divorce and separation planning have developed software programs to optimize the amounts of alimony and child support paid by the payor spouse taking into account the relative tax brackets of both parties. These programs also assign to the most appropriate party the income tax dependency exemptions for children (discussed next) and qualify the most appropriate parent for head of household tax rates. If the parties involved are willing to cooperate to design the most cost-effective option for their particular situation, they can effectively use the income tax law to minimize their overall living cost situation. It is often difficult for the spouse who is in the lower income tax bracket to understand why it makes economic sense for the payor spouse to claim most of the income tax deductions and to share that benefit with the payee spouse. All he or she sees is that the other spouse is getting all the tax breaks. A financial planner, accountant, or attorney must be able to explain how this can work to the mutual benefit of both parties.

TAX CONSIDERATIONS RESULTING FROM DIVORCE

Tax credits that are likely to change as a result of divorce or separation are the dependency exemption, the child tax credit, and the child care credit.

The Dependency Exemption

Generally, the dependency exemption ($3,100 in 2004) is awarded to the parent who has custody of the child for the greater part of the calendar year. This rule applies only if the child receives over one-half of his or her support from parents who are divorced, legally separated, or have lived apart for the last six months of the calendar year. In addition, the child must have been in the custody of one or both parents for more than one-half of the calendar year.

There are three exceptions to the general rule that a custodial parent is entitled to the dependency exemption:

- if there is a multiple support agreement that allows the child to be claimed as a dependent by a taxpayer other than the custodial parent
- if the custodial parent releases his or her right to the child's dependency exemption to the noncustodial parent in writing on IRS Form 8332 (or similarly worded release), which is attached to the noncustodial parent's tax return for each year the exemption is released
- if a pre-1985 divorce decree or separation agreement grants the exemption to the noncustodial parent and he or she provides at least $600 for the support of the child for the year in question

As mentioned previously, the determination of which parent should claim the dependency exemptions for the children should be based on the relative tax brackets of each parent.

The Child Tax Credit

Related to the issue of the dependency exemption for children is the child tax credit. The child tax credit may be claimed by a parent for a child who is less than 17 years old as of the close of the tax year and who is claimed as a dependent by that same parent. For tax years 2003 and 2004, the credit is $1,000. For tax years 2005 through 2008, the credit is $700. This credit begins to phase out when modified adjusted gross income (MAGI) reaches $110,000 for joint filers, $55,000 for married taxpayers filing separately, and $75,000 for single taxpayers. The credit is reduced by $50 for each $1,000, or fraction thereof, of MAGI above the applicable threshold amount.

The Child Care Credit

Also related to the dependency exemption for children is the child care credit. If the custodial parent is gainfully employed, maintains a household for a dependent under age 13, and incurs qualifying expenses (household services and those for the care of a qualifying child), he or she may qualify for the child care credit. The maximum amount of employment-related expenses to which the credit may be applied is $3,000 if one qualifying child is involved or $6,000 if two or more are involved less excludable employer dependent care assistance program payments. The credit is equal to 35 percent of employment-related expenses for taxpayers with AGI of $15,000 or less. For taxpayers with AGI over $15,000, the credit is reduced by one percentage point for each $2,000 of AGI (or fraction thereof) over $15,000. For taxpayers with AGIs of over $43,000, the credit is 20 percent. Qualifying employment-related expenses are considered in determining the credit only to the extent of earned income—wages, salary, remuneration for personal services, net self-employment income, etc.

Income Tax Filing Status

Even though a husband and wife are not living together on the last day of the tax year, they may still file a joint return if they are *not* legally separated under a decree of divorce or separate maintenance on that date. Spouses who are separated under what is known as an interlocutory decree of divorce are considered husband and wife and are entitled to file a joint return until the decree becomes final. But certain married individuals living apart may file separate returns as heads of household, if they meet the specific requirements, discussed next.

A portion of the benefits that the more favorable tax rates bestow upon a married couple filing a joint return are given to an unmarried individual who qualifies as a **head of a household**. Head of household rates are better than single rates but not as beneficial as joint return rates. In order to qualify for head of household status, a taxpayer must not be married or a surviving spouse at the close of the tax year. In addition, the taxpayer must maintain as his or her home a household that, for more than one-half of the tax year, is the principal place of abode of his or her child. [Actually, persons other than one's child may qualify him or her for head of household status, but here we are confining the discussion to the effect of head of household status on divorce or separation].

One's marital status, for the purpose of applying the head of household rates, is determined at the end of the tax year. A taxpayer is considered to be unmarried at the end of a tax year if his or her spouse was a nonresident alien at any time during the tax year or if he or she is legally separated from his or her spouse under a decree of divorce or separate maintenance at the close of the tax year. A taxpayer under an interlocutory decree of divorce is not legally separated. A married taxpayer will be considered unmarried and eligible for head of household status if the taxpayer's spouse was not a member of the household for the last six months of the year and if the household is the principal place of abode of a child for whom the taxpayer is entitled to a dependency exemption. However, the taxpayer will still be eligible for head of household status if no dependency exemption is available for a child because the taxpayer waived the exemption or because of the existence of a pre-1985 divorce decree or separation agreement.

An individual "maintains a household" only if the individual furnishes (with funds the source of which are attributable to the taxpayer) more than one-half the cost of maintaining the home during the tax year and if at least one of his or her children lives there for more than one-half of the year (except for temporary absence, such as time spent at school). Birth or death of a child during the year will not disqualify the taxpayer as a head of household if the person lived in the household for the part of the year during which he or she was alive.

The costs of maintaining a household include property taxes, mortgage interest, rent, utility charges, upkeep and repairs, property insurance, food consumed on the premises, and other household expenses. They do not include the cost of clothing, education, medical treatment, vacations, life insurance, transportation, food consumed off the premises, or the value of services rendered by the taxpayer or child.

Divorced spouses with or without children who do not qualify as heads of household must file as single taxpayers, unless they have remarried.

Ownership of Tax Refunds

After spouses are divorced, a tax refund may be received, based upon the filing of a joint return while they were still married, because of a prior overpayment, credits refunded, or a net operating loss carry-back. On the surface, it would appear that such a refund would be jointly held property. However, the overpayment is the property of the spouse whose income and tax prepayments created the overpayment. This is true even though spouses are jointly and severally liable for the payment of tax on a joint tax return. The refund is not joint property unless both spouses had income and both paid in a portion of the tax on the return. The portion of the tax attributable to each spouse is calculated by means of a "separate tax formula."

If tax refunds are anticipated, they should be negotiated between the spouses and included in the divorce decree covering how they will be divided between the spouses.

DISSIPATION OF MARITAL ASSETS

Many states have enacted statutes that prescribe how a court is to divide a couple's property upon divorce. Within such statutes are factors that a court takes into consideration upon its division of the parties' assets. Many times, these factors include one spouse's "dissipation" of marital or nonmarital assets. **Dissipation of marital assets** generally is defined as one spouse's expenditure of marital funds for nonmarital purposes once the marriage has irretrievably broken down. That is, if one spouse expends marital funds extravagantly, or for his or her sole benefit, and these expenditures decrease the value of the marital estate, this spouse may be charged with dissipation. Only extravagant, unusual expenditures for nonmarital purposes should be considered dissipation.

PROPERTY SETTLEMENTS

In Chapter 14, we discussed the implications of property titling. In divorce proceedings, property owned by the spouses must be classified and divided between them. Among the factors determining who currently has title to specific assets and how they will be divided is the couple's state of residence, the location of the property, and where, when, and how the assets were acquired.

As we discussed in Chapter 14, state law varies in defining **marital property**. Generally, marital property includes all property that either spouse has acquired during the marriage, except for property acquired by inheritance or gift. **Separate property** is property that each spouse has acquired before the marriage, through inheritance or gift during the marriage, and after separation. Most states assume that assets acquired during the marriage are marital. It may be necessary for a spouse to trace the origins of funds used to acquire property in order to prove that the property is separate.

Property divisions are based upon the concept of **equitable distribution**. This concept states that each spouse has a legal right during marriage to the other spouse's earnings and to the assets acquired by those earnings. Accordingly, courts must perform three tasks:
- classify all assets either as marital or separate
- value the assets
- distribute the assets equitably

Courts will consider the duration and quality of the marriage, marital fault, monetary and nonmonetary contributions to the marriage, each spouse's earning ability, separate property of each spouse, their ages and health, custody of children, and other factors. Because of the impossibility of physically dividing certain assets, such as the marital residence or a business, spouses will have to be assigned other assets in exchange or the property will have to be sold to facilitate an equitable distribution.

Sometimes it is necessary to trace separate property if, for instance, it has been used to acquire other property, it has been commingled with marital property, or if its value has increased significantly.

For income tax purposes, a transfer of property from one spouse to the other "incident to the divorce" is tax-free. This means that no gain or loss is recognized by the transferor spouse. This includes sales or exchanges of property between ex-spouses within one year of the end of the marriage and transfers pursuant to a divorce or separation agreement generally occurring within six years after the end of the marriage. Such transfers are treated the same as gifts for income tax purposes. The transferor's tax basis and holding period carry over to the transferee. Accordingly, if the transferee spouse sells the property, he or she will recognize a taxable gain or loss on the difference between the tax basis obtained from the transferor and the selling price. Because of this, a spouse who is offered a particular asset in a divorce settlement should determine the estimated taxable gain upon its potential sale in order to arrive at an after-tax value for the asset. All significant assets to be divided should be valued in this manner in order to produce an equitable distribution of assets on an after-tax basis.

MARITAL RESIDENCE ISSUES

For most couples, their marital residence is their most valuable asset. Typically, when there is a divorce or separation, one spouse remains in the home with the children, if any, while the other locates separate living accommodations. In such situations, the departing spouse may make the monthly mortgage payments on the jointly owned home until it is sold and the proceeds are divided between the parties. A taxpayer who owns a residence is deemed to use it as a principal residence when the taxpayer's spouse or former spouse has been granted exclusive use and occupancy under the terms of a divorce or separation.

In other situations, the departing spouse may transfer ownership of the home entirely to the remaining spouse. In this case, the transferee spouse's period of ownership will be increased by that of the transferor spouse. A third scenario is the immediate sale of the residence and division of the proceeds. Each of these circumstances gives rise to specific tax and financial treatment. For example, if the marital residence is jointly owned and both parties are liable for the mortgage, a departed spouse may deduct only 50 percent of the mortgage interest he or she pays. The other 50 percent of the mortgage payments made by the departing spouse is treated as alimony, deductible as such and income to the other spouse. After reporting one half of these mortgage payments as alimony income, the other spouse can deduct his or her one half of the mortgage interest paid. As a result, each spouse is considered to have paid one half of the mortgage interest.

On the other hand, if the departing spouse is solely responsible for the mortgage, then he or she is deemed to have paid all of the mortgage interest. But that does not necessarily entitle him or her to the mortgage interest deduction. Generally, a taxpayer can deduct mortgage interest paid on a principal or secondary residence. Once the departing spouse moves out of the marital residence, he or she can no longer claim that house as his or her primary residence. But he or she may be able to claim it as a secondary residence, even though he or she no longer lives there. The tax rules in this area are not clear-cut, but there is support for permitting a post-divorce departing spouse to deduct mortgage interest that he or she pays on the house occupied by his or her former spouse, if the former spouse lives in the house rent-free.

It is strongly recommended that the parties obtain competent income tax advice in this area. To avoid some of the ambiguity in the current tax rules in this area, it is recommended that the departing spouse, rather than paying the monthly mortgage payments directly, increase the amount of monthly alimony otherwise payable by the amount of the monthly mortgage payments. Of course, there should be no reference in the divorce decree or separation agreement to the fact that the amount of alimony payable has been increased for this reason. In this manner, the payor spouse may deduct this additional amount as alimony while the payee spouse must include it in gross income and, in turn, may claim a deduction for the mortgage interest.

In the situation where the residence is sold immediately and the proceeds distributed to the owners, each divorced party may exclude from gross income up to $250,000 of taxable gain from the sale, provided they meet certain residency and ownership requirements. If the parties are not yet divorced and can still qualify to file a joint return, they can exclude from joint gross income up to $500,000 of taxable gain on the sale, provided they meet the applicable requirements.

INSURANCE COVERAGE

At the time of a divorce or separation, both parties need to re-examine their respective insurance coverages. In the situation where there is a financially dependent spouse, that spouse should be advised by his or her financial planner to ascertain whether adequate life insurance currently exists on the life of the payor spouse. If the payor spouse were to die prematurely, monthly support payments to the payee spouse would cease. Accordingly, an amount of life insurance, adequate to provide a monthly income stream equal to the required monthly support payments, should be in place. The divorce decree or separation agreement should prohibit the payor spouse from changing the beneficiary on such a life insurance policy for a specified period of time. Absent such a provision in the divorce instrument, each party should change the beneficiary designation on his or her respective life insurance policies. A method of ensuring that premium payments are made when due is for each former spouse to own the policy on the other.

Likewise, disability income insurance on the payor spouse should be adequate to continue the required monthly support payments in the event of the payor spouse's disability.

With regard to medical expense insurance, a nonworking, financially dependent spouse is eligible for up to 36 months of coverage in the group plan of his or her former spouse's employer. In most cases, the premiums charged for group coverage are much less than those for individual policies. After receiving notification of eligibility for such coverage, the recipient must contact the former spouse's employer within 60 days to exercise his or her right to coverage. After securing this group coverage, the spouse should investigate other medical expense insurance options, including individual policies. In order to avoid large increases in premiums, higher deductibles or copayments or HMO options may need to be considered.

Often the noncustodial parent's medical insurance permits the children to continue being covered provided they are claimed as dependents by the noncustodial parent. This can result in a significant cost saving to the custodial parent as he or she will now need to pay for medical expense insurance only for him- or herself. As discussed earlier under Claiming the Dependency Exemption for Children, the custodial parent may need to give up the dependency exemption(s) in order to realize this potentially large insurance cost saving.

After property has been transferred to a new owner in a property settlement, it is important to modify or obtain new property insurance coverage. With regard to automobiles, title should be transferred as required by the divorce instrument and then insurance coverage changed accordingly. This may result in higher premiums due to the loss of multi-vehicle and multi-line discounts (both homeowners and auto policies insured by the same insurance company).

EDUCATION ISSUES

It is essential that divorcing couples with children make some arrangement for the education of their children. Each party should take some responsibility in the divorce instrument, which could take the form of requiring a deposit of a lump sum amount of money in a qualified prepaid tuition plan or monthly payments into a state savings plan or other vehicle. Children with special needs may require special schooling, with the necessity of a trust for that purpose. An additional education issue is the responsibility for repayment of student loans incurred by one or both former spouses.

INVESTMENT ISSUES

When a couple divorces or separates, it will be necessary to take a fresh look at the investment portfolio that each party will have. Most likely, cash flow requirements, income taxes, liquidity requirements, management needs, and risk tolerance will change. The financial planner will need to address these issues separately with each spouse. For example, the risk tolerance of the couple is probably quite different from that of each separate spouse. Investments owned may no longer be appropriate in light of their new situation.

RETIREMENT ISSUES

Divorce or separation can affect one's retirement plans in a major way. One spouse may have planned on sharing his or her spouse's pension or retirement plan benefits and Social Security benefits. For that reason, a spouse may not have contributed to his or her IRA or Keogh to an adequate extent.

In most states, the present value of a pension plan benefit is considered marital property subject to equitable distribution. It includes only the portion of the pension or profit-sharing interest that is "acquired" during marriage, based on the contributions and earnings or losses allocated to the spouse's account during marriage. In some cases, it will be necessary to determine the value of these benefits either at the date of divorce or the date of separation. This will require consultation with one's attorney and the preparation and service of a **Qualified Domestic Relations Order (QDRO)** served against the pension plan administrator to claim one's share of the other spouse's pension benefits. The recipient spouse's share of such benefits will be subject to income tax upon receipt.

If the marriage lasted at least 10 years, both parties are at least 62 years of age, and the person seeking benefits is unmarried, Social Security benefits may be payable based on the work contributions of his or her former spouse. Receipt of such benefits does not reduce the former spouse's benefits to a current spouse.

ESTATE PLANNING ISSUES

Divorce or separation is a time to examine all existing estate planning documents for possible revision. For instance, a divorced or separated spouse and his or her attorney need to make sure that the former spouse is removed as personal representative, successor trustee, holder of powers, or beneficiary on estate planning documents. Similarly, the issue of child custody succession at the death or disability of the custodial parent should be addressed in the divorce instrument.

Former spouses with large estates will have to reevaluate their estate planning in light of the loss of the unlimited marital deduction and possible decreased liquidity resulting from the property settlement. This may require the purchase of additional life insurance to assure adequate estate liquidity.

LEGAL, ACCOUNTING, AND APPRAISAL FEES

Generally, expenses related to legal, accounting, and appraisal services incurred relative to a proceeding for separation and divorce are not deductible. The determination of their tax-deductibility depends upon their categorization as trade or business expenses, expenses incurred for the production or preservation of income, expenses incurred for the determination of tax liability or tax advice, or for personal expenses. Divorce is considered to be a personal expense; as such, the associated costs of litigation are not deductible. On the other hand, counsel fees for tax advice are deductible as a miscellaneous itemized deduction (subject to the 2 percent of AGI limitation) if the taxpayer itemizes deductions. Also, if the fees are incurred in defending income-producing property from another spouse's claims, such fees may be added to the basis of the property defended. In a case in which one party agrees or is ordered to pay the other's legal fees, the deduction may be lost to both. Legal fees attributable to the production or collection of alimony are deductible; however, a deduction is not allowed for fees attributed to the collection of child support. Finally, appraisal, actuarial, and accountant's fees to determine the correct tax or to help collect alimony are deductible as an itemized deduction.

IMPORTANT CONCEPTS TO REMEMBER

Valuation of a closely held business interest

Alimony

Child support

Frontloading and recapture provisions

Dependency exemption, child tax credit, and child care credit for children

Head of household

Tax refund ownership

Dissipation of marital assets

Property settlements

Marital property

Separate property

Equitable distribution

Sale of marital residence

Deduction of mortgage payments

Life insurance issues

Qualified Domestic Relations Order (QDRO)

Income tax deductions for legal, accounting, and appraisal fees

QUESTIONS FOR REVIEW

1. What are some of the difficulties in valuing a closely held business interest?

2. What issue must be resolved prior to preparing estimates of future income and living expenses for each spouse?

3. What requirements must be met to qualify payments to a spouse or former spouse as alimony?

4. Prior to the adoption of the frontloading and recapture rules, why were alimony payments often frontloaded?

5. What is the income tax treatment of alimony payments that are reduced based on a contingency related to a child?

6. How can financial planners, accountants, and attorneys design a divorce settlement to take maximum advantage of the income tax laws and regulations?

7. What are the three exceptions to the general rule that a custodial parent is entitled to the dependency exemption?

8. What additional income tax benefits are directly related to the dependency exemptions for children of divorced parents?

9. What are the requirements to qualify for head of household tax filing status?

10. What are the general tax rules applicable to a marital property settlement?

11. How should life insurance policies on the lives of former spouses be owned?

12. What is the primary purpose of a Qualified Domestic Relations Order (QDRO)?

13. Which types of divorce-related expenses are tax-deductible?

SUGGESTIONS FOR ADDITIONAL READING

2004 U.S. Master Tax Guide by CCH Editorial Staff, CCH Incorporated, 2003.

Tax and Financial Planning Strategies in Divorce, 2nd edition, by Bruce L. Richman, CPA, ABV, CVA, Panel Publishers, a division of Aspen Publishers, Inc., 1999.

"Divorce and Taxes: Avoiding the Pitfalls" by Ginita Wall, *Journal of Financial Planning*, August 2002.

"At the Crossroads" by Heidi L. Steiger, *Financial Planning*, December 2003.

CHAPTER NINETEEN

Planning for Financial Windfalls

• • •

When a financial planner's client receives a financial windfall, either expected or unexpected, it presents financial planning opportunities as well as challenges. A financial windfall could take the form of a significant inheritance or gift, a large bonus or exercise of a stock option, a lump-sum pension distribution, a settlement of a lawsuit, or a lucky lottery ticket, among others. When a client receives such a windfall, nearly every facet of his or her financial life will change. Financial planners need to know how to counsel clients confronted with this situation.

Most people are very envious of those who have received such financial windfalls. However, not all recipients of such windfalls receive them under favorable circumstances. For instance, a client may receive a financial settlement for serious injuries suffered and catastrophic medical and other related costs incurred as the result of another's negligence. In addition, even if a windfall occurs under happier conditions, many recipients end up suffering from their good fortune because of an inability to cope with the money. Some squander it through bad investments or simply living the "high life." Their lack of experience in handling large amounts of money places them at risk.

A large windfall will probably touch every subject area of personal financial planning. Financial planners will need to evaluate each of these areas and to educate clients on both the opportunities and dangers in managing newfound wealth.

The objectives of this chapter are:

- Discuss some of the general considerations in planning for a financial windfall.
- Explain the advantages of a structured settlement in physical injury cases.
- Identify the requirements to establish a qualified assignment of a structured settlement.
- Distinguish between compensatory and punitive damages in a legal settlement.
- Compare the various life insurance death proceeds settlement options.
- Identify the principal income tax advantages of receiving an inheritance.
- Discuss the advantages to both the donor and the donee of lifetime gifts.

GENERAL CONSIDERATIONS IN PLANNING FOR FINANCIAL WINDFALLS

Before discussing the specific aspects of various types of financial windfalls, we will turn first to some general considerations that will apply to most types of windfalls. For planning purposes, the financial planner needs to obtain specific information from the client, including answers to various questions and client decisions. Listed below are some of the issues that should be addressed by the financial planner and the client:

- when and in what form the windfall will be received
- what the client has decided (at least in general terms) to do with the money
- development of a new budget or cash flow projection to reflect the expected changes in income and expenses
- development of records, if necessary, of the tax basis of the assets received
- review of the client's insurance coverage, with an emphasis on liability coverage in the homeowners, automobile, and personal liability umbrella policies
- determination of the potential benefit of retiring client debt
- development of an investment plan for the cash proceeds
- if the windfall takes the form of securities, evaluation of the securities received and their effect on the client's existing portfolio allocation, risk tolerance, and overall financial resources
- if the windfall is in the form of a single security, evaluation of the client's ability to bear the risk of having a large portion of his or her net worth concentrated in this manner
- review of the client's income tax situation both from the standpoint of the taxability of the windfall itself and from that of the client's future status
- review of the client's previous retirement planning and update, if necessary
- determination of the client's financial ability to manage a planned major expenditure, change in life style, early retirement, or other significant financial commitment

- review of the client's existing estate plan to determine the need for revision and updating, including the possible use of trusts or other strategies and the purchase of life insurance to defray anticipated estate taxes
- determination of the desirability of disclaiming all or a portion of an inheritance to pass it to a lower generation

STRUCTURED SETTLEMENTS

Since 1982, with the enactment of The Periodic Payment Settlement Act, Congress has encouraged the use of structured settlements in physical injury cases. A structured settlement is a voluntary agreement between an injury victim and the defendant in which the victim agrees to receive compensation over an agreed-upon period of time in a tax-free manner to meet the victim's future medical expenses and basic living needs. A structured settlement may be agreed to privately (for example, in a pre-trial settlement) or it may be required by a court order, which often happens in judgments involving minors.

Historically, damages paid because of an injury lawsuit were paid in the form of a single lump sum. However, this settlement method placed the injury victim in the position of having to manage a large sum of money precisely at the same time of also having to establish a new lifestyle. Further, the individual also could run the risk of resorting to public assistance in the event of financial mismanagement. Therefore, the concept of a structured, privately negotiated payment was created.

A long-term structured settlement has several advantages. First, there is the security to the injured victim of having guaranteed long-term income. Second, there is the income tax advantage of receiving 100 percent of every structured settlement payment completely free of income taxes. Congress amended Internal Revenue Code Section 104(a)(2) to provide that the investment earnings on such payments are received tax-free. In addition to personal injury cases, structured settlements are frequently used in cases involving the temporary or permanent disability of individuals, guardianship cases that may involve minors or incompetents, workers compensation cases, and wrongful death cases where the survivors need monthly or annual income.

In a physical injury case, the parties will negotiate issues such as the victim's medical care and basic living and family needs. Often an expert, such as a structured settlement broker, will be hired who will calculate the long-term cost of these needs. When there is a resolution of the benefits due the injury victim, the defendant will fund a stream of payments to meet these needs. Generally, at this point, the obligation to fund the damage payments will be transferred to a third party, such as an insurance company, through the purchase of an annuity. This process relieves the defendant of further responsibility for the payments and transfers the administration and record-keeping responsibilities. The insurance company or other assignee of the obligation usually specializes in these activities and may offer additional financial security to the injured party.

In Depth: Definition of a Qualified Assignment

In order to protect the public, Congress specified in IRC Section 130 the requirements to establish a qualified assignment. They include the following:

- the assignee assumes the liability from the defendant
- both the victim (and his or her attorney) and the defendant agree that the payment schedule cannot be accelerated, deferred, increased, or decreased
- the payment stream may be excluded from the recipient's gross income for tax purposes
- the injury must be a physical sickness or injury; and
- a highly secure funding asset (such as an annuity or U.S. Treasury obligation) must be used to fund the payments

Alternatively, a trust fund, funded by U.S. Treasury securities, may be established. In any event, this type of agreement can be very complex and should not be entered into without professional advice.

Structured settlements are very flexible and can be designed for virtually any set of needs, including those involving other than equal monthly payments. For instance, an injury victim who will need a new wheelchair every three years might elect to receive a larger payment every 36 months to help defray this cost. An attorney knowledgeable in this area or a structured settlement broker can provide valuable advice in specific cases.

In recent years, certain individual investors and firms have offered to purchase structured settlement payments from injury victims. Twelve states have enacted consumer protection statutes that establish strict conditions for these transactions. Advocates for consumers and the disabled, including the Consumer Federation of America, The National Spinal Cord Injury Association, and the National Organization on Disability, have publicly called attention to the sometimes unethical practices of firms engaged in the purchase of structured settlement payments. Injury victims should seek the advice of legal counsel and/or other appropriate experts in this area.

LEGAL SETTLEMENTS

A legal settlement for a personal injury case, absent a negotiated structured settlement, is the predominant form of settlement in the courts today. Generally, two forms of damages may result from such an action—compensatory or punitive damages. **Compensatory damages**, as the name implies, are intended to compensate the injured party for his or her loss or injury as measured by such items as directly related out-of-pocket expenses incurred and income lost. **Punitive damages**, on the other hand, are awarded to punish the wrongdoer. There may be other modifying words associated with damages, such as **liquidated** (in the case of a contract) or **treble** (which is usually a multiple of actual damages); however, these are just variations of the two previous forms.

The classification of a damage award as compensatory or punitive is important for one primary reason—taxability. Compensatory damages, those received on account of personal injury or sickness, are excludible from income taxation under IRC Section 104 (a)(2). In contrast, punitive damages are always taxable to the recipient unless received under the terms of a state's wrongful death statute where compensatory damages are not also available (a relatively small exception). While the courts may (and do) disagree at times whether damage awards are compensatory or punitive in nature, once established, the tax consequence is relatively straightforward. Accordingly, in providing financial planning services for a client who is the recipient of a personal injury award, the potential amount for investment depends greatly on the classification of damages between these two forms. Additional funds will be available where compensatory (non-taxable) damages are awarded.

LOTTERY WINNINGS

In all the excitement of being a lottery winner, it is important to recognize that such winnings are fully taxable. Therefore, the amount received will not be the total amount of money won; indeed, the amount payable will reflect a much lesser after-tax figure. Where a lottery is won by a group of individuals, the financial planning should begin before the lottery proceeds are claimed.

In addition, the recipient will immediately be faced with the question of whether he or she wishes to be paid in one lump sum or in installments over time. Normally, the state or institution awarding the payment will arrange for the purchase of an annuity should the recipient choose to take his or her winnings in installments over time. Usually, this annuity will have a fairly conservative rate of interest or return associated with it, given the guaranteed nature of the payment. The safety and security of these payments must be balanced against the **opportunity cost** of potentially gaining a greater overall return by taking a single lump-sum amount and investing it. It is here that a financial planner can prepare financial projections and provide great assistance to his or her client.

LUMP-SUM RETIREMENT DISTRIBUTIONS

At the time of their actual retirement, some retirees may be faced with the major financial decision of what form of retirement plan distribution to select. In certain types of employer plans, this may not be an issue. The historically prototypical pension plan (a defined benefit plan) may not offer the option of taking a distribution in a lump sum. Plans such as these are usually structured to provide an annuity or other periodic payment over the lifetime of the participant (and that of his or her spouse, if married). However, more and more plans—including the very popular 401(k) plan (a defined contribution plan)—do offer the alternative of a single lump-sum payment.

As with other monetary settlement options addressed in this chapter, the decision to take a lump-sum retirement distribution must give careful consideration to the impact of taxes. While the employee's cost basis (or after-tax contributions) to a retirement plan will be recovered free of income tax, any distribution in excess of this basis will be subject to income taxation at ordinary income rates.

Through 1999, many recipients of lump-sum distributions from employer retirement plans were able to use a special five-year income averaging method to calculate the income tax payable on such distributions. Starting in the year 2000, the five-year income averaging tax treatment for such a distribution was repealed. Distributees born prior to 1936 may elect one of three options: (1) include the entire taxable amount in gross income in the year received; (2) use a special ten-year averaging method; or (3) pay a separate 20 percent tax on the pre-1974 portion of the taxable amount and use the special ten-year averaging method for the post-1973 portion of the taxable amount.

A significant disadvantage to lump-sum distributions is that an employee or spouse may outlive the proceeds of the retirement plan distribution if taken in a lump sum. A second disadvantage is that a lump sum of money in the hands of some presents a great temptation to overspend, thus presenting considerable financial issues in the future. Finally, the employee/participant now has the responsibility of reinvesting this money. It is here that he or she will depend greatly on the investment acumen of a financial planner.

LIFE INSURANCE PROCEEDS

Life insurance policies provide that when the death proceeds become payable, the insured or the beneficiary may elect to have these proceeds paid either in a lump sum or according to some **optional mode of settlement**. If the proceeds remain with the insurance company under some form of settlement option, these proceeds normally are income tax-free to the beneficiary; however, any interest received on the proceeds is taxable. Where the proceeds are paid in a lump sum, they are generally fully exempt from income taxation.

One of the optional modes of settlement is the **interest option**, under which the death proceeds are left with the insurance company, to be paid out at a later time, with the beneficiary receiving only the interest earned on the principal. A minimum rate of interest is guaranteed in the policy but many insurance companies pay excess interest above the guaranteed rate if additional interest is earned by the company.

Another settlement option is **installments for a fixed period**. Under this option, the insurance company computes how much it can pay out of the policy proceeds and the interest earned on them during each of the required periods, so that the entire principal and interest will have been distributed by the end of the period. This option is most valuable where the main consideration is to provide income during some definite period, such as the child-rearing years.

Some beneficiaries may choose **installments of a fixed amount** per month for as long as the principal plus interest on the unpaid portion of the principal will last. The controlling factor here is the amount of each payment, rather than the time period over which they will extend.

Other beneficiaries may choose to have the death proceeds paid out in the form of a life annuity. There are four basic types of life annuity options.

- The first is the **straight life income option**, which pays the policy proceeds to the beneficiary on the basis of his or her life expectancy. The downside of this type of settlement option is that if the beneficiary dies during the first year of payments, the company has fulfilled its obligation and no further payments are made.

- The second option is the **life income with period certain**, which pays a life income for as long as the beneficiary lives, but guarantees a minimum number of payments (typically 5, 10, 15, or 20 years). Payments after the death of the beneficiary are made to a contingent beneficiary.

- Third is the **life income with refund option**, which pays a life income for the life of the beneficiary. If, at the time of the beneficiary's death, the policy proceeds have not been paid out, the remainder of the proceeds is paid to a contingent beneficiary, either in installments until exhausted or in a lump sum.

- The fourth settlement option is the **joint and survivor income option**. It provides a life income to two payees. At the death of the first payee, the payments continue over the life of the second payee. In some cases, the amount of the payments decreases after the death of the first payee.

The amount payable under any one of the life annuity options depends on the age and sex of the beneficiary, plus the plan selected.

A financial planner needs to proceed with caution in this area. While life insurance proceeds (the so-called "face value" of the policy) are generally free of income tax, this is not the usual result with regard to estate tax, where taxability occurs whenever the insured possessed "incidents of ownership" in the policy at his or her death. The avoidance of estate tax on insurance proceeds is a major advantage of an irrevocable life insurance trust (or ILIT).

The non-tax aspects of the receipt of life insurance proceeds in a single sum are similar to those involving retirement plan distributions. Again, the client is faced with a significant sum of money to invest for which he or she may have little expertise or interest. The role of the financial planner is to solve this problem for the client, while also attending to the psychological aspects of assisting a client who has just suffered a major human loss.

INHERITANCE

According to demographic and financial trends, for the "baby boom" generation (those born between 1946 and 1964), the transfer of wealth from their parents will be in the trillions of dollars. This is a major event—one that requires much planning between members of the respective generations. However, intergenerational planning rarely takes place. As a result, a financial planner needs to be prepared to assist in this area.

At this point, one needs to make a distinction between the terms **inheritance** and **estate**. The latter term refers to assets in the hands of the giver or, in the context of our discussion, the parents of the baby boomer. Inheritance, on the other hand, refers to the assets once received by the beneficiary (the baby boomer). Estate taxation is imposed at the federal level on the assets, in excess of a specific amount, passing from the parent to the baby boomer. If there is inheritance taxation, it will more likely occur at the state level and be a financial obligation of the recipient "boomer." With certain exceptions, there will be no income taxation imposed on the inherited assets, although once received and placed in the name of the beneficiary, income tax will subsequently be imposed upon any income from the property or upon any gain at the time of sale. A significant income tax advantage of an inheritance is that the tax basis in the hands of the beneficiary is the fair market value at the death of the deceased (or the alternate valuation date of six months after death, if elected). If the asset inherited is one that has increased substantially in value over the manner years it was owned by the deceased, the beneficiary can avoid paying income tax on this large increase in value if he or she elects to sell the asset at a price at or close to the date of death value.

GIFTS

In some cases, the baby boomer's parents may decide to make a lifetime gift of a large portion of their assets to their children and/or grandchildren in order to reduce the size of their estate upon their deaths, to provide financial assistance to their loved ones, and to see their loved ones enjoy the benefits of these gifts while the donors are still alive. Currently, donors may make gifts of up to $11,000 per year to each donee, and if their spouses agree to make a joint gift, they may transfer up to $22,000 per year to each donee. If this gifting program is conducted over several years, neither federal income nor gift tax will be payable on the significant amount of assets so transferred.

Alternatively, the baby boomer's parents may elect to make taxable gifts to these same donees in amounts in excess of the current annual exclusion amount ($11,000 or $22,000 joint per year). In fact, the parents may elect to make large gifts all in one year or over just a few years. In this case, the parents will have to file a federal gift tax return and pay gift tax on gifts in excess of the annual exclusion amount. The gift tax is calculated by adding the current year's taxable gifts to all prior years' taxable gifts and then calculating the tentative tax by applying the applicable tax rate from the unified rate schedule to the total amount of taxable gifts.

Taxable gifts are the total of all gifts made by a donor during the calendar year, less the amount of marital and charitable deductions. The gift tax currently payable is determined by applying the applicable tax rate to the sum of all prior years' taxable gifts and then subtracting that sum from the tentative tax. The tentative tax is then reduced by the amount of a unified credit (currently $1 million). Of course, using the unified credit (or a portion of it) during one's lifetime may affect the estate tax payable at that donor's death.

Generally, the recipients of such gifts, for the purposes of calculating gain on the sale or other disposition of the property, obtain the donor's tax basis. If gift tax was paid on the gift, the basis of the property is increased by the amount of gift tax attributable to the net appreciation in value of the gift. The net appreciation for this purpose is the amount by which the fair market value of the gift exceeds the donor's adjusted basis immediately before the gift. For purposes of determining loss on the sale or other disposition of the property, the tax basis is the lower of the donor's basis or the fair market value of the property at the time of the gift. If the donee is considering selling the property received by gift, these tax basis rules can have a significant impact on the decision to sell and the timing of such a sale. The tax implications of the sale of gifted property are beyond the scope of this text.

IMPORTANT CONCEPTS TO REMEMBER

Structured settlements

The Periodic Payment Settlement Act of 1982

Qualified assignment of a structured settlement

Compensatory damages

Punitive damages

Special 10-year averaging method for lump-sum retirement plan distributions

Straight life income option

Installments for a fixed period

Installments of a fixed amount

Life income with period certain

Life income with refund option

Joint and survivor income option

Income tax basis of an inheritance and of a gift

QUESTIONS FOR REVIEW

1. What are some of the general considerations in planning for financial windfalls?

2. What is meant by a structured settlement and what are its primary advantages?

3. What Internal Revenue Code requirements must be met to make a qualified assignment of a structured settlement?

4. What two primary forms of damages are often awarded in a personal injury lawsuit and how is each type treated for income tax purposes?

5. What is meant by the opportunity cost of taking lottery winnings in installments over time?

6. What type(s) of income averaging is(are) currently available for lump-sum retirement plan distributions, and who can take advantage of this income averaging?

7. What is the difference between the life income with period certain and life income with refund option forms of life insurance settlement options?

8. What would be the income tax effect of the immediate sale of appreciated property received as an inheritance versus appreciated property received as a gift?

9. Currently, how much may an unmarried donor gift to a donor each year without potentially incurring gift tax?

SUGGESTIONS FOR ADDITIONAL READING

Personal Financial Planning Handbook, 2nd edition, by Jonathan D. Pond, RIA, 2001.

Fundamentals of Risk and Insurance, 9th edition, by Emmett J. Vaughan & Therese Vaughan, John Wiley & Sons, Inc., 2003.

2004 U.S. Master Tax Guide by CCH Editorial Staff, CCH Incorporated, Chicago, 2003.

CHAPTER TWENTY

Quantitative Analysis

• • •

Quantitative analysis, as used in a personal financial planning context, is a broad term for the application of mathematical and statistical methods to analyze the reliability of projections of future results for the purpose of making better decisions. Its primary application in personal financial planning is in the area of investment planning; however, it may be used in the areas of retirement planning (retirement needs analysis), life insurance planning (life insurance needs analysis), and in education planning (education funding needs analysis), among others. Before the widespread use of personal computers, projections of future results were often made as point estimates using historical results and the judgment and experience of the forecaster, without factoring in the degree of uncertainty of future results. In the last several decades, the degree of sophistication in decision-making has made giant strides.

In this chapter, we will discuss several types of quantitative analysis including probability analysis, modeling, and simulation (including Monte Carlo simulation), sensitivity analysis, scenario analysis, and decision tree analysis.

The objectives of this chapter are:
- Define the term probability analysis.
- Explain the law of large numbers.
- Describe how empirical data are used to construct a probability distribution.
- Explain what is meant by a point estimate.
- Distinguish between the range and the variance of a group of values.

- Explain the relationship between the variance and the standard deviation of data from the mean.
- Discuss the primary use of the coefficient of variation.
- Describe the technique of sensitivity analysis.
- Compare and contrast sensitivity analysis and scenario analysis.
- Describe how decision tree analysis is used in project decision-making.
- Explain the process of Monte Carlo simulation.
- Identify some of the limitations of simulation analysis.

PROBABILITY ANALYSIS

Probability analysis is the body of knowledge concerned with measuring the likelihood that a given event will occur and then using this measurement to make forecasts of the event's future occurrence. It is based on the premise that most events are not simply a matter of chance, but rather that they tend to be repeated over a large number of trials. We could use words such as "unlikely," "almost impossible," "probable," "doubtful," or "expected" to express the degree of uncertainty of an event. However, numbers offer a much more precise way of measuring uncertainty. Probabilities are measured on a scale that runs from 0 to 1. Those events that are assigned a value of 0 are considered to be impossible, and those having a value of 1 are considered to be certain to occur. Those events assigned values between 0 and 1 are more likely to occur as their assigned value approaches 1. Historically, these values were assigned subjectively as an expression of an individual's degree of belief that a particular event would occur. More recently, the probability assigned to an event signifies the relative frequency of its occurrence that would be expected, given a large number of separate independent trials and assuming that stable conditions apply on a consistent basis. Under this relative frequency interpretation of probability, only events that may be repeated over a large number of trials may be governed by probabilities.

Using this relative frequency interpretation of probability, we can obtain an estimate of the probability of an event by one of two methods. The first involves the use of what are known as **a priori probabilities**. Under this method, we can predetermine the probabilities by examining the underlying conditions that cause an event. For example, when a coin is tossed, if we assume that the coin is perfectly balanced and fairly tossed and we reject the possibility of the coin landing on its edge, there are only two possible, equally likely outcomes. The probability of either a head or a tail is 0.5. Similarly, if we roll one die, the probability of rolling a six is 1/6, and if we try to draw the ace of spades from a standard deck of cards, we know that the probability is 1/52. These probabilities either can be calculated or are obvious from the nature of the event. Since these probabilities are determined before any trials have been run, they are referred to as a priori probabilities.

These a priori probabilities can be used to illustrate the operation of the **law of large numbers**, which in its simplest form is expressed as:

The observed frequency of an event more nearly approaches the underlying probability of the population as the number of trials approaches infinity.

Returning to our coin flip example, while we know that the probability of either a head or tail coming up is 0.5, we are not able to use this information to accurately forecast the result of a given flip. But we know that if we flipped the coin a large number of times, we would expect half of the outcomes to be heads and half to be tails. Put another way, for the 0.5 probability to be demonstrated, a large number of flips or tosses is necessary. In fact, as the law of large numbers indicates, the greater the number of trials or flips, the more nearly the result will approach the underlying probability of 0.5.

While our coin flip example is intuitive, in most cases, the underlying probability will not be known and will not be easily determined. In these cases, it will have to be estimated based on actual prior experience. Using life insurance as an example, assume that a mortality table indicates that the probability of a 21-year-old male dying before reaching age 22 is .00191. The insurance company has access to many years of actual, historical mortality data that show the following statistic: out of every 100,000 men alive at age 21, 191 have died before reaching age 22. Accordingly, we would expect, assuming stable conditions going forward, that the same proportion of 21-year-olds will die in the future. These probabilities, computed after a study of past experience, are called **a posteriori** or empirical probabilities. By observing the frequency with which the various outcomes have occurred over a long period of time under nearly identical conditions, one can construct an index of the relative frequency of the occurrence of each possible outcome. This index is referred to as a **probability distribution**. The probability assigned to a particular event is the average rate at which the outcome is expected to occur.

By making probability estimates on the basis of past experience or historical data, we are engaging in what is referred to as statistical inference. In effect, we are inferring from the sample data certain characteristics about the entire population. We use a sample because ordinarily it is not possible to examine the entire population. Taking a sample value (sample statistic) enables us to reach a conclusion about some measure of the population (a parameter). By trying to estimate the probability of an event, we are attempting to determine the event's mean or average frequency of occurrence. The basis for our estimate is the sample. In so doing, we realize that since we are not testing 100 percent of the population, our estimate of the probability may be wrong. But by applying the law of large numbers, we know that as we increase the number of trials in our sample, we will also increase the quality of our estimate of the probability. More and more trials will bring us increasingly closer to finding the true probability of an event. However, from a practical standpoint, in most cases, we are unable to take a large sample. As a result, we use the mean of the sample to arrive at what is known as a **point estimate** of the mean of the population. Next, we estimate the probability that the mean of the population falls within a certain range (margin of error) of this point estimate.

The confidence we can place in our estimate of the true probability will depend a great deal on how widely dispersed the values are that make up the mean of the sample. In those cases where we have estimated the probability using widely dispersed sample values, we should expect to have a larger variation between our probability estimate and the true probability. Through the use of probability analysis, we can measure the variation in the values that make up the sample mean and use this variation to determine the likelihood that the sample mean approximates the population mean.

We can begin by calculating the variation from the smallest value to the largest value, referred to as the **range**. However, a more important measure is the **variance**. The variance is computed by squaring the deviations of the values from the mean and then taking an average of these squared differences. The following example should help to illustrate the computation of the variance:

Assume that an investment had the following actual rates of return over the past five years: 7, 11, 10, 9, and 13 percent. Based on this information, we can calculate the variance as follows:

Year	Average Return	Actual Return	Difference	Difference Squared
1	10	7	3	9
2	10	11	1	1
3	10	10	0	0
4	10	9	1	1
5	10	13	3	9
				20

$$\frac{\text{Summation of differences squared}}{\text{Number of years}} = \frac{20}{5} = 4$$

Now assume that a different investment had the following actual rates of return over the past five years: 16, 4, 10, 12, and 8 percent. Based on this information, we calculate the variance as follows:

Year	Average Return	Actual Return	Difference	Difference Squared
1	10	16	6	36
2	10	4	6	36
3	10	10	0	0
4	10	12	2	4
5	10	8	2	4
				80

$$\frac{\text{Summation of differences squared}}{\text{Number of years}} = \frac{80}{5} = 16$$

As you may observe, both investments have a mean rate of return over the five-year period of 10 percent. The variance of the first investment's rates of return is 4, and that of the second investment is 16. The larger variance of the second investment's rates of return is an indication of the greater dispersion of the data that compose the mean of 10 percent than that of the first investment.

Using the variances just calculated, now we are prepared to calculate the most widely used and probably the most useful of all measures of dispersion—the **standard deviation**. The standard deviation is the square root of the variance. Therefore, using the information from our example, since the variance of the first investment is 4, its standard deviation is 2. The variance of the second investment is 16, resulting in a standard deviation of 4. The standard deviation, like the variance, simply measures the concentration of the values about their mean. The smaller the standard deviation, the less the dispersion around the mean and the more uniform the values. A lower standard deviation permits us to be more confident in our estimate of the population mean. But just as we discussed in our coin toss example, if we know with certainty that the mean return over the past five years for both of these investments was 10 percent, that does not mean that the return will be 10 percent in the sixth year. In what is known as a normal distribution, whereby values are dispersed uniformly on both sides of the mean, it can be demonstrated that 68.27 percent of the rates of return will fall within the range of the mean plus or minus one standard deviation. Similarly, 95.45 percent of the rates of return will fall within the range of the mean plus or minus two standard deviations. If we go to three standard deviations plus or minus the mean, 99.73 percent of the rates of return will lie in that range, bringing us to practical certainty.

In the case of the first investment in our example, where the standard deviation was determined to be 2, we can say that there is a 68.27 percent probability that the rate of return in the sixth year will be between 8 and 12 percent (i.e., 10 +/– 2), a 95.45 percent probability that the rate of return will be between 6 and 14 percent, and a 99.73 percent probability that the rate of return will be between 4 and 16 percent. In the case of the second investment, where the values were more dispersed and the standard deviation was calculated to be 4, there is a 68.27 percent probability that the rate of return will be between 6 and 14 percent, a 95.45 percent probability that it will be between 2 and 18, and a 99.73 percent probability that it will be between 0 and 22.

It should be apparent that uncertainty is inherent in predictions we may make. By simply using the historical mean return of 10 percent as an estimate of the sixth year's rate of return, we know that in the case of the first investment, we can be 99 percent certain only that the true probability lies somewhere in the range of 4 to 16 percent. This means that actual results may be expected to deviate by as much as 6 percent from the predicted 10 percent. This represents a possible deviation of 60 percent from the expected value.

Without going into the mathematics involved, the standard deviation of a distribution is inversely proportional to the square root of the number of items in the sample. This is why increasing the size of the sample actually decreases the area of uncertainty and increases the confidence level that our estimate of the rate of return approximates the true probability. It is important to realize that things may not happen in the future as they have in the past. As a matter of fact, it is likely that the true probability involved is constantly changing.

COEFFICIENT OF VARIATION

In the analysis of investments, an additional statistical measure is used to compare the relative risk of two or more investments. The **coefficient of variation** is a measure of risk per percentage of expected rate of return. It is calculated by dividing the standard deviation of an investment by its expected rate of return.

Consider the following examples for stocks A and B:

	Expected Return	Standard Deviation
Stock A	8%	6.5
Stock B	16%	10.1

An investor who is risk averse may select Stock A since it has a lower standard deviation. However, compare the amount of risk per percentage of return. Stock A's risk to return percentage is 0.81 (6.5 divided by 8 percent), while Stock B's risk to return factor is .63 (10.1 divided by 16 percent). It should be clear that Stock B incurs less risk per percentage of return to achieve its expected rate of return than does Stock A. The investor may now consider changing his or her choice of possible investments.

SENSITIVITY ANALYSIS

To best understand sensitivity analysis, assume that we are trying to determine the net present value (NPV) of a particular project. In this particular project, we know that the NPV is affected by a number of variables, such as the number of units sold, the selling price per unit, fixed costs, and variable costs. We will assign probabilities to each of these variables. Also, we know that if a key input variable, such as the number of units sold, changes, it will affect the project's NPV. However, without doing detailed calculations, we do not know how much of an effect this change in unit sales will have on the project's NPV. In order to calculate this effect, we must hold all other key input variables constant. What we are attempting to determine, through a technique known as **sensitivity analysis**, is the sensitivity of the project's NPV to various sized changes in the key input variable of unit sales. This information could be critical in determining whether to proceed with the project. If fairly significant changes in unit sales do not result in a meaningful change to the project's NPV, the NPV is said to be relatively insensitive to such changes in unit sales. This information would assist the decision maker by letting him or her know that the accuracy of the unit sales forecast is not critical to the achievement of the project's expected NPV. On the other hand, if relatively minor changes in unit sales result in significant changes in the project's NPV, then the NPV is considered to be sensitive to fairly small changes in unit sales and hence, riskier. This will indicate to the decision maker that the accuracy of unit sales forecasts is critical to this project's NPV and will cause him or her to obtain the most reliable unit sales projections available or, alternatively, to abandon the project because such highly reliable information is not available. Sensitivity analysis is, as used in this example, a technique that indicates exactly how much the NPV will change in response to a given change in an input variable, other things held constant.

In order to initiate the process, we must construct an **expected** or **base case,** using the best available estimates of input values. The next step is to ask a series of "what if" questions. For example: "What if unit sales decline 20 percent below the expected or base case level?" "What if the sales price per unit falls by a given percentage?" "What if variable costs are 70 percent of dollar sales rather than the expected 65 percent?" Sensitivity analysis provides answers to these questions.

In a sensitivity analysis, each variable is changed by specific percentages above and below the expected or base case value, with other things being held constant, to see how much the NPV of the project changes. In fact, the resulting recalculated NPVs are plotted against the variable that was changed to produce sensitivity graphs. The slope of the lines in the graphs shows how sensitive NPV is to changes in each of the input variables. In this manner, one can identify how sensitive NPV is to changes in each of the input variables.

If two projects were determined to have the same NPV, but one had steeper sensitivity lines for the key input variables, it would be regarded as riskier. That is to say, a fairly small error in estimating specific variables for this project could produce a significant error in the project's projected NPV. Sensitivity analysis enables a decision maker to identify the relative risk of different projects with similar NPVs. Spreadsheet computer programs are particularly adept at performing sensitivity analysis because of their ability to instantly recalculate NPV as each input value is changed.

One of the shortcomings of sensitivity analysis is that it fails to consider the range of likely values of the input variables as reflected in their probability distributions. A risk analysis technique that does take into account the probability distributions of the input variables is known as **scenario analysis,** discussed next.

SCENARIO ANALYSIS

In general, a project's risk depends on both (1) its sensitivity to changes in key variables and (2) the range of likely values of these variables as reflected in their probability distributions. Scenario analysis, unlike sensitivity analysis, considers both factors. Under this analysis technique, the decision maker makes projections using, on the one hand, very pessimistic assumptions with regard to the key variables and, on the other hand, very optimistic assumptions with regard to those same variables. In effect, "worst case" and "best case" scenarios are calculated and compared to the expected or base case scenario, discussed earlier. The results of the scenario analysis can be used to determine the expected NPV, standard deviation of NPV, and the coefficient of variation. We are not confined to NPV. We could also apply this analysis to the internal rate of return (IRR) or payback of the project.

The next step is to assign probabilities to the occurrence of the three scenarios (worst case, base case, and best case). For instance, we may estimate that there is a 25 percent probability of the worst case, a 50 percent probability of the base case, and a 25 percent probability of the best case. Obviously, estimating scenario probabilities is at best very difficult.

Scenario analysis does provide more information than can be obtained from using only sensitivity analysis; however, it considers only a few discrete outcomes (NPVs in this case) for a project, although there are in reality an infinite number of possibilities. This limitation of scenario analysis has led to the development of a more complex but more realistic method of assessing a project's risk.

DECISION TREE ANALYSIS

This technique is used where a decision (typically one involving a choice of investments) can result in one of several specified outcomes. It is especially useful in analyzing multistage, or sequential, decisions over a period of time. Decision problems are multistage in character when the choice of a given option may result in circumstances that will require yet another decision to be made. For instance, the first decision might be to conduct a market potential study of a particular product. At the completion of the study, depending upon the results, a second decision might be either to design and fabricate several prototype products or to discontinue the project. Depending upon reaction to the prototypes, a third decision might be either to build a production plant or to discontinue the project.

Each branch of the decision tree is assigned a probability and the joint probability of occurrence of each final outcome is determined. The joint probability is determined by multiplying together all probabilities on a particular branch of the decision tree. Each subsequent decision is based on the conditional probabilities of the preceding decision. Therefore, the decisions made at the different points in time are interconnected. In an investment context, a very practical question that derives from a decision tree analysis is "[W]hat is the probability of losing money if I make this investment?" This question can then be taken to its next logical extreme: "[W]hat is the probability that I will lose $100,000 (or any given amount) if I make this investment?"

Decision trees are models, and as such, are simplifications of the real problem. This simplification is the very strength of the modeling process because it fosters an understanding and insight that would be obscured by detail and complexity. It allows a complex decision problem to be analyzed as a series of smaller decision problems.

STOCHASTIC MODELING AND SIMULATION

The quantitative analysis techniques discussed so far are what may be characterized as deterministic, in which fixed relationships are assumed to exist between the input variables and the calculated NPVs. And we have seen that these assumed deterministic relationships do not necessarily result in accurate forecasts.

In this section, we will discuss so-called stochastic (random) modeling and simulation where the relationships between input variables and results are either not understood or are complex (as in the real world). These models also assume that the input variables are influenced by chance (referred to as quantum mechanics) or are estimated with uncertainty (e.g., attempting to forecast the investment markets).

A form of modeling and simulation currently very much in vogue is **Monte Carlo Simulation (MCS)**. While many consider MCS to be a relatively new simulation technique, it dates from about 1944 and the Manhattan Project at Los Alamos National Laboratory (development of the first atomic bomb). It was named by John von Neumann and Stanislaw Ulam during the Manhattan Project and was first used in finance by The Hertz Corporation in 1964. It became more popular in the 1970s with the advent of computing power and the theory of computational complexity. In the institutional arena, Monte Carlo analysis of investment returns and cash flow assumptions has been in use since the 1960s for pensions and endowments.

This type of analysis, named after the city in Monaco, grew out of work on the mathematics of casino gambling. The roulette wheel was considered, in theory, to be a random number generator. MCS ties together sensitivities and input variable probability distributions and can be run on the more powerful personal computers.

The first step in a computer simulation is to specify a probability distribution for each of the key variables in the analysis. For purposes of discussion, let us return to the project analysis discussed under **Sensitivity Analysis**. One of the key variables in that analysis was the sales price and in order to determine the NPV of the project we would have determined an expected sales price. However, for the purposes of MCS, we need to determine a range of sales prices from the lowest possible price to the highest. Then, for each possible sales price, we need to assign a probability. Next, for each possible sales price and related probability, we assign a series of random numbers. If, for instance, the probability of the lowest possible sales price is 5 percent (.05), five digits are assigned to that possible price. If the next highest sales price has a probability of 20 percent (.20), we assign 20 digits to that price, and so on for the other possible prices. Once the probability distributions and associated random numbers have been specified for all the key variables (including sales quantity, unit variable costs, construction costs, and so on), the computer simulation can begin.

Computers either have stored in them, or they can generate, random numbers. The numbers generated by computers are, strictly speaking, pseudorandom because they only have the appearance of being random. If someone had access to the logic of the software program used to generate such numbers and the initial number, he or she could predict the series of numbers to be generated. On the first trial run, the computer selects a different random number for each uncertain variable.

Depending on the random number selected, a value is determined for each variable. Once a value has been established for each of the variables, the computer generates the NPV for the computer's first run. The NPV so generated is stored in memory and the computer then proceeds to the second trial run, using a different set of random numbers. The NPV generated in the second trial run is again stored, and the model proceeds on for perhaps 500-1,000 runs. If we are concerned only with average performance around expected NPV, then a relatively few samples are appropriate. However, if we are looking for outlying statistics, as would be the case with a highly volatile investment, then many more samples are necessary. [This is the premise of Latin Hypercube sampling, which is designed to reduce the number of samples required. See **Suggestions for Additional Reading** at the end of this chapter.] If we repeat this process a large number of times, then it is to be expected that the more likely combinations of NPVs will occur most often, while the unlikely combinations will occur relatively infrequently. Thus the probability of a particular NPV occurring can be estimated from the frequency with which it occurs in the simulations.

While this sounds like a long and tedious process, modern computers can complete this operation almost instantaneously. All of the stored NPVs, in this case, are then printed out in the form of a frequency distribution, together with the expected NPV and the standard deviation of this NPV. Applying this to financial planning, once the perhaps thousands of runs have been generated, the program starts calculating the odds of reaching a particular outcome (e.g., rate of return). MCS will often change a financial planner's or client's decision about whether, for instance, the client can retire at a particular level of annual income.

In a personal financial planning context, this procedure may be used in a variety of engagements including retirement planning, insurance needs analysis, education funding needs analysis, and estate planning, among others. The primary advantage of simulation is that it shows us a range of possible outcomes, with attached probabilities, and not just point estimates. In our earlier example, the expected NPV can be used as a measure of the project's profitability, while the variability of this NPV as measured by its standard deviation can be used to measure risk. By dividing the expected NPV's standard deviation by the expected NPV we can calculate the coefficient of variation (CV) and use the CV to compare the relative riskiness of various projects. Again, in a financial planning context, a MCS can take into account returns, volatility, correlations, and other factors, all based on historical statistical estimates.

One of MCS's main benefits is that it helps people think about investment and long-term planning in terms of probability and alternate outcomes rather than certainty. Also, it can provide a link between portfolio construction, client goals, circumstances, and preferences and a platform to illustrate the tradeoffs between risk and return that is generally more meaningful and pertinent to clients.

Limitations of Simulation Analysis

One of the basic assumptions of simulation analysis is that the input variables are independent of one another. However, some variables may in fact be correlated. Returning to our earlier example, it may be that unit sales and sales prices are correlated. For example, if demand is weak, sales prices may be depressed, suggesting that if unit sales are low, a low sales price should also be used.

Moreover, simulation assumes that the values of each variable, and hence the bottom line result (NPV in our example) are independent over time. It would appear more reasonable to assume that high sales in the early years of a project imply market acceptance and hence high sales in future years, rather than to assume that sales in one year are not correlated with sales levels in other years.

While MCS software permits the use of correlations between input variables and between years, it is very difficult to specify what those correlations should be. It is important not to underestimate the difficulty of obtaining valid estimates of probability distributions and correlations, if any, among the variables.

Another shortcoming of MCS, as well as scenario and sensitivity analysis, is that some software packages may ignore the effects of diversification. As a result, if a particular investment is projected to have highly uncertain returns, but those returns are not correlated with the returns on the investor's other portfolio investments, then the investment may not be very risky in terms of the investor's risk tolerance or market risk. If the investment's returns are negatively correlated with the returns on the investor's portfolio's other investments, then it may actually decrease the investor's overall risk. In fact, the larger its standard deviation, the more it will reduce the investor's overall risk.

Also, some experts have indicated that spreadsheet software random number generators may repeat after as few as 20,000 numbers. Of even greater significance, experts who have evaluated stochastic planning programs have determined that none of the programs examined had built-in statistical validity tests. As a result, planners who use stochastic simulation planning models must realize the results may produce outlying data that have not been tested for statistical validity.

Moreover, MCS software generally uses arithmetic average annual rates of return rather than annualized compound returns over the life of a portfolio. The data used by financial planners and other advisers to evaluate historical performance and to project future portfolio performance is reported almost exclusively in terms of annualized compound return. The difference in these two values can be as much as two percent. MCS, unlike the historical single-point analysis approach (which uses a single constant value for return), assumes variations in return over the life of the portfolio.

An additional shortcoming of MCS is that it has been developed for use with financial analyses by mathematicians with training and expertise in these techniques, which have been used and refined for years in a number of other industries. While these mathematicians are knowledgeable in this area, they are generally not experts in the subject matter that provides input for financial analyses. On the other hand, financial advisers are experienced in the gathering and use of these inputs, but generally not familiar with the mathematical principles embodied in MCS. As a result, there has been a lack of an effective knowledge bridge between these two types of experts, resulting in some fundamental errors in the design of MCS software to perform financial analyses, such as the use of arithmetic average annual returns rather than annualized compound returns discussed in the previous paragraph.

Financial planners need to exercise care in the use of MCS output. If they treat the information developed by MCS by communicating to clients an absolute result, such as a specific percentage probability that they will achieve a particular goal, they have misused MCS. The real probabilities of achieving a particular goal are unknown. MCS simply enables one to make an educated guess, often with questionable assumptions.

Finally, failing to run an adequate number of trials can lead to inaccurate results. For instance, in 1987, a MCS using 500 to 1,000 simulations would have failed to predict the stock-market crash of that year. It would have taken 100,000 or more simulations to forecast this event. However, for most financial planner uses, experts recommend about 1,000 trials, with more than 3,000 considered to be overkill.

IMPORTANT CONCEPTS TO REMEMBER

Probability analysis	Coefficient of variation
A priori probabilities	Sensitivity analysis
The law of large numbers	Scenario analysis
A posteriori probabilities	Decision tree analysis
Probability distribution	Stochastic modeling and simulation
Point estimate	Monte Carlo simulation
Variance	Random numbers
Standard deviation	Limitations of simulation analysis

QUESTIONS FOR REVIEW

1. What is meant by the term quantitative analysis?

2. What is meant by the term probability analysis?

3. What is the basic premise of the law of large numbers?

4. What is another name for an index of the relative frequency of the occurrence of particular events?

5. How is the variance calculated?

6. What is the relationship between the variance and the standard deviation?

7. What does the coefficient of variation attempt to measure?

8. If two projects had the same net present value but one had steeper sensitivity lines, what conclusion can be drawn about that one project?

9. In what way does scenario analysis differ from sensitivity analysis and in what way is it similar?

10. Which quantitative analysis technique is especially useful in analyzing multistage or sequential decisions over a period of time?

11. What are the steps in creating a Monte Carlo simulation?

12. What is the primary advantage of a Monte Carlo simulation?

13. What are some of the limitations of simulation analysis?

SUGGESTIONS FOR ADDITIONAL READING

Decision Analysis for Management Judgement by Paul Goodwin & George Wright, Chichester John Wiley & Sons, Ltd. (UK), 1999.

An Introduction to Management Science: Quantitative Approaches to Decision Making by David Ray Anderson, Dennis J. Sweeney, & Thomas Arthur Williams, South-Western College Publishing, 2000.

"A Better Way to Size Up Your Nest Egg" by Christopher Farrell, *Business Week*, January 22, 2001.

"The Full Monte" by J. Harold Bell & Robert C. Rauf, Jr., *Financial Planning*, June 2002.

"Modeling the Future: The Full Monte, the Latin Hypercube and Other Curiosities" by Glenn Kautt & Fred Wieland, *Journal of Financial Planning*, December 2001.

"Monte Carlo for Financial Planners" by H. Lynn Hopewell, available at www.montecarlo-simulation.com.

"Modeling the Future" by Glenn Kautt & H. Lynn Hopewell, *Journal of Financial Planning*, October 2000.

"The Problems with Monte Carlo Simulation" by David Nawrocki, *Journal of Financial Planning*, November 2001.

"Financial Planning in Fantasyland" by William F. Sharpe, 1997, available at www.stanford.edu/~wfsharpe/.

"Sensitivity Simulations: A Faster Alternative to Monte Carlo" by Gobind Daryanani, CFP, Ph.D., *Journal of Financial Planning*, September 2002.

"An Integral Approach to Determining Asset Allocations" by Ton vanWelie, Ronald Janssen, & Monique Hoogstrate, *Journal of Financial Planning*, January 2004.

Appendix A

• • •

PERSONAL FINANCIAL PLANNING QUESTIONNAIRE

Please complete the following information as completely and accurately as you can.

Personal Information

	Client	Spouse
Name		
Address		
Home/cell phone numbers		
Prior Residence (by state)		
Birthplace		
Birthdate		
Current age		
Social Security number		
Occupation		
Employer		
Length of Current Employment (years)		
Business Phone Number		
Current Marital Status		
Prior Marriages (yes/no)		

Family Members Who Depend on Your Support

Please list any family members or individuals that you wish to plan for.

Child/Grandchild	Birthdate	Birthplace	Social Security number
Other Individuals/ Dependents	**Birthdate**	**Birthplace**	**Social Security number**

Family Health Issues

Do any family members/dependents have significant health problems? If so, please explain.

Family Member	Health Issues(s)

Family Advisors and Representatives

	Name	Phone Number
Attorney		
Banker		
Doctor		
Executor(s)		
Financial Planner		
Guardian(s)		
Insurance Agent		
Investment Advisor		
Minister/Rabbi		
Tax Preparer		
Other:		
Other:		

Family Goals

Please list all of your financial planning goals and a timeframe for when you wish to begin implementing them.

Family Goals	Sense of urgency (immediate, within 3 to12 months, or 1 year or later)
Client's Individual Goals	
Spouse's Individual Goals	

Family Objectives

Please indicate which of the following objectives are important for your family

Objective	Important to the Client (yes/no)?	Important to the Spouse (yes/no)?
Saving for education (yourself, children, grandchildren, etc.)		
Saving for retirement		
Being able to retire early (age 55 or earlier)		
Minimizing income taxes		
Minimizing estate taxes		
Providing support for an aging parent/relative		
Improving investment returns		
Improving insurance coverage		
Supporting a favorite charity		
Planning for your estate		
Improving your standard of living		
Changing or improving your employment situation		
Other:		
Other:		

Taxable Assets

Please list the current value for each of the following and provide the latest account statement available.

Account/Investment	Client	Spouse	Joint
Cash on hand			
Checking account			
CDs			
Money market			
Savings account			
Life insurance cash surrender value			
Stocks:			
Bonds:			
Mutual funds:			
Closely held business interest			
Limited partnership interest			
Other:			
Other:			

Retirement Accounts

Please list the current value for each of the following and provide the latest account statement available.

Account	Client	Spouse
IRAs:		
401(k)/403(b)		
Pension plan		
Profit-sharing plan		
Stock options		
Deferred compensation		
Other:		

Real Estate

Please list the current value for each of the following.

Type	Ownership (client, spouse, or joint)	Cost (in dollars)	Market Value (in dollars)	Loan Balance (in dollars)	Monthly Payment (in dollars)
Primary residence					
Vacation home					
Rental property					
Other:					
Other:					

Personal Property

Please list the current value for each of the following.

Type	Ownership (client, spouse or joint)	Market Value (in dollars)	Loan Balance (in dollars)
Aircraft			
Art and antiques			
Automobile			
Automobile			
Automobile			
Boat			
Collectibles			
Fur(s)			
Household goods			
Jewelry			
Other:			
Other:			

Liabilities

Please list the current balance for each of the following.

Type	Ownership (client, spouse, or joint)	Balance Due
Alimony/child support		
Bank loans		
Charitable pledge		
Credit cards		
Home equity loan or line of credit		
Installment loan		
Insurance policy loan		
Investment debt (margin)		
Personal loan		
Retirement plan loan		
Student loans		
Other:		
Other:		

Credit Ratings

What is your current credit rating or score?	
When was the last time you pulled a copy of your credit report?	
Have you ever filed for bankruptcy?	
What is the date when you last prepared a family balance sheet?	

Income

Please list the following sources of income in annual amounts.

Type	Client	Spouse	Joint
Employment Income			
Annual salary			
Bonus			
Commissions			
Self-employment			
Other:			
Investment Income			
Dividends			
Interest–taxable			
Interest–tax-free			
Rental income (net)			
Annuities			
Other:			
Miscellaneous Income			
Alimony			
Trusts			
Child support			
Estates			
Gifts			
Retirement accounts			
Sale of property/ investments			
Social security payments			
Other:			
Other:			
Do you expect a significant change in income over the next two to three years? (if so, estimate amounts)			

Expenditures

Please list the following current estimated expenditures in annual amounts.

Type	Amount
Charitable contributions	
Clothing	
Education	
Employment-related	
Food	
Gifts	
Home improvements/repair/maintenance	
Income and other payroll taxes	
Insurance:	
Auto	
Homeowners	
Disability income	
Life	
Medical	
Long-term care	
Personal liability	
Other:	
Medical expenses (unreimbursed)	
Mortgage/rent	
Personal expenses	
Recreation:	
Dining out	
Vacations	
Other:	
Savings	
Taxes:	
FICO	
Income	
Property	
Telephone	
Transportation:	
Auto fuel/repairs/maintenance	
Auto payments	
Utilities	
Other:	
Other:	

What is the date when you last prepared a family budget?

Insurance Coverage

Please list the following types of coverage.

Type	Amount	Owner	Insured	Beneficiary
Life				
Group term				
Term				
Universal life				
Whole life				
Disability				
Short term				
Long Term				
Medical				
Health care				
Long-term care				
Liability				
Umbrella				
Professional				
Property				
Auto				
Homeowners				

Are you or your spouse engaged in any professional activities, paid or unpaid, outside of your main employment (e.g., moonlighting, board memberships, volunteer work, professional association memberships, etc.)? If so, please explain.

Client or Spouse	Professional Activity

Retirement Planning

Question	Client	Spouse
At what age do you plan to retire?		
Where will you retire?		
Have you made an estimate of income needed for retirement? (If so, list estimated annual amount in today's dollars.)		
Are you eligible for Social Security? If so, list estimated annual amount.)		
What savings, if any, have you already made for retirement expenses?		
What savings vehicles are available to you through your employer?		
Are you taking maximum advantage of your employer's savings plans?		
How many years do you anticipate living in retirement?		
What do you expect the inflation rate to be during your retirement?		
What rate of return do you expect to earn on your investments during retirement?		
What preparations, if any, have you made for long-term healthcare needs?		
Do you expect to receive any inheritances?		

Please describe your plans and dreams for retirement.

Estate Planning

Document	Client	Spouse
Do you have a current will?		
Do you have a letter of instruction to assist your executor(trix) in administering your estate?		
Have you discussed your inheritance plan with your adult children and other potential heirs?		
Do you have a guardian for your children?		
Do you have a living will?		
Do you have a healthcare power of attorney?		
Do you have any trusts established?		
Do you wish to make charitable bequests at your death?		
Have you made known (or communicated) to others your preferences for funeral arrangements?		

Please describe the details of any trusts affecting you or your family.

Trust Name	Owner	Beneficiary	Purpose

Education Planning

Question	Response
Do you intend to send your children to college?	
Will this be a public or private institution or some combination?	
Have you completed an education cost needs analysis?	
Have you made an estimated Expected Family Contribution calculation?	
Do you anticipate the need for financial aid?	
What savings, if any, have you already made for college expenses?	
Is borrowing for college (student loans) an acceptable option?	
Do you expect your children to pay for part or all of their college educations?	

Tax Planning

Question	Response
Who prepares your tax returns?	
What is your marginal federal tax bracket?	
Do you have adequate documentation to support your returns in the event of an audit?	
Do you expect to be in a higher or lower tax bracket in retirement?	
Do you normally receive a federal tax refund each year?	
Are you taking advantage of all of the tax benefits available through your employer (cafeteria plan, retirement plan, etc.)?	

Please attach a copy of your last two years' tax returns.

Investment/Risk Tolerance Questionnaire

1. (a) What is the approximate value of your investment portfolio $_____

   (b) What percentage of your total investments is represented by this portfolio?   _____%

2. (a) Is there an immediate or near term (i.e., within 5 years) need for income from this portfolio?   Yes___ No___

   (b) If yes, when will the income be needed?   _____years

3. Will significant cash withdrawals of principal and/or contributions be made from this portfolio over the next 5 years?   Yes___ No___

4. (a) Is this a taxable or partially taxable portfolio?   Yes___ No___

   (b) If yes, what income tax rate should be used for planning purposes?   _____%

5. What is your portfolio's investment time horizon?

   Note: Investment time horizon refers to the number of years you expect the portfolio to be invested before you must dip into principal. Alternatively, how long will the objectives stated for this portfolio continue without substantial modification? Please mark your choice.

Three Years	_____
Five Years	_____
Ten Years	_____
Over Ten Years	_____

   If you have indicated less than ten years, please explain when the funds will be needed: _____

6. My (our) goal for this portfolio is an annual return of :   _____%
   This is based on an expected inflation rate of: _____%

7. For each of the following attributes, circle the number that most correctly reflects your level of concern. The more important, the higher the number. You may use each number more than once.

	MOST				LEAST	
Capital preservation	6	5	4	3	2	1
Growth	6	5	4	3	2	1
Low Volatility	6	5	4	3	2	1
Inflation Protection	6	5	4	3	2	1
Current Cash Flow	6	5	4	3	2	1
Aggressive Growth	6	5	4	3	2	1

8. ASSET CLASS CONSTRAINTS

ASSET CLASSES	Provide Any Asset Class Limitations (OPTIONAL)	
	Minimum	Maximum
T-bills, CDs, money market		
Intermediate government bonds		
Intermediate corporate bonds		
Intermediate municipal bonds		
Long term government bonds		
Long term corporate bonds		
Long term municipal bonds		
Foreign bonds		
Domestic equities, S&P 500		
Domestic equities, OTC		
Foreign equities		
Real estate		
Precious metals		

9. What percent of your investments are you likely to need within 5 years?   _____%

10. Up to what percentage of this portfolio can be invested in long term investments (i.e., over 5 years)?   _____%

11. Investment "risk" means different things to different people. Please rank the following statements from 1 (the statement that would worry you the most) to 4 (the statement that would worry you the least).

    I would be very concerned if I did not achieve the return on my portfolio that I expected, i.e., my target rate of return.   1__2__3__4__

    I would be very concerned if my portfolio was worth less in "real" dollars because of inflation erosion.   1__2__3__4__

    I would be very concerned with short term volatility, i.e., if my portfolio dropped substantially in value over one year.   1__2__3__4__

    I would be very concerned with long term volatility, i.e., if my portfolio dropped in value over a long period of time (i.e., five years and longer).   1__2__3__4__

12. Except for the "great depression", the longest time investors have had to wait after a market "crash" or a really bad market decline, for their portfolio to return to its earlier value has been: 4 years for stock & 2 years for bond investments. Knowing this, and that it is impossible to protect yourself from an occasional loss, answer the following question:

    If my portfolio produces a long term return that allows me to accomplish my goals, I am prepared to live with a time of recovery of:

Less than one year	_____
Between one and two years	_____
Between two and three years	_____
Over three years	_____

    If you selected less than "between two and three years", are you prepared to substantially reduce your goals?   Yes___ No___

13. Please check the statement that reflects your preference.

    I would rather be out of the stock market when it goes down than in the market when it goes up (i.e., I cannot live with the volatility of the stock market).   _____

    I would rather be in the stock market when it goes down than out of the market when it goes up (i.e., I may not like the idea, but I can live with the volatility of the stock market in order to earn market returns).   _____

14. Several portfolio performance projections are listed below. Assuming that inflation averages 3 1/2%, check the portfolio that most nearly reflects your goal for your portfolio.

Overall Risk Level	Expected Compounded Return (Inflation = 3 1/2%)	Expected Annual Range of Returns*		"Worst Case"**	CHECK
Low/Low	6.5%	-2.0% to	13.0%	-4.0%	
Mod/Low	7.5%	-3.0% to	16.0%	-9.0%	
Mod/Low	7.7%	-4.0% to	19.0%	-10.0%	
Mod/Low	8.0%	-4.5% to	20.0%	-11.0%	
Mod/Mod	8.3%	-5.0% to	21.0%	-13.0%	
High/Mod	8.5%	-6.0% to	22.0%	-14.0%	
High/Mod	9.0%	-7.0% to	24.0%	-20.0%	
High/Mod	9.5%	-8.0% to	25.0%	-24.0%	

* These estimates are based on a statistical measure of one standard deviation. This means that based on the assumptions used in developing these projections, the portfolio returns will fall within these ranges two out of every three years.
** We use the term "worst case" to describe the worst annual return that a portfolio is likely to experience 90% of the time.

15. Please answer either (a) or (b) to the following two questions.

    Question #1. (Choose (a) or (b))

    (a) You win $80,000   _____

    (b) You have an 80% chance of winning $100,000
        (or a 20% chance of winning nothing)   _____

    Question #2. (Choose (a) or (b))

    (a) You lose $80,000   _____

    (b) You have an 80% chance of losing $100,000
        (or a 20% chance of losing nothing)   _____

16. Do you consider yourself a risk taker or a risk avoider? Please explain:

    Client_____

    Spouse_____

17. On a scale of 1 to 10 (with 10 being an ability to accept a high degree of risk), how would you rate your risk tolerance level?

    Client_____

    Spouse_____

18. Do you have certain investments you would or would not want to sell or reposition due to past performance, personal preference, social issues, or any other reasons? If so, what are they?

    Client_____

    Spouse_____

19. Which investments have been most financially rewarding?

    Client_____

    Spouse_____

20. Which investments have been most disappointing?

    Client_____

    Spouse_____

21. How active would you like to be in the management of your investments?

    Client_____

    Spouse_____

Document Storage

Please identify the location for the following documents, if applicable to your situation.

Document	Location
Bank statements	
Birth certificates and passports	
Business documents	
Credit card statements	
Employee benefit handbooks	
Household budget	
Insurance policies	
Inventory of household furnishings and possessions	
Inventory of wallet/purse contents	
Investment statements	
Loan documents	
Marriage license	
Personal financial statements	
Property titles	
Retirement plan statements	
Tax returns	
Trust documents	
Wills	
Other:	
Other:	

Accuracy of Information You Provided

How would you characterize the quality of the information you provided?

- ☐ Very accurate
- ☐ Based on estimates that are reasonably accurate
- ☐ Based on rough estimates

Comments: _____

_____

_____

_____

_____

Appendix B

Figure B.1

STATEMENT OF PERSONAL FINANCIAL POSITION, OR PERSONAL BALANCE SHEET		

Name _____   Date _____

ASSETS		LIABILITIES AND NET WORTH	
Liquid Assets		**Current Liabilities**	
Cash on hand	$	Utilities	$
In checking		Rent	
Savings accounts		Insurance premiums	
Money market funds and deposits		Taxes	
Certificates of deposit (<1 yr. to maturity)		Medical/dental bills	
Other		Repair bills	
Total Liquid Assets		Bank credit card balances	
Investments		Dept. store credit card balances	
Stocks		Travel and entertainment card balances	
Bonds		Gas and other credit card balances	
Certificates of deposit (>1 yr. to maturity)		Bank line of credit balances	
Mutual funds		Other current liabilities	
Real estate		**Total Current Liabilities**	
Other		**Long-Term Liabilities**	
Total Investments		Primary residence mortgage	
Retirement Funds		Second home mortgage	
Vested employer pension benefits		Real estate investment mortgage	
IRAs		Auto loans	
Rollover IRAs		Appliance/furniture loans	
Other		Home improvement loans	
Total Retirement Funds		Single-payment loans	
Personal Use Assets		Education loans	
Primary residence		Other long-term loans	
Second home		**Total Long-Term Liabilities**	
Auto(s):			
Auto(s):			
Recreational vehicles			
Household furnishings		**(II)Total Liabilities**	$
Jewelry and artwork		**Net Worth [(I) – (II)]**	$
Other			
Total Personal Use Assets		**Total Liabilities and Net Worth**	$
	(I) Total Assets	$	

Figure B.2

PERSONAL CASH FLOW STATEMENT		
Name(s) _____		
For the _____	Ending _____	
CASH INFLOWS		
Wages and salaries	Name:	
	Name:	
	Name:	
Self-employment income		
Bonuses and commissions		
Pensions and annuities		
Investment income	Interest received	
	Dividends received	
	Rents received	
	Sale of securities	
	Other	
Other income		
	(I) Total Income	$ _____
CASH OUTFLOWS		
Housing	Rent/mortgage payment (include insurance and taxes, if applicable)	$
	Repairs, maintenance, improvements	
Utilities	Gas, electric, water	
	Phone	
	Cable TV and other	
Food	Groceries	
	Dining out	
Autos	Loan payments	
	License plates, fees, etc,	
	Gas, oil, repairs, tires, maintenance	
Medical	Health, major medical, disability insurance	
	(payroll deductions or not provided by employer)	
	Doctor, dentist, hospital, medicines	
Clothing	Clothes, shoes, and accessories	
Insurance	Homeowner's (if not covered by mortgage payment)	
	Life (not provided by employer)	
	Auto	
Taxes	Income and social security	
	Property (if not included in mortgage)	
Appliances, furniture, and other major purchases	Loan payments	
	Purchases and repairs	
Personal care	Laundry, cosmetics, hair care	
Recreation and entertainment	Vacations	
	Other recreation and entertainment	
Other items		
	(II) Total Expenditures	$ _____
	CASH SURPLUS (OR DEFICIT) [(I) – (II)]	$ _____

Figure B.3

CASH BUDGET: ESTIMATED INCOME														
Name(s) _____														
For the _____							Ending _____							
Sources of Income		Jan.	Feb.	March	April	May	June	July	August	Sep.	October	Nov.	Dec	Total for the year
Take-home pay	Name:													
	Name:													
	Name:													
Bonuses and commissions														
Pensions and annuities														
Investment income	Interest													
	Dividends													
	Rents													
	Sale of securities													
	Other													
Other Income														
TOTAL INCOME														

Figure B.4

CASH BUDGET: ESTIMATED EXPENDITURES

Name(s) _____

For the _____ Ending _____

Expenditure Categories		Jan.	Feb.	March	April	May	June	July	August	Sep.	October	Nov.	Dec	Total for the year
Housing	Rent/mortgage payment (include insurance and taxes, if applicable)													
	Repairs, maint., improvements													
Utilities	Gas, electric, water													
	Phone													
	Cable TV and other													
Food	Groceries													
	Dining out													
Autos	Loan payments													
	License plates, fees, etc.													
	Gas, oil, repairs, tires, maintenance													
Medical	Health, major medical, disability insurance (not provided by employer)													
	Doctor, dentist, hospital, medicines													
Clothing	Clothes, shoes, and accessories													
Insurance	Homeowners (if not covered by mortgage payment)													
	Life (not provided by employer)													
	Auto													
Taxes	Income and social security													
	Property (if not included in mortgage)													
Appliances, furniture, and other	Loan payments													
	Purchases and repairs													
Personal care	Laundry, cosmetics, hair care													
Recreation and entertainment	Vacations													
	Other recreation and entertainment													
Savings and investments	Savings, stocks, bonds, etc.													
Other expenditures	Charitable contributions													
	Gifts													
	Education loan payment													
	Subscriptions, magazines, books													
	Other:													
	Other:													
Fun Money														
TOTAL EXPENDITURES														

Figure B.5

CASH BUDGET: ESTIMATED EXPENDITURES		
Name(s) _____		
For the _____	Ending _____	

	Expenditure Categories*	Annual Amounts
Housing (12-30%)	Rent/mortgage payment (include insurance and taxes, if applicable)	$
	Repairs, maintenance, improvements	
Utilities (4-8%)	Gas, electric, water	
	Phone	
	Cable TV and other	
Food (15-25%)	Groceries	
	Dining out	
Autos (5-18%)	Loan payments	
	License plates, fees, etc.	
	Gas, oil, repairs, tires, maintenance	
Medical (2-10%)	Health, major medical, disability insurance (amount deducted from payroll checks or neither purchased nor provided by employer)	
	Doctor, dentist, hospital, medicine	
Clothing (3-8%)	Clothes, shoes, and accessories	
Insurance (4-8%)	Homeowner's (if not covered by mortgage payment)	
	Life (not provided by employer)	
	Auto	
Taxes (N/A)	Income and social security	
	Property (if not included in mortgage)	
Appliances, furniture, and other major purchases (2-8%)	Loan payments	
	Purchases and repairs	
	Other:	
Personal care (1-3%)	Laundry, cosmetics, hair care	
Recreation and entertainment (2-8%)	Vacations	
	Other recreation and entertainment	
Savings and investments (3-10%)	Savings, stocks, bonds, etc.	
Other expenditures (1-10%)	Charitable contributions	
	Gifts	
	Education loan payment	
	Subscriptions, magazines, books	
	Other:	
	Other:	
Fun money (1-5%)		
	TOTAL EXPENDITURES	$

* Percentages noted parenthetically in the first column are suggested spending guidelines.

Figure B.6

CASH BUDGET: MONTHLY SUMMARY

Name(s) _____

For the _____ Ending _____

Income	Jan.	Feb.	March	April	May	June	July	August	Sep.	October	Nov.	Dec	Total for the year
Take-home pay													
Bonuses and commissions													
Pensions and annuities													
Investment income													
Other income													
(I) Total Income													
Expenditures													
Housing													
Utilities													
Food													
Autos													
Medical													
Clothing													
Insurance													
Taxes													
Appliances, furniture, and other													
Personal care													
Recreation and entertainment													
Savings and investments													
Other expenditures													
Fun Money													
(II) Total Expenditures													
CASH SURPLUS (OR DEFICIT) [(I) - (II)]													
CUMULATIVE CASH SURPLUS (OR DEFICIT)													

Figure B.7

BUDGET CONTROL SCHEDULE

Name(s) _____

For the _____   Months Ending _____

	Month:				Month:				Month:			
	Budgeted Amount (1)	Actual (2)	Monthly Variance (3)	Year-to-Date Variance (4)	Budgeted Amount (5)	Actual (6)	Monthly Variance (7)	Year-to-Date Variance (8)	Budgeted Amount (9)	Actual (10)	Monthly Variance (11)	Year-to-Date Variance (12)
Income												
Take-home pay												
Bonuses and commissions												
Pensions and annuities												
Investment income												
Other income												
(I) Total Income												
Expenditures												
Housing												
Utilities												
Food												
Autos												
Medical												
Clothing												
Insurance												
Taxes												
Appliances, furniture, and other												
Personal care												
Recreation and entertainment												
Savings and investments												
Other expenditures												
Fun Money												
(II) Total Expenditures												
CASH SURPLUS (OR DEFICIT) [(I) - (II)]												
CUMULATIVE CASH SURPLUS (OR DEFICIT)												

APPENDIX C

• • •

TIME VALUE OF MONEY FORMULAS AND LOGIC OF CALCULATIONS

Note to readers: this information is made available to you to enhance your understanding of the mathematical relationships behind many of the calculations used in Chapters 10 and 11 of this text. This information is provided for those of you who want to understand what is behind the keystrokes used in this text.

For all of the following formulas, variables are defined as follows:

FV = future value (or FV on the calculator)

PV = present value (or PV on the calculator)

n = number of years (or N on the calculator)

i = interest rate or rate of return (or I/YR on the calculator)

pmt = payment amount (or PMT on the calculator)

I = inflation rate

d = dividend

g = growth rate expected

r = required rate of return

Future Value (FV) $= \text{initial investment} \times (1 + i)^n$

Logic: This is a formula for considering how much one dollar is worth when it is compounded over time. The initial investment can also be called the present value (PV).

Example: If $100 is deposited in an account earning 8 percent for 3 years, how much will the account be worth? Using the formula,

$\quad$ FV $= \$100 (1 + 0.08)^3$

$\quad$ FV $= \$100 (1.2597)$

$\quad$ FV $= \$125.97$

The table below shows the value of $ 100 compounded at 8 percent over various periods of time:

Value today	In 1 year	In 2 years	In 3 years	In 4 years
$100.00	$108.00	$116.64	$125.97	$136.05

Present Value (PV) $= \dfrac{\text{future value}}{(1 + i)^n}$

Logic: Each payment to be received in the future earns a certain amount of interest, depending on the number of time periods over which the payments are received. Further, the interest earned may also earn interest (this is compounding), depending on the length of the holding period.

Example: A certificate of deposit will be worth $200 in 4 years. If you can earn 6 percent on your money from alternative investments, how much is the CD worth to you today? Using the formula,

$\quad$ PV $= \dfrac{\$200}{(1+0.06)^4}$

$\quad$ PV $= \dfrac{\$200}{(1.2625)}$

$\quad$ FV $= \$158.42$

The table below shows the value of $200 discounted at 6 percent over various periods of time.

Value today if to be received in 4 years	Value today if to be received in 3 years	Value today if to be received in 2 years	Value today if to be received in 1 year	Value in the future
$158.42	$167.93	$178.00	$188.68	$200.00

Future value of an ordinary annuity (FVOA)

$$\text{FVOA} = \text{pmt}\,(1 + i)^0 + \text{pmt}\,(1 + i)^1 + \cdots + \text{pmt}\,(1 + i)^{n-1}$$

Logic: Each payment to be received in the future earns a certain amount of interest, depending on the number of time periods over which the payments are received. Further, the interest earned may also earn interest (this is compounding), depending on the length of the holding period.

Example: If $500 is deposited annually at the end of each year (ordinary annuity) in an account that earns 4 percent interest, how much will the account be worth at the end of 3 years? Using the formula,

$$\text{FVOA} = \$500\,(1 + .04)^0 + \$500\,(1 + .04)^1 + \$500\,(1 + .04)^2$$

$$= \$500 + \$520 + \$540.80$$

$$= \$1{,}560.80$$

Future value of an annuity due (FVAD)

$$\text{FVAD} = \text{pmt}\,(1 + i)^1 + \text{pmt}\,(1 + i)^2 + \cdots + \text{pmt}\,(1 + i)^n$$

Logic: Each payment to be received in the future as well as a payment received immediately earns a certain amount of interest, depending on the number of time periods over which the payments are received. Further, the interest earned may also earn interest (this is compounding), depending on the length of the holding period.

Example: If $500 is deposited annually at the beginning of each year (annuity due) in an account that earns 4 percent interest, how much will the account be worth at the end of 3 years? Using the formula,

$$\text{FVAD} = \$500\,(1 + .04)^1 + \$500\,(1 + .04)^2 + \$500\,(1 + .04)^3$$

$$= \$520 + \$540.80 + \$562.43$$

$$= \$1{,}623.23$$

Notice the difference between the account value for an ordinary annuity (shown above to be $1,560.80) and the annuity due ($1,623.23). In the examples shown, receiving the first $500 payment today meant the account was worth $62.43 more than if we had waited one year to receive the first payment. In this short 3-year example, waiting one year to make a deposit cost over $62. Imagine the impact waiting just one year will have over longer holding periods, such as the 10 or 20 years or more a retirement investor might have.

Present value of an ordinary annuity (PVOA)

$$PVOA = \sum_{t=1}^{n} \frac{pmt}{(1 + i)^t}$$

Logic: Each payment to be received in the future is worth a certain value today, depending on the number of time periods over which the payments are received. Further, the interest that could have been earned on interest (this is discounting) has value as well, depending on the length of the holding period.

Example: If $700 is received annually at the end of each year (ordinary annuity) in an account that earns 9 percent interest for 3 years, how much is the account worth today? Using the formula,

$$PVOA = \frac{\$700}{(1 + 0.09)^1} + \frac{\$700}{(1 + 0.09)^2} + \frac{\$700}{(1 + 0.09)^3}$$

$$= \$642.20 + \$589.18 + \$540.54$$

$$= \$1,771.92$$

Present value of an annuity due (PVAD)

$$\sum_{t=0}^{n-1} \frac{pmt}{(1 + i)^t}$$

Logic: Each payment to be received in the future, as well as a payment to be received today, is worth a certain value today, depending on the number of time periods over which the payments are received. Further, the interest that could have been earned on interest (this is discounting) has value as well, depending on the length of the holding period.

Example: If $700 is received annually at the beginning of each year (annuity due) in an account that earns 9 percent interest for 3 years, how much is the account worth today? Using the formula,

$$PVAD = \frac{\$700}{(1 + 0.09)^0} + \frac{\$700}{(1 + 0.09)^1} + \frac{\$700}{(1 + 0.09)^2}$$

$$PVAD = \$700.00 + \$642.20 + \$589.18$$

$$PVAD = \$1,931.38$$

Notice the difference between the account value for an ordinary annuity (shown above to be $1,771.92) and the annuity due ($1,931.38). In the examples shown, receiving the first $700 payment today meant the account was worth $159.46 more than if we had waited one year to receive the first payment. In this short 3-year example, waiting one year to make a deposit cost over $159. Again, imagine the impact waiting just one year will have over longer holding periods, such as the 10 or 20 years or more a retirement investor might have.

Present value increasing/growing annuity (PVIA), ordinary annuity

$$PVIA_{ord} = pmt \left(\frac{1 - [(1 + \text{inflation rate})/(1 + \text{interest rate})]^n}{\text{interest rate} - \text{inflation rate}} \right)$$

where pmt is the first cash flow. Stated a little more simply in symbolic terms,

$$PVIA_{ord} = pmt \left(\frac{1 - [(1 + I)/(1 + i)]^n}{i - I} \right)$$

Logic: Each cash flow is increasing by a set percentage per time period (in this text, each payment increases by the rate of inflation). Each of those growing payments to be received in the future is worth a certain value today, depending on the number of time periods over which the payments are received. Further, the interest that could have been earned on interest (this is discounting) has value as well, depending on the length of the holding period.

Example: Your son will attend a state university for four years. The first payment of $15,000 will be due at the end of your son's freshman year and is expected to increase by 6 percent after that (hence this is an increasing ordinary annuity). How much money do you need today if you can earn 8 percent on your investments?

$$PVIA_{ord} = 15,000 \ \left(\frac{1 - [(1 + .06) / (1 + .08)]^4}{.08 - .06} \right.$$

$$= 15,000 \ (3.6021)$$

$$= 54,031.50$$

Below is a table showing how each year's payment is affected by the inflation rate and the discount rate that will be earned by the investment. The final answer may differ from the above answer due to rounding.

	Year 1, the end of your son's freshman year	Year 2, the end of your son's sophomore year	Year 3, the end of your son's junior year	Year 4, the end of your son's senior year
Payment amount due (increasing by 6 percent per year)	15,000	15,000 × 1.06 = **15,900**	15,900 × 1.06 = **16,854**	16,854 × 1.06 = **17,865.24**
Present value today (discounted at 8 percent)	FV 15,000 N = 1 I/YR = 8 PV = **13,888.89**	FV 15,900 N = 2 I/YR = 8 PV = **13,631.69**	FV 16,854 N = 3 I/YR = 8 PV = **13,379.25**	FV 17,865.24 N = 4 I/YR = 8 PV = **13,131.48**
Sum of all the present values	**54, 031.31**			

Present value increasing/growing annuity (PVIA), annuity due

$$\text{PVIA}_{\text{due}} = \text{pmt} \left(\frac{1 - [(1 + \text{inflation rate}) / (1 + \text{interest rate})]^n}{\text{interest rate} - \text{inflation rate}} \right) (1 + i).$$

where pmt is the first cash flow. Stated more simply in symbolic terms,

$$\text{PVIA}_{\text{due}} = \text{pmt} \left(\frac{1 - [(1 + I) / (1 + i)]^n}{i - I} \right) (1 + i).$$

Logic: To convert the ordinary annuity formula to an annuity due formula, we simply multiply the right-hand side of the equation by (1 + interest rate); this multiplication effectively gives the "ordinary annuity" answer one additional compounding period at the stated interest rate.

Each cash flow is increasing by a set percentage per time period (in this text, each payment increases by the rate of inflation). Each of those growing payments to be received in the future is worth a certain value today, depending on the number of time periods over which the payments are received. Further, the interest that could have been earned on interest (this is discounting) has value as well, depending on the length of the holding period.

Example: The college inflation rate is 6 percent, and your son will attend a state university for four years. The first payment of $15,000 is due today at the start of his college term (hence this is an increasing annuity due). How much money do you need today if you can earn 8 percent on your investments?

$$PVIA_{due} = 15,000 \left(\frac{1 - [(1 + .06) / (1+.08)]^4}{i - I} \right)(1 + .08)$$

$$= 15,000 \, (3.6021)(1.08)$$

$$= 58,354.02$$

Below is a table showing how each year's payment is affected by the inflation rate and the interest rate that will be earned by the investment. The final answer may differ from the above answer due to rounding.

	Year 0 (today), the start of your son's freshman year	Year 1, start of your son's sophomore year	Year 2, start of your son's junior year	Year 3, start of your son's senior year
Payment amount due (increasing by 6 percent per year)	15,000	15,000 × 1.06 = **15,900**	15,900 × 1.06 = **16,854**	16,854 × 1.06 = **17,865.24**
Present value today (discounted at 8 percent)	FV 15,000 N = 0 I/YR = 8 PV = **15,000**	FV 15,900 N = 1 I/YR = 8 PV = **14,722.22**	FV 16,854 N = 2 I/YR = 8 PV = **14,449.59**	FV 17,865 N = 3 I/YR = 8 PV = **14,182.00**
Sum of all the present values	**58,353.81**			

Future value increasing/growing annuity (FVIA), ordinary annuity

$$FVIA_{ord} = pmt \left(\frac{(1 + \text{interest rate})^n - (1 + \text{inflation rate})^n}{(\text{interest rate} - \text{inflation rate})} \right)$$

where pmt is the first cash flow. Stated more simply in symbolic terms,

$$FVIA_{ord} = pmt \left(\frac{(1 + i)^n - (1 + I)^n}{(i - I)} \right)$$

Logic: Each cash flow is increasing by a set percentage per time period (in this text, each payment increases by the rate of inflation). Each of those growing payments to be received in the future will be worth a certain value in the future, depending on the number of time periods over which the payments are made. Further, the interest that will be earned on interest (this is compounding) has value as well, depending on the length of the holding period.

Example: Jerry contributes $ 1,000 at the end of each year for the next 3 years. He will increase the amount of each year's contribution by 4 percent (beginning with the contribution made at the end of the second year), to keep up with inflation. If Jerry earns 9 percent on his money, how much will he have at the end of 3 years?

$$FVIA_{ord} = 1,000 \left(\frac{(1 + .09)^3 - (1 + .04)^3}{(.09 - .04)} \right)$$

$$= 1,000 \, (3.4033)$$

$$= 3,403.30$$

Below is a table showing how each year's payment is affected by the inflation rate and the compounding rate that will be earned by the investment. The final answer may differ from the above answer due to rounding.

	End of Year 1	**End of Year 2**	**End of Year 3**
Contribution amount (increasing by 4 percent per year)	1,000	$1,000 \times 1.04 = $ **1,040**	$1,040 \times 1.04 = $ **1,081.60**
Future value (increasing by 9 percent per year) *at the end of year 3*	PV = 1,000 N = 2* I/YR = 9 FV = 1,188.10 * This contribution is made at the end of Year 1 and grows for 2 years to the end of Year 3.	PV = 1,040 N = 1* I/YR = 9 FV = 1,133.60 * This contribution is made at the end of Year 2 and grows for only 1 year until the end of Year 3.	PV = 1,081.60 N = 0* I/YR = 9 FV = 1,081.60 * This contribution has no earnings growth at all, because it isn't made until the end of Year 3.
Sum of all the present values	**3,403.30**		

Future value increasing/growing annuity (FVIA), annuity due

$$\text{FVIA}_{\text{due}} = \text{pmt} \left(\frac{(1 + \text{interest rate})^n - (1 + \text{inflation rate})^n}{(\text{interest rate} - \text{inflation rate})} \right) (1 + \text{interest rate})$$

where pmt is the first cash flow. Stated more simply in symbolic terms,

$$\text{FVIA}_{\text{due}} = \text{pmt} \left(\frac{(1 + i)^n - (1 + I)^n}{(i - I)} \right)(1 + i)$$

Logic: To convert the ordinary annuity formula to an annuity due formula, we simply multiply the right-hand side of the equation by (1 + interest rate); this multiplication effectively gives the "ordinary annuity" answer one additional compounding period at the stated interest rate.

Each cash flow is increasing by a set percentage per time period (in this text, each payment increases by the rate of inflation). Each of those growing payments to be received in the future will be worth a certain value in the future, depending on the number of time periods over which the payments are made. Further, the interest that will be earned on interest (this is compounding) has value as well, depending on the length of the holding period.

Example: Jerry contributes $1,000 at the beginning of each year for the next 3 years. He will increase the amount of each year's contribution by 4 percent (beginning with the contribution made at the beginning of the second year), to keep up with inflation. If Jerry earns 9 percent on his money, how much will he have at the end of 3 years?

$$\text{FVIA}_{\text{due}} = 1,000 \left(\frac{(1 + .09)^3 - (1 + .04)^3}{(.09 - .04)} \right) (1 + .09)$$

$$= 1,000 \, (3.4033) \, (1.09)$$

$$= 3.709.60$$

Below is a table showing how each year's payment is affected by the inflation rate and the compounding rate that will be earned by the investment. The final answer may differ from the above answer due to rounding.

	Beginning of Year 1	Beginning of Year 2	Beginning of Year 3
Contribution amount (increasing by 4 percent per year	1,000	$1,000 \times 1.04 =$ **1,040**	$1,040 \times 1.04 =$ **1,081.60**
Future value (increasing by 9 percent per year) *at the end of year 3*	PV = 1,000 N = 3* I/YR = 9 FV = **1,295.03** * This contribution is made at the beginning of Year 1 and grows for 3 years to the end of Year 3.	PV = 1,040 N = 2* I/YR = 9 FV = **1,235.62** * This contribution is made at the beginning of Year 2 and grows for 2 years until the end of Year 3.	PV = 1,081.60 N = 1* I/YR = 9 FV = **1,178.94** * This contribution is made at the beginning of Year 3 and grows for 1 year until the end of Year 3.
Sum of all the present values	**3,709.59**		

General observations about solving increasing annuity problems (only) with an HP 10BII calculator

- Always keep the calculator in the BEGIN mode, whether you're solving annuity due or ordinary annuity problems.

- To solve an ordinary annuity problem, follow the keystrokes to solve the problem as if it's an annuity due problem. Then divide your final answer by (1 + interest rate) to convert the answer to an ordinary annuity. That's it. Recall that in the formulas above, we multiplied an ordinary annuity by (1 + interest rate) to convert it to an annuity due. Because of the programming in the calculator, we reverse this process to convert an annuity due to an ordinary annuity. In other words, divide your final answer from the annuity due keystrokes by (1 + interest rate) to convert it to an ordinary annuity.

- Always divide the interest rate (or rate of return) by the inflation rate when calculating the inflation-adjusted rate of return. Even if the inflation rate is greater than the interest rate (what appears to be a "negative" I/YR), the calculator will still solve the problem correctly.

Net present value (NPV)

Rather than reinvent the wheel, turn to Appendix B in the HP 10BII calculator owner's manual for the formula for NPV. The logic is similar to solving the present value of an annuity (shown above), except that the payments are unequal amounts (and the payments may come sporadically over time).

Internal rate of return (IRR)

$$\text{Purchase price today} = \frac{\text{1st period cash flow}}{(1 + IRR)} + \cdots + \frac{\text{cash flow } n}{(1 + IRR)^n} + \frac{\text{sales price } n}{(1 + IRR)^n}$$

Logic: The internal rate of return is the interest rate necessary to produce a net present value of zero for a series of cash inflows and outflows. The unknown variable, IRR, can be solved on a manual basis by trial and error, using many different interest rates. Fortunately, your financial function calculator can solve this problem for you much more quickly.

Example: Debbie bought shares in a stock mutual fund for $1,000. The fund paid her a quarterly dividend of $20, $20, then $30, and then another of $30, and then she sold her shares for $1,040 three months later. What is her internal rate of return?

$$\$1,000 = \frac{20}{(1 + IRR)} + \frac{20}{(1 + IRR)^2} + \frac{30}{(1 + IRR)^3} + \frac{30}{(1 + IRR)^4} + \frac{1,040}{(1 + IRR)^5}$$

As you can see, trying to guess the IRR can be a tedious process. Using a calculator, we come up with a quarterly IRR of 2.77 percent, which equals an annual rate of 11.09 percent. To verify the math, we can plug the quarterly rate into the above equation resulting in the following:

$$\frac{20}{(1 + .02773)} + \frac{20}{(1 + .02773)^2} + \frac{30}{(1 + .02773)^3} + \frac{30}{(1 + .02773)^4} + \frac{1,040}{(1 + .02773)^5}$$

$$\frac{20}{1.0277} + \frac{20}{1.0563} + \frac{30}{1.0855} + \frac{30}{1.1156} + \frac{1,040}{1.1465}$$

$$= 19.46 + 18.94 + 27.64 + 26.89 + 907.11$$

$$= \text{approximately } \$1,000. \text{ which was the original purchase price}$$

Annualized rate of return $= \dfrac{\text{return}}{\text{number of days held}} \times 365$

Logic: When an investment is held for less than one year, its rate of return can be converted into an annual figure by using the above formula. If an investment was held for 1 month, you'd simply multiply its rate of return by 12 to annualize it. If the investment was held for 3 months, you could multiply its rate of return by 4 to annualize it. To be more precise, you can use the actual number of days an investment is owned and divide it by 365, the number of days in a year.

Example: Jamie has made 6 percent on her investment, which she has owned for 60 days. What is her annual rate of return on her investment?

Annualized rate of return $= \dfrac{6}{60} \times 365 = .10 \times 365 = 36.5\%$

Holding period rate of return (normally used for a time period of less than one year) $= \dfrac{\text{current period income} + \text{current period capital gain or loss}}{\text{starting investment value}}$

Logic: This measure of return only takes into account the cash flow and change in value of an investment. You can determine the holding period return by adding any cash inflows (such as interest or dividends) to the change in value of an investment for a set time period, and then dividing this result by the original investment value.

Example: Aaron bought a share of stock for $25. Since he purchased it, the stock has paid a dividend of $1.00, and the stock's price is now $30. What is his holding period rate of return?

Holding period rate of return $= \dfrac{(1 + 5)}{25} = \dfrac{6}{25} = 24\%$

After-tax rate of return (federal only) $=$ return $\times$ (1 − federal tax rate)

Logic: Depending on your marginal tax rate (at the federal level), you will lose a certain percentage of any return to taxes. For instance, assume you earn $1 from an investment and that your tax bracket is 15 percent. You must pay the government 15¢ of your dollar, meaning you have 85¢ left over to keep. Thus to determine your after-tax rate of return, you can multiply your earnings by 1 − your federal tax rate.

Example: Tara is in the 27.5 percent tax bracket and has earned 7 percent on her investment for the past year. What is her after-tax rate of return?

After-tax rate of return $= 7 \times (1 - .275) = 7 \times .725 = 5.08\%$

After-tax rate of return (state and federal)

= **return** × (1 − [**federal tax rate** + (**state rate** × (1 − **federal rate**))])

Logic: Because of the nuances of the tax code, state income taxes, since they are deductible for federal income tax purposes, do not increase total income taxes by the amount of the nominal state income tax rate. In other words, a taxpayer does not effectively pay the full nominal state income tax rate because of the fact that he or she obtains a federal income tax benefit by deducting the state tax on his or her federal income tax return.

For example, assume you had total earnings of $200 from a savings account. In the 28 percent tax bracket, your federal taxes would take $56 of your earnings, leaving you with a net amount of $144. If you live in a state where your earnings are taxed at say, 4 percent, the $8 of state income tax ($200 × 4%) will be deducted on your federal income tax return, thereby saving you $2.24 ($8.00 × 28% federal tax rate) on your federal tax bill. As a result, the "net" state income taxes paid are actually $5.76 ($8.00 − $2.24). When this $5.76 is added to the $56 of federal income taxes, the total income taxes are $61.76. Thus you would have a total of $138.24 left over ($200.00 − $61.76). In effect, your combined federal and state tax rate is 30.88 percent.

Notice you **cannot** simply add the federal and state tax brackets together (28 percent + 4 percent = 32 percent), because that would overstate the impact of the taxes on your investment return.

Example: Tim is in the 15 percent federal tax bracket and the 5 percent state income tax bracket. If he owns a CD paying 6 percent, what is his after-tax rate of return?

After-tax rate of return (state and federal) =
$6 \times (1 - [.15 + (.05 \times (1 - .15))]) = 6 \times (1 - [.15 + .0425]) = 6 \times (1 - .1925) = 6 \times .8075 = 4.845\%$

Inflation-adjusted rate of return

$$= \left[\left(\frac{1 + \text{rate of return}}{1 + \text{inflation rate}} \right) - 1 \right] \times 100$$

$$= \left[\left(\frac{1 + i}{1 + I} \right) - 1 \right] \times 100$$

Logic: Inflation erodes the purchasing power of a dollar over time. Thus, in 1988, a dollar would buy four postage stamps. In 2001, that same dollar would almost buy three postage stamps. Inflation also erodes investment returns over time. In essence, you have a "three steps forward, two steps back" effect taking place. While the investment return increases the nominal value of the investment, inflation erodes the underlying value of the principal.

Simply subtracting the inflation rate from the nominal investment rate of return will bring you intuitively close to the "real" rate of return (after netting out the effects of inflation), but to be precise we need to use the equation above.

Example: Julie thinks she will earn 8 percent on her corporate bond fund for this year. If inflation runs at 4 percent, what will Julie's inflation-adjusted rate of return be?

$$\text{Inflation-adjusted rate of return} = \left[\left(\frac{(1+.08)}{(1+.04)}\right)-1\right]\times 100 = [1.0385-1]\times 100$$

$$= 3.8462\%$$

$$= 3.85\%$$

Taxable equivalent yield of a tax-exempt security

$$\text{(federal only)} = \frac{\text{yield of tax}-\text{free security}}{1-\text{federal tax rate}}$$

$$\text{(federal and state)} = \frac{\text{yield of tax -free security}}{1-[\text{federal tax rate}+(\text{state rate}\times(1-\text{federal rate}))]}$$

Logic: In order to compare apples to apples, tax-free yields (such as municipal bond yields) need to be converted to a taxable yield. Doing so allows an investor to compare the yield of a municipal (tax-free) bond to a corporate (taxable) bond. This calculation allows the investor to choose the type of return that generates the most after-tax income, given a particular tax bracket.

Example: Bailey owns a municipal bond paying 5 percent, and he is in the 36-percent federal tax bracket. What is his taxable equivalent yield for this bond?

$$\text{Taxable equivalent yield} = \frac{5}{1-.36} = \frac{5}{.64} = 7.81\%$$

If Bailey finds a taxable bond yielding 7.81 percent after taxes, he will be in the same position as if he owned a tax-free bond yielding 5 percent. To check the math, use the after-tax rate of return calculation: $7.81 \times (1-.36) = 7.81 \times .64 = 5\%$.

Intrinsic Value of common stock

$$= \frac{\text{dividend} \times (1 + \text{growth rate expected})}{\text{required rate of return} - \text{growth rate expected}}$$

$$= \frac{d(1 + g)}{r - g}$$

Logic: As this is one of many investment-related formulas discussed in most investment planning textbooks, the reader is referred to such textbooks for an explanation of its rationale.

Example: Paul owns stock ABC which paid a $2.00 per share dividend last year. He expects the dividend to grow at a rate of 7 percent. If Paul has a 10 percent required rate of return, what is ABC's intrinsic value?

Value of ABC $= \dfrac{2.00 \times (1 + .07)}{.10 - .07} = \dfrac{2.14}{.03} = \$71.33$

Index

• • •

N

Q

W

Z

NOTES